Six Minutes in Berlin

STUDIES IN SPORTS MEDIA

Edited by Victoria E. Johnson and Travis Vogan

Six Minutes in Berlin

Broadcast Spectacle and Rowing Gold
at the Nazi Olympics

MICHAEL J. SOCOLOW

UNIVERSITY OF
ILLINOIS PRESS
Urbana, Chicago, and Springfield

© 2016 by the Board of Trustees
of the University of Illinois
All rights reserved
Manufactured in the United States of America
1 2 3 4 5 C P 5 4 3 2 1
♾ This book is printed on acid-free paper.

The cataloging-in-publication data is available
on the Library of Congress website.

Contents

Acknowledgments

This book began on a trip to the Library of Congress in the spring of 1999. One day, while awaiting the retrieval of requested books, I wandered around the alcoves in the Jefferson Building's Main Reading Room. A series of identical volumes carrying what looked like an Olympic logo caught my eye. I looked through them and found an oral history by Gordon B. Adam. I found Adam's memories of his experience visiting Berlin for the Olympic Games—and his description of the final race itself—riveting. I photocopied the interview and tucked it away, thinking that one day I would research and write this story.

I wrote a doctoral dissertation on radio history, moved my way through academia, and started a family. All the while, however, I "collected string" on this incredible story. Before they died, I interviewed Robert Moch and Jim McMillin, and I remain grateful for my correspondence with Moch before his death in 2005. I located a recording of the gold medal race as it appeared on CBS in the NBC collection at the Library of Congress, and I traveled to Seattle to research and interview people about the events. The debts I owe for assistance over the last seventeen years as I researched, composed, and now published *Six Minutes in Berlin* are legion.

I was trained as a historian at Georgetown University. I remain grateful to Dorothy Brown, R. Emmett Curran, Richard Duncan, Michael Kazin, Joe McCartin, James Shedel, and John Tutino for their guidance as mentors and to Peter

Cole, Jennifer Hull Dorsey, Gillian McGillivray, Jeff Taffet, and Theresa Alfaro Velcamp for their collegial support and friendship.

For assistance in securing access to archival recordings and other materials I am indebted to Bryan Cornell and Janet McKee of the Recorded Sound Reference Center at the Library of Congress. Mark Ekman of the Paley Center for the Media in New York City also helped track down Olympic broadcast recordings and arrange scholar listening privileges. Nora Patterson provided research assistance in Madison, Wisconsin, as did Laurel O'Connell in Seattle.

I particularly would like to thank Dan Raley, the former sports editor of the *Seattle Post-Intelligencer*. Dan not only inspired me as an author but also graciously shared materials—including his interviews with Joe Rantz, Roger Morris, and others—with me. Others sharing their knowledge and experience in interviews include Michael Moch, Barbara Moch, and Bill Pickard of the George Pocock Rowing Foundation. Pickard, in particular, helped me understand the developmental history of the rowing technique in Seattle. Mike Dirks, the grandson of Seattle sportswriter Clarence Dirks, alerted me to sources I would otherwise have missed. The staff at the Mystic Seaport Museum and Library helped me find much relevant material in the Mendenhall collection, and the staff at the George Pocock Rowing Center also helped me locate materials. I'm grateful that Stanley Wertheim shared memories of his cousin Ted Husing with me as well. For translation assistance, I thank Justus Hillebrand, Laura Lindenfeld, Anette Ruppel Rodrigues, and Google Translate.

Josh Levin, the executive editor of *Slate*, encouraged this project by publishing an excerpt tied to the London Olympic Games in 2012. I'm also grateful for the close reading and helpful suggestions offered by the anonymous reviewers evaluating the manuscript for the University of Illinois Press. Daniel Nasset from the University of Illinois Press was a supportive and attentive editor, and the efforts of Geof Garvey and Tad Ringo improved this book. For assistance securing images and other materials, I'd like to thank Anne Mar and Dale Stieber of the Special Collections Department at Occidental College Library; Bruce Levy of the Steven Spielberg Film and Video Archive at the United States Holocaust Memorial Museum; Joe McCary from Photo Response (www.photoresponse.com); and Susanne Hennings of the Deutsches Rundfunkarchiv in Frankfurt am Main. I also received help from Adam Paul in the Collaborative Media Lab of Fogler Library and Duane Shimmel of the University of Maine's Faculty Development Center. Jennifer Bonnet, the University of Maine's Social Sciences and Humanities Librarian, provided much research assistance. The University of Maine Humanities Center facilitated publication with the award of a publication subvention in 2016, and I am also grateful for financial support provided by the

University of Maine's College of Liberal Arts and Sciences and Department of Communication and Journalism.

I'm lucky to be involved with a supportive community of radio and broadcast scholars such as James Baughman, Cynthia Meyers, Kathy Newman, Elena Razlogova, Alex Russo, Shawn Van Cour, and David Weinstein. Parts of this manuscript were composed in a writing group consisting of Nathan Stormer, Constanza Ocampo-Raeder, and Liam Riordan. I am particularly indebted to Liam for making a key organizational suggestion. I've benefited enormously from the support of former colleagues in the American Studies Department at Brandeis University, including Joyce Antler, Jerry Cohen, Tom Doherty, and Steve Whitfield and from the support of my current and former colleagues in the Department of Communication and Journalism at the University of Maine, including Paul Grosswiler, Sunny Skye Hughes, Kristin Langellier, Jennifer Moore, Joshua Roiland, Eric Peterson, Laura Lindenfeld, John Sherblom, and Nathan Stormer.

Friends, family, and colleagues who knew of this project and supported it over the years include Tom Auth, Marc Duby, Amy Fried, Alex Grab, Cary Hall, Ed Hewett, Matt Hook, Chuck Jettmar, Andrew Levitt, Ethan Melone, Stephen Miller, Janice Min, Lesa O'Connell, Martin O'Connell, Eric Schiff, Howard Segal, Peter Sheehy, Susan Thibedeau, and Jerry Von Dohlen. Brooks Moriarty and Charles Forcey endured far too much of my frustration with typical good humor and wonderfully encouraging words.

My family, including my brother, Jonathan Socolow, sister, Elisabeth Socolow Vucinic, and mother, Anne K. Socolow, were always supportive of my work, as were my brothers-in-law Bruce Babij, Chip Fussell, Hughes Kraft, Dan Sievers, and Sasha Vucinic, my wife's parents, Suzanne and George J. McVey, and her siblings Pam Babij, Mimi McVey, Mary McVey, Karen Fussell, and Amy McVey. The Mack Road Irregulars of Clove Valley, New York, consisting of Somers Cooper, Chase Cooper, Ellis Cooper, Richard Greene, Nathaniel Greene, Daniel Krulewitch, David Krulewitch, Drew Krulewitch, Peter Krulewitch, Geo Socolow, Jono Socolow, Simon Socolow, and the late Sandy Socolow always enjoyed chats about history in general, and a certain failed housepainter from Austria in particular.

When an excerpt of *Six Minutes in Berlin* first came out in *Slate*, my good friend Evan Schultz pointed out something I'd not realized. The story I wrote encompassed three of my life's most formative and passionate interests: rowing, broadcasting, and history. I rowed at Columbia University and later for the King's Crown Rowing Association. I worked as an information manager for the host broadcast organizations at the Barcelona, Atlanta, and Sydney Olympic

Games, and my father's life and career were shaped by global broadcasting. He was executive producer of the CBS Evening News with Walter Cronkite and London bureau chief of CBS News. In 2001, I earned my doctorate in history. All research is, indeed, ultimately "me-search," and it is therefore to my family that I owe my greatest debts. This book would not have been written without the love and support of my wife Connie McVey or without the advice and wise counsel of our sons Simon McVey Socolow and George McVey Socolow. *Six Minutes in Berlin* is dedicated to the memory of my late father, Sanford Socolow. Dad once admonished me when I complained about the project. "Look," he said, "you are either going to write the book, or you are not going to write the book." Dad: The book is written.

Six Minutes in Berlin

Prologue

Olympic Regatta Racecourse
Grünau, Germany
14 August 1936
5:30 p.m.

César Saerchinger was anxious. He checked his watch. Under the cloudy gray skies plaguing the Berlin Olympics, Saerchinger stood next to Bill Henry, sports editor of the *Los Angeles Times*, on a small platform above a grandstand along the Langer See, a branch of the Spree River. A huge crowd—estimated at more than 75,000 spectators—overflowed a floating grandstand across the river, crowded the promenade below, and lined both banks. Saerchinger and Henry were only minutes away from starting CBS's broadcast of the final contest in the Olympic rowing competition, but CBS's European correspondent realized there was a timing problem. The circuit booked for the live broadcast of the Olympic regatta's final race was scheduled to open at precisely 6:15 p.m. Berlin time (1:15 p.m. in New York City), but that contest, the eight-oared crew final, would almost certainly start earlier. With less than an hour to go before air time, it appeared the race would end before the CBS program opened. Saerchinger pleaded with a nearby German radio official to open the circuit early. The answer was no.

Frantically, Saerchinger jumped past the German official and raced down the stairs. He shouldered his way "past Nazi guards into the clubhouse," where he "grabbed a telephone and asked for New York," he later recalled. Bystanders thought him crazy. When he finally connected with CBS's headquarters, the network's control-room engineers confirmed their ability to reschedule the program and relay the shortwave signal early. Pushing the broadcast up fifteen minutes saved the highly anticipated program. Bill Henry, who had followed Saerchinger down the stairs, watched his colleague hang up the telephone and then together they trudged back out into the cold drizzle and up the stairs to their broadcasting platform.[1]

Saerchinger and Henry did not broadcast the earlier races—mostly won by German rowers—because the U.S. listening audience was almost exclusively interested in the eight-oared crew championship. Had the U.S. broadcast started earlier, American listeners would have heard the amazing results compiled by the Germans. German oarsmen won five of the six gold medals awarded in the regatta, and in the sixth race they captured the silver. With one race left, it was already the most remarkable display of rowing dominance in Olympic history. Those results cheered Chancellor Adolf Hitler, Hermann Göring, and the other Nazi dignitaries watching from a special box atop a boathouse by the finish line. With each German victory, the oarsmen gave the Nazi salute, two anthems were played (the German national anthem, *Deutschland über Alles*, and the Nazi party anthem, the *Horst Wessel Lied*), and several rowers enjoyed brief personal congratulations from the Führer in a small office inside the boathouse.

The terrifically successful day for German rowers proved to be the opposite for Germany's top filmmaker, actress/director Leni Riefenstahl. She originally envisioned filming the Olympic rowing finals by building a series of towers next to the racecourse and recording the boats in succession as they moved down the course. But that plan became too costly and impractical, and so she decided to use a balloon tethered at the halfway mark to follow the race from above. With cameras mounted on the grandstand, she would capture the racing in progress and at the finish line. But the rain that morning carried a threat of lightning, and Olympic officials forced Riefenstahl to lower the hydrogen-filled balloon. She threw a tantrum, but "her hysteria did not change the minds of the authorities." The balloon's descent did not go well; gas escaped too quickly and the unlucky cameraman, Walter Frentz, plunged into the Langer See.[2]

A few hours later, with the Germans having already compiled one of the most impressive regatta records in Olympic history, Riefenstahl's twenty-one cameramen stood ready to shoot. Radio reporters from England, France, Germany, the United States, and elsewhere stood perched on an elevated platform, chatting rapidly into their microphones, preparing millions of listeners around the globe for the latest sensational Olympic contest. The six eight-oared shells completed their warm-ups and arrived at the starting line to position themselves for the race. The tension drew everyone's nerves tight. Even the enormous crowd, many waiting patiently under umbrellas, quieted noticeably as the regatta's finale neared.

Two thousand meters downriver, in the low-profile racing shell built by Seattle's master boatwright George Pocock, the eight oarsmen and one coxswain representing the United States prepared for the challenge of their lives. They had never lost a race together, and as they finished their warm-up, the rowers shared a sense of purpose and confidence. Yet the oarsmen also felt something wasn't right in the boat. Their shell felt a bit sluggish and heavy. With the most important race of their lives about to start, an unaccustomed concern arose in each of their minds. It wasn't exactly doubt, but rather, an anxiety about the boat's feeling in the water. They also worried about their teammate, the boat's stroke Don Hume.

Hume had been sick even before the regatta started, and a brutal qualifying heat severely worsened his condition. Hume's job as stroke was to set the pace for the men behind him; to take the coxswain's verbal demands and translate them into rhythmic movements followed by the rest of the oarsmen. Hume barely responded to coxswain Bob Moch's calls in the warm-up. Something was clearly amiss. With the most important race in their life about to begin, this annoyance added additional tension to an incredibly intense moment. "I don't think we were that confident on the final day," Gordon Adam, sitting in the three seat, would later remember. "We were running scared from start to finish, believe me."[3] Sitting in the five-seat, two seats down the shell from Adam, Jim McMillin, the crew's captain, tried to banish such thoughts. "I had felt that if we rowed the best we knew how, we could get there," he remembered almost seventy years later. But "everything went wrong from that point on."[4]

Introduction

Six Minutes in Berlin is the story of an event lasting a bit more than six minutes between 6:02 p.m. and 6:08 p.m., European Central Time, on 14 August 1936. In those moments an Olympic event was beamed across the globe, relayed to broadcast transmission towers, and listened to by tens of millions—if not hundreds of millions—of people simultaneously. The event was the eight-oared crew race concluding the Olympic rowing regatta. That race is mostly forgotten today, but in its day it was covered extensively by the U.S. press and networks, and it would later be remembered and celebrated in magazine articles, radio programs, and other media. Legendary sportswriter Grantland Rice called it the "high point" of the Berlin Olympic Games, and CBS's Bill Henry labeled it "the outstanding victory of the Olympic Games."[1] As a compelling patriotic drama, the race and its media coverage (both contemporaneous and historical) were a harbinger of the world's media future. In recounting the national celebrity of the squad from Seattle, and its relationship to the origins of sports broadcasting, *Six Minutes in Berlin* contextualizes this historical event portending the future development of globalized electronic media spectacle.

The race on that rainy day in Berlin was an important event in the history of U.S. Olympic triumphs. The story of the University of Washington's Berlin victory anticipates the U.S. media's later glorification (and commercialization) of such Olympic celebrities as Dorothy Hamill, Bruce [Caitlyn] Jenner, Mary

Lou Retton, and the 1980 "Miracle on Ice" hockey team. Turning Olympic victors into media celebrities antedated the Berlin Games—Johnny Weissmuller, for example, converted swimming gold into a lucrative Hollywood career—but the addition of live radio coverage intensified and extended the popularity of Olympic heroes. Electrified memories shaped by radio's intimacy and immediacy resounded in Germany, the United States, Japan, Argentina, and elsewhere around the world. The race in Grünau would remain etched in the minds of all those who experienced it, either in person or over the airwaves. "I saw the University of Washington crew win its race," Thomas Wolfe, the bestselling U.S. novelist, later told a reporter, "and that's a sight I'll never forget."[2] Like Wolfe, millions of U.S. listeners recalled the race over the next few years as newspapers, magazines, newsreels, and radio broadcasts periodically revisited the memorable Olympic victory. The scope and ephemerality of this new type of Olympic celebrity, catalyzed by the newest mass medium, makes the University of Washington crew an especially illustrative and revealing case study of the nexus of new telecommunications technology, mass-mediated spectacle, and the evolution of athletic fame. The legacy of the crew is both indebted to, and intertwined with, the broadcasting innovations making the Berlin Games one of the most vivid radio experiences in history.

The Berlin Games represented the first alignment of multilateral global broadcast technology with sophisticated propaganda technique. The combination of compelling sports narrative and new modes of modern telecommunication created the blueprint for all future sports broadcasting. Before the widespread implementation of refined shortwave intercontinental and transoceanic relay, the live spectacles we now expect with each quadrennial Olympiad were impossible. After Berlin and after the Second World War, the resumption of the games (in 1948) established one of the world's most important, and lucrative, recurring global broadcasts. Every four years the Olympics leverage the most innovative and sophisticated communication technologies to give global citizens new memories of athletic achievement. The Olympic Games as live global spectacle, replete with intertwined political and athletic meaning, originated in Berlin.

Our understanding of the 1936 Olympics remains centered on the brilliant achievements of Jesse Owens and the filmmaking of Leni Riefenstahl. Other U.S. stories from Berlin, including the triumphs of U.S. sprinter Helen Stephens and the last-minute removal of Sam Stoller and Marty Glickman, the two Jews on the U.S. 400-meter relay team, would later be remembered. With few exceptions, however, the rowing event and its broadcast remain largely unknown.[3] For most historians and scholars, the 1936 Games provided an ominous prelude to later Nazi villainy. They offer an early harbinger of the power of propaganda to mask heinous crimes committed in the name of race and nation.

For these and other reasons, the Berlin Games continue to fascinate. They echo across the decades, their clash of ideologies and athletics offering a bloodless preview of the twentieth-century's most titanic conflict. Many Olympic traditions debuted in Berlin, with the torch relay from Mt. Olympus in Greece, the professionalization of "amateur" athletics, and live, multilateral global broadcasting all being inaugurated in summer 1936. The German Reich Ministry for Public Enlightenment and Propaganda (often referred to as the Propaganda Ministry) used the media—particularly the Reichs-Rundfunk-Gesellschaft (RRG), Germany's National Broadcasting Company—to disseminate to the world an illusion of a "new" Germany. The RRG leveraged the games to showcase some of the world's most sophisticated and extensive broadcasting systems. Local television broadcasts to movie theaters and other dedicated locales throughout Berlin, demonstrating the media future for both Germans and tourists alike, were the promotional focus of the RRG's efforts. The Germans and the British had been racing since 1932 to be the first to introduce television to the masses. "The new Hitler administration has put itself squarely behind the development of television as an outstanding German achievement," reported *Electronics* in early 1935, "and neither money nor effort are being spared to bring about this realization."[4] The emphasis on primitive television eclipsed other innovative German broadcast technologies—including the installation

A cartoon in the *Berliner Illustrierte Zeitung* predicts the future of the Olympics. By the year 2000, television and loudspeaker technologies will make Olympic stadia obsolete.

of massive directional antennae at the shortwave plant in Zeesen—that made the games a truly global event for the first time.[5]

Because television would later become integrally linked to the mass audience's experience of the Olympic Games, most scholarship on the media and the Berlin Games emphasizes press reports, cinematic accounts (Leni Riefenstahl's *Olympia*, in particular) and rudimentary television.[6] Despite the widespread publicity surrounding television, Berlin's television broadcasts were considered disappointing. Bad weather and overcast skies created almost impenetrable gray shadows that often obscured the athletes. Described as "faulty," the German technical standard of 180 lines at 25 frames per second resulted in "onlookers" seeing only "shadowy and distorted forms." The German post office provided twenty-five viewing rooms and two motion picture theaters for the television broadcasts, but "only a single water polo game proved clear." "The audiences," reported *Broadcasting*, "were disappointed with the results."[7] Nor would Riefenstahl's *Olympia* immediately entertain. The film was not completed and released for almost two years. Yet, despite these facts, popular memory of the Olympic Games remains primarily visual. The iconic photographs of Adolf Hitler in the Olympic stadium, the torch relay through Berlin, Jesse Owens and German long jumper Lutz Long awaiting their turns, and other images instantly signal—and structure—the perception of the games across the decades. Visual memories of the Berlin Olympic Games have clearly outdistanced any auditory recall.

Yet, in Berlin and around the globe, the medium that mattered was radio. For all the scholarship on Riefenstahl's *Olympia*, on newspaper coverage of the games, on the reactions of tourists in the stadia and on the streets of Berlin, it remains the magic of radio that created the Olympic spectacle for the vast majority of people experiencing the 1936 Games. Because the Berlin Olympics were the first truly global "media event," the worldwide radio audience estimated at 300 million listeners was enabled to participate in a media spectacle as never before.[8] This global audience for the Berlin Games comprised by far the largest cohort of humanity to participate in a single event up to 1936. For listening audiences that spanned Japan, Australia, Africa, the United States, and Latin America, radio established a mental bridge to Berlin. In those Berlin radio broadcasts we find the seed that would flower into global sports broadcasting as we know it today. They involved listeners directly and immediately as no newspaper account could. Radio, as a medium, is alive, experiential, participatory, and ephemeral.[9] It is intrinsically electrifying and, unlike film and print, cannot duplicate its personal, psychological, or mass impact in stored or recorded form. Capturing and re-presenting the experience of radio listening remains particularly difficult in media studies because of its ethereal quality. At its best, radio's characteristic connective power engages listeners' imaginations precisely because both audience and broadcaster know the communication occurs in real time—like a conversation. This shared valorization of immediacy—what radio scholars have come to describe as radio's "liveness"—is precisely why so many people loved listening in on Berlin in 1936.[10] But it's also why so many scholars bypass radio in favor of other media.

In 1936, the excitement of listening to live sporting events occurring on the other side of the globe thrilled millions. Most of the global audience had never visited Berlin or knew much about the "new" Germany. Radio provided passports, transport, and tour guides. Sporting events catered to patriotic rooting interests, while promotional articles, programs, and advertisements primed global audiences for novel listening experiences. "Listen to the Olympics!" commanded a General Electric (GE) advertisement in Toronto's *Globe and Mail*. "You'll be particularly thrilled with the broadcasts of the Olympic Games from Germany if you replace all weak and noisy radio tubes with General Electric Micro Sensitive Radiotrons," read the ad. "They ensure better reception as you follow Canada's athletes in this big international sports event." Like GE, The National Broadcasting Company (NBC) advertised Olympics programming in trade journals to spur receiver sales during the summer—a traditionally slow marketing season.[11]

The radio broadcasts from Berlin captivated listeners for other reasons as well. Live broadcasting is always simultaneously connective and suspenseful. Listeners remain tightly engaged because they sense potentialities in live broadcasting unavailable elsewhere in the media. Live broadcasts, whether on television or radio, can effectively transmit indelible moments of history in real time, or they might fail spectacularly from technical difficulties. They can also do both simultaneously, as when failure itself becomes historic—such as when the 1989 Loma Prieta earthquake interrupted a live broadcast of Major League Baseball's World Series. "Well folks," ABC's Al Michaels told the audience seconds after the network's video transmission disappeared, "that's the greatest open in the history of television—bar none!"[12] Because the Berlin broadcasts comprised the most complex series of live relay transmissions attempted up to 1936, they included both remarkable successes and less well remembered failures. This is the dual nature of liveness. The transmission of every live sports event creates implicit—and often unconscious—audience expectation of both excellence and error. Suspense exists, in other words, in both the medium and the message. True broadcast perfection can be attained only retrospectively, through the employment of recordings and sophisticated technology. And even then—as with NFL replay and other officiating controversies—slippage can occur.[13]

The prospect of excellent live transoceanic programming produced through new technologies excited CBS and NBC executives in 1936. Because the Germans required no rights fees and offered free technical, engineering, administrative, and logistical assistance, both CBS and NBC seized the unprecedented opportunity. The rivalry between the two U.S. chains in both sports coverage and transoceanic broadcasting intensified significantly in 1936.[14] The Berlin events combined the drawing power of athletics with popular curiosity about German politics and culture, making "competition between American broadcasters" during the games "keener than ever."[15] One NBC executive later estimated that the network carried seventy Olympic broadcasts in 1936 (including coverage of the winter games, also held in Germany), and a CBS publication noted almost forty separate Olympic broadcasts from Germany. Measured in total transoceanic airtime, the Berlin Olympiad was the most important global broadcast on the U.S. airwaves in 1936.[16] And that year provided by far the most international programming ever heard on U.S. radio. "During 1936," a CBS promotional pamphlet explained, "the number of trans-oceanic broadcasts of the Columbia Broadcasting System was almost double that of any preceding year."[17]

The Berlin Games helped CBS, which trailed the more popular and respected NBC in network broadcasting's first decade, establish a brand identity for global news and special events coverage. Before 1936 CBS executives had been hampered in their attempts to bring German programming to the United States. NBC's exclusive agreement with the RRG resulted in significantly more German programming airing on the senior U.S. chain. In 1932, for example, NBC aired forty-five programs originating within Germany, and CBS just eleven.[18] Though NBC's exclusive contract with the RRG lapsed without renewal in 1934, both networks continued honoring it in principle. Relegated to working with the German post office's inferior studios and equipment, broadcasts from Germany airing on CBS lacked the quality of NBC's offerings.[19] To generate prestige and good publicity in the United States, however, the RRG agreed to collaborate closely with CBS and treat it almost as NBC's equal during the games.[20] The junior chain ultimately leveraged its excellent Berlin coverage to match NBC in international sports programming. This rivalry between the two broadcasting corporations undoubtedly increased audience interest in the games as both networks tried to outperform their rivals.

Around the globe, other national networks and stations worked diligently to leverage the popularity of the Olympics into higher audience numbers. The Germans, for instance, introduced a new, battery-powered portable radio receiver named the *Olympiakoffer* ("Olympic Case") in conjunction with the games. Though somewhat expensive, the new radio's portability allowed listeners to catch broadcasts in parks or at the beach. "The Olympic Games was a seminal moment in the development of [German] radio," writes historian Roger Moorhouse. They represented "a moment when many, especially the apolitical and those in rural areas, were first made aware of the enormous potential of the medium." Similarly, Japan's NHK flooded the domestic airwaves with Olympic broadcasts in 1936. In Argentina, Radio Prieto leveraged the games to attract listeners throughout South America. In the global context, there can be little argument with Olympic historian Arnd Krüger's assertion that the Berlin Games constituted "by far the largest media event of the world to that time."[21]

Scholars have analyzed the Berlin moment from a variety of angles, asking fundamental questions about the role of international athletic competition, the politics of sport, and the ideological, social, and cultural meaning of the games both in Germany and in the United States.[22] While such dynamic issues as racism and nationalism have been examined in detail, many human stories of athletic achievement have received far less attention. Yet their contemporary obscurity does not diminish their symbolic meaning, for either the participants or the new global radio audience. The success of Jesse Owens has been chronicled by scholars and authors precisely because his athletic triumph not only rebuked racist ideologies, but because in the rivalry occurring between nations struggling through the Depression, the sprinter symbolized U.S. vitality and democracy. But Owens's monumental legacy has eclipsed other remarkable and compelling stories from the summer of 1936—including those deemed equally impressive by contemporaneous reporters.

The eight-oared crew final was just such an event. By contextualizing that seminal athletic contest as a case study of Olympic celebrity, *Six Minutes in Berlin* simultaneously explains the arrival of global sports broadcasting while describing the Berlin Games on a human scale. In chronicling the story of the University of Washington crew—many of whom had never left the state of Washington before taking up rowing—this study establishes their legacy at the nexus of U.S. sports history and U.S. media history. Today it might seem incongruous to interweave the story of a champion rowing squad with an important moment in media history. But intercollegiate rowing, during the interwar years, was enormously popular. Each June, CBS, NBC, and several top New York stations broadcast the intercollegiate rowing championships live from Poughkeepsie, New York, to audiences in the millions. One hundred thousand spectators regularly lined the shores of the Hudson River, or rode observation trains, or stood by the rail of tour boats or on bridges, to watch eight-oared shells from top U.S. universities duel the four miles from Krum's Elbow to the finish line in

Poughkeepsie. Newspapers from across the continent sent reporters to cover races on the East and West Coasts. Popular magazines such as *Collier's, Harper's, Esquire, Life,* and the *Saturday Evening Post* published rowing features. Both the *New York Times* and the *New Yorker* assigned columnists to cover the rowing season. Newsreels brought all the big races and regattas to movie audiences.[23] By the late 1930s, CBS and NBC fought for exclusive broadcast rights to the national rowing championships.[24] Radio executives and sportscasters wrote books in this period noting rowing's importance on the broadcast schedule.[25] The University of Washington squad was the most important crew when rowing achieved its zenith in national popularity. Many U.S. listeners tuning into the Berlin regatta were acquainted with the Washington oarsmen, having heard earlier victories on their radios or read about them in magazines or newspapers or watched racing highlights in newsreels. By the time they raced in Berlin, they were featured in a national breakfast cereal advertisement and their names appeared in newspaper headlines throughout the United States.

Today we take global media spectacles such as the Olympics, royal weddings, or other ceremonial occasions for granted. But only a series of fortuitous circumstances created the opportunity for global broadcasting of the 1936 Olympic Games. Just four years earlier, NBC and CBS dropped live coverage from Los Angeles when the cash-strapped Olympic organizing committee demanded exorbitant rights fees at the last minute. The shrewd German regime, however, understood the propaganda value of the games. They invested heavily in production technologies and subsidized broadcasters by providing everything they needed for free or significantly reduced prices. The Reichs-Rundfunk-Gesellschaft not only spent an estimated 2 million 1936 Reichsmarks (more than $800,000 1936 U.S. dollars, or $13.6 million in 2015) to cover the games and subsidize global broadcast production, but it even supplied multilingual sports announcers for any foreign network unable to send its own broadcasters.[26]

This collaborative attitude allowed a U.S. audience to listen to the games live for the first time. For the University of Washington rowers and their coaches and all the other U.S. athletes, these live, heavily promoted broadcasts catalyzed new opportunities and celebrity. They also linked participants to their U.S. homes, where friends, family, and communities shared in their achievements. These radio experiences offered a brief respite from the constant drumbeat of dispiriting economic news and reports of social tension on the airwaves. The celebration of the Olympics on the radio created, around the world, a new venue to enjoy heroic narratives while debating national superiority. And on the global airwaves, one nation appeared to lead all others in culture, innovation, and athletic achievement: Germany.

In this sense, the Berlin Olympics were, above all, a singularly effective propaganda triumph for the Nazi regime. "Foreigners who saw Germany on exhibit were impressed by its prevailing order, by its bustling economy, by the endless spectacles of triumph," remembered German historian Fritz Stern, who, as a ten-year-old Berliner, personally experienced the games. "If Hitler had died that summer of 1936," Stern concluded, "he would probably still, in today's Germany, be hailed as a hero—a murderer of thousands, yes, but the savior of millions." The French ambassador to Germany in the 1930s, André François-Poncet, agreed. The Berlin Games, he wrote, represented "a climax of sorts, if not the apotheosis of Hitler and his Third Reich."[27] Hitler later recalled the games in a private conversation as "a unique opportunity . . . a splendid chance of enhancing our prestige abroad." He remembered rebuking officials of the Ministry of the Interior for being too penurious in their initial budget. They offered "a good example of the tendency of Germans to do things on a niggardly scale," he told his lunch companions on 12 April 1942. "On occasions of this sort," he continued, "one must aim for the greatest success possible, and the proper solution of the problem demands thinking on a grand scale."[28]

In 1936 Hitler had yet to become widely known as the murderous tyrant we recognize today. U.S. radio executives struggled to balance the more unsavory reports emanating from the Third Reich with news of Germany's rebirth in this period. For example, the NBC collection at the Library of Congress holds the prescripted obituary for Adolf Hitler, to be aired across U.S. airwaves in the event of his death. Originally composed by NBC's Program Department on 5 February 1934, the obituary was turned over to the News and Special Events Department on 7 April 1936. When read today, one is struck by its valedictory and benevolent tone. "Tonight Adolf Hitler, the idol of a nation, lies dead," the program begins. "To millions, he symbolized the restoring of a people's courage. He was the living expression of German patriotism. The world unites in sympathy for Germany in the loss of her leader."[29]

The neutrality of this memorial program (which unfortunately never aired) reveals the confused response to the Nazi revolution within NBC. By promoting the games, remaining neutral on the Nazis, and working cooperatively with the Reich Ministry for Public Enlightenment and Propaganda, the U.S. networks furthered the communicative aims of the German government in 1936. In doing so, CBS and NBC broadcast Olympic programs that often countered critical reporting Americans read in their newspapers. Such positive coverage was the payoff for the substantial German investment to facilitate broadcasting the games. The Olympics provided CBS and NBC goodwill advertising unobtainable through other channels while also allowing the German regime to exploit the credibility and prestige of the U.S. networks. Berlin thus created the model for transforming global sporting events into political weaponry, and the Nazis' shrewd utilization of sports journalism remains the model for contemporary dictatorships.

While global sports broadcasting as we know it today was born in Berlin, several earlier intercontinental sports broadcasts had been relayed successfully. A few weeks before the Berlin Olympics, for example, German heavyweight Max Schmeling knocked out Joe Louis in a broadcast transmitted back to multiple European nations from New York City.[30] Four years earlier, in June 1932, Schmeling's championship bout with Jack Sharkey was used to test a simultaneous shortwave relay to Europe and South America. RCA employed German sportswriter Harry Sperber to call the fight live for Germany while an unnamed Spanish language announcer broadcast simultaneously to South America.[31] These programs built upon earlier experiments, such as the successful relay of the Jack Dempsey–Gene Tunney bout and Westinghouse's transmission of a U.S. golf tournament to the BBC, both occurring in 1927.[32]

The first intercontinental sports broadcast produced by the U.S. corporate radio industry is most likely the shortwave experiment conducted by Westinghouse on 11 September 1924. That night Luis Firpo—the so-called "Wild Bull of the Pampas"—fought U.S. contender Harry Wills in Jersey City, New Jersey. Westinghouse hired an announcer to call the fight in Spanish, rented telephone lines to relay the signal to their Pittsburgh plant, and then converted the signal for shortwave transmission to La Nación, a station run by a newspaper company in Buenos Aires. La Nación reconverted the signal and broadcast it to its Argentine audience. In lauding the program's success, the New York Times called it "one of the greatest radio feats yet attempted."[33]

The relay of the Firpo–Wills fight would have been impossible without the encouragement of shortwave experimentation at Westinghouse under the direction of engineer Frank Conrad. Much of the professional radio community in the early 1920s dismissed Conrad's work on shortwaves. Standard belief held that only massive amounts of power and gigantic antennae transmitting "long" waves would be capable of transoceanic relay. Shortwaves were rejected by most of the corporate broadcast community (and left to the amateur hams) because of their unreliability over short distances and the atmospheric effects that occasionally distorted or weakened their reception. But long-wave transmission demanded huge amounts of power coursing through aerials elevated high off the ground on enormous towers with wires radiating out great distances. GE's first intercontinental transoceanic broadcasting experiments required the construction of a giant plant at Rocky Point, Long Island (New York), costing millions.

Unfortunately for GE, the Rocky Point plant became obsolete before being put into operation. But GE's technicians had been warned. In 1922, the great Serbian-American engineer Nikola Tesla toured Rocky Point. GE's engineers showed Tesla their six-hundred-foot-tall antenna, with its wires spreading out more than a mile and a half. "You know," Tesla told them, "it's not going to be very long, I'll take a lamp post for an antenna and I'll communicate just as far as you will with this big antenna." Conrad's Westinghouse shortwave work verified Tesla's prediction sooner than anybody imagined possible. "We all thought [Tesla] was crazy," one GE engineer, who participated in Tesla's tour, later remembered.[34]

Because Westinghouse (along with GE) owned part of RCA, Frank Conrad worked closely with his RCA and GE colleagues. Refusing to be discouraged by their dismissal of his work, Conrad arranged stunts to prove shortwave's utility. A few weeks before the Firpo–Wills fight, for instance, Conrad and RCA's David Sarnoff traveled to London for a radio conference. The gathering's goal was to establish regular radio transmission between Europe and South America. The attendees uniformly agreed that only "ultra-long wave transmission" would be suitable, at the prohibitive cost of $4 million per transmitter. But Conrad knew transoceanic relay need not be so expensive or inefficient, and he knew how to prove it. He brought to London his portable shortwave receiver, and late one night he lugged it to Sarnoff's hotel room. Coupling the receiver to the shower rod in the bathroom (for an antenna), Conrad successfully tuned in Westinghouse's experimental shortwave station 8XS from Pittsburgh. A shocked Sarnoff clearly heard the announcer at Westinghouse's Pittsburgh plant read off that day's baseball scores and other news items. Perhaps the live report of those baseball scores, rather than the Firpo–Wills fight, should be considered the origin of global sports broadcasting. But because the signal was not converted for transmission on the standard band, and the audience was so minuscule, Conrad's demonstration for Sarnoff is perhaps best considered developmental.[35]

Westinghouse and Conrad continued experimenting with shortwaves and shortwave relay throughout the mid-1920s. Sporting events proved ideal for testing technology. In 1925 Westinghouse technicians successfully employed shortwave to relay baseball's World Series between the Pittsburgh Pirates and the Washington Senators back to Pittsburgh from the nation's capital.[36] Earlier that year RCA engineers began their own shortwave testing. They selected a rowing race on the Harlem River in New York City for experimentation, and the event marked the first employment of a portable shortwave relay transmitter in U.S. broadcast history. The race call was transmitted from the water to a station on shore and then relayed to the RCA network.[37]

RCA's network (known as the WJZ network, named after its key station) would merge with AT&T's WEAF network one year later to create the National Broadcasting Company. The merger paved the way for commercial network broadcasting and was part of the general consolidation of the radio broadcasting industry in the United States between 1926 and 1934.[38] By the time of NBC's establishment it was clear that all future transoceanic intercontinental broadcasting would be accomplished through shortwave relay. Throughout 1927 and 1928, foreign engineers visited the United States while U.S. radio technicians traveled abroad to confirm cooperative experimental standards. In 1928, RCA collaborated with the British Broadcasting Corporation (BBC), the Philips Company in Holland, and the RRG to exchange special programs "to determine the usefulness of long distance, trans-oceanic, short wave transmission for rebroadcasting." On 1 February 1929, a live symphony broadcast from London was successfully carried on the U.S. airwaves over the two networks operated by NBC, inaugurating an international program series that remained active until the outbreak of the Second World War. On 25 December 1929, a full program exchange with Dutch, British, German, and French broadcasters included the initial nonexperimental U.S. network program sent East across the Atlantic to European audiences.[39] CBS's Continental Representative, César Saerchinger, later claimed the first transoceanic sporting events brought to the U.S. airwaves from overseas were soccer's Football Association Challenge Cup final at Wembley and horse racing's Derby Stakes, run at Epsom Downs in June 1930.[40] By the end of that year, all the technologies required for successful global sports broadcasting—portable shortwave transmitters for on-scene reporting and large intercontinental shortwave transmission plants—had been developed and implemented.[41] The 1932 Lake Placid Winter Olympic Games created further opportunities to refine shortwave technique and increase global sports broadcasting collaboration and exchange.[42] Between 1930 and 1935 the majority of transoceanic sports broadcasts airing on the U.S. airwaves originated in Great Britain, with the Wimbledon tennis championships and the Oxford–Cambridge Boat Race annually featured.[43]

International programming exchanges revealed myriad differences in national broadcast policies, priorities, and production standards. For example, U.S. network broadcasters were alone in prohibiting the use of transcribed (electrically recorded) materials on the national airwaves. To ease the merger creating NBC, corporate radio interests essentially bribed AT&T out of the network business by promising to exclusively rent telephone lines to connect stations. All U.S. network programming would, from then on, be carried live across telephone lines. CBS later abided by this policy, ensuring that A&T

transformed from potential network rival to a partner in limiting competition on the national airwaves. This requirement that all transoceanic broadcasting be produced live severely limited the opportunities for global programming growth in the United States. Aside from time-zone complications, shortwaves often reacted sensitively to atmospheric disturbances. Bright sunlight regularly caused problems. Over time, it was discovered that the most effective periods for live, transoceanic broadcasting occurred when both transmitter and receiver shared the same atmospheric conditions. This usually meant late afternoon (daytime) broadcasts from Europe airing in the mornings in the United States. As sunlight increased in the summer, these windows for transoceanic broadcasting expanded. But when atmospheric conditions differed considerably, or when one transmitter sent a signal from the dark evening to a receiver in a sunny daytime location, the probability of interference increased.[44] This is not to say that fine—even excellent—broadcasts could not occur even under adverse conditions. But the requirement that all programming be live, rather than recorded when conditions proved most advantageous and played back later, hindered the expansion of international program exchange in the United States.

Technological policies constituted but one noticeable difference between national broadcasting systems. Cultural assumptions, public institutions, audience relations, and performance standards further differentiated national systems.[45] In sports programming, announcing styles evolved separately around the globe, as did the popularity of specific sports. Different nations favored different events; for example, the Tour de France bicycle race proved by far the most popular sports broadcast in prewar France; the British favored cricket, soccer, and rowing; the Japanese began with baseball and sumo wrestling; Canadians favored hockey; and U.S. fans preferred boxing, horse racing, baseball, and college football.[46] But even among these four sports, boxing reigned supreme in the United States. The fights provided unity, catharsis, and distraction for the suffering U.S. public during the Depression. In Olympic sports, U.S. audiences were particularly interested in track and field, swimming, and rowing—the three sports widely viewed as most likely to result in gold-medal performances by U.S. athletes.

Producing and coordinating multiple simultaneous broadcasts in different languages across the globe proved a herculean task for the RRG. Often the same running race, boxing match, or sailing event needed to be broadcast simultaneously to two or more countries by multiple announcers. And broadcast styles differed noticeably; some announcers yelled and others narrated events calmly, requiring careful modulation for each individual signal. Germany's own international shortwave broadcasts, produced for every event and sent around the globe, added significantly to the endeavor. These were offered in multiple languages and often duplicated (or substituted for) the broadcasts of various nations.[47] The massive Zeesen shortwave transmission plant, the world's most sophisticated, beamed broadcasts around the world twenty-four hours a day. This multiplicity of signal distribution resulted in global audiences being able to catch the Berlin games via a variety of outlets. In the United States, some local stations (such as WBNX, New York) relayed the RRG English shortwave signal to their audiences in order to compete with CBS and NBC, and those equipped with shortwave receivers could enjoy BBC and RRG Olympic programs directly.[48]

The scope of this duplicative and multilateral coordination distinguished the Berlin game broadcasts from all previous radio events. By 1936 global transmission of boxing matches, tennis tournaments, and golf contests had just barely become routine. But such programs were unilateral; that is, they were generally transmitted from a single nation to another through standard program exchange channels. The Berlin experience was truly global, with listeners simultaneously enjoying the same events in New York City, Buenos Aires, Tokyo, and Sydney. "Other broadcasts have a higher interest value for individual countries, and even groups of countries, but never before has there been such a concentration of the world's broadcast commentators in one country," noted one BBC publication. "From a technical point of view the Berlin Olympic Games are the biggest job of its kind that broadcasting has ever tackled."[49] Because the 1936 Games lasted two weeks, with events occurring throughout the days and evenings and occasionally overlapping, broadcasters additionally scheduled daily summary programs. Production took place throughout the city and suburbs of Germany's huge capital, requiring an extensive local relay network and multiple studio facilities to ensure consistent levels of professional production. This is not to say every broadcast went off perfectly; occasional errors and technical difficulties arose throughout the two weeks. A few important moments were marred by production or technical issues, and some failed to air entirely. But the RRG's efforts were remarkably innovative, creative, and successful, and the broadcast of the games proved a milestone in the history of communications technology. Despite this fact, U.S. and British radio scholars remain reluctant to revisit this landmark achievement, most likely because they occurred under Nazi direction. German scholarship on the broadcasting of the Berlin Games mixes admiration for technical achievement with revulsion at the Nazi administration.[50]

The RRG's broadcast accomplishments greatly add to the historical importance of the Berlin Games. In the fields of propaganda, documentary film, and global broadcasting, the 1936 Games remain a seminal moment in twentieth-century history. "In Berlin," notes one history of the period, "the entire world was the audience."[51] And the international ramifications of this Nazi achievement continue to resonate. But we should remember that the 1936 Olympic Games played out simultaneously on the global stage and at the personal level. The experiences of athletes and journalists, tourists and citizens, radio listeners and broadcasters, all capture this vital twentieth-century moment in detail. In their stories the future of Olympic athletics, global celebrity, media innovation, and sport rivalry can all be clearly discerned.

For eight U.S. oarsmen, one coxswain, and their coach, Berlin crystallized the realization of a dream. It represented the culmination of years of labor and countless hours of practice. On the evening of 14 August 1936, they prepared to etch their names into history. Years, months, days, and hours now boiled down to a contest that would last between six and seven minutes. Back in Seattle, their families, and much of the community, listened anxiously to their radios, as did millions of other Americans. Linked by invisible waves, the next few minutes would prove electrifying and heart-stopping. But to properly understand this feeling and its place in the history of Olympic celebrity and global sports media, one must return to the Montlake Cut, in Seattle, Washington, on the chilly morning of 23 March 1936.

CHAPTER 1

Rowing, Radio, and American Sports Broadcasting, 1925–36

The late-March morning dawned cloudy over the gray hills of Seattle. Down at the boathouse, the University of Washington oarsmen gathered for the first of two practice rows on Monday, 23 March 1936. The oarsmen milled about, checking their names on the board where daily lineups were posted. The varsity, or first boat, looked strong. It was filled with experienced, powerful oarsmen, including the squad's captain, Walter Bates. But the lineups had been fluid, as every rower had experienced elevation and demotion on the board that month. The seats in the varsity for the 1936 racing season remained wide open.

The first boat went hands-on first. At their coxswain's command, they synchronously pulled the delicate cedar shell off the rack, swung it overhead, and carried it down the dock where they gently placed it in the water. The other oarsmen watched enviously. The first boat retrieved their oars, placed them in the oarlocks, took their seats, and shoved off. Waiting on the water in his coach's launch was Alvin Ulbrickson. There was almost no wind, and the long practice row was scheduled to carry the eights west through the Montlake Cut and out toward the Ballard Locks.

As the varsity shoved off the dock, coxswain Robert Moch called his rowers together by their shell. He could read it in their faces; they shared a mix of frustration, wounded pride, and determination. They were a good boat—James McMillin, sitting in the five seat, and Charles Day, in the bow pair, rowed in the previous year's varsity. Joseph Rantz, the muscular engineering student in the seven seat, had never lost a race. Gordon Adam rowed in the freshman crew that easily captured the national intercollegiate championship the year before, and that boat had been stroked by Donald Hume from Olympia, Washington, who was now assigned to this squad. They knew each other well, having spent most of the previous three months rowing in different combinations while synchronizing their styles. In fact, the same lineup, but with Donald Hatch in place of Joe Rantz in the seven seat, and a different coxswain, rowed together once at the end of the previous week. On that cold Friday afternoon, their second boat had slightly outperformed the varsity over a long practice row. They gained even more speed the next day when Ulbrickson swapped out Hatch for Rantz. The rowers rested on Sunday, and on this Monday morning, with Bob Moch in the coxswain's seat and Joe Rantz rowing behind Don Hume, the lineup that eventually won Olympic gold prepared to pull together for the first time.[1]

As Moch called out for his oarsmen to go hands on the shell, an unaccustomed quiet pervaded the shell bay. Usually, the oarsmen joked with each other or quietly chatted before hitting the water—especially if Ulbrickson was not within earshot. But on this morning—Moch remembered almost seven decades later—the boathouse and the dock were almost eerily silent. Being stuck in the second boat bothered these oarsmen. An unspoken but palpable tension was evident.

Yet the oarsmen shared another feeling as well. They shared a collective respect for and confidence in each other. They realized something escaping their coach: They possessed the strength, skills, and confidence to easily eclipse Ulbrickson's favorites. The rowers knew they were the best crew the University of Washington would boat that day. "I remember that day very distinctly," Jim McMillin recalled. "I looked up and down the boat—this was the first time we rowed together—and we thought to ourselves, you know, maybe we got something here. So it didn't take long for us to get organized, and we started to beat the hell out of the varsity." Moch recalled his crew silently watching the varsity row off the dock that morning. "We were standing about a little bit after we put the oars in the oarlock, and somebody said, 'you know this thing is going to fly.' And from the very moment that we were put together we knew that we were going to go fast."[2]

The boats rowed evenly on the run out toward Ballard Locks. But on the return back to the boathouse, rowing smoothly and powerfully, Moch's shell led comfortably all the way. Coach Ulbrickson took note. That afternoon the second boat again dominated. Going out from the boathouse—in a strong southeasterly wind—the crew coxed by Moch led by seven boat lengths by the time the shells turned around to return to the boathouse. Over the next few weeks Ulbrickson kept this eight together and watched them gain speed. He soon sensed that his career might be riding on this crew. With the Berlin Olympics looming, the veteran coach knew the 1936 varsity boat would determine his future. Washington's national reputation for rowing excellence, propagated in newsreels, discussed on local and national radio programs, and chronicled in newspapers and popular magazines, had been largely eclipsed by the success of the University of California's Golden Bears. Coach Carroll M. "Ky" Ebright's crews had won the two previous Olympic gold medals, and, in 1935, captured their third straight national championship.

Rowing, in the United States in 1936, was an enormously popular sport. Over the previous fifty years, crew races evolved into one of the country's most entertaining athletic spectacles. Regattas drew huge crowds as each new medium, whether the small magazines in the 1890s, the newsreels of the 1910s, or radio in the 1920s, exploited and increased the sport's national following.

Rowing in U.S. Popular Culture, 1852–1936

"It all started with a boat race." So wrote *Los Angeles Times* sportswriter Jim Murray in 1985. Rowing, Murray explained, "is the oldest intercollegiate sport anywhere in the world." Intercollegiate athletics can be dated to the institution of the Oxford–Cambridge boat race in England in 1829, with the U.S. version, embodied by the Harvard–Yale race, starting in 1852. "Long before the campus hero was the All-American halfback, he was the stroke oar on the crew," explained Murray. "Long before the Four Horsemen or the Seven Blocks of Granite, the Harvard Eight with cox was considered the epitome of athletic excellence. . . . The whole notion of collegiate competition began with crew. It opened the way to the Rose Bowl, Final Four, Big Ten, Ivy League, We're No. 1, Betty Coed, Boola Boola, Alma Mater Dear—the whole hoopla of my-school-can-beat-your-school."[3]

Modern intercollegiate athletics developed in the last quarter of the nineteenth century. During this period, the popularity of rowing races—both professional and intercollegiate—for spectators and gamblers continually increased. Regattas drew enormous crowds to places like Saratoga Springs, New York; Springfield, Massachusetts; and Philadelphia, Pennsylvania. An estimated twenty-five thousand people turned out in Saratoga to watch the 1875 championship race, contested by thirteen eastern colleges. By the late 1870s, intercollegiate rowing emerged as the premiere athletic endeavor of eastern colleges, with newspapers regularly devoting multiple pages to the sport and its stars.[4] This was rowing's first golden age, as professional oarsmen, revered in the media for herculean feats of endurance, became celebrities appearing in advertisements and on cigarette trading cards. Sculling races drew gambling activity, excited drunken crowds, and occasionally ended in violence. It was during this period, Robert Kelley wrote, that "clergymen and educators deplored the evils attendant on the [rowing] exhibitions; and the entire country took sides" between amateur collegiate oarsmen and professionals. Sensing an opportunity to capitalize on the sport's popularity while helping to improve its reputation, James Gordon Bennett Jr. (publisher of the *New York Herald*) began sponsoring a championship cup for the top collegiate rowing teams in the 1870s. By the 1890s, the Hearst newspapers were promoting their exclusive rowing columnist, Ralph Paine of Yale University. Rowing's immense popularity helped inspire the creation of dedicated sports pages, and later sections, in U.S. newspapers.[5]

Between 1870 and 1895 the development of an organization tasked with administering a national championship in intercollegiate rowing proved difficult. The first series of conferences, held in 1870 and 1871, resulted in the creation of the Rowing Association of American Colleges (RAAC).[6] A surprise victor captured the first championship when the unheralded University of Massachusetts crew won on 21 July 1871. In the regatta's first five years, champions included Massachusetts, Amherst College (1872), and Cornell University (1875 and 1876). Between them, Yale and Harvard won only a single national championship (Yale's 1873 victory), which led the two schools to jointly withdraw from the RAAC and resume their exclusive duel in 1877.[7] That same year the RAAC collapsed.

Throughout the 1880s, both Harvard and Yale invited various eastern schools to race in preparatory regattas before their annual contest. Columbia, Cornell, and the University of Pennsylvania all rowed against the Crimson and the Elis in various combinations throughout the decade. Attempts to revive the RAAC, or start a new "Inter-Collegiate Rowing Association" foundered when Harvard and Yale continually refused to join.[8] By the end of the decade, preliminary racing had ended, leading Columbia, Cornell, and Pennsylvania to organize their own racing series. These contests drew huge crowds and media attention, leading local booster organizations in Minneapolis (1893), Philadelphia (1894), and elsewhere to pay for the privilege of hosting college racing. Finally, in December 1894, representatives from Columbia, Cornell, and Penn met in Poughkeepsie, at the invitation of local civic leaders, to establish an organization dedicated to developing technical standards and rules, protecting amateurism, and administering a national championship.[9] That meeting led to the establishment of the Poughkeepsie Regatta, an annual championship to be contested on the Hudson, but it also ultimately created a distinct cleavage in U.S. intercollegiate rowing.

Henceforth, every rowing season ended with two separate championships: the intercollegiate championship in Poughkeepsie and the Harvard–Yale race at New London.[10]

Poughkeepsie proved an inspired spot. Perched atop a cliff just east of the Hudson River, the town's architecture and culture retained much of its Dutch-German atmosphere. Just north of the town lay a series of estates—including ones owned by the Vanderbilts, the Astors, and the Roosevelts—that lent the area a pastoral, and somewhat European, sensibility. Easily accessible by rail from eastern metropolitan areas, Poughkeepsie's civic leaders agreed to provide accommodations for the collegiate squads. The racecourse was framed by beautifully imposing bluffs and green hills that gave this stretch of the Hudson the nickname "America's Rhineland."[11]

The Hudson racecourse was historic. Sailing races on the four-mile stretch of river descending from the bend called Kromme Elleborg ("Krum's Elbow") had been organized by Dutch sailors as early as 1609. Dutch colonists called this stretch of the Hudson De Lange Rak ("The Long Reach"), and by 1837 the straight run, descending from Hyde Park to New Hamburgh, hosted rowing competitions. On 18 July 1865, the U.S. rowing championship, with its $6,000 in prize money (and more than $100,000 in legal wagering) occurred on the course. With its rich rowing history, its central location, its communication and transportation links, and its community support, the three collegiate representatives—Thomas Reath from Pennsylvania, Charles Tremaine from Cornell, and Columbia's Frederick Sill—agreed Poughkeepsie would be an ideal permanent host.[12]

The inaugural regatta, scheduled for 21 June 1895 and occurring just seven months after the association's organization, exceeded expectations. More than thirty thousand people traveled to Poughkeepsie for the weekend race, filling up hotels, restaurants, and bars and crowding the riverside park. The observation train, created when the West Shore Railroad placed grandstands on flatbed railcars, sold three thousand tickets, and thousands more spectators jammed the decks of massive excursion boats. Yachts and pleasure boats lined the racecourse.[13] All of Poughkeepsie's top establishments—the Nelson House Hotel, the Smith Brothers Restaurant, and the many shops lining Market and Main streets—were jammed.[14]

An unfortunate precedent was set even before the race began. The inaugural regatta's honored guest was the former vice president of the United States and current governor of New York, Levi P. Morton. Morton planned to use the regatta as an early presidential campaign event for 1896. As he waved to the crowds from a tugboat's deck, the boat's captain created a huge wake by steaming up the Hudson too quickly. The wake hit the Penn shell and smashed it against the floating dock, causing damage so substantial that Penn could not race. When the Columbia and Cornell oarsmen heard of the incident, while waiting at the starting line, they refused to race. The referees protested, but to no avail, and to the disappointment of tens of thousands of spectators the race was postponed until Monday, 24 June 1895, so that Penn's shell could be repaired.[15] From then on, the regatta would be scheduled on a weekday when less boat traffic plied the Hudson. But even with weekday racing, unexpected delays due to weather, equipment problems, or other issues plagued the regatta over the next fifty years.[16]

The initial regatta set other precedents. After Columbia's victory, the celebration would be long remembered for its riotous atmosphere. Most of the competitors got drunk, brawls broke out, and Columbia's oarsmen smashed apart the dining room of Poughkeepsie's top hotel. The police were called to put an end to the partying. Thus, from its inception, the Poughkeepsie Regatta earned a reputation for its rambunctious atmosphere. "Rowing races," one history of Poughkeepsie notes, "tended to be quite rowdy affairs, with much gambling and drinking." "Violence, [and] drunkenness," another states, "was endemic to race day in Poughkeepsie."[17] This party atmosphere continued to grow; by the late 1920s, the actual racing, for many attendees, merely provided a pretense for dodging prohibition, showing off leisure craft and yachts, and making the society pages of the *New York Times* or *Herald-Tribune*.

Gambling remained popular throughout the regatta's first decades, leading to rumors that certain coaches not only bet on races but manipulated odds by using the press.[18] The gambling community's presence always concerned collegiate authorities. In 1919 the chairman of the University of Pennsylvania's Council on Athletics announced his preference that the Quakers abandon Poughkeepsie. Dean William McClellan complained of what he termed "the professional instinct" occurring on the Hudson. He argued the training camp and regatta, occurring outside "term-time" made oarsmen "vulnerable to societal pressures" more closely monitored when students lived under close supervision. His effort to end Pennsylvania's participation, like other attempts to clean out the gambling element, went for naught.[19]

Not everyone in the rowing community loved Poughkeepsie's party atmosphere. Many complained that partying and socializing eclipsed racing. Poughkeepsie became a New York society spectacle, where a first-class seat on the observation train, or an invitation to the right dance, represented an important status marker. Like Wimbledon, or the Masters golf tournament, just the name "Poughkeepsie" sparked associations about class and wealth. Predictably, as the event grew, so did the blowback. "The most overrated spectator sport I know of is college rowing," Paul Gallico, one of the top U.S. sportswriters, argued:

> How it manages annually to attract the vast crowds that go to see it has mystified me ever since in my early youth as number six in the Columbia shell I rowed four miles down the Hudson past banks solidly black with people. The regattas are difficult to get to and even more difficult to get away from. If you haven't a seat on the observation train—and the supply of seats is limited—you see perhaps one minute of the race. . . . Most of the spectators are pretty bored . . . but go for the party and in order to be able to say that they've been.[20]

Jimmy Cannon, the *New York Post*'s veteran sports columnist, complained about the reverence with which sportswriters approached the race. Unlike most athletic contests, "the crew races at Poughkeepsie were described with dignity by the awed journalists." Such reporting, he suggested, was the result of a lazy reliance upon dramatic clichés and a class bias in which this "purest of amateur sports" was "untouchable" because of its identification with U.S. university culture. Disdaining the conventions hindering accurate race reporting, Cannon recalled one particularly telling experience:

> As Navy won the varsity race, one of the journalists said: "The Navy stroke collapsed." Someone remarked that the unidentified young man was erect and fresh-looking in the boat. "How can you write a story without having the winning stroke collapse?" the rowing expert asked. "You'd get fired in a minute. That's always part of the story."[21]

Cannon, like Gallico, never considered crew an engaging spectator sport. "No matter where you were," he recalled, "it was almost impossible to see the small flat shells until they were very close to you."[22] Even one of Poughkeepsie's civic leaders later admitted that "watching a Regatta is not a very exciting way to spend an afternoon."[23] But the crowds, festivities, gambling, parades, and bands marching down Main Street to the river turned the event into a spectacle. The regatta's reputation as a place to see and be seen increased throughout the interwar years. When New York governor Franklin Roosevelt—who had served on the civic committee hosting the regatta and attended regularly as a guest of the stewards—was elected president, the event gained even more national prominence.

Attendance kept growing. By the middle of the 1930s, more than a hundred thousand people annually lined the banks of the Hudson; stood atop the High Bridge at the three-mile mark; crammed the decks of riverboats, sightseeing cruisers, yachts, and other pleasure craft; or watched from the mobile grandstands on the forty-car observation train. Routines became enshrined; a signal system to name the victor for the enormous crowd—and the gamblers—was in place by 1910: Mike Bogo, a local tavern owner, ignited a series of bombs to indicate the champion's lane number.[24] The system worked wonderfully from its inception—with one major mishap. In 1935 a duel between California and Cornell ended in a very tight finish. Because of the twilight darkness and the angle of the finish line, most observers could not discern the victor. The popular consensus was that Cornell passed California at the line, and Bogo sent up that signal. Regatta officials, however, soon ruled that California had, in fact, held off Cornell. Word was quickly sent up to Bogo on the bridge, but it was too late. Gamblers and bookies had already begun paying off Cornell tickets when they were suddenly besieged by California's bettors. Confusion reigned. One unlucky bookmaker claimed to have lost $30,000. Going into the 1936 race, Bogo was warned only to light his bombs upon receipt of official results.[25]

Like that 1935 varsity final, racing in Poughkeepsie could be tense and dramatic. But during the regatta's first three decades, one team distinguished itself by its dominance. Cornell University lost the initial regatta but soon thereafter made finishing first or second in Poughkeepsie an annual tradition. The custom of winning resulted from the coaching of Charles E. ("Pop") Courtney, the greatest professional sculler in the last quarter of the nineteenth century. Courtney won hundreds of thousands of dollars in sculling purses and was already a national sporting celebrity before agreeing to coach in Ithaca. After Columbia won in 1895, the reign of Courtney's Cornellians began. In 1896, when Yale abandoned Harvard to participate in the English Henley Regatta, the Crimson traveled to Poughkeepsie where Cornell easily beat them. Cornell's dominance enabled Poughkeepsie to overshadow the Harvard–Yale race.[26] In 1897, to establish a true national champion, two Poughkeepsie Regattas were held. One featured Cornell, Yale, and Harvard and the second Cornell, Columbia, and Pennsylvania. Cornell easily swept both. Cornell's dominance enhanced its reputation, attracted national media attention, and catalyzed interest in participation from other schools. Georgetown University sent its first crew in 1900, and Syracuse University's application for admission was accepted in 1901. The United States Naval Academy sent a crew in 1907 (but would not return until 1921), and Stanford University—the first representative from the Pacific Coast—was admitted to the 1912 race. The University of Washington arrived in 1913, and California's Golden Bears participated for the first time in 1921.[27]

Regional press interest grew with each additional competitor. The regatta became a truly national sport spectacle long before Major League Baseball or the National Football League posted teams to the West Coast. The decade of the 1920s saw a tremendous upsurge of interest in collegiate athletics—particularly football—as the development of "intersectional" rivalries paralleled and facilitated the growth of national radio networks. By the mid-1920s, the general narrative of Poughkeepsie competition was established. The racing provided a confrontation between eastern schools rowing with a British, and later, American, rowing style versus the more natural and physical Pacific Coast schools practicing a western stroke.[28] The eastern style, which became distinctly American under the coaching innovations of Richard Glendon, powered one of the greatest Olympic champions, the "Miracle Crew" from the United States Naval Academy that captured gold in 1920. Glendon became a famous figure in U.S. athletics, publishing a popular book in 1923 and having his maxims and aphorisms widely reprinted in the press.[29]

This East versus West narrative encompassed the nation and explains the event's popularity as new national media such as newsreels, the small magazines, and eventually radio came into being. The regatta became so famous that popular magazines such as *Collier's Weekly, Harper's, Scribner's,* and others published both fictional and nonfictional stories set during the training camps for the race. *Literary Digest, The Outlook,* and other national magazines condensed newspaper reporting about the regatta. *The New Yorker* began reporting on college rowing in the late 1920s, and by the mid-1930s "The Oarsmen" column had become a regular feature. The race showed up in less expected media venues as well; Seattle sportswriter Clarence Dirks sold a story to the pulp magazine *Dime Sports* that pivoted upon a fictionalized version of Al Ulbrickson's legendary performance stroking the Washington varsity to victory with a torn arm muscle in 1926. The stories emerging from the regatta tended to be romantic and consisted chiefly of predictable morality tales about sacrifice and teamwork. The authors—with the notable exception of Alastair MacBain, who won the regatta twice as a Columbia oarsman—usually used the event as a prop to anchor universal themes of love, competition, cooperation, collaboration, and sacrifice. One old-time coach decried "the crews of fiction" appearing in magazines "somewhere in the issues between May and June" because the stories were so formulaic and (to any real rower) humorous in their overdramatized romanticism.[30] None of these stories can be considered a classic; several are well-written, however, and accurately relay the experience of rowers as evidenced later in memoirs and interviews. The mere existence of so many stories attests to the regatta's national popularity.[31]

Ultimately radio broadcasting, with its ability to report the Poughkeepsie races live across the continent as they unfolded, elevated the regatta's—and rowing's—national profile to its historical apex. The excited announcers and roaring crowds, the intersectional rooting interests, and the dramatic races all combined to create one of the most important sporting spectacles of the inter-war years. Rowing and radio, in many ways, were ideally matched.

Rowing and American Sports Broadcasting, 1925–36

From Seattle to Boston, Chicago to Atlanta, millions of U.S. listeners tuned in every June to CBS and NBC to listen to racing on the Hudson. And just as radio heightened rowing's popularity, rowing played an influential yet forgotten role in the development of U.S. sports broadcasting.

Broadcasting and rowing were particularly well suited during U.S. network radio's developmental decade between 1926 and 1936. Before advertising agencies captured control over production and scheduling of programming on the U.S. airwaves, the networks sought low-cost, high-interest "sustaining" (non-commercial) programs capable of growing network radio's national audience.[32] Coverage of rowing in allied media provided free promotion for network radio's regatta programming. The sport was often practiced in major urban areas, near broadcasting facilities, keeping production costs low. Unlike boxing matches or baseball games, crew races had predictable (and short) durations, allowing radio executives to confidently slot them into fifteen-minute or thirty-minute programs. The races also proved useful for experimenting with new technologies. U.S. broadcasting's first test of portable shortwave (wireless) retransmission from an outdoor pickup occurred when Radio Corporation of America (RCA) engineers placed a transmitter aboard a yacht following the Child's Cup race between Columbia, Princeton, and the University of Pennsylvania on the Harlem River racecourse. "We were desirous of broadcasting certain important shell races—that is, college boat races—during the early years of broadcasting," remembered RCA research engineer Raymond F. Guy, "but we had no way to transmit from the water. So in our laboratory I developed a portable transmitter which we could put on a boat and then send the program over the radio relay to the shore line where it would be picked up and forwarded." That successful broadcast, with J. Andrew White at the microphone, occurred on 23 May 1925. It paved the way for all future portable wireless relay broadcasting, including coverage of political conventions, parades, sports, and other events unreachable by wired microphones. "Boat races were considered exceptionally suited to radio reporting," remembered RCA's chief engineer in 1930.[33] Broadcasters in England and Germany concurred. Germany's first sports broadcast consisted of a rowing race in 1925, and the BBC first employed portable shortwave relay transmission with the broadcast of "The Boat Race" in 1927.[34]

Because Poughkeepsie sat less than 100 miles north of the networks' central offices in New York City and had excellent broadcast relay wire facilities, it was quickly identified as an ideal event for testing live coverage techniques. Memoirs by network executives detail regatta coverage extensively. For NBC's A. A. ("Abe") Schechter, the head of News and Special Programs (NBC Sports did not yet exist as a network division), and CBS's Ted Husing, the network's top sports announcer and later Director of Sports, racing stories provided colorful anecdotes illustrating the rivalry between America's initial radio networks.

The earliest Poughkeepsie Regattas were broadcast by local stations on an experimental basis in 1921 and 1922.[35] These reports, however, were problematic for several reasons. "We had to do it by telescope from long distance and weren't always sure which boat was in the lead," explained RCA's Guy. After constructing the first portable shortwave relay transmitter, and after employing it successfully to cover the 1925 Child's Cup race, Guy and his RCA engineering team brought the transmitter to Poughkeepsie for the 1925 regatta:

> By virtue of this radio relay it was possible to do a perfectly wonderful job of describing [the] race. . . . It was broadcast from the boat to the nearby shore—a fraction of a mile—and then it was picked up and sent by wire line to the station. The only difficulty we ran into was the rocking of the boat. When the boat rocked, the frequency would change because the antenna would move down and change capacity to the action of the water. We found out how to fix that in short order.[36]

Between 1925 and 1930 the regatta grew in popularity as NBC, and then CBS, continually improved the required technical infrastructure. The local telephone company, hired by the networks, employed "scores of radio and telephone experts" to install new equipment. At one point they built "a radio control point in an old mansion on the eastern side of the river" in order to amplify and modulate shortwave relay signals for transmission down the Hudson to New York City control rooms.[37] Network radio's two top sports announcers—Husing and Graham McNamee of NBC—began making the annual trek to Poughkeepsie to cover the race. In 1930, to prepare for the regatta, Husing "spent four days at the training quarters of various crews, riding in the coaching launches and learning just what makes the wheels go round in the well-oiled human mechanism which propels the delicately balanced shell."[38]

The 1929 regatta transmission was particularly remarkable. Both CBS and NBC broadcast the races, and Husing later called it "the most exciting half-hour of sports broadcasting I ever knew or maybe ever will know." Equipped with a portable shortwave transmitter, sitting in the bow of the yacht the *Maid Marian*, Husing prepared to call the varsity race. This on-the-water report gave

CBS's broadcast an advantage over NBC's program, which relied on McNamee calling the race from the rail of the Mid-Hudson Bridge. CBS's edge would be the proximity to the action; remembering the program, Husing crowed that McNamee "couldn't see any of the agony, even through binoculars," from such an elevated perch.[39]

But the weather did not cooperate. Just before the race was to start, the wind began blowing as "a big thunderstorm was brewing off to the west. The sky was black in that direction," recalled Husing. A false start delayed the race, and the water became rough. The *Maid Marian* collided with Cornell's shell and split it in two. The race then began just as a massive squall hit the river and rain cascaded from the black sky. Shells filled with water, and identifying the crews became impossible. One by one boats started sinking. Across the course, oarsmen and coxswains required rescue. Six of the nine starting crews sank, and the race was "won" by a Columbia team that taped up its outriggers, creating rudimentary splashboards before the race began. The broadcasts were a mess. Husing blindly called the race, constantly qualifying assertions with remarks about the lack of visibility. McNamee confused the Columbia shell with M.I.T.'s squad, ultimately calling "an astonishing radio victory for the Engineers." The following day the *New York Times* reported the difficulties faced by the radio announcers. "We could scarcely see what was going on," one told the *Times*. Both networks signed off without obtaining the official results. Listeners complained to the networks and the press about the programs because the announcers hedged every comment with "seems," "appears," or "perhaps." In Seattle, a crowd listening to the broadcast on loudspeakers outside the *Seattle Times* building cheered when news that California sank came over the loudspeaker.[40]

Royal Brougham, sports editor of the *Seattle Post-Intelligencer*, traveled to Poughkeepsie annually where CBS (and later NBC) employed him to call the races. Though he attempted to remain impartial on the air, Brougham occasionally showed favor to the western crews. This bias was particularly evident in the 1934 broadcast.[41] That 1934 race would also be one of the final sportscasts for Graham McNamee, the pioneering U.S. sportscaster. McNamee caused a scene and was almost fired for his stumbling, almost incoherent, and likely inebriated race report. *Sports Illustrated* later recounted the event:

> For some reason McNamee decided to call the race from a rowboat at water level. He arrived late and had trouble getting his bearings. . . . Visibility was poor, particularly so from McNamee's boat. In addition, an incorrect rumor seeped down that one of the shells had sunk, and McNamee kept trying to place the missing crew. He maintained a brave chatter of rowing jargon . . . while he tried to identify the various eights flashing by. When the blur reached the finish line

he had to make a decision, and he named Navy. Actually, California was first by ¾ of a length, Washington second and Navy third, ¼ length behind Washington. One onlooker seems to remember that McNamee, straining to get the finish, fell into the water.[42]

NBC received numerous letters of complaint about McNamee's performance. "I think your man on the observation train did an excellent job," wrote one Chicago listener. But "a very poor job was done at the finish line by your star reporter, Graham McNamee." A chastened McNamee wrote a three-page memo to NBC management blaming the Coast Guard, the judges, spectators, and others for his mistakes. The 1934 regatta proved the last in a series of erratic performances by McNamee, and NBC management spent the rest of 1934 auditioning replacements for their top sportscaster.[43]

No ratings exist for the Poughkeepsie broadcasts because they aired as "sustaining" or unsponsored special event programs. Yet the national popularity of the broadcasts can be measured by the reports of audience interest in newspapers and broadcast industry magazines, the annual renewal, and the bids eventually placed for exclusive rights to the event.[44] The regatta's peak in national

Throughout the 1920s and 1930s, rowing races appeared regularly on U.S. network radio. Here Ted Husing and Franklin Delano Roosevelt Jr. (who rowed at Harvard) call the 1938 Columbia–U.S. Naval Academy race for CBS. (CBS publicity photograph.)

popularity occurred between 1935 and 1940, at precisely the time when competition between CBS and NBC for exclusive sports programming first emerged.

The emerging rivalry between the two national networks in sports broadcasting resulted from a combination of factors. Broadcast advertising's growth
from the trough of the Depression in 1932–33 enabled the chains to sell more
programs, and the improvement in technology for remote broadcasting facilitated an increase in outside production. But the chief spur to national sports
broadcasting occurred when the networks decided to enter the arbitrage business of directly purchasing broadcast rights and reselling them to advertisers.
Except in special circumstances (primarily heavyweight championship boxing
matches), neither network paid directly for exclusive national sports broadcasting rights before 1935. In 1932, for instance, when the Los Angeles Olympic
Committee sought to negotiate a rights fee to cover its deficits, the offended
radio companies colluded in a boycott of live coverage of the games rather than
engage in a bidding war.[45] By 1935, however, the advertising climate for commercial broadcasting had improved. Network executives watched as advertisers,
with their agencies, started buying national sports programming. Particularly
eye-opening was the purchase from Major League Baseball, by the Ford Motor
Car Company, of the broadcast rights to the 1934 World Series for $100,000.[46]

CBS and NBC management realized profits could be earned should the radio
networks themselves purchase exclusive rights, which could then be sold off
to advertisers. In September 1935 CBS executives informed John Royal, NBC's
head of programming, that they intended to end the three-year "understanding"
between the networks that they "would not buy sporting events of any kind for
sustaining [noncommercial] purposes." The issue was simple: CBS had never
aired a heavyweight championship fight, and NBC's success in obtaining and
selling exclusive rights to the most popular program on the U.S. airwaves hurt
CBS financially. To Royal, the timing of the change was suspicious; he was
convinced that CBS intended to purchase the 1935 World Series directly from
Major League Baseball before lining up a sponsor—something neither chain
had ever done. "We must meet this challenge," Royal told the general manager
of NBC:

> They have thrown down the gauntlet and I think we should give them a darn
> good licking. My suggestion is that we go out and buy all the important events
> now. Most of them we can sell. We might have to take a loss on one or two, but
> in the long run we will keep NBC out in front where it belongs.[47]

Royal's plan was soon implemented. Both networks started buying sports
events throughout 1936 and into 1937. With rowing's huge popularity—and

the promotional boost offered by enormous newspaper and magazine coverage—the Poughkeepsie Regatta made an obvious target for CBS management.

The problem for CBS was that the race occurred in public space, over a four-mile course, and there was no way to prevent NBC from access. So CBS negotiated a deal with the Intercollegiate Rowing Association to purchase exclusivity in reporting from the judges' float at the finish line and from aboard the observation train. Upon initially hearing the erroneous rumor that CBS purchased exclusive rights to the entire regatta, NBC's Schechter was "apoplectic" about "this outrage." The Hudson River, he argued, was public domain, and nobody could "own" the rights to an event occurring upon it. When informed that the rights were simply to broadcast exclusively from the observation train and float, Schechter calmed down. "Obviously, if we had the foresight to sew up the observation train, Columbia would have screamed that *they* had been outraged," he admitted.[48]

Despite CBS's exclusive contract, in 1937 disguised NBC employees boarded the observation train with hidden transmitting equipment. The railroad ejected the NBC personnel, but NBC did everything else possible to negate CBS's broadcasting advantage. "We got our lines up along the river . . . about a mile apart and at these points we stationed announcers with powerful field-glasses," Schechter recalled, explaining that NBC also arranged with the New York Central Railroad to have an observer "on a convenient trestle that would enable him to see the boats coming down the river." NBC chartered an airplane to circle the racecourse with Royal Brougham transmitting from above. The race was delayed by rain and wind, and the airplane continued circling, occasionally running into turbulence. "Mr. Brougham heroically stuck to his task," Schechter recalled, "with only an occasional burp to indicate that he . . . was air-sick." When the program ended, Schechter called it "undoubtedly the finest description of a Poughkeepsie Regatta by a man in the throes of vomiting in the whole history of radio."[49]

While the Poughkeepsie Regatta represented the most important annual rowing event on the national airwaves, other races—including the Harvard–Yale duel—were also regularly broadcast. But just as Poughkeepsie achieved its apex of national popularity between 1930 and 1940, the Harvard and Yale crews proved less competitive with the squads from California, Cornell, Columbia, Navy, and Washington. Neither the Crimson nor the Elis had a realistic chance to represent the United States in 1936 as the eight-oared crew in Berlin.[50] In contrast, both the 1935 and 1936 Poughkeepsie Regattas drew additional media attention because of the upcoming Olympic Games. In 1935, after California barely edged out Cornell, the Golden Bears and their coach appeared on Al Jolson's popular NBC variety program, "Shell Chateau." Ky Ebright and Reggie

Watt ("the coach and the coxswain of the famous University of California crew") were interviewed, followed by Jolson introducing a skit parodying sportscasters titled "The 2,000-Meter Race."[51] The Poughkeepsie racecourse was four miles, but the Olympic distance was 2,000 meters. Everyone, it seems, was looking ahead to 1936.

Assembling Olympians: The 1936 University of Washington Crew

Al Ulbrickson felt the pressure. The University of Washington crew, victors of three national championships over four years in the mid-1920s, had not returned from the Hudson with a title since his senior year in 1926. During the previous three decades the university's crew enjoyed a national reputation for excellence. The media regularly attributed the development of modern U.S. intercollegiate rowing to the team from Seattle. The university's "new" campus, built in 1905 off Union Bay, offered perhaps the best geography for rowing in North America. Washington's crew tradition emerged just as outdoor recreation became a big business and vital civic endeavor in the largest city in the Pacific Northwest.[52]

The university's new campus was situated perfectly for rowing. Once the Montlake Cut, with its canal, was completed in 1916, Washington's oarsmen enjoyed access to some of the finest waterways on the continent. Crews could venture into Lake Washington, but if whitecaps or swells prevented practice, they could row west toward the Puget Sound through the Montlake Cut and then make a curve, going through Portage Bay and Lake Union, just north of the main part of Seattle, out to the Ballard Locks. Seattle's temperate climate provided the opportunity for year-round, on-the-water conditioning and technique drills. Unlike eastern schools, the Huskies were never iced in. "Washington is superbly situated for rowing," noted *The Outlook*, and "the men of Seattle are out on the water literally months ahead of any other crews."[53]

Yet geography does not fully explain the University of Washington's rowing success. Washington's crew community proved exceptionally unified. The squads were generally composed of Washington State natives with little rowing experience. These athletes tended to be older and more mature, with many having taken time off to work in physically demanding jobs to earn tuition. Many oarsmen were first-generation college students from working-class families. Unlike eastern rowers, of whom many first rowed in prep school, Washington's athletes were coachable blank slates, ready to be trained in the technique known as the "Conibear" stroke or "western" rowing style. Many rowers lived in the Varsity Boat Club, a cooperative student-athlete house. "The quarters are ample, the food of the best, the living co-operative and as cheap as it can be made," noted *The Outlook* in 1925, and "during months of living together the crew squad becomes one big family."[54]

Local media supported the team. Rowers became regionally famous, with profiles regularly appearing in Seattle's newspapers. Alden Blethen, publisher of the *Seattle Daily Times*, insisted that sports editor George Varnell provide ample rowing coverage, and the *Post-Intelligencer*'s Royal Brougham was also a regular presence at the boathouse.[55] Such publicity furthered Washington's success by producing huge numbers of participants in the annual crew "turnout." As many as 250 aspiring oarsmen might show up on the first day of the season. Every fall, Tom Bolles, the coach of the freshman team between 1927 and 1936, boated enormous numbers of would-be oarsmen.

The consistent excellence of University of Washington rowing can be attributed to these factors, but it was the presence of a tall, austere British boat builder named George Pocock that distinguished the Huskies from their rivals. Pocock's "value to Washington is immeasurable," one newspaper account reported without exaggeration.[56] Pocock's knowledge of rowing, his craftsmanship and boatbuilding technique, and his inspirational (if occasionally intimidating) presence structured, animated, and inspired Washington rowing throughout the twentieth century.

Born in 1891, Pocock immigrated to Canada from England as a teen. He was the son, and grandson, of famous boat builders. His father served as Eton's boatwright, and his uncle owned a boat-building shop under London Bridge. George and his brother, Dick, were raised on the water. Upon turning fourteen, George and Dick joined their father's Eton workshop as apprentices. For five years the brothers assisted their father as he carefully honed and shaped wood, assembling the slim, delicate crafts with precision. They also rowed whenever given the chance, and in 1910 Dick Pocock won the prestigious Doggett's Coat and Badge race, a contest on the River Thames originating in 1715. Aaron Pocock unfortunately lost his position at Eton in 1910, and the boys went to London in search of employment, only to move on to Canada when word of an opportunity reached them. They traveled to Vancouver, where a former Cambridge University oarsman paid them to build sculls for the Vancouver Rowing Club. Within a few months, additional boat orders arrived from Victoria, British Columbia, and elsewhere in the Pacific Northwest.[57]

The brothers' reputation reached Seattle. One morning in 1912, a "strange visitor" rowed up to the Pocock's shop. "My name's Hiram Conibear," he announced. Conibear told the brothers he'd begun assembling a prestigious crew at the University of Washington. He wanted the school to become the

"Cornell of the West"—a young university with an unbeatable crew enhancing its national reputation. Conibear promised more orders than they could fill if the Pococks would move to Seattle. The delighted brothers headed south.[58]

George Pocock and Hiram Conibear possessed opposite personalities yet collaborated to revolutionize rowing. Described by the *Saturday Evening Post* as "a tall, slender, gray-eyed chap with a mop of unruly hair," Conibear's presence was kinetic. Although rowing existed at the University of Washington before his 1906 arrival, the initial efforts were mostly intramural with inconsistent intercollegiate racing. Conibear brought to Seattle outsized aspirations for the little-known university. Born in Illinois in 1871, at a young age Conibear went to work in a watch factory. The manufacturer switched over to bicycles to capitalize on the national craze for six-day bike races, and Conibear managed and trained the company's cycling team. The success of that team caught the eye of Amos Alonzo Stagg, the University of Chicago football coach, who hired Conibear to train Chicago's football and track teams in 1896. Working for Stagg paid off. Five years later Conibear was named track coach and head trainer at the University of Illinois. After an unsuccessful stint as athletic director of Montana State University, Conibear returned to Chicago to train the 1906 World Series champion White Sox.[59]

That fall a former Washington football star studying medicine in Chicago contacted Stagg looking for a recommendation for a trainer. Stagg suggested Conibear, who accepted the university's offer and moved west. The university, Conibear soon learned, needed a rowing coach. "I'd make a good one," he told athletic director Lorin Grinstead. Even though Conibear admitted not knowing "one end of a boat from another" Grinstead hired him. An autodidact, Conibear read rowing books voraciously and pressed any visiting easterner with rowing experience for information. He tinkered constantly in his quest for the most efficient stroke. He "never taught the same stroke two years running," one of his oarsmen recalled. Conibear's inventiveness eventually led to the development, in collaboration with George Pocock, of the "Conibear" or "western" or "Washington" stroke that came to dominate U.S. rowing. Oarsmen rowing the stroke won the eight-oared championships in the Olympic Games of 1924, 1928, 1932, and 1936. The coaches of those Olympic champions—Ed Leader at Yale (1924), Ky Ebright at California (1928 and 1932), and Washington's Ulbrickson (1936)—learned the technique in Seattle. Once a stable iteration of the stroke was established, about 1916, it achieved remarkable results. University of Washington crews captured intercollegiate rowing titles three times in four regattas in the mid-1920s. Washington became known as the "mother church" of U.S. rowing when coaches teaching the stroke were hired throughout the nation.[60]

The stroke's chief innovation resulted from the recognition that the long-layback commonly used in eastern rowing was inefficient and counterproductive. While the eastern style kept the oar in the water longer, extending propulsion and limiting the oar's time out of the water ("on the recovery"), it could place too much pressure on the stomach and back muscles. It also often caused the oar's speed to slow in the water and "pinch" upon release (that is, check the speed of the boat by making extraction from the water too slow). Conibear's curiosity about mechanics inspired him to think about how the stroke and recovery (the time when the oar is out of the water) might be combined holistically so the whole process blended seamlessly. In other words, he wondered where the most efficient application of power would be in order to keep the boat moving at uniform speed. According to legend, he discovered his secret by turning over a bicycle and patting a wheel as it spun. The key moment, he realized, occurred when his open palm first struck the already spinning wheel. The parallel moment in rowing was when the oar initially contacts the water as the shell moves—the moment known as "the catch." Through a series of experiments, including one involving a skeleton borrowed from a laboratory, Conibear created his new stroke.[61]

The emphasis on a clean and aggressive catch was but one of Conibear's innovations. He also favored a quick, almost chopping, release at the finish of the stroke. The combination of speed and precision at both ends of the stroke meant his technique required disciplined hand movements. The Conibear technique soon became distinguishable by its quick hand-catch, with the oar slashing directly into the water, and its short, rapid oar extraction at the finish. Length of time in the water mattered less to Conibear than the intensity of the application of power. But that intensity needed to be blended with a smooth recovery to keep the boat gliding.[62] The paradox of the western stroke is that it was at once more mechanistic and more fluid than either its predecessors or contemporaneous practice in eastern (U.S.) rowing. The precise timing of each segment of the stroke was crucial; any slightly jerky or asynchronous movement between the hands, legs, arms, and back could frustrate both the individual and the crew as a whole. Only by voluminous practice could rowers habituate the sequence of movements. And even after weeks and months of repetition, proficiency required an unconscious mastery embedded in muscle memory.[63]

Between 1907 and 1917 Hiram Conibear and George Pocock built the foundation of Washington's rowing program. Conibear implemented the new stroke, successfully raised funds, and improved the profile of the sport and the university. He organized the Varsity Boat Club, had a new boathouse built in 1910, and pressed the university and Seattle's civic leaders to fund trips to Poughkeepsie starting in 1913. But in 1917 intercollegiate racing was suspended because of World War I, and the Pococks went to work for Bill Boeing's aircraft concern. One day that spring, Conibear fell from a ladder in his backyard, broke his neck, and died instantly. The rowing community memorialized Conibear by naming the stroke for him, but precise authorship of the innovative technique must be attributed to both Pocock and Conibear.[64]

Yet, for all its success, the stroke that launched the University of Washington to national athletic prominence failed to deliver the Huskies an intercollegiate championship between 1926 and 1936. Ulbrickson started coaching the team in fall 1927 when Rusty Callow, a popular veteran of Conibear's crew, left Seattle for the University of Pennsylvania. Ulbrickson—like Conibear, Ed Leader (who left Washington for Yale and took Dick Pocock with him), and Callow before him—relied heavily on the expertise of George Pocock. Ulbrickson and Pocock were both quiet, pensive, and thoughtful men. But underneath his tough exterior, Ulbrickson could be wracked by anxieties and indecision. He loathed changing lineups and demoting rowers, for instance, and would invite Pocock to take a break from boat building to attend practices. Pocock would then make the difficult decisions, and oarsmen soon learned to fear the British man's presence in the coaching launch. But that fear also intermixed with respect, as Pocock's few words of encouragement carried tremendous weight.[65]

Rowing, for Pocock, was transcendently mystical. It shifted its practitioners to higher realms of existence, teaching them soulful lessons unavailable elsewhere in life. For him, rowing offered the finest combination of individual athleticism and teamwork, an endeavor where the singular melding of consciousness and feeling could occur. The drive to row perfectly—an impossible goal—represented to Pocock a spiritual, technical, and physical quest. Ulbrickson's orientation proved more grounded. Shortly before starting high school, Ulbrickson's family moved from Seattle to Mercer Island. No bridge linked the island and the mainland at the time, and so throughout his high school years he spent countless hours rowing between his island home and the city's lakeshore. After graduation, Ulbrickson spent a year working physically demanding jobs in order to earn enough money to enroll at the University of Washington. After stroking his freshman eight to a national freshman championship in 1923, he led the 1924 and 1926 Husky varsities to national championships. He rowed with grace, employing a natural stroke honed by the hours on Lake Washington. Ulbrickson's handsome but impassive face hid a quiet intensity. Always laconic, he seemed old for his age. His quiet demeanor and deadpan look later earned him the sobriquet "the Dour Dane," in the national media.[66]

Ulbrickson believed his 1928 and 1932 crews possessed legitimate opportunities to represent the United States in the Olympics, but in both years California took Poughkeepsie and the Olympic trials. By fall 1933, Ulbrickson and Pocock were already thinking about Berlin. Oarsmen were closely evaluated for qualities both tangible and intangible; character and drive as well as physical strength and rhythmic grace. The first iterations of 1936's varsity crew contained few—and sometimes none—of the men eventually venturing to Berlin. This was the great irony of Washington's most successful season: the coach originally preferred different oarsmen. Ulbrickson called his 1933 varsity—denied the opportunity for an intercollegiate championship by the suspension of the Poughkeepsie Regatta—"by far, the best crew I ever put together."[67] The publicity surrounding that crew made the freshman turnout in fall 1933 the largest in history.[68] The following spring, Tom Bolles's freshman crew easily won the freshman championship on the Hudson. One observer called that 1934 squad "perhaps the best that ever rowed in the preliminary two-mile race in Poughkeepsie." The freshman victory contrasted sharply with the 1934 varsity and junior varsity results, leading Pocock and Ulbrickson to favor this group of rising sophomores going into the 1935 season. "Ulbrickson sees in his sophomores the Olympic champions of 1936," the *New York Times* reported that year.[69] Calling the sophomores "potentially the greatest crew I've ever coached," Ulbrickson admitted that he "shunted experienced men into the background." "Those sophomores in a year or two may be the fastest crew that ever rowed a race," he told one magazine.[70]

Early in 1935 Ulbrickson named the sophomores the varsity crew. He rarely switched lineups, and his veterans grew frustrated. Making matters worse, Royal Brougham regularly lauded the sophomore oarsmen as Seattle's new heroes in the *Post-Intelligencer*. Resentment intensified, making 1935 a tense and unsuccessful season. Intrasquad time trials became battles. Team unity evaporated. Soon the older, more experienced oarsmen began beating the vaunted sophomores, but Ulbrickson refused to demote his Olympians. Agreeing to a time trial before the California race on the Oakland estuary, Ulbrickson promised his squad the fastest boat would be named varsity. "We [the veteran crew] beat them down in California," Bob Moch remembered, "and Al . . . didn't know what to do really, because he was just so imbued with the idea that this was going to be his Olympic crew." Sheepishly, Ulbrickson reversed himself. The following day the sophomores raced as the varsity. "We beat those guys," Jim McMillin recalled. "But he didn't switch boats—and that really made us mad." But the coach's decision was vindicated when, in front of 50,000 spectators, his sophomore varsity came from behind to defeat an excellent California crew by six seconds.[71]

But victories—the freshmen and junior varsity also beat the Golden Bears—calmed nobody. "When we got back to Lake Washington, and started practicing for Poughkeepsie, we really handed it to them," McMillin recalled.[72] The oarsmen in Moch's crew derisively called the sophomores "Brougham's boys." "We got to the point that we didn't like [Royal] Brougham at all," Moch recalled. "He kept touting this crew that they should be the varsity." The tension between the two shells reached its zenith when teammates stopped talking to each other. "It was a very, very bad situation," Moch remembered. The antagonism damaged the team, and though the 1935 freshmen cruised to victory on the Hudson, Washington's varsity finished a disappointing third. California looked well prepared for the Olympics, as its victorious time of 18:52 was the second-fastest ever rowed over the Hudson course.[73]

The following fall Ulbrickson realized time was running out. Integrating sprinting exercises into fall practice, he openly discussed Berlin with the press, his oarsmen, and Seattle's civic community.[74] In spring 1936, throughout the initial practices, Ulbrickson mixed and matched his oarsmen. He soon settled on a particular type: tall, but not too tall; strong, but not too muscle-bound; and graceful on both ends of the stroke. On 23 March 1936, he boated a squad including John York, the veteran stroke, Delos Schoch, Sid Lund, Walter Bates, and Don Coy—all experienced rowers sharing the right height, shape, grace, and potential. His second boat's oarsmen were more idiosyncratic. Jim McMillin, who, at 6'5", occasionally appeared too tall and awkward while rowing, was in the five seat. Roger Morris, in the bow, seemed too thin to propel a varsity shell. Joe Rantz, a man of enormous strength, could not nail the proper technique. This second boat had potential but lacked the polish of Ulbrickson's chosen crew. Within a few days, however, the speed of this second boat was unmistakable. That crew's velocity emerged from a shared mentality—part resentment against the coach, part confidence in their individual and collective skill, but mostly a deep commitment to each other. "From the very moment that they were put together they thought they were a good crew," Moch remembered.[75]

In the bow seat rowed Herbert Roger Morris. Morris was the quietest member of the crew, showing up for the original turnout because his friend Joe Rantz suggested giving rowing a shot. Morris was born in 1916 in Fremont, a Seattle neighborhood, and graduated from Lincoln High School. Like many families in Fremont, the Morris family was poor, and the university—just a few miles east of his home—represented an opportunity for social mobility.[76] Morris's rowing stroke was particularly graceful and consistent, and from his arrival at the university in fall 1933 he made a strong impression on his coaches. He was, the *Post-Intelligencer* recorded, "the smoothest oarsman in the boat."[77]

In the two seat rowed Charles Ward "Charley" or "Chuck" Day. Born in Colville, Washington, he moved with his family to Seattle as a young child. After graduating from Roosevelt High School he matriculated at the University of Washington in fall 1933.[78] Day was a "tall, skinny, blue-eyed chap" that the *Post-Intelligencer* described as "bespectacled, noisy, and bubbling over with fight and pepper." He loved joking around, and Ulbrickson considered Day the "clown of the outfit." Bob Moch called him the "most effervescent" member of the crew, a "volatile, fun guy" who was always ready to "have a good time."[79] Day's superstitions were legendary. "Most oarsmen are superstitious," Al Ulbrickson once told a reporter, but Day's were particularly intense. He surreptitiously attached his lucky charm—a rabbit's foot—below his slide. At first, few of his teammates knew it was there—but as the season progressed, rather than ridicule him, they quietly joined him. "During workouts when the 'swing' was bad," Ulbrickson remembered, Day "waited until a halt was called, then unfastened the rabbit's foot, passed it up and down the shell, telling each man to take a rub. Each one did." Day's personality made him "the inspirational leader" of the boat, remembered teammate George Hunt.[80]

Gordon Adam rowed in the three seat, directly in front of Day. Adam radiated a calm, confident presence. His teammates always respected him—he was captain of the 1934 champion freshman crew, and later the 1938 varsity—and Royal Brougham once noted that he "pulls more for his weight than any man on the river." He was also extraordinarily tough. In the 1935 California race he cut his thumb almost to the bone but "laughed it off." Born in Seattle in 1915 to a father who immigrated from Scotland and a mother from Minnesota, Adam's family operated a mom-and-pop grocery store until purchasing a dairy farm in the Nooksack Valley near the Canadian border. After graduating from high school he canned salmon in Alaska, earning enough tuition money to matriculate at the University of Washington in 1933. He originally tried out for—and made—the freshman football team but decided (at his mother's urging) to switch to rowing.[81]

In front of Adam, in the four seat, rowed John Galbraith ("Johnny") White Jr. White differed from his teammates in many ways. He did not grow up impoverished, nor was he a first-generation college student. His father, John G. White Sr., graduated from the University of Pennsylvania, where he excelled as a sculler. After assuming a series of executive positions in the steel (and related) industries, John G. White Sr. arrived in Seattle in 1904 to open an import-export business. He enjoyed a sterling reputation in the Seattle business community. His son, born and raised in Seattle, was tall, quiet, strong, and "a very intelligent fellow," recalled Bob Moch.[82]

In the five seat rowed James McMillin. Born and raised on Queen Anne Hill in Seattle, McMillin recalled seeing the Washington crews rowing on Lake Union in his childhood. Despite his height and athleticism, he never participated in high school sports. In fall 1933, however, he was ready to try out for a team after enrolling at the university. "Somebody said, well why don't you turn out for crew—they start you right at the bottom," he remembered. Jim McMillin's

The 1936 intercollegiate and Olympic rowing champions from the University of Washington: From left: Don Hume, Joseph Rantz, George E. Hunt, James B. McMillin, John G. White, Gordon B. Adam, Charles Day, and Roger Morris. At center front is coxswain Robert G. Moch. (Photo courtesy of University of Washington Libraries, Special Collections, UW2234.)

great advantage was his height. At almost 6′6″, McMillin was much taller than the typical Washington oarsman. This initially proved disadvantageous, as McMillin resembled a cramped stork wedged in the boat, with arms and legs akimbo, as his body folded into the catch and unfurled to the layback. He looked uncomfortable as he rowed; his face, the *Post-Intelligencer* reported, "goes through a few . . . contortions every time he reaches for a bladeful of water." After failing to win a spot in the 1934 freshman crew, he almost quit, but Ulbrickson personally asked him to return that fall. "I thought, well, maybe in another three years I might be able to make the JV or something and get a trip to New York. I'd never been out of state," he recalled. McMillin tended to be the most serious oarsman in the shell. He spoke little in practice and rarely joked with the others.[83]

In front of McMillin rowed George "Shorty" Hunt. Standing almost 6′5″ with a thick, muscled body, Hunt, at nineteen years old, was the youngest member of the boat. He rowed beautifully and powerfully. "The strongest guy on the crew was Shorty Hunt," Moch remembered. Hunt "has that rare combination of qualities, power, good oarsmanship, and fire," Brougham wrote, calling him "one of the best men on the squad." Hunt had been born in Seattle but moved to Puyallup as a child, where he played basketball and football in high school.[84]

Joe Rantz rowed in front of Hunt. Though his stroke lacked finesse, Rantz possessed a singular ability to effectively propel boats. By the time he graduated in 1937, Rantz compiled, along with Roger Morris, one of the most astonishing records in rowing history: He never lost an intercollegiate race. Rantz's early life was heart-breaking. His mother died when he was three; his father was an erratic, peripatetic presence in his childhood. Abandoned by his family at 15, he went to live with an older brother while completing high school in Seattle. One day, while visiting the school, Al Ulbrickson stopped by a gymnasium where he noticed Rantz's flexibility, agility, and strength while doing a gymnastics workout. He suggested Rantz come to the university and row. Described as "tough as rawhide," Rantz compensated for his inconsistent form with power, an intense commitment, and a gymnast's balance. But his unorthodox rowing stroke always bothered Ulbrickson, who several times demoted Rantz. But with each shift, the new shell would move noticeably faster and the boat Rantz vacated would slow down.[85]

George Pocock called Don Hume, the boat's stroke, "a natural." Hume's form required minimal coaching, but his real gift was timing. He could curl and unfurl his body in a steady and precise rhythm, setting the perfect pace for his crew. Like a metronome clicking back and forth, Hume's easy stroke and natural recovery never varied no matter how long practice extended. Hume "just rows and rows, and by watching his face you'd think he was taking a stroll in the park," wrote one columnist. Although he was slightly shorter—and much lighter—than his teammates, Hume's smooth recovery on each stroke let the boat run beautifully. "In the middle of a race," wrote a *New Yorker* columnist, "Hume can produce a long, effortless stroke that saves his men but seems to eat up distance." As the stroke oar, Hume made everyone more efficient and the boat faster. "Hume was ideal for that crew, there is no question about that," Moch recalled. Born and raised in Olympia, Hume's wide, toothy smile was often hidden behind a set of "marble features." Like Ulbrickson, Hume's natural countenance was a drawn, deadpan poker face.[86]

Perched in front of Hume, in the coxswain's seat, sat Bob Moch. The only senior in the boat, Moch was the most experienced member of the crew. Blond-haired, handsome, and intense, Moch arrived on campus in 1932 from Montesano, Washington. His father, Gaston Moch, a French immigrant, owned the local jewelry store. Gaston Moch married the daughter of Montesano's banker, and Bob proved a gifted and motivated student throughout high school. He continued his academic success at the university, where he earned the Schaller

Trophy for the highest grade-point average on the crew three years in a row. His experience, his air of command, and the way he coached in the shell combined to instill in his teammates an enormous trust. "You had complete confidence in Bob knowing when and what to do during a race," Joe Rantz remembered. "He had a tremendous spirit," George Pocock recalled, "which spread the length of the boat. A winning spirit."[87]

Moch, Day, and McMillin rowed in the 1935 varsity. They provided a steadying influence on their younger teammates as the crew coalesced. With each practice, the boat came closer and closer to achieving the perfect rhythmic swing that makes a crew stronger than the sum of its parts. By the end of March, Ulbrickson knew what he had. In long, exhausting rows up and down Lake Washington, the coach caught glimpses of the greatest crew he'd ever seen.[88]

Every rowing squad dreamed of the Olympics as the 1936 collegiate rowing season opened. Uncharacteristically candid, Ulbrickson told one reporter his team "stands an excellent chance of making the trip to Berlin." California or the Naval Academy would be his crew's toughest competition. But even while contributing to it, Ulbrickson fretted over the media attention. "I want to warn you about taking all this publicity seriously," he told his crew. "The newspapermen mean well . . . but they seem to have some far-fetched idea that we can easily reach out and snatch a world's champion from some bush—well, that's not so. . . . According to all advance notices, we are going over to Berlin and walk away with the world's crown. Remember: we must have a mighty good crew to even get beyond the trials." On 28 March at the boathouse, a dedication ceremony for the Huskies' newest shell occurred. As George Pocock prepared for the occasion, he started to "think: Berlin . . . Olympic Games . . . German . . . *sauerkraut!*" He procured a can of sauerkraut juice, which he poured over the shell's bow in front of the small crowd. "I christen this boat *Husky Clipper*. May it have success on all waters it speeds over. Especially Berlin," he said. "It smells like sauerkraut," somebody in the audience called out. "It is," Pocock replied, "to get it used to Germany." The crowd laughed. On the *Husky Clipper*'s inaugural run the new shell "flew over the water."[89]

On 15 April California's crew arrived in Seattle for the annual Pacific coast duel. The Golden Bears varsity contained six rowers who had won the national championship in Poughkeepsie one year earlier, four of whom also had triumphed on the Hudson in 1934. Coach Ebright considered his varsity boat "slightly better than the boat which won at Poughkeepsie last year." Two days later the two favorites for Berlin raced for the first time in 1936 on Lake Washington's Sheridan Beach racecourse. Despite slight rain showers, a sold-out observation train filled with students and fans left the Northern Pacific depot at precisely 2:15 p.m. The lake surface remained calm, with only a slight tailwind pushing up the course. About 60,000 spectators arrived by boat, train, bus, and car by the time racing began. Sheridan Beach, near the finish line, was jammed.[90]

From the start of the varsity race, Washington rowed a lower stroke rating and looked more relaxed and powerful than California. A small lead in the first mile lengthened in the second as the Huskies moved steadily and relentlessly. With one mile left, California raised its stroke rating to claw back into the race, but the Huskies responded. "Not an inch" of the lead was given back. The men of the *Husky Clipper* moved as one, driving like pistons firing back and forth, with perfectly syncopated leg drives followed by identical back swings and folding arms. The oarsmen, Clarence Dirks wrote, were "merged into one smoothly working machine; they were, in fact, a poem of motion, a symphony of swinging blades." When they crossed the finish line, a large white flag signaled the Huskies' triumph. Horns blasted and the crowd roared. Three boat lengths separated the two crews by the time California finished. The Huskies covered three miles in 15:56, or more than 37 seconds faster than was ever recorded for the course. Washington's speed and power "positively stunned" Ebright. The Huskies, he told the press, were a "great crew." Newspapers throughout the country made Washington the favorite to represent America in Berlin.[91]

The squad then turned their attention to the Hudson. The 1936 trip east felt different for Washington's veterans. The rally to send the Huskies off at the Great Northern depot was "the greatest ovation ever given a Hudson-bound squad."[92] Leaving on 10 June 1936, the Seattle contingent packed for a longer trip than usual. After Poughkeepsie would come the Olympic trials in Princeton, followed, it was hoped, by the trip to Berlin. If all went as planned, the oarsmen, their coach, and George Pocock would not be returning to Seattle for more than two months. The group was one of the largest ever sent. It included Ray Eckmann, the university's new athletic director, and Earl "Click" Clark, the university's athletic trainer. All three boats—the freshman, junior varsity, and varsity—traveled as well. Washington's junior varsity, filled with experienced oarsmen including the team's popular captain, Walter Bates, might have been the second-fastest shell in the United States. They strengthened the varsity by challenging them in practice, and Ulbrickson even hinted to the press that his junior varsity might compete at the Olympic trials.[93]

The transcontinental train ride could be tiring, but it also allowed the oarsmen time to think, rest, and recuperate from the semester's stress. Joe Rantz brought along his guitar, the rowers played pranks on each other, and card games filled the time. George Pocock regularly checked on his shells in the baggage car. Meals were excellent; the oarsmen, one reporter wrote, were "exceptionally well fed." Ulbrickson explained that he expected his oarsmen to gain three or four pounds over the four days, in order to pack away the "extra fuel" as "weight to burn in hard training on the Hudson." In Chicago the team detrained to row a short practice in Lincoln Park lagoon. They enjoyed a luncheon at a local country club where Catherine Conibear, Hiram Conibear's daughter, wished them luck. Then it was off to the overnight train.[94] At 7:30 a.m. on the misty Sunday morning of 14 June 1936, the Huskies arrived in Poughkeepsie. As the rain started falling, they unloaded their shells, carrying them carefully the quarter-mile from the train station to their new boathouse.[95] Arriving that same morning were Cornell and the U.S. Naval Academy teams. California had come a week earlier, and their early time-trials impressed the media. Bookmakers made California, Washington, and Cornell the favorites in early betting.[96]

The regatta committee assigned Washington much nicer and more modern quarters for 1936 than in previous years. The new quarters were spacious, comfortable, and allowed for cool breezes to sweep through. On that gray June morning, the varsity and freshmen oarsmen were assigned cots in the second-story dormitory, and the junior varsity found their beds in an open space in the shellbay. For the first time, Washington rowers would have hot showers, heat if needed, and electricity. Shortly after settling in music could be heard wafting out the window and down to the river. One of the rowers plugged in a radio—a luxury unavailable to earlier generations of Washington athletes. There was only one drawback to the new quarters: They were directly next door to California's boathouse. The West Coast rivals shared a dock. Worse yet, only a single, party-line telephone was installed for the two boathouses to share. Significant interaction with the enemy before race day would be unavoidable, but Ulbrickson loved the new place.[97]

For the Golden Bears, the 1936 race meant more than avenging the loss in Seattle or preparing for the Olympics. A victory by California would make four intercollegiate championships in a row, solidifying Berkeley's claim as heir to the Cornell legacy. Ky Ebright grew confident watching his men practice. Shortly after Cornell, Navy, and Washington arrived, The *New York Times*'s John Kieran found Ebright upstairs in the California boathouse, finishing a letter, and asked him whether he had mentioned the Olympics to his rowers. "It might have been discussed," the smiling coach replied. But Ebright also concealed a secret from his rivals and the press. His number-five oar, Al Daggett, had injured himself in a motorcycle accident before leaving California. Daggett assured Ebright he felt fine and the crew showed no ill effects in initial workouts. But Ebright wondered whether Daggett's ribcage would hold up under the stress of four miles.[98]

Washington's late arrival concerned George Pocock. They had only one week of training before the regatta and "seven days isn't long enough at Poughkeepsie," he lamented. Making matters worse, choppy conditions hindered practice in the middle of the week. Ulbrickson could not hide his frustration. "We haven't had enough work for them to throw off the effects of the train trip from Seattle," he complained. "Unless we can get some long rows in I'm afraid that the varsity boat will be far from its normal form in the regatta." Of the eastern teams, Cornell and the Naval Academy looked strong while training for the race.[99] As race day drew near, Ulbrickson complained about media coverage and constant questions about Berlin. He ultimately imposed a media blackout. "We never saw a sports page," McMillin recalled. "We'd get the newspapers, the manager would go up into town and bring us the newspapers, but Ulbrickson would have him take out the sports section so we would never have a feel for what the writers were doing. We didn't know."[100]

The media distraction was but one of the psychological concerns Ulbrickson and his crew faced. He knew his varsity shell tended to start slowly, and so he and the crew came up with a mantra: "Mind in Boat" or M-I-B. Moch would remind his oarsmen during practice to keep their focus only on their own shell on race day. Ulbrickson believed deeply that a winning crew rows its own race and imposes its will on others. To get his oarsmen accustomed to starting out behind, throughout the practices on the Hudson he would start the varsity well behind the junior varsity and freshmen. He watched for loss of composure as the varsity boat clawed back toward the others. The key to victory for the Huskies would be its ability to retain confidence in victory no matter how far behind the boat fell. By keeping M-I-B, the team would remain unfazed even as it trailed others. "We vowed not to look at another boat," recalled Don Hume.[101]

Race day dawned dry and clear, with the early sun illuminating a scene the *New York Post*'s sports editor called "one of the world's premiere social and collegiate events . . . [with] more than a touch of Coney Island and a county fair" feeling everywhere. Unlike most recent years, President Franklin Roosevelt was unable to attend the regatta. He sent his personal regrets to Maxwell Stevenson, chairman of the Intercollegiate Rowing Association, who invited Roosevelt to once again share his customary viewing spot aboard the SS *Tara*. "I do wish I could come," the president wrote, "but I must remain here in Washington. I even have to abandon New London, where F.D.R. Jr. is rowing again [in the Harvard–Yale Regatta] on the Junior Varsity." After losing to Yale, the president's son and his teammates traveled to Poughkeepsie to watch the regatta aboard the sold-out observation train. The gamblers and bookmakers were out in force. In just a few moments Hugh Bradley of the *New York Post* witnessed one bookmaker take $600 worth of bets—mostly placed on Cornell and California.[102]

Most of the crews waited quietly for the races in their boathouses, resting and eating a large mid-day meal several hours before the 8 o'clock start. The observation train, in 1936, consisted of twenty-three cars (eight more than in 1935), and tickets ran a pricey $4.75 per seat. Yachts lined the racecourse, and although they were neither as numerous nor as ostentatious as the ones dotting the river during the 1920s, they still impressed. Light music wafting across the water could occasionally be heard from radio loudspeakers on the yachts or the bands parading on Main Street. A hulking gray Navy cutter, by far the biggest boat on the river, sat anchored by the finish line to inspire the Midshipmen.

Al Ulbrickson wore a striped sweater, a white cap, and the lucky purple tie given to him by Dr. Loyal Shoddy, one of Washington's most dedicated alumni. He enjoyed watching Washington's freshmen, and then junior varsity, demolish the competition. He paced nervously around the boathouse, chewing gum and occasionally smoking, until the varsity held their prerace meeting shortly before shoving off for the warmup. Meeting in a tight circle, he reminded them of the importance of keeping their minds in the boat, ignoring the competition, and rowing their own race. Then he pulled Moch aside to reiterate the race strategy one final time. The Huskies, he instructed, were to stay around thirty strokes per minute for the first two miles—no matter what occurred with the competition. In the third mile, Moch was to take the rating up two to thirty-two, and then raise it again heading into final sprint. With one mile left, Moch was told to "cut it loose." But he also warned his coxswain not to let California gain more than a full boat length on the Huskies early in the race, as more distance could swing confidence and momentum to the Golden Bears. Finally, he warned his coxswain to stay inside of his lane when approaching the pier below the High Bridge at the three-mile mark. The Huskies had drawn the far outside lane—lane 7—which was considered the worst on the course because of swirling eddies kicked up by the bridge supports.[103]

Ulbrickson left to join his rival coaches on the press car in the center of the observation train. They chatted quietly with reporters as the train slowly crawled up to Krum's Elbow. Soon the crews arrived. The river—and observation train—fell silent. It was about 7:50 p.m., and all the eights were lined up and awaiting orders from the referee. The surface remained flat as the shells aligned and rowers shifted into their starting crouch. Each coxswain was polled on his readiness, and then a booming "ready all!" was heard. The sharp snap of the starter's pistol sent the boats rocketing off the line. It was a clean start.[104]

Soon the shells settled down to their cruising pace. Columbia, Pennsylvania, and Navy pushed their bows slightly ahead, but they also were rowing more strokes per minute. Washington drifted back, settling into last place, but clearly rowing the fewest strokes per minute among the shells. The Huskies looked smooth, strong, and confident even while trailing. The only discordant note occurred when the referee warned Moch he was steering his shell too close to Syracuse in lane 6. The Washington coxswain pulled the *Husky Clipper* back to the center of his lane as Syracuse—and the rest of the field—started moving further away.[105]

At the first mile mark Washington was alone in last place. Yet the boat was rowing beautifully. The problem was that Hume settled too low—at 28 strokes per minute, rather than 30. "Of course, that was too low," Bob Moch recalled:

> But they were rowing well, really well. The boat felt good, it was going a pretty good clip for 28, and they were not even breathing hard. It was really running. . . . I did not want to disturb that, so I tried a lot of little tricks of the trade to get the stroke to come up, and it would come up a little one or two strokes . . . but then it would come right back down to 28. So what was I going to do? I either force it up, or I leave it alone. So I left it alone. And we were way behind—somebody once said we were eight lengths behind at the halfway mark—and I think that's about right, some others said five, but we were way back.[106]

California looked strained while pushing itself into the lead by the end of the first two miles. Passing Columbia, Penn, and Navy had taken a toll. The Golden Bears were ahead but struggling, not looking as smooth or as polished as the Huskies. The distance between California in front and Washington in last place remained about five lengths as the High Bridge drew near. Watching from the observation train, Ulbrickson started to sweat. His varsity still looked good but the space opened up by California also appeared substantial. Ulbrickson later admitted feeling "scared to death." He "chewed gum mechanically," one reporter noticed. "There was a stupefied look in his eyes. Every now and then he passed a trembling hand across his brow."[107]

Inside the *Husky Clipper,* all was calm. "We didn't pay attention to the rest of the crews and had no idea California was so far ahead," Don Hume remembered. The boat moved with grace and power, maintaining a low, controlled stroke rating. "I was still breathing through my nose at the end of three miles, we were in such good condition," McMillin recalled. Each oarsman retained fuel in the tank. The only question was when Bob Moch would shift gears. Moch never mentioned how far behind they had fallen. "If we had known that at the time we would probably have turned around and gone back to the boathouse,"

McMillin remembered. "Now we know Moch was a little fibber, but his fibbing probably saved us the race," added Hume. "If we had known . . . that California and Navy were four lengths to the good we'd have collapsed."[108]

As the race closed upon the High Bridge, Moch acted. "I yelled at the fellows, 'take it up to 34 and don't get below it.' The stroke went up to about 34 and we just flew. The crew just . . . mowed them down."[109] Like tightly wound springs, the oarsmen exploded off their foot stretchers and bounded into their sprint. Coming under the bridge, Moch again called the stroke rating up. Don Hume and Joe Rantz, the stroke pair, responded with a smooth, almost imperceptible transition. They went under the bridge at 34 and emerged at 36 strokes per minute. By then they had caught the boats in the trailing pack.

For the crowd on the observation train, the thousands on the yachts and lining the banks, it looked as though the Washington shell had suddenly awoken. They started passing other crews in a smooth, almost robotic charge. "Don't ask me what they did," wrote Bill Henry of the *Los Angeles Times*. "It was something imperceptible, uncanny—like opening up a valve in a steam engine." The boat, he continued, started "hurling along the surface like a skipping stone." Ulbrickson would later recall this moment. His crew was cruising much faster than any other shell in the race. Maintaining his poker face Ulbrickson got a "chilled spine."[110]

There was a haunting beauty to the finish. The rowers' legs driving like pistons, their bodies uncurling in perfect rhythm, the 80,000 spectators watched the Huskies row down the other crews stroke by stroke. California's coxswain Grover Clark yelled at his oarsmen to answer Washington's challenge. For a few strokes they arrested the Husky charge, matching their speed with a furious drive. But there was little fuel left, and California faltered. Washington pounced and moved its bow into the lead for the first time. The last quarter-mile concluded one of the finest races ever rowed. With Cal passed, only open water and the finish awaited Washington's rowers. Their shell planed beautifully over the water.[111] The crowd's roar grew steadily, engulfing the *Husky Clipper*. "When we slid into the last 400 yards," Shorty Hunt recalled, "I could hear the radios on the yachts alongside screaming about the race. I remember trying to catch the announcer's words, to see if we were leading." The 1936 regatta would be the latest ever started, with the finish occurring in a dusky twilight after sunset. The "thick gloam," wrote one reporter, "gave the effect of a ghostly armada."[112]

The crowd in the observation train originally cheered wildly for different teams. But as the Huskies' awe-inspiring sprint impressed the crowd they "swung from their obvious allegiance to the eastern crews to cheers for the all-conquering Husky oarsmen."[113] "Even the Cornell rooters," one reporter noted, "cheered the Huskies lustily." Ulbrickson's face broke into a wide grin as he hugged Bolles and Rusty Callow, disembarked, and then rushed back to the dock. The crowd on both banks continued to roar, with shrill whistles, horns and bells blasting out of yachts and boats, and signal bombs filling the air with noise. Although they did not set a course record, the dash from last to first astonished everyone.[114]

Witnessing Washington pass his crew—and watching his rowers scramble to meet the Husky challenge—sickened Ky Ebright. He knew his oarsmen were excellent but something was clearly lacking. They failed to match the intensity of Washington's challenge when it mattered most. "We went good the first three miles," Ebright asserted, "but then we sort of went to pieces." The lost composure frustrated Ebright. "We didn't think they could do it from so far behind, and we were upset by it," he told one reporter. "That's a remarkable crew," he told another.[115]

Ebright returned to Cal's boathouse. The eight paddled up to the dock and Ebright noticed something amiss. In the five seat, Al Daggett was in terrible pain. In a brief conversation Daggett finally admitted to having "rowed the four-mile race with broken ribs." He had never told Ebright the full truth about the motorcycle accident in California, assuming his ribs would heal in time. The stress of the race, however, proved too much. Cal's strongest oar essentially collapsed in the last mile. Ebright was furious. With the Olympic trials around the corner he was now forced to find a replacement.[116]

Sportswriters and coaches were impressed with the Huskies. "What could any crew do in the face of an outfit that could come up from seventh-place to beat a crew like California?" the Naval Academy's Buck Walsh asked. Grantland Rice, watching the race from the observation train, immediately established the Huskies as the favorites for the Olympic trials. He noted that the Washington crew's final, victorious sprint was of "just about the Olympic distance."[117]

"I've brought eight crews here and I can honestly say that for the first time, I really thought I would win," Ulbrickson admitted later. "All season they have been confident that no crew could outsprint them," he said, "and they proved it tonight." Staying true to form, he said little to the many well-wishers near the boathouse. "It was a pretty good day," he conceded before returning to the boathouse to collect his things.[118] Along with Pocock and Moch, he was headed to New York City for newspaper and radio interviews.

The drama of the 1936 championship ensured good reviews for the regatta's broadcasts on CBS and NBC. One noted the call from the observation train had been clear, precise, and surprisingly accurate. "An observation train . . . is noisy and the shifting angles of the river are likely to be confusing," noted the *New York Post*, but on CBS the program was exciting and vivid. Royal Brougham, certain of Washington's victory, had scheduled a special CBS network broadcast that night. Back in Seattle, listeners tuned into CBS affiliate KOL to catch the victors. "It was a great—my greatest thrill—to [be] gunning across the line a winner," Moch told Brougham and the national audience.[119]

CHAPTER 2

"Let's Go to Berlin"

The Olympic Trials, the Boycott Movement,
and Broadcast Preparations

The Washington rowers rested the day after their Poughkeepsie triumph. Practice resumed on the choppy Hudson shortly after Moch, Ulbrickson, and Pocock returned from New York City. The Olympic trials, scheduled to commence on Independence Day in Princeton, New Jersey, awaited the Huskies.

The squad spent their week of practice on the Hudson addressing the challenges of sprint racing: the need for faster starts, higher stroke ratings, and smooth power application under intense time pressure. The mental and physical dynamic of sprint racing differed considerably from the long-course racing they had mastered that spring. The brevity of sprint racing magnified the value of each stroke. With so much at stake in so little time the slightest mishap might cost the Huskies their ticket to Berlin. "I wish the distance were a little longer than 2,000 meters," Ulbrickson told a reporter toward the end of their Poughkeepsie stay. "One bad stroke can ruin a boat in a race of that distance." The initial time trials on the Hudson, however, pleased Ulbrickson. On a choppy surface, against the wind, his Huskies pulled a 6:30 while looking "noticeably smoother than at any time this year" to an onlooking reporter.[1]

Despite his concerns, Ulbrickson knew—as did his oarsmen—that they were prepared. He monitored the rowers carefully in each practice as they swept up and down the tidal Hudson. Comparing notes with George Pocock and Bob Moch, he appreciated his crew's ability to adapt so quickly to rowing the new pace. They were a smart group of boys, and they handled the transition remarkably well. He also allowed them some time to rest and recuperate—both mentally and physically—with outings in the Hudson Valley. On 24 June, after practice, the team motored up to West Point to receive a tour of the military academy and watch the cadets drill on the parade ground. They then returned to Poughkeepsie, where dinner awaited at the Nelson House, a stately red-brick landmark hotel that opened in 1876 and was one of President Franklin D. Roosevelt's favorite spots in town. "No more play now," Ulbrickson told George Varnell of the *Seattle Times* after dinner. "The lads are rested up and ready for their biggest assignment, the Olympic trials."[2] By the time they packed their bags, loaded the *Husky Clipper* in the baggage car at Poughkeepsie's train station, and departed the Hudson Valley, Ulbrickson radiated an unusual confidence and calm.

Technique, power, and racing strategy were not Ulbrickson's only worries in those balmy days at the end of June. The heat and humidity, first in Pough-keepsie, then down in Princeton, had climbed to uncomfortable heights. His oarsmen started losing weight. In the case of Don Hume and Roger Morris, the two lightest rowers in the boat, this development presented a serious prob-lem. Ulbrickson talked to both about maintaining their weight while noting the drop-off in power and stamina caused by shedding pounds from their slender frames. To beat the heat he moved practices earlier in the morning and later in the afternoon. He also decided that all hard practicing and time trials would occur on the Hudson, both because he wanted to taper his crew and because he did not want the other teams to witness his squad's sprint speed. "When we leave we will have all our hard work behind us," he told a reporter. "We will do no more than paddle after reaching Lake Carnegie."[3]

On the hot evening of 1 July 1936, the Huskies' train from New York pulled into the Princeton train station. Ulbrickson wanted to familiarize his rowers with Lake Carnegie as soon as possible, and so he ordered them to the boat-house. Even before checking in to the Princeton Inn, the crew headed down to the shell bay, where they rigged up the *Husky Clipper* and rowed. Barely forty minutes off the train, the Huskies found themselves paddling down the lake.[4] During breaks in the abbreviated practice, the rowers admired Lake Carnegie's beauty, its calm surface, and the tall oaks, elms, and the occasional willow lin-ing its banks. Andrew Carnegie gave Lake Carnegie to Princeton's crew three decades earlier, and the sheltered conditions and calm water made it an ideal regatta locale. The Huskies rowed through the gentle bends heading east and then sharply turned north, where the lake's straightest run—its sprint course—opened up for three miles. They paddled down the course, but not all the way to the lake's terminus at a dam, before returning to the boathouse.

By the time the Washington oarsmen arrived the University of California crew had already been practicing on Lake Carnegie for three days. Their earliest rows clarified Al Daggett's situation. Although the boat still moved impressively, Daggett's face registered pain whenever the crew tested their power. Moving Daggett out of the boat would be tricky at this point because the five seat, in the middle of the boat, was the heart of the "engine room." Generally, a coach will put his finest technicians—the rowers with the smoothest strokes and most sensitivity to balance—in the bow pair. The stern pair is reserved not only for skilled rowers, but masters of rhythm, as these two oarsmen translate the coxswain's commands into the crew's stroke rating. In between the bow and stern pair sit four oarsmen considered the "engine room." These four tend to be the biggest—and least technically adept—oarsmen in the shell (coaches will try to hide their strongest, but least smooth, oarsmen in the three and four seats). The engine room oarsmen earn their seats primarily—but not exclusively—by the amount of power they can apply on their oar blade.

Daggett was the key cog in Berkeley's engine room. Knowing the pressure of sprint racing could aggravate the damage to Daggett's ribcage, Ebright ordered his massive oarsman to the hospital for X-rays. The results were clear: one of Daggett's ribs was broken. To allow him to stay in the boat would cripple the Golden Bears' chance of earning the Berlin bid. But to replace him at this point meant tinkering with an excellent boat's chemistry. Coach Ebright made his decision, and a heartbroken Daggett was pulled from the eight. Even if Berkeley won the title, Daggett would not race in Berlin. On the last day of June, Cal's new lineup rowed down Lake Carnegie for their first trial run.

Ebright chose a curious replacement. Daggett, despite being the youngest member of California's eight, was the tallest (at 6'3½"), heaviest (188 pounds), and most powerful oarsman on the squad. Frank Dunlap, who stood exactly six feet tall and weighed twenty pounds less than Daggett, moved into the five seat. Dunlap had spent the 1936 season rowing in the bow seat of California's junior varsity. As a sophomore, Dunlap rowed in California's national champion varsity eight, and Ebright selected Dunlap primarily because his finesse promised the least disruption to the crew's rhythm. With three years of experience under his belt, Dunlap was a reliable, known commodity. The decision to insert Dunlap over a more powerful, but less skilled, replacement would later haunt Ebright. But the crew rowed well in its initial practices.[5]

California was not Ulbrickson's sole concern before the trials. The undersized U.S. Naval Academy crew surprised observers with a strong third-place finish on the Hudson. Though lacking the power of the Huskies and Golden Bears, the Midshipmen benefited from the savvy coaching of Buck Walsh. Inconsistency

marked the Naval Academy's results during Walsh's first few years, but some-
how he tended to find the words to motivate his men to row well under pressure.
To improve his squad for the Olympic trials, Walsh brought back Victor "Brute"
Krulak as coxswain. Krulak—who would go on to become a legendary Marine
Corps general—had been the first coxswain in the history of Navy rowing to be
named captain of the crew. That occurred in 1934, during his senior year. Walsh
also daringly swapped out his stroke and seven-man for the stronger, but less
smooth, junior varsity stern pair the week before the trials.[6]

The other eastern boat of concern was Rusty Callow's University of Pennsylvania eight. Any team coached by the widely respected Callow would be
formidable. In 1935 and 1936 he had compiled the enviable record of five wins in
six sprint match races. Penn's improvement had been widely noted in the press.
"The past two seasons . . . have been the most successful that Pennsylvania
has enjoyed in the last decade," noted the Intercollegiate Rowing Association
regatta program.[7] Yet Penn finished a disappointing sixth in Poughkeepsie. Callow, however, had three aces up his sleeve for the Olympic trials. Their names
were Joe Burk (captain of Penn's 1934 crew), Charles Swift (captain of Penn's
1935 crew), and Dick Jordan (captain of Penn's 1933 crew). Burk, Swift, and
Jordan sculled and occasionally substituted into the Penn varsity during the
Poughkeepsie training camp, as Callow previewed the speed they would add
for the Olympic trials.[8] With the collegiate season over, Callow pulled three of
his undergraduate oarsmen and substituted his veteran rowers, all of whom
had been rowing regularly with the Pennsylvania Athletic Club.[9]

Callow and Ulbrickson shared a long personal friendship dating to the 1923
season when Ulbrickson rowed for Callow at Washington. Callow had hired
Ulbrickson to coach Washington's freshmen, and upon accepting Penn's offer in
1927, Callow personally recommended the young and inexperienced Ulbrickson
as his successor. Their mentor–mentee relationship always added poignancy
to their competitions. Ulbrickson suspected—correctly—that his mentor would
have tactical solutions to Penn's challenge of being undersized in comparison
to the Huskies and the Golden Bears. When he got to Princeton and eventually
saw Pennsylvania's new lineup, Ulbrickson knew they had gained significant
speed since Poughkeepsie.[10]

As the racing drew near, the Olympic trials started feeling like a Pennsylvania
home race. Henry Penn Burke, the chairman of the Olympic Rowing Committee
and chief official for the regatta, was not only a Penn alum, but also the chairman and steward of the Pennsylvania Athletic Club. The rotund and officious
Burke hand-selected Philadelphia native and three-time gold medalist Jack
Kelly—the father of actress Grace Kelly—to join him as the official referees for

the Olympic trials. The University of Pennsylvania's campus sat less than fifty miles from Lake Carnegie. With an undistinguished Princeton varsity given little chance, Pennsylvania had all the advantages of a home favorite. For Burke and Kelly, the memories of the 1932 Olympic trials still stung. Four years earlier, on Philadelphia's Schuylkill River, the Pennsylvania Athletic Club eight fell to Ebright's Golden Bears by 0.2 seconds in an amazingly close finish.[11] That California crew went on to collect gold in Los Angeles.

None of these peripheral issues, however, seemed concerning to the Huskies. They enjoyed meeting Kelly, who was a top rowing star in the 1920s, and the *Husky Clipper* continued sailing through sprint practices. As a group, they remained far more relaxed and upbeat than their coach. In the shell they looked sharp, even as they practiced the weakest part of their racing: their opening sprint. But even this weakness could be transformed into an advantage: The Huskies gained by knowing not to panic no matter where they stood at the start of a race. The air of nonchalance and confidence permeating the crew was unmistakable to reporters in Princeton, who more than once caught them singing the World War I ditty "On to Berlin" while walking around. The rowers' confident and calm demeanor contrasted sharply with Ulbrickson's permanently anxious state. "I'm wondering if we can get started fast enough," Ulbrickson told the press, candidly admitting his crew's chief flaw. "You can't spot anybody more than half-a-length of a 2,000-meter race and expect to catch them." While working on raising the stroke rating, Ulbrickson preached strategic consistency. The Huskies' sprint racing strategy would simply be a condensed version of their long-course plan. He instructed his crew to again settle below their competition and conserve energy for a powerful sprint in the final quarter of the race. Or, as Gordon Adam later told an interviewer, they were instructed to turn "it on at the finish."[12]

Sportswriters, impressed by the final sprint at Poughkeepsie, generally picked the Huskies. Grantland Rice, who traveled to Princeton to report the race, prophesied a Washington, California, and Navy order of finish.[13]

Aside from California, Navy, Pennsylvania, and Princeton, the Huskies faced one more entrant at the Princeton trials. A boat composed of older athletes from the New York Athletic Club (NYAC) entered the trials without much experience or skill—but plenty of muscles. Labeled the "most interesting boat in the lake," the self-described "old men from Manhattan" pounded up and down Lake Carnegie in preparation for the racing. "They are not long on technique," the *Seattle Post-Intelligencer* noted, "but they fairly rock the lake with the ferocity of their blade work," demonstrating "astonishing power" as they slugged their way down the course. Joe Rantz later remembered his first thoughts upon seeing the NYAC eight: "we were scared to death of them." Yet the NYAC eight had just finished a terrible season, getting easily beaten in late May at a Philadelphia regatta, and few gave them any chance. "They were just a big bunch of muscle men," Jim McMillin recalled. "A lot of them had posed for *Physical Culture* magazine and all this stuff, and here we were, a bunch of skinny tall kids from the Northwest, and we used to kid, 'hey, don't beat us too bad!' They thought they were going to beat us, but hell, they weren't even in the same water." None of the collegiate coaches were much concerned with the musclemen from Manhattan.[14]

Al Daggett's injury had been Washington's first stoke of good luck. The second arrived with the announcement of the heats. The Huskies drew Princeton and the NYAC boat in the first race, with the Quakers, Golden Bears, and Midshipmen composing the second heat. Only one boat from each heat faced elimination; thus, an inferior Princeton or NYAC eight was guaranteed a spot in the finals. Not drawing California, Navy, or Penn delighted Ulbrickson, who immediately understood the ramifications. He told his oarsmen to win but to row a low stroke rating throughout the contest. He instructed Moch not to call a sprint if the lead was substantial toward the end of the race.

Ebright knew his draw spelled trouble. Both Pennsylvania and Navy could knock off his California squad if Frank Dunlap proved an inadequate substitute for Al Daggett. The quality competition, however, also offered the first real test for his new lineup. A strong showing might intimidate either the Quakers or Middies, whichever boat might join the Golden Bears in the next day's finals.

Independence Day dawned clear and hot over Princeton. The heats were scheduled to begin at 5 p.m. The grandstand erected on the shore was crowded with spectators enjoying the holiday in their shirtsleeves, and across the lake people leaned against their parked cars or sat on their car's bumpers to take in the day's racing. The Huskies spent most of the morning lounging at the Princeton Inn before heading down to the boathouse after lunch. The mercury continued to rise, as did the humidity, and clouds threatened a thunderstorm that never arrived. By the time Washington's oarsmen pulled the *Husky Clipper* from its rack and headed out to warm up, the air had become oppressive and the temperature remained stuck the high eighties.[15]

Ulbrickson's prediction about the woeful Princeton and NYAC shells was vindicated in the first minute of racing. He was not sure whether his Huskies would actually lead off the line, as they still started (relatively) slowly, but within two hundred meters the *Husky Clipper* was smoothly sailing ahead of the other two boats. Settling down to a surprisingly comfortable 36 strokes per minute, they kept lengthening their lead. Princeton's shell rowed efficiently but slowly, dropping behind the furiously pounding NYAC boat. Watching the Huskies extend their lead to a full length—with even a little open water—by the thousand-meter mark, one reporter later described the Washingtonians as dispatching their rivals with "almost ridiculous ease." In the second half of the race, Washington continued lowering the stroke rating—and gaining space—on the other shells. "Don't any of you guys go to sleep while you're rowing!" yelled Moch as he called the boat's pace down, first to 34 and then 32 strokes per minute. The *Husky Clipper* skimmed along the clear, flat surface of Lake Carnegie, each stroke rhythmically pulling the bow up and over the water. For most of the race's second half the Huskies stroked a rating lower than they had been practicing. Without sprinting, the *Husky Clipper* crossed the finish line in 6:17.8, a fast time considering the minimal effort expended. It was the easiest race the Huskies rowed in 1936. "There was never any doubt about this test," the *New York Times* reported.[16]

The second heat unfolded completely differently. Twenty minutes after the *Husky Clipper* eased over the finish line, California's Golden Bears and Penn's Quakers found themselves locked in a furious duel. Penn's smaller oarsmen—averaging ten pounds less per man than California—maintained a lead throughout the first half of the race by rowing a higher stroke rating. For the first three minutes Cal stalked the Quakers from about one half-length behind. Both boats rowed with speed and grace, pulling away from the overmatched Naval Academy. The Middies eventually finished a distant third, their Berlin dream over.

Both Penn and California tried moves and countermoves in the second half of the race, but their relative positions remained stable until California finally managed to edge into a tie heading into the final sprint. The two boats matched each other stroke for stroke in a dynamic charge for the line. Finally, with only a few seconds and five or six strokes left, California pushed its bow in front to win by a deck-length, or perhaps five feet. The oarsmen in both shells recoiled as they passed the line, collapsing over their oars or lying backward in the shell.[17]

Ebright knew immediately he had made a mistake. Both Penn and his Golden Bears rowed ten seconds faster than the Huskies in identical conditions—but at the cost of far more energy, both mental and physical. Once Navy faded, both boats were assured spots in the following day's finals. Ebright expected to beat the Quakers but did not foresee such a tight contest. The Quakers, not the Bears, walked away from the contest with the psychological edge; not only could they stay with the bigger Cal crew, but the next day's race offered a chance to avenge their failed sprint. The winning time of 6:07 impressed everyone. Duplicating that speed the next day would give any boat a good shot at Berlin. The upside for Ebright, however, was not inconsequential: Dunlap held up well.

The morning of 5 July 1936 dawned hot and hazy again over Princeton. The forecast called for more of the same—intolerable humidity and higher temperatures—with only the hint of a chance of a thunderstorm to break the heat. When the clouds burst open in a torrential midmorning rain, everyone thought it might cool the area. But by noon the storms and most of the clouds were gone, and the temperature and humidity escalated quickly. The Huskies tried to rest and stay cool. When they finally put their shell in the water to warm up, Jim McMillin could not believe the heat. "It was 105 in the shade, and there was no shade," he recalled.[18]

The boats were seeded according to their preliminary times. California and Pennsylvania earned the middle lanes (2 and 3), with the NYAC crew on the inside (lane 1) and the Huskies on the outside (lane 4). Only NYAC had no chance. After witnessing the previous day's racing, Ulbrickson felt assured the bad blood between California and Pennsylvania would keep those crews bunched tightly down the course. The outside lane would not be too much of a problem, as Lake Carnegie again provided perfect rowing conditions. The surface was not quite the glassine perfection the lake could occasionally present, but the very slight tailwind barely pushed tiny ripples on the water.

By the time the boats reached the starting line, an estimated ten thousand spectators lined the course. A troop of Boy Scouts circulated, soliciting donations for the United States Olympic Committee. Most fans stayed in the shade under the broad elms and maples rather than broiling on the exposed grassy bank, as the temperature hovered near one hundred degrees. Curled at the catch, awaiting the starter's call, all the oarsmen were covered in sweat. Jack Fraser and Bill Slater prepared to call the race for NBC from the grandstand.[19]

The crews rifled off the line. Pennsylvania, rowing 39 strokes a minute, dashed out to a half-length lead over the NYAC eight, which struggled to match the high rating. California sat half-a-boat-length behind, also rowing an exacting 38 strokes per minute. Washington was slightly off the pace, rowing only a 34 and looking relaxed. In the second five hundred meters, Washington surged over the flailing NYAC shell, and California, surprisingly, began to falter. But the rowers in the top three squads kept firing their bodies like pistons, curling at the catch and unfurling into the finish, moving their shells with a machinelike cadence down the racecourse.

As the boats closed in on the halfway mark, Penn pulled away slightly and California fell back to Washington. The Golden Bears were slowing. "Here's California!" Moch yelled. "Here's where we take Cal!" he shouted, calling for a move. The Huskies edged in front of the Bears, stroke by stroke, moving up on Penn. The thousand-meter marker flashed past. Washington was still rowing a solid 36 strokes per minute, almost 3 beats less than Penn, while looking strong.[20]

The *Husky Clipper* surged forward with a smooth efficiency, but the game Pennsylvanians countered the Huskies' first move and maintained their lead. The Quakers were racing as well as they did the day before, leading the pack less than three minutes from the finish line—and Berlin. Penn took a move and extended its lead by another seat. Jim McMillin quietly called on Washington's engine room to counter. He "mumbled . . . 'let's test a couple.'" "We really bore down there for five or six strokes, and we just [saw] that other boat come right back. So we settled back down again," he recalled.[21]

The facility with which the Huskies stopped the Quakers' momentum in the third five hundred meters offered a powerful portent. Heading into the final five hundred meters, the Huskies "really went to work." Moch called the stroke rating up two, and the *Husky Clipper* reeled in the Penn squad. The Washingtonians passed the Pennsylvanians "like a graceful swan," one newspaper reported the next day. Another described the Huskies passing the Quakers like "the Queen Mary going by a lighthouse." Penn's oarsmen had no answer for the Huskies' charge; their reservoir of energy, already badly depleted the day before, bottomed out with less than two minutes to go. With only about two hundred fifty meters left, and the Huskies lengthening their lead to a full length, Moch again called the rating up. Amazingly, the spacing between the oar blade puddles— which usually shortens when the stroke rating goes up, because recovery time between strokes is lost—maintained its impressive ratio. The boat was running between strokes at 40 strokes per minute at about the same spacing as 36 strokes per minute; in other words, they were flying. One observer was particularly impressed with their ability to seamlessly shift stroke ratings, noting that the transition to the final sprint was as effortless as "a star violin player who could handle any tempo at any time."[22]

The *Husky Clipper* knifed across the finish line, having put open water between themselves and the dispirited, deflated Penn boat.[23] California trailed Penn by more than a length, with the NYAC boat paddling in well after the others. As each boat crossed the line, their balletic synchronicity broke down, with each oarsman loosening his grip on his oar and writhing in pain. Their shells drifted, and all that could be heard were the cheers from the shore echoing across the lake and the soft purr of the officials' motorboats. The Huskies patted each other on the back and congratulated one another. Broad smiles creased their faces.[24]

They did it.

They were the fastest boat in the United States.

They were going to Berlin, to become the fastest boat in the world.

Sitting in the *Husky Clipper* on the placid waters of Lake Carnegie, beneath a broiling sun, they almost could not believe it. They had realized a dream. From early in the season, the oarsmen had developed a mantra: L-G-B. When asked, they told people it meant *Let's Get Better*. Between themselves, the shared an alternative understanding: *Let's Go to Berlin*. They were now going to Berlin.

A few minutes after the triumph, NBC's Bill Slater flagged down Al Ulbrickson, who spoke a few words to the national audience about his crew and his delight at the prospect of going to Berlin.[25] Ulbrickson later told the press that his crew's complete belief in each other—their almost spiritual unity—provided significant advantage:

> Our varsity crew has the finest mental attitude of any boat I ever saw, and I've seen some pretty good ones. Every one of our eight oarsmen, and the coxswain, has absolute confidence in every one of his mates. They work together as a flawless unit—as a perfect rowing machine. There are no prima donnas in the shell. Every man considers himself just a cog, and does the best job he can to help the others.[26]

Rusty Callow was crushed by the defeat. He knew this crew represented Penn's best chance to make the Olympics. He believed, right up until the last two minutes of the race, that he was going to Berlin. He could hardly speak as the crew loaded their shell on the trailer for the short ride back to Philadelphia. In a private conversation, in the shade by the side of the Princeton boathouse, Callow told his boss that he was finished. With tears in his eyes, he tendered his resignation. Leroy Mercer, the chair of the Department of Physical Education, begged Callow to reconsider. Callow withdrew his resignation the following morning.[27]

While crediting the Huskies with a brilliant and dominating sprint, most newspaper coverage the following day stressed the role of the brutal Cal–Penn duel in the final result. The Pennsylvania boat proved to be the "sensation of the races," according to one report, because of the remarkable smoothness of their rowing style. "Only weight [was] lacking to carry them to victory," the *Christian Science Monitor*'s reporter concluded. But others felt that both Pennsylvania and California doomed their own chances with poor planning. Bill Henry wrote in the *Los Angeles Times* that California's poor effort resulted from Coach Ebright's "tactical error." Caught up in the spirit of racing, the Bears made the mistake of "fighting too hard for victory in the semifinals."[28]

The winning time of 6:04.8, in almost perfect conditions, was blazing fast. Many of the top U.S. rowing officials considered it the fastest recorded time for the U.S. sprint distance of 1¼ miles.[29] The Huskies now were moving ever closer to the ideal, almost unattainable, time of six minutes flat. Although boats had rowed wind-aided six-minute races before, and different conditions always make comparing racing times difficult in rowing, no boat had ever rowed 2,000 meters in six minutes in the Olympics. The fastest time clocked on the Grünau racecourse, where the Olympic sprints would be raced, was the 6:09 rowed by a powerful Hungarian eight in the European championships earlier that summer. Like the four-minute running mile, the six-minute race in flat conditions was a magical goal. The Huskies were now below 6:05 and moving closer to establishing themselves among the greatest crews in the history of the sport.

Back at the dock awaited the press, officials, George Pocock, Al Ulbrickson, and the few Washington rowing supporters braving the transcontinental trip to support their crew. Henry Penn Burke, dressed in a handsome white double-breasted blazer fastened around his ample waist, with his cleanly pressed white trousers and perfectly shined black shoes, started the ceremonial program. Standing with Roger Morris, Charles Day, Gordon Adam, and John White on his right, Robert Moch next to him, and Jim McMillin, Shorty Hunt, Joe Rantz, and Don Hume on his left, Burke started talking about the glory that is crew racing, the fantastic event everyone had just witnessed, and the victory he expected in Berlin. He talked. And talked. And talked. And gestured, smiled, and kept talking. The sun broiled the dock as he held up the ceremonial cup awarded to the nation's top crew. The Husky oarsmen, completely exhausted, started to sway; they had raced without their shirts and now stood bare-chested facing the press and photographers. Burke kept rambling on, praising the Huskies, the Bears, but most especially, his beloved Pennsylvania Quakers. Bob Moch had enough. He reached over and grabbed the handle on the cup opposite the one Burke held. "I gave a little tug on it, on the cup. And it came off—he let go of it," Moch remembered. "He still continued to talk. So we just walked away from it. That's the kind of a guy he was: a blowhard." The oarsmen, then the crowd, and finally the press drifted away as Burke eventually stopped talking and called the ceremony to a close.[30]

But Burke quit speaking without imparting the day's most important information. The Olympic Rowing Committee met in Princeton on the eve of the regatta to assess its financial resources and calculate the cost of sending the full contingent of almost thirty oarsmen (including scullers, small boat rowers, spares, and coaches) to Berlin. The American Olympic Committee (AOC) warned the Olympic Rowing Committee that it would require five hundred dollars per person to cover travel and expenses for Berlin. The Olympic Rowing Committee needed to figure out how to raise the funds, as the AOC had its own sizable financial problems. The Olympic Rowing Committee members concluded they could subsidize the oarsmen to the tune of about $150. This left a gap of $350 per oarsman needing to be covered by donations, fundraising, or the personal savings of the athletes. Burke knew the bad news would need to be released as soon as one crew won the trials. But he decided to keep the dispiriting secret as long as possible. He also knew, should the University of Pennsylvania earn the berth, that he could easily induce Philadelphia's civic leaders to sponsor the Quakers. So the financials were kept quiet until an hour after the racing ended, when Burke called a meeting with Al Ulbrickson, George Pocock, and the University of Washington's athletic director, Ray Eckmann. Burke told them the news and they sat stunned. The long silence in the room made everyone uncomfortable. Ulbrickson's ashen faced looked even more pained than usual, and finally it was Eckmann who broke the silence.

"How much do we have to raise?" he asked.

"Five or six thousand dollars," Burke answered. Ulbrickson, Pocock, and Eckmann looked at each other.

"How long do we have to raise it?"

"One week," replied Burke, looking straight at Eckmann.[31]

The men filed out of the room, with Eckmann charging up the hill to the Princeton Inn to start the telephone calls and telegrams back to Seattle. Eckmann's first call was to I. F. Dix, the head of the Seattle Chamber of Commerce and one of the most important backers of University of Washington athletics. Dix led the fundraising for the Poughkeepsie regatta each year and he knew more than anybody in Seattle about organizing fundraising drives in a hurry.

Dix and Eckmann called everyone. Paul Coughlin, the president of the University of Washington alumni, heard from them that evening, as did Vernon Lattimore, a well-connected alumnus with wealthy contacts throughout the state. Within the hour the organizing committee for the fundraising drive was established, with Dix directing. It included Carl Kilgore, assistant athletic director of the University of Washington, Christy Thomas and Foster McGovern of the Seattle Chamber of Commerce, and Lattimore, representing the university's alumni. They met that evening and sketched out a plan to be finalized at the Chamber of Commerce luncheon the next day. The headquarters for the campaign would be the Washington Athletic Club in downtown Seattle.[32]

Back in Princeton, Ulbrickson and Pocock walked up the hill to a celebratory dinner in honor of Seattle's Olympians. Ulbrickson's mind turned to the meeting he held with his oarsmen after the race. He had told them how proud he was of them for rowing faster than they ever had in practice, and he finished by telling them they were the greatest crew Washington ever produced—even better than the legendary 1926 champions with which he stroked to victory, something that pained him to admit.[33]

Now the oarsmen were back at the hotel, changing into their nice clothes for the dinner, and he would have to tell them about the financial crisis. But he was also confident the people of Seattle would rally, just as they always had, for Washington's crew. As Pocock and Ulbrickson walked silently, lost in their own thoughts, suddenly Ulbrickson stopped. He held out his hand and their eyes met. "Thanks, George, for your help," said the Dour Dane, quietly surprising the man whom he knew deserved an enormous amount of credit for the day's result. "Coming from Al," Pocock recalled, "that was the equivalent of fireworks and a brass band."[34]

At the Princeton Inn, where the sports editors for both of Seattle's major newspapers were staying, "disturbing rumors" were already flying.[35] The first was perhaps the most distressing: that because the University of Washington could not afford the trip, Pennsylvania would be sent to Berlin as the U.S. crew. The news was a "staggering blow, to say the least," to the Washington rowers.[36] It is difficult to imagine the frustration felt by the crew to hear such news in their moment of triumph. While they had confidence in the people of Seattle, five thousand dollars represented an enormous sum to solicit during the Depression. That nobody from the Olympic Rowing Committee had informed the Washington contingent of the funding shortage until that evening was particularly maddening. Washington's rowers were not a privileged lot; they were paying their own way through college and could barely afford meal money on any given day. Gordon Adam worked as a janitor, scrubbing floors and washing windows on campus for fifteen dollars a month, a salary paid by the National Youth Administration, a New Deal agency. Jim McMillin and John White also worked as janitors, sweeping out the pavilion after basketball games, helping to clean and sod the football field, and even selling tickets and ushering at various events.[37] They could not afford to pay their own way to Europe.

The rowers wanted more information, or at least confirmation, as soon as possible. Royal Brougham of the *Post-Intelligencer* and George Varnell of the *Seattle Times* searched out Burke for confirmation, and a little after 7:30 p.m. they—and other members of the press—found him. Burke held an impromptu press conference.

First, he confessed the embarrassing financial situation. He told the reporters the Olympic Rowing Committee could afford only about six thousand of the sixteen thousand dollars required to take the full team, for all events, to Berlin. It was up to each athlete, coach, or official to quickly make up the difference. The S.S. *Manhattan* would sail for Europe in ten days, carrying only athletes paid in full. "We hope and will work desperately to raise additional funds for oarsmen in all crews that are scheduled to go to Berlin," Burke told the press. "I can guarantee no more than $4,000 will be necessary to complete the sum needed for Washington's eight, and it may be less." Burke's next comment infuriated the Washingtonians:

> It is a sin and a shame to say this; but if Washington cannot help out to raise the funds for its men to make the trip . . . then we must ask Pennsylvania, the crew that finished second in the trials, to attempt to raise funds to represent us in Berlin.[38]

Everyone present knew of Burke's stature in the rowing community in Pennsylvania. With just a few telephone calls he could easily land the funds for his Ivy League squad. And everyone at the press conference—as well as the University of Washington oarsmen—understood the message.[39]

Brougham and Varnell telephoned their editors, and the decision was made to feature the plight of the Huskies on the front page of both the *Times* and the *Post-Intelligencer* the next day. Upon hearing the news, the publisher of the *Times* contacted Dix to donate the initial five hundred dollars to the campaign, even before it was officially organized. Photographs of Don Hume and the crew splashed over the front pages the next day, with the heartening news that more than seventeen hundred dollars had been raised in less than twenty-four hours.[40]

Pocock and Ulbrickson arrived at the Princeton Inn for the celebration and greeted the oarsmen, officials, and administrators. On the way up the hill, they had passed the train station and watched the dejected California crew loading their shell into a baggage car for the transcontinental trip home. As the meal wound down, the sponsor of the dinner, Dr. Loyal Shoudy, rose to say a few congratulatory words. He then turned to Ulbrickson, who stood up to address the gathering. Earlier that day, Ulbrickson explained, he had counted the ballots for team captain that had been tendered in Poughkeepsie. He was pleased to announce that the captain of the 1937 University of Washington crew would be Jim McMillin. He did not say the next part, because he did not need to. Everyone in the room knew. Because the 1936 team captain, Walter Bates, had not made the varsity, McMillin would be the crew's leader for the Berlin trip. His captaincy actually started at that moment.[41]

After dinner Ulbrickson chatted with Royal Brougham. "Hume stroked the perfect race," he said, grinning a bit. "I think this crew will give a good account of itself in Berlin." Brougham updated Ulbrickson with the news from Seattle. It was a few minutes before 10 p.m., and Brougham assured Ulbrickson, "the chances look good for . . . [the] trip to Berlin." In fact, less than three hours after their victory, the word from Seattle was that "prominent Seattle citizens" guaranteed the trip, and that Ulbrickson and the rest of the squad "could make plans to sail next Wednesday" for Europe.[42]

The next morning the crew was driven to New York City, and on their day off several of them did a sightseeing tour of Manhattan. The boys took in the Empire State Building, climbed up the Woolworth Building for a panoramic view of the city, and marveled at the lights of Broadway. Back in Seattle the fundraising drive shifted into high gear. Other administrative details fell into place, as Ulbrickson received word that all his oarsmen were approved to receive their passports before departure, easing another worry.[43]

At the Seattle Chamber of Commerce luncheon, as the campaign neared the two-thousand-dollar mark, it was decided multiple, simultaneous solicitation campaigns would be used. Dix, Lattimore, and others would use their personal connections to solicit funds via telephone. Washington students would join the newsboys on the streets selling fifty-cent ribbons or tags reading "Send the Huskies to Berlin." Every chamber of commerce in the state would be canvassed for pledges, a separate citizen's committee would be assembled, and American Legion representatives would contact every post in the state—more than a hundred sixty of them—to solicit contributions. Everyone in Seattle was talking about the campaign during the next two days. At a wrestling match in Civic Arena, grappler Roscoe "Torchy" Torrance asked his fans to support the crew, and $143.55 was collected. Seattle's radio stations regularly interrupted their programming for spot announcements soliciting funds. The money poured in. By the end of the second full day of fundraising, 8 July, it became clear the Huskies would go to Berlin.[44]

The Huskies were not the only cash-strapped athletes treated poorly by the Olympic committee. To understand the fundraising challenges facing the American Olympic Committee in 1936, one must conceive of a world where Olympic officials disdained corporate sponsorship, advertising, or anything that might be construed as professionalism. Avery Brundage, the chairman of the AOC, believed in a virtuous amateur ideal that required vigilant safeguarding. Despite his millions—Brundage's wealth came largely from government engineering and construction contracts in Chicago—he dismissed sponsorship out of hand and turned expenses for participation over to the athletes and their sport governance organizations. Brundage was a brittle and uncompromising man, called by one scholar the "Iron Chancellor of amateur sport" for his rigid posture on the purity of amateurism.[45]

Brundage did not foresee, however, the myriad new financial challenges facing the AOC in 1936. While 1932 was also a depression year, the Olympic Games occurred in Los Angeles, facilitating travel for the U.S. team. When the

Nazi government offered to subsidize the transoceanic voyage if the U.S. team used a German ocean liner, the U.S. government intervened by prohibiting the committee from accepting the offer. As the games drew closer, the price tag for the AOC skyrocketed to more than $50,000. The deficit prompted a "wild scramble during the last few weeks before the team departed to raise the necessary funds," Brundage recounted in the AOC's official report.[46]

The most difficult obstacle to fundraising between 1932 and 1936 proved to be the boycott movement, a protest against the Nazi regime receiving significant publicity in fall 1935. The movement had begun once the Nazi government assumed power in 1933, but in the intervening years it garnered more support across the U.S. political spectrum. The Nazi persecution of the Jews, poor treatment of the Catholic Church, and other repressive moves were widely reported in the U.S. press. By fall 1935, a U.S. boycott of the 1936 Olympics seemed entirely possible, and even likely. Sociologist Maxine Davis found it a regular topic of debate on college campuses.[47]

Westbrook Pegler, a popular United Features syndicated columnist, stood out as the most famous media figure promoting the boycott. He regularly attacked the Nazi regime for politicizing the games and called on the AOC to reject Germany's invitation.[48] Throughout 1935, as the boycott movement gained popularity, Pegler and CBS's Bill Henry (who maintained his full-time employment with the *Los Angeles Times*) publicly dueled in print. "Nothing would be gained" by a boycott, Henry argued, explaining that such a move would probably benefit Germany, as contests usually dominated by U.S. athletes might be won by Germans. Pegler responded by pointing out Henry's trips to Germany and his official ties to Berlin's organizing committee.[49]

The radio networks covered news of the boycott movement as it grew more timely. Occasionally the Olympics appeared in other programming as well. When NBC invited Hendrik Willem van Loon to deliver a series of talks placing current events in historical context, the Dutch-born author narrated a brief, colorful history of the modern Olympic movement on the evening of 1 August 1935. Van Loon lamented that the ideals propounded by the Olympics' founder, Baron Pierre de Coubertin, had become perverted by "international rivalry and hate." The games, by linking the "determination to win at all costs" with "our present-day nationalistic feelings" created a "fine old mess." The boycott campaign, in this sense, was only part of the tension created by the Olympic movement. "Enough bitter comment has already been printed in the press of all the diverse participating nations, a year almost before the Games are to take place, to make the average citizen take a vow that no matter what happens, he will give the next Olympic Games a very wide birth," van Loon explained, before decrying such an attitude. "That," van Loon continued, "would be too bad, for think of all the *belegte brötchen* [German idiom: "finished bun" or completed works] that have been already prepared for the coming myriads of visitors and of all the extra barrels of beer, now being brewed in happy Munich for the anticipated thirst!" Facetiously, van Loon concluded by suggesting scrapping all the current Olympic events in favor of a single grudge contest. "All nations are expert at carrying chips on their shoulders," he explained. "Why not drop all the other minor sports and have a chip-carrying race?" The games could then end in a "free-for-all fight, during which the worst chip-carriers mutually assassinate each other." [50]

Van Loon's sarcasm was rare on NBC's airwaves (his program was one of the very few to escape network censorship, he explained in a letter to President Roosevelt). [51] He managed to castigate both the boycott movement and the Nazi regime for raising international tensions and corrupting the Olympic spirit. While Van Loon's script evaded NBC editorial control, internal memos in the NBC archives reveal how network executives, sensitive about their power over U.S. public opinion, extensively debated the question of boycott coverage. A few months after Van Loon's broadcast, John Royal, NBC's chief programmer, asked his management team to downplay the Olympics as a special event and "keep as far away from any controversy as possible." [52] David Sarnoff, the chairman of the board of NBC, offered confidential guidance on boycott coverage in a memo to the network's general manager:

> My personal view is that this is "news" in which the American public will naturally be interested and therefore it should be handled as you would normally handle it, regardless of the present controversy which surrounds the Olympics but as the games do not take place until the middle of next year, we will naturally want to look at the situation as it exists then. [53]

Olympic officials disdained NBC's cautious attitude toward publicizing the games. On 15 November 1935, Gustavus Kirby, treasurer of the AOC, met with NBC's Royal to discuss "the entire situation." Kirby accused NBC of supporting the boycott movement. Royal objected, telling Kirby that "no one had attempted to interfere with my judgement of what we would put on from the Olympics" and that he was, in fact, in favor of participation. Although Royal did not inform Kirby, the NBC executive had already secretly started preparing supportive information should the boycott movement fail and the American Athletics Union (AAU) vote to participate in Berlin. Royal ordered an assistant to compile a list of the Jews representing the United States in the 1932 winter and summer games. That information, Royal thought, might prove useful in rebutting criticism of NBC's future collaboration with the AOC and the Berlin organizing committee. With the official vote on the boycott only weeks away, Royal ultimately convinced Kirby that it was in the AOC's best interest that NBC "not put anything about the Olympics on the air until a final decision is made." The boycott, Royal reminded Kirby, had achieved impressive popularity. Were the AOC allotted air time, Royal continued, NBC policies required the network to turn over its microphone to the boycott movement as well.[54]

CBS management remained silent on the boycott. William S. Paley, the network's owner, had evidenced sensitivity about public discussion of his Judaism, and he was stung when *Fortune*, in early 1936, informed its readership that Columbia, unlike NBC, was "under Jewish control."[55] Dealing with the boycott movement could exacerbate the issue of Jewish media ownership in a period of rising anti-Semitism, and so Paley and his management team avoided engaging the subject. CBS sportscaster Ted Husing, however, did offer his personal opinion on the controversy to a Jewish newspaper in late 1935. Husing "says America should enter the Olympics because 'it drags the world into common fellowship,'" reported the *Jewish Standard*.[56]

On 1 August 1935, Bill Henry appeared on CBS with a glowing report from Berlin's "vast, partly finished" Olympic stadium. "If you could stand with me right now on the concrete gallery of the Olympic Stadium in Berlin," he said, "you would realize that great things are soon to happen." Calling the preparations for the games "unsurpassed," Henry prophesied that the Berlin Olympiad would be the greatest ever staged. Henry then interviewed Dr. Carl Diem, the general secretary of the Olympic Organizing Committee, to ascertain how the "work is coming along." "Our task is made easy by the energetic supports of the government and the interest shown by the German people," he explained.

HENRY: How is the Government helping?

DIEM: Most important, of course, is that it is constructing the entire sports stadium. At the wish of our Führer, the Reichsports Field—which was originally a race course—is being expanded by the government to meet the needs of the Olympic Games.[57]

The broadcast only obliquely referred to any tension surrounding the games. "I assure you that everybody from whatever country he may come and irrespective of his race and faith, will be treated as a welcome guest," Diem promised the U.S. audience. "Our people and government welcome the opportunity to demonstrate our wish to live at peace and harmony with all nations, as so often expressed by our Chancellor and Führer," he explained.[58] Henry then transferred the broadcast back to New York, where Avery Brundage then spoke to CBS listeners.

CBS sportscaster and *Los Angeles Times* sports editor Bill Henry (far right) participates in a morning run with the Berlin Olympic Organizing Committee on the track of the Olympic stadium (under construction), 1935. (Photo from the Pat Yeomans Collection on Bill Henry and the History of the Olympics, Courtesy of Occidental College Special Collections and College Archives.)

Upon his return to the United States, Henry wrote a widely distributed "special" column for the Associated Press about the games and the boycott movement. "In the light of the terrific excitement [surrounding the games] evidenced by some people in the United States," the boycott movement, he claimed, "doesn't seem to add up and make sense."[59] Claiming that "both Jewish and Catholic faiths are strongly represented in the Olympic committee membership," he argued that such members were "far better informed than anyone in this country" and they "enthusiastically urged participation in the games." If Americans truly sought to embarrass Germany, he concluded, they would send an unbeatable team of top athletes with the result that "German spectators would wind themselves into a state of physical and nervous exhaustion rising up a dozen times a day while a German band played the 'Star-Spangled Banner' in celebration of American athletic triumphs."[60]

On 31 October 1935, NBC turned over its microphone to American IOC member General Charles Sherrill to address the national audience about his recent trip to Berlin. Speaking before the Advertising Club of New York, Sherrill promoted participation in the games, and his talk was relayed by shortwave to Germany.[61] "I am today astonished that anybody can today, think me anti-Jewish," Sherrill began defensively, mentioning the threats he had received for publicly supporting participation. But he also praised the tenor of the debate, expressing his gratitude that both sides were being presented fairly. This slightly surprised him because "many warnings . . . [had] been received by me that the Jewish press and radio would fight me," he said. He then specified numerous Jewish media executives for praise:

> Never have I seen any question treated with such ultra-American fairness as has been shown by the *New York Times*, that monument to the late, lamented Jew, Adolph S. Ochs, and now conducted by his son-in-law, Arthur Sulzberger, and his nephew, Julius Adler, and let me remind you that I am today speaking to you over WOR, controlled by the Jewish group headed by Mr. Bamberger, and WEAF, an NBC connection, of which Mr. David Sarnoff—another Jew—is Chairman of the Board.[62]

Sherrill's praise was likely calculated, for it could easily be construed as a warning. By explicitly naming, on the national airwaves, specific Jewish leaders in the U.S. media, Sherrill clearly hoped to disarm criticism and weaken systematic media support of the boycott movement.[63]

Arthur Garfield Hays, who had served as an attorney in the Reichstag fire case in Berlin, gave an immediate reply to Sherrill's talk. But while Sherrill spoke to the nation through NBC, Hays was given only a local microphone by New York City's WHN. Hays claimed the U.S. IOC member sought to "make a question of principle appear to be solely a Jewish question." Later that night, station WEVD (New York) aired a commentary by Matthew Woll, the vice president of the American Federation of Labor. Woll "declared that 4,000,0000 American workers in the federation unequivocally opposed this country's participation in the Olympics." The Olympic Games, Woll asserted, would be viewed in Germany and across the world as an endorsement of the repressive Nazi regime.[64]

Just as the U.S. networks were forced to respond to the boycott movement, the management of the British Broadcasting Corporation (BBC) also received pressure to reconsider its participation in the Berlin Games. The boycott movement in Great Britain never achieved the strength of its U.S. counterpart, but nevertheless BBC broadcast management faced a dilemma in 1935 that had no U.S. equivalent. They needed to decide whether Harold Abrahams, the Jewish 1924 Olympic hundred-meter champion, would serve as the network's chief sports commentator in Berlin. Abrahams originally supported the British boycott movement but later changed his mind and publicly urged participation. "I naturally feel very strongly that the total negation of all liberty in Germany is a deplorable thing," Abrahams wrote in 1935, adding that, rather than a boycott, "a dignified appeal to Herr Hitler . . . would tend to do much more good than many people imagine or even hope."[65]

Within the BBC, management worried that employing Abrahams would insult the Germans. In late 1935 Abrahams pressed the BBC to clarify his status. Cecil Graves, the BBC's controller of programs, wrote a memo dated 6 December 1935, summarizing the quandary for his colleagues:

> The point about this is, of course, that Abrahams is a Jew. He is our best commentator on athletics. Apparently if we are prepared to come out into the open and label him the BBC Commentator for the Olympic Games he is quite ready to go to Germany. The question arises as to whether or not we should do this. We all regard the German action against the Jews as quite irrational and intolerable and on that score we ought not to hesitate. But should we, as between one broadcaster and another, put aside all views of this kind and take the line that however irrational we regard another country's attitude to be, it would be discourteous to send a Jew commentator to a country where Jews are taboo?[66]

In the end, a BBC program revisiting the controversy in 2011 explained, the British network "fudged it." "Officially, Abrahams went to the Games as an Assistant Manager of the British Athletic Team" although he actually worked almost exclusively as a newspaper journalist and BBC commentator.[67]

Thus, within the U.S. and British radio community in late 1935 and early 1936, the issue of collaborating with the Nazi regime created ethical and moral misgivings. But such qualms were balanced against the opportunity of delivering to millions of interested listeners one of the most sophisticated and attractive broadcast productions ever attempted. This balancing act meant that leading right up to the Winter Olympics in Garmisch-Partenkirchen, neither CBS nor NBC dedicated significant efforts to promoting the financial interests of the AOC—or even their own scheduled coverage of the games. Both CBS and NBC offered airtime to both boycott supporters and those supporting Olympic participation, and the networks officially assumed neutral public positions favoring neither side.

The U.S. boycott movement was finally defeated when Avery Brundage's savvy political maneuvering at the Amateur Athletic Union Convention in late 1935 resulted in a vote supporting participation. That so many AAU officials supported the boycott demonstrates how deep the cleavage ran through the U.S. athletic community.[68] Brundage, a truculent and arrogant anti-Semite, blamed a conspiracy for the boycott's popularity. Judge Jeremiah T. Mahoney, a famous

Roman Catholic, had led the boycott movement, yet Brundage publicly blamed Jews and Communists for the agitation. After the AAU vote, he told the press that "certain Jews must now understand that they cannot use these Games as a weapon in their boycott against the Nazis."[69]

Brundage's position won support among most of the top U.S. athletic administrators. "The games this summer have erroneously been referred to as the 'German Olympics,'" Harvard University's director of athletics wrote. "They are no more the 'German Olympics' than they were the 'American Olympics' in 1932. . . . The games were awarded to Berlin in 1932, long before Hitler came into power."[70] Many in Seattle also dismissed the boycott. "In my opinion, America should participate in the Olympic Games because the Olympics themselves are bigger than any one nation," the *Seattle Times*'s George Varnell told an interviewer. "It is silly to suppose the Nazi government can actively control the games." "It would be most unfair to discriminate against our own athletes because of a political situation in Germany," said Clarence "Hec" Edmundson, Washington's basketball and track coach. "What Germany does with her own athletes is none of our business."[71]

Memoirs and oral histories from participants in the 1936 Olympics reveal generally apolitical attitudes among the athletes. "The controversy about boycotting the Games didn't make much of an impression on me or most of the athletes striving to make our Olympic team," one U.S. team member recalled. "There never was any question in my mind about going to Germany."[72] According to gold medalist John Woodruff, the boycott "was never discussed amongst team members. We heard something about it, but we never discussed it. We weren't interested in the politics you see, at all, we were only interested in going to Germany and winning."[73] The oarsmen agreed. "We were not politically-minded," Joe Rantz recalled. "We were not aware there was a contrast in the [kind of] government, that Hitler was any different than anyone else who was head of a state." "We, as athletes, or at least on my part, didn't think much about the political aspects," Gordon Adam agreed.[74] "I didn't give a damn about Hitler," Bob Moch explained:

> We didn't care whether he existed or not. We were there to do a job. That was all. At that level, with the determination and the intensity, if you are going to be good, it is something, just intangible . . . you realize . . . that the determination and intensity is terrific. It is not just in rowing. At that level it has got to be every competitor that really wants to medal. If he really wants to medal, and get that gold, or silver, or bronze medal in the Olympics, he has to focus, he has to be determined, and the intensity has to be all-consuming.[75]

Ultimately, the greatest distraction for the athletes proved not to be the boycott movement and Hitler's politics, but rather, the AOC's economic desperation. In the case of the University of Washington's oarsmen, the citizens of Seattle and Washington came together to alleviate the financial anxiety. But for many others—including such famous athletes as sprinter Helen Stephens, the so-called "Fulton Flash"—paying for the Berlin trip required time and attention away from preparation. And then there were those athletes who, despite earning spots on the team, never boarded the S.S. *Manhattan* because they could not afford the tickets.[76]

The desperation of the AOC to secure funding took absurd turns. At one point, long after NBC concluded its agreements with Germany's Reichs-Rundfunk-Gesellschaft (RRG) and the Berlin Organizing Committee to broadcast the games, AOC treasurer Gustavus Kirby approached the network to demand one hundred thousand dollars. Kirby explained that the AOC would not allow its athletes to appear in retransmitted programs on the North American airwaves without the payment. Shocked NBC officials contacted their German RRG partners and the Berlin Organizing Committee forced the AOC to drop the demand.[77] The financial outlook appeared so bleak in fall 1935 and early 1936 that the AOC seriously debated whether to bring women to compete. The fundraising fiasco continued right until the eve of departure. "It was literally not known until the day before the boat sailed whether or not some squads could be taken," Brundage explained in the final report of the AOC. "This is a national disgrace and the American Olympic Committee must solve this problem [in the future]." The treasurer of the committee went further, noting "that waiting until the eleventh hour to raise funds for Olympic competition is not only wrong in theory but worse in practice."[78]

Complicating the problem, the AOC decentralized fundraising for the first time in 1936 as an "experiment." The committee required "those interested in each sport on the program to finance the team in that sport."[79] This new system, however, was poorly communicated to each of the governing bodies, and the miscommunication resulted in the rowing committee not tabulating its shortfall until 3 July 1936—the night before the Olympic trials began in Princeton. Thus began the chain of events that led to University of Washington students working alongside newsboys and local businessmen, World War I veterans, and even professional wrestlers to send the crew to Berlin.

The Washington state fundraising campaign proved an overwhelming and immediate success. While the oarsmen rested and relaxed at the New York Athletic Club's facilities on Travers Island, just outside New York City, so much money poured in that the committee announced the additional funds would subsidize other athletes from Washington going to Berlin. The five-thousand-dollar goal was passed on 9 July, three days after the campaign was announced and four days since the Huskies first heard the news, and the next day a check was sent to the Olympic Committee.[80] Despite the campaign's success, the sports editor of the *Seattle Times* published a scathing column on 10 July condemning the AOC. "What is wrong with the Olympic committee?" George Varnell asked. They had created a "financial emergency" threatening not just the Huskies, but all U.S. Olympic athletes. Worse still, they failed to communicate their dire financial situation before California and Washington crossed the continent to fight for a trip to Berlin.

The same Friday on which the check left Seattle, NBC aired its most ambitious pre-Olympic promotional program. Tied to the track-and-field tryouts on Randall's Island, in New York City, the show—titled "Olympics Past and Present"—aired over the stations of the NBC Blue Network from 10:30 to 11:00 p.m. Graham McNamee and a few actors opened the show with a series of dramatizations from the ancient games, followed by a roundtable discussion of the U.S. team's prospects. Featuring "the human, intimate side of the Olympic Games—little flashes that never got into the books," the program then moved to interviews with Mel Sheppard, two-time gold medalist in track at the 1908 games, Johnny Hayes, the U.S. marathon gold medalist in 1908, and Lawson Robertson, the track coach of the 1936 U.S. team. The program closed with the recitation of the Olympic oath.[81]

"Olympics Past and Present" was but one component of NBC's promotion of the games. Throughout spring 1936 the network promoted its coverage with a variety of programs and series. "Olympic Prospects with Bill Slater" started in April and brought a new athlete or team before the microphone every Wednesday evening to discuss preparation for Berlin.[82] As the festival drew closer, the number of programs increased. For two weeks before the U.S. team arrived in Germany, NBC (and CBS) regularly broadcast from locales between Olympia, Greece, and Berlin as the inaugural Olympic torch relay moved north.[83] Executives at both CBS and NBC were excited to cover the Olympics live for the first time, as advancements in shortwave transmission technology, combined with significant assistance from German broadcasters, transformed the dream of extended live coverage into reality. The Berlin organizers went to great lengths to welcome and assist the U.S. broadcasters in their promotional broadcasts leading up the games, giving CBS access to the Olympic Village for a special tour broadcast and helping NBC with the complex logistics involved in covering the torch relay.[84] While the Huskies rested on Travers Island, transoceanic Olympics coverage started floating across the U.S. airwaves with some regularity.

The boys fondly recalled the week before departure. The accommodations in the New York Athletic Club's boathouse and clubhouse on Long Island Sound were "excellent"; Bob Moch called it a "nice place, a lovely place." The boys swam, sunbathed, and generally relaxed while waiting for Pocock and Ulbrickson to finish sanding and revarnishing the *Husky Clipper*. For two days they did not even row. Gordon Adam recalled it as "a nice, cool place to stay," as breezes coming off the sound tempered the scorching weather. The squad became more famous as its national media profile grew; one afternoon, a *New Yorker* journalist interviewed Bob Moch shortly after cameramen from Grantland Rice's *Sportlight* newsreel captured the squad's rowing form for movie audiences.[85] In general, they relaxed and were cheered by the updates flooding in from Seattle. When the campaign wrapped up, they had more than enough money to send not only Moch and the eight oarsmen, but Ulbrickson, George Pocock (as the U.S. team's boatwright) and two spares—Don Coy and Delos Schoch—to Berlin. In all, thirteen Huskies crossed the Atlantic aboard the S.S. *Manhattan*. After the intensity of Poughkeepsie and the Olympic trials, the Travers Island vacation was idyllic. Yet not rowing the *Husky Clipper* in practice bothered some of the oarsmen, as did the heat, and there was some concern that the crew began losing its edge awaiting departure.[86]

The moment for embarkation aboard the S.S. *Manhattan* quickly approached. Ulbrickson and Pocock concerned themselves with the onerous task of maneuvering the *Husky Clipper* from the Bronx, through Manhattan, to Pier 60 on West Twentieth Street and the Hudson River. Once on the pier, placing the sixty-five-foot-long delicate shell on the top (Hurricane) deck of the *Manhattan* would have to be figured out. Pocock did not trust the ship's deckhands with his precious boat, and so after carefully placing it on an NYAC trailer the day before departure, the team drove down to the pier and looked for a way to thread the shell up to the top deck. On one side of the giant liner was the passenger pier, filled with booths, offices, shipping packages, and milling people. On the other side of the giant liner no such obstacles were apparent—but also no obvious conveyance to hoist the shell aboard. Finally somebody "spotted a baggage shoot slanting down from dock to street level where we were," Ulbrickson recalled. "Up we struggled, holding the shell at arm's length." Dressed in their street clothes, nervous about their precious cargo, the rowers drenched their shirts with sweat. They boosted their shell "up from one deck to another up to the top." The on-board process was cumbersome but not nearly as nerve-wracking as the initial threading up the baggage ramp. Once the shell passed the elevated upper deck and was safely aboard the *Manhattan*, "it was no problem." Pocock and Ulbrickson tied the *Husky Clipper* onto blocks and then threw a canvas cover

over it. They hoped nobody would mistake the shell for a bench and accidently sit on it during the voyage to Europe.[87]

The squad then headed uptown to the Lincoln Hotel on Eighth Avenue and West Forty-Fourth street to join the assembling U.S. Olympic traveling party. In the lobby of the hotel they stopped at the desk and received their official American Olympic Committee Handbook. They signed the form regulating everything from their use of the Olympic team uniform to their agreement to "refrain from smoking and the use of intoxicating drinks and other forms of dissipation while in training."[88] They received Olympic passports and Olympic identification cards. Once the administrative tasks were completed, the rowers joined their Olympic teammates for a catered lunch in the hotel's dining room. While waiting, they introduced themselves to other athletes and enjoyed the excited atmosphere pervading the hotel. The air of anticipation, the feelings of giddiness and excitement permeating the lobby of the Lincoln were infectious.[89]

Departure the next morning was a madhouse. The athletes were offered breakfast in the hotel before boarding buses at 9:30 a.m. for the drive down to the pier. But many were too excited, preferring to grab an early cab or stroll the mile down to the boat. They found a mob at the end of West Twentieth Street, composed of travelers, newspaper reporters, film crews, radio engineers, sailors, dockhands, onlookers, and autograph hounds. From the sidewalk to the gate at the end of the pier, as many as ten thousand people jammed the small area. As departure time grew closer—the athletes had to be checked in and aboard no later than 10:30 a.m.—the crowd grew more animated. One witness noted the "enthusiastic delegation from Harlem," which came down to "do honor to the Negro [team] members."[90] Hollywood stars Mary Astor and Helen Hayes moved through the mass and climbed the gangplank, as did NBC's Bill Slater, accompanied by an engineer wearing a backpack-sized shortwave transmitter.

On the deck of the ship, one hour before departure, Slater transmitted the excitement live to a national audience by interviewing athletes and coaches. Slater's CBS rival, Robert Trout, also broadcast live from the deck with the assistance of a producer wearing a portable shortwave transmitter. Slater disembarked when whistles warned of the giant ship's impending departure, but Trout remained on the air as the *Manhattan* moved into New York Bay on its way to the Ocean. He had arranged his return to the dock by tugboat, giving CBS an advantage in the competing departure broadcasts.[91]

Everything about the departure was festive and Olympic-themed; the United States Lines even painted the funnels of the giant ship red, white, and blue for the team. Barely noticeable amid the throng at the pier was a single protestor, wearing a sandwich board reading "Boycott Hitler Germany: Fight for

Tolerance, Freedom and Liberty."[92] Absent from the departure ceremony were any high-ranking federal officials. President Roosevelt, to steer clear of the boycott controversy, declined to state a public position and even refused to issue the Olympic team a farewell message.[93] But on this busy, brutally hot morning hardly anybody noticed or cared. A slight breeze cooled the athletes and tourists lining the decks of the *Manhattan* as it navigated the waters out of New York harbor. First the city, then the Statue of Liberty, receded over the horizon.[94]

The athletes eventually found their shared quarters in the bowels of the ship, below the waterline, in third class. The Olympic entourage comprised 688 passengers (out of 1,064 total), and they dominated the ship from the minute the journey began. The first problem cropped up when Helen Stephens, discus hurler Gordon "Slinger" Dunn, and others discovered propaganda pamphlets surreptitiously planted in their rooms discussing the Nazi treatment of minorities while urging athletes to sabotage the games with protests. The athletes turned over the pamphlets to Olympic officials immediately. Providing a final coda to the boycott movement, the pamphlets reminded the departing Olympic contingent that they could not ignore their representational role as political—and national—symbols. Despite their attempts to be as apolitical as possible, the pamphlets reminded the athletes that the trip signified more than athletics and tourism.[95]

At the first two meals, it quickly became apparent that the athletes would be treated differently from the other passengers—and Olympic officials—aboard the ship. Not only were they stuck in third class, but Olympic Committee officials limited both the selection and portion size of their meals. They also had a 10 p.m. curfew and bed checks to monitor compliance. Several athletes bristled, and when word reached Avery Brundage, a meeting was scheduled to address the issues. Brundage announced that henceforth each team's coach—rather than Olympic officials—would supervise their athletes' diets from the ship's regular offerings. But at the same meeting, he again warned the athletes about their behavior, reiterating the importance of the curfew and asking the athletes to refrain from gambling at cards or dice. Brundage was not all threats and bluster, however. "There's no objection if the athletes in some sports, such as the track and field events, indulge in an occasional smoke or glass of beer if they are accustomed," he later told the press, recounting what he had said at the meeting.[96]

Brundage's relaxation of the dietary restrictions had no effect on the rowers. From the start of the season, Ulbrickson monitored his oarsmen's weight carefully. His logbooks regularly noted pounds gained or lost, and he often instructed his rowers on proper eating habits. The outstanding rower, Ulbrickson once wrote, will "confine his diet to lean meat and plenty of green vegetables, and he must stay away from pastries and other rich foods." On the ship, Ulbrickson was particularly concerned about the lavish buffets, and so he "put the boys on a more rigid Spartan diet than ever." One morning McMillin awoke early and snuck over to the ship's dining room. He ordered a double stack of pancakes "generously coated . . . with butter." He poured a "golden flow of syrup" over the pile, only to have Ulbrickson swoop in and pull the plate aside. "Thanks a million, Jim, for fixing those for me," the smiling coach said. McMillin made do with dry toast and orange juice.[97]

Other members of the crew, however, needed to gain weight aboard the ship. At various times during the eight-day voyage, Don Hume, Roger Morris, and John White got seasick. Hume and Morris were already the lightest members of the crew, and the hot weather workouts in Pelham Bay had cost them pounds before the trip commenced. Ulbrickson hoped the lavish meals and forced inactivity aboard the *Manhattan* would bring them back to weight, but beginning on the second day of the trip nausea kept Hume and Morris confined to their cots. They were not the only athletes suffering from seasickness; it was a major concern for the whole Olympic team.[98]

The team received their official uniforms aboard the *Manhattan*. Each athlete received "a double-breasted blue serge coat with [U.S.] emblem on left breast and six Olympic buttons, white trousers, white shirt with red, white and blue striped necktie, straw hat with blue band and emblem, white sleeveless 'V'-necked sweater trimmed in red and blue with shield in center, white sport shoes and white sox." Two tailors from the Smith-Gray Corporation of New York were aboard ship to make any necessary alterations. The athletes also received their uniforms for competition, as well as dark blue sweat suits with "U.S.A." printed on the front.[99]

The AOC sought to provide the athletes with both opportunities to train and special amusements—such as movies, music, and dances—on the crossing. Although the ship mounted a few rowing machines on the deck, the Washington oarsmen did little crew training. The rowing machines employed a pulley system to provide resistance, and although the scullers worked out on them, Ulbrickson did not like their mechanics. The oar handles, for instance, did not move vertically, and this threatened to worsen his oarsmen's technique. After watching the unnatural stroke channeled by the machine, Ulbrickson told his crew to "forget it." He ordered them to walk the decks a few times each day. "That was the only training," McMillin recalled.[100]

Amid the boredom of the repetitive blue horizons, the men found ways to amuse themselves. "The Washington eight walk[ed] the promenade deck in formation from Coxswain Bob Moch and piano-playing stroke Don Hume down the line to Herbert Morris, bow oar, counting the rhythm of their beat," J. P. Abramson of the *New York Herald-Tribune* reported. One day the rowers discovered the ship's dog kennel on the boat's top deck. Inside the big metal cage the dogs were surprisingly sedate as they endured the trip. One day the oarsmen invited an unaware Bob Moch to take a walk with them on the top deck, and when their coxswain was not looking, they jumped him and stuffed him in the cage with the pooches. They ran down to Ulbrickson's room to tell him if he headed up to the top deck he would discover something of interest. "I found Bob on his hands and knees in the cage, peering out through the netting, between a mournful-faced St. Bernard and a quizzical little fox terrier," Ulbrickson recalled.[101]

Meeting and mingling with their Olympic teammates proved to be one of the most exciting aspects of the voyage. "It was a great thing for us to meet [the other athletes]," Gordon Adam remembered. "Some of them were well-known names, world-record holders like Glenn Cunningham, Bill Sefton and Earle Meadows in the pole vault, and other people like that who were already known names in track and field." Bob Moch also remembered meeting Jesse Owens and other famous athletes aboard the *Manhattan* as one highlight of the voyage.[102] "It was a zoo, an incredible spectacle," remembered Harvard coxswain Edward H. Bennett, a member of the U.S. Olympic four-oared crew:

> You had the walking team striding by, with that peculiar waddling gait. The boxing team—a bunch of lowlifes if you ever saw them—were shadow-boxing on the deck. The high divers were insufferably vain. They postured and posed on the diving board for an hour at a time. One of the weightlifters was even worse—on deck he wore a silk wrapper and a blue hairnet so the wind wouldn't muss his coiffure.[103]

The boat was filled with amusements and entertainments for the oarsmen, including movies, dances, live music, a putting green, and an indoor gym. The Olympic team held their own beauty contest, crowning a most beautiful female athlete and most handsome male athlete, and officials looked the other way when an unofficial "casino night" found many athletes gambling at craps and card games.[104]

But officials could not ignore the actions of one athlete. The beautiful, flirtatious Eleanor Holm Jarrett was the world's finest backstroke swimmer (she won gold in Los Angeles) and a woman who loved to party. The twenty-two-year-old flouted all the prescribed rules of behavior, regularly traveling up to the A deck to drink and dance with first-class passengers. The journalists and celebrities loved her cheeky personality, her beauty, and her confidence. "I train on champagne and cigarettes," Jarrett told reporters.[105] During the voyage athletes and officials often found her drunk, being carried back to her cabin in the mornings, and generally carrying on inappropriately. When she ignored a warning, Brundage called on AOC officials to dismiss her from the team. Most, but not all, of the athletes supported her, even going so far as to create a protest letter demanding her reinstatement. But Brundage argued the AOC was simply protecting "the image of American Olympism," and the appeal went nowhere.[106]

The athletes heard conflicting reports about the exact action causing Jarrett's banishment. Some heard she had been gambling; some that she had been seen drinking champagne, and others that she was thrown off the team merely for being on the A deck, rather than in third-class with her colleagues. "We were on board when Eleanor Holmes [sic], got sandbagged by the journalists," Bob Moch remembered. "They got her drunk, and they kicked her off the squad while she was on the boat, they told her she was off the squad. Those newspapermen were responsible for that."[107] Jarrett made the most of her expulsion; rather than returning immediately to the United States (as Brundage commanded), the Hearst newspaper chain hired her to report from Berlin.

After stopping in Ireland, then Plymouth, England, the *Manhattan* reached the mouth of the Elbe River on the evening of 23 July. The AOC had arranged with the Germans and the United States Lines to delay disembarkation until early the following morning, however, because a full slate of activities was scheduled for the official arrival. The huge liner eased slowly down the river as the sun set and night fell. The athletes lined the deck as the boat moved into Germany. "What I remember so distinctly was going up the river, from the time you entered the river that goes to Hamburg. It was at night, and pitch black, and the people, apparently, along the river in those days there were a lot of individual residences as well as businesses, and as we would approach it, as the boat came up the river, the lights came on in all of these buildings. That was pretty impressive. It made you feel welcome," Moch recalled. George Hunt was also mesmerized by the view. As the boat passed the beer gardens on terraces nestled against the hills, the lights flashed and "people along . . . the banks were yelling all kinds of words of encouragement." Two Olympic flags and the U.S. flag were bathed in searchlights, Hunt recalled, so that "there was no mistaking our mission or who we were." The athletes finally went to bed when the boat glided to a stop around 11:30 p.m.[108]

The following morning the rowers were back up at 5:00 a.m. After breakfast they watched as the *Manhattan* slowly edged into its Hamburg berth. The ship properly secured, the gangplanks were lowered and the pier exploded into action with deckhands and stevedores hustling about. The team had been instructed to wear their blazers and boaters and line up properly for disembarkation.

George Pocock and Lawrence "Monk" Terry, the coach of the U.S. entry in the four with coxswain competition, stood together at the rail of the giant ship, watching the chaotic scene unfold. The oarsmen had been instructed to handle the *Husky Clipper* carefully and make sure the German dockworkers did not touch the precious shell. The rowers carefully threaded the boat down two decks, where it was secured on slings and "hoisted over the side with a derrick." After the oarsmen departed to join the other athletes preparing to disembark, Terry and Pocock watched the shell rock back against the *Manhattan's* rail. The bump tore a twenty-five-inch crack in the boat's delicate skin. Terry looked at Pocock, who was staring at the workers as the hoist lowered the damaged shell down toward the pier. After an extended silence, Pocock spoke. "Those fellows need more practice unloading boats," he said quietly. Terry was amazed at Pocock's stoic self-control.[109]

The excited oarsmen, dressed in their blazers and sporting their white boaters, lined up with the rest of the U.S. athletes, preparing to disembark. The huge covered pier loomed over them as they marched down the ramp and into the massive warehouse, two or three abreast. Over the archway where the gangplank met the dock hung a banner flanked by two large flags—on the left, the swastika of Nazi Germany and on the right the stars and stripes. Between the two flags a horizontal white banner with Germanic script greeted the team. It read, in English: "Welcome to Germany."[110]

CHAPTER 3

Berlin 1936 as Global Broadcast Spectacle and Personal Experience

The tear in the delicate skin covering the *Husky Clipper* seemed an ominous harbinger for Al Ulbrickson, George Pocock, and the Washington squad. In addition to the sicknesses bothering John White, Donald Hume, and Gordon Adam, this new problem made the Olympic odyssey seem cursed. By the time the U.S. squad, smiling and dressed in their blazers and boaters, descended the gangplank to the festivities in Hamburg, Ulbrickson sensed the myriad challenges—logistical, physical, and psychological—he would face over the next month. The quiet, anxious, and intense Ulbrickson had begun smoking after finishing his career in the shell, but now he found himself self-medicating with tobacco more regularly. His desire for an uneventful (and even enjoyable) capstone to one of the most brilliant racing seasons in U.S. rowing history would be denied. He later labeled this confluence of troubling events beginning aboard the S.S. *Manhattan* as the team's run of "pre-Olympic bad luck."[1]

Yet not all was ominous. The S.S. *Manhattan* docked at Hamburg's wharf 13, and everyone noticed. By this point in the season Ulbrickson and his superstitious oarsmen joked that thirteen was the team's lucky number. Ulbrickson was not sure exactly when thirteen became lucky, but he remembered that trunk thirteen held his team's suits going east to New York, and he slept in train car thirteen on that same trip. It had been thirteen years since he had married his wife Hazel, and they would celebrate the anniversary in Berlin. He and the team were therefore naturally delighted to notice the "13" in the window of the gray bus they boarded to head over to Hamburg's City Hall. George Hunt even considered the rain, which had started to fall from the overcast skies, as promising. "It was raining the day we arrived at Poughkeepsie," he recalled. Bad weather did little to deter the crowds lining the wharves, docks, and streets of Hamburg as the buses filled with U.S. athletes and officials made their way through the curving streets. "When the ship docked in Hamburg there was an enormous crowd at pierside," Gordon Adam recalled, remembering the "bands and welcoming speeches. I don't know whether the citizens were ordered out to attend the event or whether they were just that enthused about the Olympics and the American team." Getting into the spirit, a few U.S. athletes blurted out "*heil!*" as they descended the gangplank, though "they made no salutes." [2]

After leaving the ship, buses ferried the Olympic group to the Rathaus, or city hall, where a celebration was scheduled. The team filed through the huge entranceway and up a wide staircase to a spacious reception hall. An honor guard of Hitler Youth, frozen at attention, lined the wide staircase and awed George Pocock. "These uniformed youngsters were something to behold: straight as ramrods, blooming cheeks, close-cropped hair and bare, tanned arms and legs," he recalled. A noise erupted behind the rowers; some boxers laughed and pushed members of the guard, seeing if they could budge their stone-faced expressions. But the Hitler Youth members just jumped back up and returned to rigid attention as though the boxers' antics never occurred. The rude behavior embarrassed Pocock. In the high-ceilinged gilded parlor, the mayor welcomed the team in German and English. Avery Brundage followed with a few pleasant words, then cigars, cigarettes, fruit punch, and orange juice (for the athletes) were passed around.[3]

In Hamburg, and later Berlin, the number of uniforms worn by the Germans impressed the U.S. athletes. "One of the first things we noticed" in Berlin, George Hunt wrote to his family, "was the presence of so many uniforms." Yet Germany's overt martial spirit had actually toned down since the winter games took place at the Bavarian resort of Garmisch-Partenkirchen earlier in 1936. Global reporting from those games revealed the new Germany's militaristic spirit and its attempts to hide Nazi anti-Semitism from public view. The reporting from Garmisch-Partenkirchen infuriated Dr. Joseph Goebbels, the Nazi propaganda minister, who almost expelled (after publicly excoriating) Bill Shirer of the United Press for publishing one especially critical piece. Goebbels and his staff decided to remedy the problem for the Berlin Games in a few ways. Orders descended from his office to the Nazi party organization, local governmental offices, and elsewhere that fewer uniforms should be in evidence; consequently, Berlin's traffic police "put aside their stiff uniforms and weapons and appeared in light, comfortable attire." Racial problems, the ministry ordered, were never to be discussed in public. Less than a month before the opening ceremonies, the Nazi party and Propaganda Ministry jointly announced that all Nazi party meetings scheduled between 1 August and 7 September 1936, would be postponed, and all party members were "instructed to spare their energy for a new propaganda campaign to be launched after the Olympics." Goebbels's newspaper, *Der Angriff*, told its readers and Germany's visitors that the nation would show "the most beautiful sports arena, the fastest transportation, and the cheapest currency" to the world.[4]

Yet Goebbels's demand that the citizenry appear less uniform and more diverse and spontaneous failed. Everywhere one looked Germans were uniformed, from the bus drivers to the Hitler Youth, and also the soldiers, sailors, and even street sweepers. The whole country seemed "uniform" in every sense: The people were regimented, the towns clean, charming, and orderly, and the media and government functionaries were conspicuously welcoming. "Our first and deepest impression of the country was the total patriotic hold Hitler had over the people. Red and white flags bearing the Nazi hooked cross were everywhere," George Pocock recalled. But German patriotism was neither condescending nor exclusive. Rather, to many U.S. visitors German nationalism appeared intertwined with genuine warmth. Friendly, helpful attitudes were on display everywhere. Even the uniforms did not bother everybody. Berlin was "magnificently dressed for the big show," sports columnist Paul Gallico reported. "The Germans," he continued, "are being wonderfully polite and cordial and helpful to the Americans."[5]

Immediately after the Hamburg reception, the team boarded buses, were driven to the Bahnhof, and loaded onto two special reserved express trains for Berlin.[6] The oarsmen sat together, watching the countryside fly by outside their windows, as CBS's Bill Henry, using a portable shortwave transmitter, conducted the first live interviews from Germany with U.S. Olympic athletes (an attempt to speak with the athletes earlier in Hamburg had failed). The interviews were beamed live back across the Atlantic and aired coast to coast. For thirty minutes, with the sound of the train motoring and the wheels clicking on the tracks in the background, Henry discussed the trip and previewed the games with athletes and officials. When the train arrived in Berlin, NBC's broadcasters were surprised to find themselves scooped by CBS.[7]

The two trains rocketed south, past farmers' fields, forests and woods, and charming towns. Looking out the window, George Hunt noticed "the absence of underbrush" in the forests. Hunt detected planting and forestation patterns that seemed to him "very much like those out toward Spanaway and Fort Lewis" back home. The speeding train occasionally slowed as it moved in and out of towns. Hunt noticed the many small houses and shacks bordering the tracks—which he compared to Hoovervilles in the United States—"except they are very clean and all have a small garden." Finally slowing as it moved into the suburbs of the capital, the train pulled up with a hiss of its pneumatic brakes at the Lehrter Bahnhof (Berlin Central Station). Passengers, newspaper and radio reporters, officials, and athletes all piled out onto the long cement platform. Smiling and joking, the U.S. Olympians walked into the station, where a huge crowd and marching band awaited them under the gigantic vaulted roof. Officials, newsreel cameramen, radio technicians, and newspaper photographers, reporters, and onlookers all crowded around the standing microphones for the brief arrival ceremony. Hunt recalled it as "quite a pompous affair." Young English-speaking Germans—both girls and boys—accompanied the U.S. athletes to translate and indicate the various key figures at the station's brief reception ceremony.[8] The athletes made their way through the crowd and out to the street, where they were surprised by the "biggest crowd of people you ever saw in your life." Thousands of welcoming Berliners swarmed the sidewalks, plaza, and street where gray buses idled in neutral, waiting for their U.S. passengers. The buses had their convertible tops rolled back, so the U.S. athletes "laughed, sang and waved" at the boisterous crowds. "The greatest crowd in the history of Unter den Linden filled that famous avenue to overflowing today," the *New York Times* reported, estimating that 24,000 people (or more) jammed the street. "I could easily say 100,000 people lined that parade route just to welcome the team to Berlin," remembered Gordon Adam. The crowd was so dense, George Hunt recalled, "you couldn't see the pavement. I don't think I've ever seen so many people." As the gray army buses slowly made their way down Berlin's overflowing streets, the athletes were amazed. Soon they arrived at city hall.[9]

Berlin was magical, festive, and electric. Everything about the city was transformed; clean, neat, and orderly; the movie theaters, nightclubs, and restaurants extended their late night hours to keep the parties running every night. Slums were nowhere to be seen. Nor was graffiti, pollution, garbage, or prostitution visible. Huge flags and banners draped down from the light posts lining every major thoroughfare. Smiles were plastered on faces everywhere—despite the well-known reputation of Berliners as surly and curt. Tourists from around the world later remembered the city in July and August 1936 as the greatest advertisement the Nazi government ever produced. The sheer number of published remembrances of those summer days attests to the deep impression that the games made. Howard K. Smith, later to become a Rhodes scholar and newscaster working with Edward R. Murrow at CBS during World War II, spent the summer of 1936 studying and traveling in Germany. He remembered his first vision of Germany that summer as "captivating," and though he could not afford tickets to the events, he would visit the Olympic stadium and neighboring Maifeld just to participate in history.[10]

The emotional intensity of Berlin's Olympic welcome stunned visitors. "Men who had been with former Olympic teams said that this was by far the greatest reception ever given an Olympic team," one athlete remembered.[11] As tourists from across Germany and the world descended upon the German capital, the Nazi hosts cleverly exploited every opportunity to generate much-needed foreign currency and goodwill from international travelers. Special "Travel Marks" offered discounted currency when purchased abroad, allowing the Reichsbank to leverage the games in order to exploit the foreign exchange opportunity. "Foreigners were forced to purchase their tickets in their home currencies," a *New Yorker* correspondent reported. "The Games were managed as a brilliant banking coup which, with the excitement about how far and fast athletes could run and jump and swim over and under things, no one seemed to notice." Though discounts on hotels and railway tickets abounded, the flood of foreign and domestic tourists more than recouped the Reichsbank's subsidy of Travel Marks. German credit on international markets improved significantly.[12]

The Olympic Games, it was clear, had been transformed. In 1936 they became more broadly experiential, more nationalistic, and they served new purposes unrelated to athletics. This intensification included higher emotional stakes for audiences around the world, stoked by the new level of global media attention. Even the classic amateur ideal—so treasured by Avery Brundage—underwent a transition in Berlin. Hitler rewarded his athletes lavishly both before and after the games with money and promotions, and after the games several medal winners were awarded six-month vacations subsidized by national corporations.[13] Before Berlin, the Olympic Games served as a festival of athletic contests produced by local boosters seeking publicity for a variety of purposes. It was the Nazi government, the Reichs-Rundfunk-Gesellschaft (RRG), and Berlin's organizing committee that transformed them into the professional globalized spectacle we know today.

The conflation of sport with politics, business, tourism, and propaganda had evolved as a component of the Olympics since their inception. But nothing—not even the Los Angeles games four years earlier—could compare with the German effort. The brilliant efficiency of the Berlin Games offered a stark contrast to the shoddiness of the Los Angeles Olympiad. The Los Angeles Olympics occurred in the depths of the worldwide economic depression. The lack of sponsors and access to governmental financial assistance combined with enormous expenses made the Los Angeles Olympic Committee—and American Olympic Committee (AOC)—beg for money and visitors. The cash-strapped governments of California and the United States did little to alleviate the pressure as the 1932 games neared. At one point, the organizers turned to Hollywood. They arranged national and international advertising broadcasts in which film celebrities implored tourists to visit southern California for the games. Europeans "should close up your shops this summer and come on over, 'cause you aren't doing anything anyway," Will Rogers, the famous humorist joked, "and bring your customers with you." He even went so far as to poke fun at the global reputation of the United States. "We're broke over here now," he said, "and so we're humble. You better come and see us quick before we get rich again!"[14]

This desperate push for revenue resulted in the organizing committee notifying both CBS and NBC only weeks before the Los Angeles games that Olympic radio coverage would require rights payments. The broadcast networks considered coverage of the Olympics an unsponsored news and special-events production—much like coverage of other events of national interest such as a presidential inauguration or celebratory parade. To have $100,000 demanded in summer 1932—shortly after CBS fired more than one hundred employees and ordered all remaining workers to accept a 15 percent pay cut, and NBC fired 195 workers—infuriated network executives.[15] Live broadcasts, they argued, would promote the games widely and induce listeners to purchase tickets and travel to Los Angeles. This impasse was never resolved; CBS and NBC sent their top sportscasters hoping the organizing committee would rethink their demands, but Grantland Rice (NBC) and Ted Husing (CBS) were reduced to broadcasting only results and summaries every evening. "Radio," historian Barbara Keys notes, "was the one area where organizers [of the Los Angeles Games] stumbled."[16]

Despite the tensions between CBS and NBC and the AOC and Los Angeles Olympic Committee, 1932 did prove to be a milestone year in international global shortwave sports broadcasting. Selected events and athlete interviews from the winter games, held in Lake Placid, were relayed successfully to Europe by RCA and NBC.[17] In Los Angeles, the Bell System collaborated with RCA Communications to deliver the best sports coverage possible in light of the very tight restrictions. Ultimately, both the Lake Placid and Los Angeles broadcasts were largely experimental. Transoceanic relay and reception often proved satisfactory in 1932, but the broadcasts were few in number, went to only a handful of countries, and were short in duration.

Berlin would be completely different. From the organizing committee's inception, decisions at the highest level of the German government (both before and after the Nazi government assumed power) to support the games eased the economic and logistical burdens for everyone involved. The games would be a media spectacle on an entirely new scale. Improvements in filmmaking and the new reliability of broadcasting technology ensured that audiences for the games would no longer be confined to stadia in and around the capital city. Hundreds of millions of people around the world, the German organizers understood, could be influenced to look at the "new" Germany with respect and admiration. Tourists could be lured, positive impressions made, and the contrast between an "open" or cooperative authoritarianism such as Germany practiced versus the "closed" or intransigent Soviet authoritarianism could be illuminated. Nor were the benefits limited to publicity. Hard currency, in the form of tourist dollars, and direct investment from impressed international manufacturers and business leaders, provided an opportunity for the German government to leverage the Olympic Games into a profitable return on its investment. "The Olympic Games afforded us a unique opportunity to amass foreign credits, and, at the same time, a splendid chance of enhancing our prestige abroad," Adolf Hitler recalled years later.[18]

To the athletes and officials who attended the games in Los Angeles, Amsterdam, and even Paris, the change in tone and scale was immediately apparent. CBS's Bill Henry estimated that the Los Angeles committee spent approximately $2.5 million on facilities for the 1932 games. After touring the Berlin facilities as an adviser in 1935, and then again in early 1936, Henry estimated that the Germans spent more than $10 million (they ultimately spent an estimated $30 million).[19] Everything about the games had become more cosmopolitan, more refined, more impressive, and more luxurious. The athletic facilities, technical apparatus, and accommodations were the finest in the world for the athletes, spectators, and media personnel.

Most modern of all, the Berlin Olympics were explicitly designed to generate popular global support for a new political regime. "All over Berlin . . . wherever you went or whoever you bumped into, nobody said hello, nobody said good morning; they said, 'Heil Hitler,'" Gordon Adam remembered. The presence of the Nazi dictator was everywhere and inescapable. For the rowers from the Pacific Northwest, such humorless idolatry seemed alien. "The standard greeting was 'Heil Hitler,'" Adam recalled. "We, of course, got smart once in a while and would answer them, "'Heil Roosevelt,' which I don't think they noticed." Some Australians also took to parodying the Nazi salute. "Some of us did it, only ironically, and when you were supposed to say 'Heil Hitler' we used to say 'Haile Selassie,' or 'hailstones'—we wouldn't do it properly," Australian wrestler Dick Garrard remembered. Misbehavior by visitors, which could be unruly and even criminal, was often ignored by Berlin's police. "The Olympic visitor to Berlin can do no wrong," wrote the United Press's Henry McLemore. "He may yank down flags, uproot trees on the Unter den Linden, bump people off the sidewalk, bop waiters in the eye and make himself thoroughly objectionable without a fear of being tossed in the calaboose."[20]

This touristic euphoria bothered those U.S. visitors who knew Nazi Germany well. Reporters, diplomats, and expatriates, disturbed by the sheer fraudulence of the façade, tried to convince their countrymen that all was not what it appeared under the hooked cross. "The Games themselves were . . . beautifully organized and staged," Bill Shirer remembered, but "Hitler saw to it that the country was on its best behavior; no persecution of the Jews. No action against unruly Catholics and Protestants. No savage attacks against the 'decadent' Western democracies and 'Jewish-dominated' America. All was, for the moment, sweetness and light."[21] Max Jordan, NBC's Continental Representative, also abhorred the façade. He had been dealing with Nazi bureaucracy for three years by the time the Olympics began. Negotiating with the RRG had proven far more contentious since the Nazi party asserted control over radio. First came the firing of non-Nazi personnel in spring 1933—a group of veteran radio executives whom Jordan respected. In particular, the forced resignation of Kurt Magnus, the founding director of the RRG, and his colleague Hans Bredow shocked Jordan and his NBC colleagues. Not only were they replaced by inexperienced Nazi party loyalists, but within a few months both men were imprisoned in concentration camps on fabricated embezzlement charges.[22] Perhaps most shocking was the fate of RRG chief engineer Walter Schaeffer. Beginning in September 1931, Schaeffer coordinated "What America Talks About," a bimonthly RRG program produced in cooperation with NBC. Well liked and respected by his U.S. colleagues, Schaeffer regularly hosted and participated in annual exchange tours. But soon after his firing by the Nazi administration, the despondent Schaeffer committed suicide in his apartment in Berlin.[23]

Fanatical devotion to Nazi ideals proved the key qualification for the men selected to replace the RRG's veteran management team. By 1934 the RRG was under the direction of Eugen Hadamovsky, a formerly unemployed auto mechanic who joined the Nazi party in 1930 and proved to be a skillful organizer and administrator in the party's central propaganda office. Hadamovsky possessed undeniable talent for planning large-scale broadcasts and handling acoustic production at huge Nazi rallies. But he lacked the experience, collegiality, and intellect of his predecessors at the RRG.[24] A shrewd opportunist, Hadamovsky pleased Goebbels by energetically pursuing the propaganda minister's goal of placing a radio set in every household in the Reich. To that end,

Hadamovsky worked closely with the Reich Radio Association to speed the sale and distribution of radio receivers. Radio loudspeakers were placed atop pillars in public spaces, and community listening to important programs was encouraged. The rapid rise in German radio set ownership between 1934 and 1936 significantly increased revenues available for RRG broadcast production and technical improvements while furthering the reach of Nazi propaganda campaigns. As one RRG employee proudly noted in a U.S. journal, within two years of the Nazi takeover of the RRG, German broadcasting techniques, policies, and program models became widely imitated in neighboring European nations.[25]

Few U.S. broadcasters cooperating with the RRG between 1934 and 1941 worked closely with Hadamovsky. Preoccupied primarily with domestic radio, Hadamovsky left international broadcasting to others. U.S. broadcasters encountering Hadamovsky (whom they referred to as "Hada") considered the RRG director a party hack most notable for his sarcastic, conceited, and belligerent manner.[26] His arrogance was best displayed in the study he published on radio and nation in 1933: *Propaganda und Nationale Macht: Die Organisation der Öffentlichen Meinung für die Nationale Politik* ("Propaganda and National Power: The Organization of Public Opinion for National Politics"). *Propaganda und Nationale Macht* offers the most precisely delineated Nazi perspective on broadcasting and propaganda ever expressed. "The task of radio is to form the will of the nation," Hadamovsky explained, while emphasizing propaganda's more general goal of exploiting all media to unite the citizenry in opposition to "forces of internationalism that would destroy our people."[27] Echoing Goebbels, Hadamovsky asserted the supremacy of radio as the propagandist's most persuasive tool.[28] The key, according to Hadamovsky, was to exploit radio properly. Because matching "the forces of race and blood that lie hidden in the subconscious mind" to the proper national aesthetic constituted the essential task of the propagandist, broadcasters needed to carefully consider the most appropriate stimuli at all times. This is undoubtedly why, on 13 October 1935, Hadamovsky famously banned jazz music from the German airwaves. "As of today," he proclaimed, "Nigger jazz [*sic*] is finally switched off on the German radio."[29] "Nigger jazz music [*sic*] will cause different reactions than a Beethoven symphony," he had written earlier in *Propaganda und Nationale Macht*, explaining that music's inherent power to transport listeners to "a world of pure phantasy and rhythmical animation" made jazz especially dangerous.[30]

Hadamovsky carefully concealed his toxic racism and xenophobic nationalism during the Olympics. Praising peace and harmony, he officially welcomed the world's broadcasting community to Berlin. "Your radio," he explained, is "linked high above all frontiers, mountains, and oceans, directly with the Olympic arena." Radio would inspire the imagination "to expand the vast space of the arena, with its more than one hundred thousand seats, into a gigantic forum in which all the peoples of the Earth" would be "participators and listeners at the Olympic Games." Such participatory experiences would "serve perfectly the peaceful union of nations, and is proved a most powerful instrument of peace."[31] In this spirit of cosmopolitan internationalism, Hadamovsky even supported the Propaganda Ministry's lifting of the ban on jazz music for the duration of the games. But he and Dr. Goebbels would go only so far. Only "German jazz," or jazz music played by "a few American orchestras consisting only of whites" was permitted in the clubs and on the airwaves.[32]

Permitted jazz was only a small part of Germany's cultural inversion occurring during the Olympic pause. Indeed, revisionist historians have argued that the implicit—and occasionally explicit—repudiation of Nazi ideals occasioned by the games made the Olympics far less politically successful than is commonly believed.[33] The tolerance of competing value systems, such as those structuring the political economy of international trade and market consumerism, combined with the banishment of racism and xenophobia, represented a clear rebuke to National Socialism. German businessmen seized the opening to promote imported goods within the domestic market using new techniques. Such activity countered the ideal of autarky heavily promoted in Nazi propaganda. The Nazis rallied the German citizenry around tension and conflict, but the Olympics fostered an atmosphere of tolerance, respect, and interchange. Joining their German colleagues, foreign businessmen also took advantage of this Olympic inversion. Especially helpful, in this regard, was Rotary International. The Berlin chapter hosted and assisted foreign business interests throughout the games, only to be outlawed by a Nazi court the following year.[34]

No international business exploited the Berlin Games more effectively than Coca-Cola. The Atlanta-based soft drink company first moved in to the European beverage market in a large way during Amsterdam's summer Olympic Games. In 1928, "the Company's new Foreign Department sent a thousand cases of the soft drink along with the U.S. Olympic team to Amsterdam, where special Coca-Cola kiosks staffed by vendors with Coca-Cola caps and coats wooed more customers than competing 'health drinks'," Barbara Keys notes.[35] "Sports provided a means by which to introduce Coca-Cola, to spread the word," remembered Walter Oppenhoff, the attorney who incorporated Coca-Cola GmbH in Weimar Germany in 1930.[36] Throughout the 1930s, Coca Cola was marketed in Nazi Germany as *rein und gesund* ("pure and wholesome") and the corporation regularly sponsored athletic events to build sales and brand recognition. Coca Cola's president, Robert Woodruff, journeyed to Berlin, accompanied by several top executives, but proved unable to secure exclusive beverage vending rights at the venues through the organizing committee. The Nazis reserved those rights for the German brewery Schultheiss. Historian Jeff Schutts notes, however, that Coca-Cola GmbH was authorized "to provide supplementary 'refreshment service' from sidewalk stands outside the Olympic venues."[37] The ubiquitous presence of Coca Cola in Berlin's restaurants and cafés became a powerful harbinger of the Olympic movement's future. Just as fascist regimes emphasized athletics as symbolic of national power in the 1930s, the U.S. shaping of international sport also could first be felt emerging in this period. As Barbara Keys concludes, the primary U.S. influence on global athletics in this period was "the transformation of international sport from an elite cultural pursuit to a mass cultural phenomenon based on commercialism and the new consumer culture."[38] The consumerism in Berlin was negligible, however, in comparison with that of later Olympic festivals. It required the defeat of the fascist regimes and the emergence of the Cold War to produce the final fusion of nationalism and consumerism marking the contemporary Olympic movement.

The propagation of that synthesis is unimaginable without reference to Olympic broadcasting's maturation in Berlin, where both the Nazi authorities and U.S. marketers shared a desire to use radio to influence and persuade mass audiences. In this sense, the RRG under Hadamovsky had more in common with U.S. commercial networks than with national broadcast organizations committed to educational uplift, such as the BBC and Japan's NHK. In both Germany and the United States, radio authorities sought to significantly grow listening audiences through the widespread distribution of low-cost receivers. As both network systems matured in the early 1930s, the imperative of unified popular appeal to propagate national values largely superseded older models of classic moral and ethical instruction.[39] In both countries, for example, radio authorities increased the amount of popular contemporary music (including folk genres) while decreasing classical concerts on the airwaves.[40] The role of women, as both consumers and producers of broadcasting, developed a new importance in both nations. "Women's relationship to radio was deemed to be of key ideological and practical importance in the Third Reich," notes Kate Lacey, echoing the work of U.S. radio historians who have detailed the catalytic role of women in structuring U.S. network broadcasting's first two decades.[41] Yet one can extend these parallels too far; Hadamovsky never jettisoned his elitist and hierarchical perspective on radio, and he always disdained bourgeois "democratic" applications of the medium.

U.S. broadcasters saw little of Hadamovsky during the Olympics. Most contact with the RRG occurred through a managerial group assembled by the network and the Propaganda Ministry. This team included Kurt von Boeckmann, Kurt Rathke, Horst Cleinow, and Harald Diettrich. The group worked out of a special Olympic office near the Haus des Rundfunks and Olympic stadium in West Berlin. NBC's Max Jordan and CBS's César Saerchinger both knew von Boeckmann and Rathke well, having collaborated with them on broadcasts over the previous five years.[42] Jordan was fond of Rathke, one of the few senior RRG managers to antedate the Nazi takeover and survive the broadcast management purge of 1933. But Rathke was the exception; the Nazi takeover of German radio in 1933–34 so distressed Jordan that by 1935 he moved NBC's continental operation to Basel, Switzerland, just across the German border. In Basel he hired Mathilde Baier, a young multilingual Swiss woman, to be his assistant. As the Olympics neared, both Jordan and Baier traveled to Berlin frequently. Despite his aversion to Nazi management, Jordan's relations with RRG employees remained professional, and in May 1936 he collaborated with von Boeckmann on broadcasts from the new German dirigible *Hindenburg* during its maiden transatlantic crossing.[43] Baier's work for NBC in the 1930s is largely forgotten, but her facilitation of communication with the RRG and other European broadcast systems played an important role for NBC News as the decade wore on.[44]

Jordan and Baier were assigned to assist NBC's top sportscaster Bill Slater upon his arrival in Germany. Slater would cover live events and relay daily summaries of the results and interviews late at night, while the RRG's Eduard Roderich Dietze would report events and cover the broadcasts that Slater could not attend. In 1936 Slater was a rising star in the new field of sports broadcasting. In 1933 NBC executives began planning to replace the pioneering but erratic Graham McNamee but had little luck until they heard the CBS broadcast of the Army–Navy football game at the end of that year.[45] Slater, a 1924 graduate of West Point, teamed with Ted Husing for that program, and the quality and clarity of his voice was memorable enough for NBC to offer him a part-time contract in 1934. Slater's full-time position was serving as headmaster of Adelphi Academy, a private school in Brooklyn, New York. Slater began his radio career while teaching at the Blake School in Minneapolis in the 1920s, where as a hobby he broadcast high school and college football games. As he sharpened his skills and honed his delivery, professional broadcasters began taking notice. He moved to New York City both to serve as headmaster at Adelphi and improve his work opportunities in sports broadcasting. "Brisk and informative," was one assessment of Slater's style, but NBC's management was particularly interested in

Slater for another reason: His voice and delivery were almost indistinguishable from those of Ted Husing.[46] Both men enunciated clearly and rapidly, adding a natural enthusiasm and excitement to their sports programs. Although Husing was the most critically acclaimed sportscaster of the era (as demonstrated in polls of newspaper radio editors), Slater's delivery was also appreciated and praised. "Ted Husing at times becomes too erudite," wrote one radio critic, but "Bill Slater has a more polished and suave approach." Slater "was very lyrical," remembered veteran sportscaster Chris Schenkel. "His voice was up and down like a good opera singer." Though he "lacked charisma," according to sportscaster Marty Glickman, Slater "was a very good announcer" who could be relied upon for a serious and steady delivery. In 1934 Slater began working for NBC on unsponsored (sustaining) sports broadcasts that did not conflict with his headmaster's job, and by 1936 he was widely known for his proficiency as an announcer and commentator.[47] Both NBC and radio-set manufacturers seeking to exploit the Berlin Olympic Games for high ratings and sales increases promoted Slater's Olympic broadcasts. "Fleet-footed Finns . . . English hurdlers . . . Japanese swimmers . . . American sprinters . . . match their might. Bill Slater will be there . . . sending vivid word pictures by radio across the Atlantic to be broadcast throughout America. Philco will bring these broadcasts through a nearby station," read a full-page Philco advertisement appearing in several magazines in summer 1936.[48]

Shortly after Slater arrived in Berlin, Jordan conferred with him to go over logistics, information, and general administrative issues. Slater confessed surprise about Germany; his initial impressions, he told Jordan, simply did not match the image presented in the U.S. media. The people were friendly and welcoming, and the government efficient and helpful. "It's hard to believe that this country is in the throes of a violent revolution," he explained. "Why, if the people didn't speak German, and if there weren't all these swastikas around, you'd almost think you were back home."[49]

Max Jordan was tired of hearing such sentiments. In various ways, U.S. journalists like Jordan, William Shirer, and others who knew the reality of the Nazi dictatorship attempted to educate their countrymen. Earlier, at the winter Olympics, Shirer arranged a luncheon in which Douglas Miller, the U.S. Embassy's business attaché (and future author of *You Can't Do Business with Hitler*), revealed the multitude of ways the Nazi government restrained freedom in everything—including commercial business. Miller's talk—much to Shirer's disappointment—convinced none of the guests. Later, during the Berlin Games, Shirer again shared a meal with several prominent U.S. businessmen. "The genial tycoons" told Shirer they knew "the situation in Nazi Germany." "They liked it, they said. The streets were clean and peaceful. Law and Order. No strikes, no trouble-making unions."[50]

The Nazi propaganda ministry not only influenced these U.S. business-men within Germany but also sought to persuade U.S. citizens back in North America of Germany's good intentions. They pursued this goal in a variety of ways. Propaganda books and pamphlets extolling both the revitalization of Germany and the peaceful and cooperative nature of National Socialism were distributed to foreign journalists, athletes, and officials. When reporters first visited the nation for the winter games, they found press liaisons to be friendly, useful, and efficient. Later, however, when cables mysteriously vanished and reports were "lost" in transmission (sometimes without the correspondent being notified), journalists felt chagrined at their naïveté. A few weeks after leaving Garmisch-Partenkirchen, Paul Gallico was surprised to discover that "apparently anything I sent that criticized the running of the winter games, or *Der Führer,* was simply filed in the waste basket in Garmisch."[51]

Not every visitor was taken in. Visiting Berlin for the Olympic festival was the famous author and playwright Thomas Wolfe. He chronicled the games in "The Dark Messiah," a key chapter in *You Can't Go Home Again,* his 1940 bestseller. Using the pseudonym George Webber in his autobiographical novel, Wolfe notes that newspaper articles about the "new" Germany left him in "amazement, shock, and doubt."[52] Wolfe loved the Weimar Republic he had visited a few years earlier, and so he decided to return for the Olympic festivities. Once in Berlin, Wolfe noticed that "the sheer pageantry of the occasion was overwhelming" to the point of oppression. "One sensed a stupendous concentration of effort, a tremendous drawing together and ordering in the vast collective power of the whole land," Wolfe wrote. "And the thing that made it seem ominous was that it so evidently went beyond what the games themselves demanded. The games were overshadowed."[53]

For Wolfe, all Berlin became "a kind of annex to the stadium," as loudspeakers spaced a thousand feet apart up and down the Kurfürstendamm piped "in the results from the stadium as they occurred."[54] For Berliners and visitors, par-ticipating in the Olympic Games became mandatory and inescapable, whether via radio, newspapers, or loudspeakers. But the tone and tenor of the German mass media changed perceptibly that July. "The radio and the newspapers calmed down and even Goebbels dribbled less of his poison," remembered one Berliner.[55]

Some Berliners discovered that the games offered an opening for surrepti-tious resistance. Peter Gay was a Jewish adolescent growing up in Berlin. He would later immigrate to the United States, become Sterling Professor at Yale

University, and establish an international reputation as one of the foremost historians of modern European thought. But as a Jewish teenage sports fan in 1936 Berlin, he remembered the feelings of oppression felt by his family and the relief and joy offered by the Olympic festival. Gay's father, a businessman, purchased tickets to Olympic stadium events in 1935 but had wisely done so during a visit to Hungary. Inside the giant stadium Gay and his father sat in a section filled with Hungarians. They enjoyed cheering for anybody but the Germans without arousing suspicion. Evidence exists that Gay was not alone; other Germans, also bothered by the Nazi destruction of democracy, secretly wished that foreigners would leverage the sports festival to pressure the German government. For much of Berlin's youth, however, the Olympic Games were less a political event than the occasion of a unique opportunity to marvel at foreigners and participate in the kind of international interchange frowned upon by the Nazi regime. Joachim Fest, later to become chief editor of North German Broadcasting, recalled his delight in traveling downtown "looking for Negroes round about the Brandenburg Gate."[56]

This official celebration of cultural exchange and global amity worked against those, like Shirer and Jordan, who hoped to influence U.S. media coverage of the new Germany by providing reportage with more contextual depth. One veteran sportswriter similarly angered by his Berlin experience was John Tunis. Shortly before the Olympics, Tunis published a perceptive and critical analysis of athletics under dictatorship in *Foreign Affairs*.[57] Five years later, in 1941, he appeared on the NBC radio program "Speaking of Liberty," where he excoriated the credulous and naïve reporting from Berlin in a conversation with Ben Grauer:

> JOHN TUNIS: There was only one newspaperman, or American radio commentator, at Berlin, who had the nerve to say, "Hey! Wait a minute! This thing's a racket!"
>
> BEN GRAUER: Who was that, Mr. Tunis?
>
> JOHN TUNIS: Westbrook Pegler. There must have been a hundred American sports commentators and radio men there at the time, and he was the only one—Westbrook Pegler was the only one—who spoke his piece and showed up this racket in sports.[58]

As Tunis noted, Pegler's reporting on the Nazi regime and its exploitation of the Olympic festival was noteworthy for its critical independence. Pegler—a difficult, irascible man—insulted German security guards to their faces, regularly pushed his way into prohibited areas, and generally acted rude throughout the duration of the festival. "Pegler infuriated Goebbels," Holocaust historian

Deborah Lipstadt wrote, by publishing withering commentary before, during, and after the Olympic Games.[59] Pegler's efforts received much attention both at the time and in retrospect, but other visiting columnists also tried to publicize the Nazi regime's barbarity. The *New York World-Telegram*'s Joe Williams picked up a German newspaper one day during the Olympic festival and was shocked by the sensational report of a convicted kidnapper's execution by beheading. Incensed that U.S. newspapers dedicated far more space to covering a "rather pointless" exhibition baseball game than to report the story of the "ghoulish" execution of Hans Giese, Williams argued that such editorial choices kept it "impossible for Americans to understand the modern Germany."[60]

Pegler and Williams were exceptions. Far more common was the foreign media's promotion of the messages dictated by the Berlin organizing committee under Theodor Lewald and the information provided by the Reich Ministry for Public Enlightenment and Propaganda. Shortly after the Nazis assumed control in 1933, Lewald met with Hitler to secure the regime's support and patronage of the games. Soon thereafter, Lewald met with Goebbels. The propaganda minister recognized the value of the games and promised significant assistance in numerous areas. Goebbels and Lewald agreed on the centrality of worldwide radio to the goal of the Berlin Olympics. From 1935 on, the Propaganda Ministry and Berlin Organizing Committee worked cooperatively to promote the games widely on the radio. Germany began sending its European neighbors regular programs previewing the games, and the ministry established a promotional news service to issue news bulletins and updates in multiple languages. These public relations campaigns proved effective, as newspapers throughout the world started promoting the live radio broadcasting of Olympic events as a remarkable innovation.[61]

The public relations blitz did not inform everyone about the new Germany. NBC's Slater arrived in Berlin with little real knowledge of the Reich. It fell to Max Jordan, who grew up in Germany, earned a Ph.D. from Jena University, and started his journalism career at *Berliner Tageblatt* in 1920, to educate his NBC colleague. Named NBC's first European representative in 1931, Jordan set up office in Berlin and worked closely with Magnus, Bredow, Rathke, and others at the RRG.[62] Jordan knew the Germans as well as any American in Berlin during that summer of 1936, and he was friends and acquaintances with both members of the regime and opposition figures. When Jordan heard Slater's praise for Nazi society, he decided to invite his NBC colleague to dine with a prominent professor in the Friday Circle of underground opposition. Professor Karl Nord explained to Slater how Germany, though appearing "free" and "buoyant" on the surface was, in reality, a land of "terrorism with mass arrests." The difference between Slater's first experiences and Nord's descriptions proved so vast that, at first, Slater remained skeptical. By the time their dinner ended, however, Slater had changed his mind. He and Jordan walked quietly back to their hotel. "Bill said not a word as we walked down the street," Jordan remembered. "He was greatly upset by all he had heard." Slater professed his difficulty believing that the U.S. media had so completely erred in reporting on the true story of Nazi Germany. Jordan explained how the censorship regime evolved and expanded to such an extent that even countries neighboring Germany knew little about the occurrences across the border. Visitors also could be easily hoodwinked, Jordan continued. Tourism into Nazi Germany had been widely encouraged for the hard currency it reaped, and so visitors were generally not "forced to salute in the Nazi style" and were the "recipients of special attention . . . [and] given every privilege." Jordan termed this Germany's "sleeping powder propaganda" and explained how Goebbels was the world's finest practitioner. Slater's interactions with the Nazis eventually proved the veracity of Jordan and Nord's claims.[63]

Unlike NBC's Slater, CBS's Ted Husing knew the regime's repressive nature before his arrival in Berlin. Husing, though the top U.S. sportscaster in 1936, was originally not scheduled to broadcast the games. His life had fallen apart in the first six months of 1936. He was drinking heavily, and his wife of less than a year moved to Reno for a divorce just one month before the games.[64] With his failing marriage making headlines, he sought escape. He booked a trip to Europe as a vacation—not even a working vacation—so that he could return refreshed to the grind of his weekly college football broadcasts. "He has been very much under the weather," reported *Variety*, "and it's his first vacation in a couple of years." Husing "had been ill all winter and pretty much down in the dumps to boot." To substitute for him in Berlin, CBS set up a tryout for several New York sportswriters during the Princeton Invitational Track Meet in Palmer Stadium. CBS executives, listening in at headquarters in New York on a rented closed circuit, were disappointed. "Not one suited," wrote William L. Stuart. Then they heard of his vacation plans. "He wasn't planning on" covering the games, the *Brooklyn Daily Eagle* reported, "but when his bosses discovered his secret plans for a summer vacation in Europe, they asked, 'why not?'" The CBS team in Berlin, composed of Henry, Husing, and Saerchinger, would prove more flexible, experienced, and skilled than their NBC rivals in covering the full scope of the games. Because NBC centered its broadcasts on Bill Slater with supplemental coverage by Max Jordan and RRG announcer Eduard Roderich Dietze, CBS possessed clear promotional advantages for its broadcasts.[65]

Husing's excursion to Germany that summer was motivated as much by personal as professional responsibilities. Although the popular sportscaster had never visited Germany, he knew the country well. His parents were German immigrants, and as a child their native tongue was spoken in the home. Years later, Husing ruefully admitted that throughout his childhood he was ashamed of his parents' German accent, even though it was common in his New York City neighborhood.[66] Because Husing sought to visit relatives in Germany and tour Europe, he left aboard the S.S. *Normandie* two weeks before the U.S. team crossed on the S.S. *Manhattan*. He traveled first to Berlin and then spent a week relaxing in London before returning to Germany to cover the games.[67]

Husing had grown up hiding a family secret: His mother, Bertha, had converted from Judaism to marry his father, a Lutheran named Henry Husing. Ashamed of his Jewish heritage, Husing told nobody of a familial obligation he sought to fulfill in Germany. Husing, who was always very close to his mother, had a cousin living in Warburg, Westphalia. He had never met Max Wertheim, a decorated veteran of the Imperial army in World War I, but on this trip to Germany he would meet with his first cousin to plan the Wertheim family's escape. Wertheim, a secular Jew proud of his military service, was ambivalent about leaving the country he loved. But the military governor of Westphalia, an old family friend, warned Wertheim of his dismal future under Nazi rule. With his wife Lotte, Max Wertheim began planning escape. A meeting between first cousins was arranged in Berlin. The CBS correspondent told nobody of these efforts and fretted the risk of imprisonment, or being fired, for such risky personal activities while working on a journalist's visa. "Ted got very nervous about it," remembered Stanley Wertheim, Max Wertheim's son. "He told me later that he told my father, 'you know, my chauffeur here is a Gestapo agent, the maid in my hotel is a Gestapo agent,' and my father didn't quite realize how dangerous it was, you know, coming from a little town" to Berlin. These unauthorized Berlin meetings risked Husing's press credentials, his presence in Germany, his freedom, and even his CBS job. Husing agreed to help Wertheim secure the required affidavits for immigration, but explained that everything had to be handled under Henry Husing's name. His assistance was to be kept entirely secret.[68]

Bill Henry's Berlin trip lacked the drama of his CBS colleague's. He visited the German capital in both 1935 and early 1936, each time offering German officials technical advice based on his experience as sports technical director of the Los Angeles Olympiad. These trips were expensive and not entirely subsidized by either his full-time employer, the *Los Angeles Times*, CBS, or the Germans. Henry "saved dimes from 1928 to 1936" to finance his trips to Berlin and also pay for his family to tour Europe around his work at the Olympics. To earn more money for the trip, Henry agreed to collaborate with the American Express Company to lead "The Bill Henry Tour of Europe." "Forty-five avid sports fans" paid for the privilege to "see Europe and the Olympics" alongside CBS's lead reporter.[69]

Upon arrival in Berlin, the U.S. reporters were greeted by the most techno-logically sophisticated broadcast operation ever assembled. Under the mam-moth bowl of the Reichssportfeld, directly below the Führer's loge, a control room had been installed to centralize, coordinate, and distribute simultaneous feeds arriving from multiple locations and going out to numerous transmitters and control rooms. The centerpiece of the "beehive" control room was called the "40-Nations Switchboard," a switching device that was as tall as the wall and twenty-one meters in length, and it contained no less than ten thousand circuits.[70] Before it was actually put into use, the RRG estimated one hundred simultaneous broadcast feeds could be distributed to transmitters in Germany, Europe, and around the globe. In actual practice, because of a variety of technical issues, the 40-Nations Switchboard could coordinate only eighteen simultane-ous European feeds with ten simultaneous relays to shortwave transmitters for overseas service. But even these numbers are misleading, in that the control room could route overflow directly to the nearby Haus des Rundfunks on Adolf Hitler Platz, where additional personnel and transmission apparatus could be employed. Recording equipment was available as well, so that broadcasters could wire interviews or accounts into the control room for later distribution, and the RRG provided a fleet of mobile recording units in case certain venues required more than the dedicated number of direct microphone lines. The con-struction and installation of such sophisticated facilities in a building remote from a broadcasting headquarters had never been attempted. The *New York Times* called the broadcast installation "a remarkable nerve center for the whole globe that has never been equaled before in its scope" and marked its completion as "an astonishing feat."[71]

The RRG's engineering report called "the foundation of the technical orga-nization . . . the centralization of the complete system of relay lines" in the sta-dium's production center. This "system of relay lines" was a widespread network of sixty-eight transmission points stretching around the city, north to Kiel (the yachting venue), southeast to Grünau for rowing, and across the city for various other events, including the marathon and cultural festivals occurring in con-junction with the games. This web, installed by Telefunken in cooperation with the RRG and Conrad Lorenz, GmbH, was reciprocative and dynamic; any point could communicate with any other point individually, in selective groups, or across the entire system. It required no less than seventeen substations scattered throughout the city and a parallel network made up of forty-six interconnected wire recording machines called "Textophones" designed to rapidly distribute results and facilitate communication. The Textophone could be used as a telephone or voice recorder because it contained a steel wire recording machine. Textophones made delivering Olympic news and information, and coordinating broadcasts, "rapid and efficient." The work of cabling together these tremendous Olympic webs was remarkable; one estimate claimed the networks required four thousand miles of dedicated cable to cover everything.[72]

The speed of circuit changes throughout the assembled networks was greatly enhanced by the invention of an "ultra-rapid switching" technique tied to coded transmission shortcuts. A broadcaster, for example, could place an order for a program to originate in a booth within the Olympic stadium, then move seamlessly (perhaps with a short musical interlude or theme—the RRG provided selections) to another commentator elsewhere in Berlin for an additional report. Such innovative production could be done, simultaneously, for dozens of broadcasts being relayed live across the globe. To ensure fidelity through incoming circuits, one hundred seventy speech input amplifiers (Lorenz V35 models— the world's most advanced) were installed across the network, including at the distant venues in Kiel and Grünau.[73]

This web, however, was not fully automated. The network required human intervention to maximize flexibility. Adaptability, and even improvisation, symbolized the technical paradox at the heart of the Berlin broadcasts. The Olympic network simultaneously required stability and plasticity on a level never before attained in broadcasting. "The total technical organization must be created as elastic as possible," noted a German radio periodical when defining this challenge. The engineers had to ensure "flexibility while everything remains perfect and ready."[74] Estimates for the number of engineers employed to modulate incoming audio and outgoing relays, monitor and switch network circuits, supervise recordings, and handle all hardware issues—including quickly fixing or replacing broken equipment—ranged from three hundred to five hundred eighty.[75] Even before the games began, more than forty-five hundred relays had been booked, to air across more than eighty foreign broadcast organizations, in a period of about two weeks. And this schedule did not include the RRG's own foreign-language service. The German broadcasting company employed several multilingual engineers and reporters to assist the global broadcasting community, but it also maintained its own regular schedule of shortwave broadcasts to Latin and North America during the games—productions in Spanish and English. These broadcasts were available for free retransmission, and there is some evidence a few small U.S. stations pulled them in from the short waves, converted them to the standard band, and aired them to listeners in direct competition with CBS and NBC.[76] The goal of producing a full domestic schedule of

Olympic broadcasts, combined with RRG overseas productions while facilitating the work of numerous visiting broadcasting organizations had never been attempted by a single broadcast organization before 1936. "The [German] radio organization as a whole," the *New York Times* reported, "will have no rest either night or day."[77]

The RRG and Telefunken innovations were not entirely network-related. In an effort to improve the fidelity of transmissions from outside broadcasts, new noise-reducing condenser technology was tested and installed in Siemens microphones.[78] This new type of microphone, developed by Lorenz, was plugged into an innovative "commentator's transmitter" and designed to maximize clarity. Ultimately, these new microphones and transmitters proved too effective at removing ambient sounds, and so to allow the "listeners to still be able to recreate the atmosphere of the competition venues at home" dedicated "noise" or crowd microphones were installed at various intervals around each venue. Engineers at the switchboard under the stadium would then mix feeds and control levels to produce the most engaging and vivid portrayal of an event as possible. The employment of sophisticated microphone technology and crowd mixing not only ensured the finest-quality retransmission but also proved futuristic in establishing the standard model for future live sports broadcast production.[79]

The comparison with technologies utilized four years earlier in Los Angeles was stark. The Bell System constructed a primitive network in 1932 for the Los Angeles games that included a modified standard switchboard possessing two hundred seventy telephone circuits. These circuits routed everything— telephone calls for newspaper reporters, broadcast transmissions, and even signals to six teletypewriters for distribution of results and information. The entire network employed only two miles of dedicated underground and aerial cables that were then linked into existing radiating lines.[80] The lack of immediate access to Los Angeles–based shortwave transmitters, combined with the organizers' general distrust of live radio, further hindered global transmission. Japan's NHK sportscasters, for instance, were unable to relay live programs despite substantial investment. Reporter Norizo Matsuuchi would carefully take notes during events and then drive to NBC's Los Angeles studio, where he would "produce 'virtual commentary' broadcasts . . . as if [he] were speaking live from the stadium." This occasionally produced unintentionally humorous results, as when a recreated call of the hundred-meter sprint final—a race that lasted barely more than ten seconds—took almost one full minute to describe.[81] These fabricated programs needed to be piped north to San Francisco for shortwave relay across the Pacific. Despite some popularity with Japanese listeners, these broadcasts—according to the network's official history—were a "debacle." Ultimately, the NHK ended up being the only foreign broadcast network that covered the Los Angeles games; the BBC originally planned to carry the CBS signal from Los Angeles, but when that option fell through, the British broadcasters skipped the games entirely.[82]

Four years later, live overseas feeds out of Berlin would be accessible via the RRG's shortwave transmitter plant in Zeesen, a suburb just south of Berlin. In 1935, the Germans began installing five new additional shortwave towers, raising the total in Zeesen to eight. Engineers modified the standard shortwave transmitters, adding the newest quartz control apparatus, to make them deliver each signal to specific areas of the globe more effectively—an innovation building upon the experimental directional antenna work being done in England and the United States at the time.[83] The technical sophistication of the new transmitting equipment, combined with the favorable seasonal atmospheric conditions in Berlin (i.e., more daylight) for shortwave transmission meant "the world at large" would not "be expected to experience much trouble in eavesdropping on 'the games of nation'," a *New York Times* preview explained.[84] The "new and improved short-wave stations at Zeesen," reported *Radio-Craft*, "will probably give Germany the most advanced short-wave transmitting facilities in the world."[85] The additional transmitters and Olympic upgrades, CBS's Saerchinger argued, catapulted Zeesen past the BBC's Daventry plant as "the largest and most potent propaganda machine in the world."[86] The cumulative labor on television, transoceanic shortwave relay, multi- and unilateral domestic and European network distribution, and other innovative technical and programmatic endeavors marked the Berlin Olympic Games as a milestone in the history of telecommunication. According to Olympic scholar John McCoy, the broadcast of the games was unquestionably "the largest task undertaken to that stage by the radio industry."[87]

That broadcast work began in earnest once national teams started arriving in Berlin. Teams traveling the farthest distances arrived first, and so CBS and NBC began their program schedules the week before the opening ceremony, as did Japan's NHK. For teams coming from closer locales—such as the British and French—Olympic programming started with the opening ceremonies.[88] For many broadcasters, including those from the United States, arrival day proved a key promotional introduction for subsequent programs to follow. The NBC and CBS teams, joined by newsreel and newspaper reporters, tracked the U.S. athletes minute by minute on 24 July as they traveled down from Hamburg to Berlin and on to the Olympic Village. U.S. officials were asked to speak a few words at each stop, with the day's final broadcast and newsreel recordings occurring from the Olympic Village. The U.S. officials continually expressed their gratitude toward their German hosts. At Berlin's City Hall, the team was celebrated in a ceremony presided over by Reich Commissar for the City of Berlin, Julius Lippert. Amid the "spacious, magnificent reception room," Lippert presented Avery Brundage with a commemorative medal. Several Nazi functionaries attended, and—with all the uniforms, formality, and lavish surroundings—the little celebration had more than a hint of an official state ceremony. Most of the U.S. attendees did not understand a word of the German being spoken. Brundage, carried away by all he had seen that day, raised eyebrows among his compatriots when he told his hosts that "no nation since Ancient Greece has captured the true Olympic spirit as has Germany."[89] Luckily for the athletes, few of whom had slept much the night before, the Berlin welcome was cut short and they were allowed back to their buses for the final trip to the Olympic Village or other quarters.

For the oarsmen, the long day ended with a bus trip out to their Olympic residence at the Köpenick police barracks near Grünau. Two buses carrying the U.S. *Ruderer* headed across Berlin and into the southern suburbs, to the island town of Köpenick at the juncture of the Dahme and Spree rivers, where home for the next few weeks would be the Polizei Offizier Unterkunft.[90] The Police Officer Training school was a squat, modern, rectangular building that had not originally been requisitioned for the games. All rowers and canoeists had been slated to bunk in the imposing Köpenick Palace, a baroque castle sitting on an immaculately landscaped island in the Dahme. But as the games drew near, it became clear the palace could not accommodate all the participants for Grünau.[91] Organizers scrambled to find additional space, finally settling upon two nearby schools, one of which was the Police Training Academy. The three locales complicated the original plan of ferrying participants the four miles to the racecourse in motorboats. A circular bus route was established between the three locales instead, with the German army providing seven gray buses at no cost. Each team also had a dedicated bus and driver for its use during the games as well.

The Washington oarsmen were pleased with the Polizei Offizier Unterkunft; its big windows allowed much light to bathe the spacious rooms, and the ground floor contained large and pleasant dining halls and recreation rooms.[92] "There were a few of the police about with their vehicles and horses," remembered Gordon Adam, "but they had been moved out or detailed elsewhere so that we got their barracks for the duration." In the evenings and mornings the rowers would hear the click-clack of police training drills occurring on the grounds through their open windows.[93] Shortly after arrival at the police school on that first night in Germany, the men from Washington went to sleep. The day's excitement seemed to exacerbate the illnesses of Don Hume, Gordon Adam, and John White.

For the next few days, the team recuperated, rested, and explored Grünau while George Pocock repaired the damage to the *Husky Clipper*. The team became accustomed to their routine, which included morning rows, three delicious meals, and as much as fifteen hours of rest in their bedrooms or common rooms per day. The food, served by waiters and prepared by chefs from the North German Lloyd Company, was rich and delicious. For coach Ulbrickson, that was precisely the problem. He called over the team's assigned interpreter in the dining hall after watching his oarsmen eat too much for the first few days in Germany. Speaking slowly, Ulbrickson told the interpreter to instruct the chef and waiters that the rowers "were not to be given second helpings." The Germans did not understand. The organizers had brought in the finest chefs and supplied excellent meals to ensure that the oarsmen would experience the same fine dining served at the much larger Olympic village back in Berlin. A second interpreter joined the conversation as the curious rowers looked on. An insistent Ulbrickson would not leave the dining hall until his orders were clarified. The Germans, he later told a U.S. reporter, were "trying to kill his boys with kindness." Their huge portions and all-you-can-eat generosity would slow his crew, he explained, and he would have none of it. It took almost thirty minutes of discussion for Ulbrickson to feel secure that his orders would be respected.[94] But soon thereafter he caught his oarsmen sneaking additional helpings and took matters into his own hands. "Al served all the plates personally" from that point on, another coach recalled, "with a weight chart at his side." To drink, his squad was allowed only water and a "very little milk in the morning, none at noon, and a good portion at night," George Hunt remembered. While restricting butter, oils, and fats as much as possible, Ulbrickson permitted his rowers to pack away carbohydrates with almost unlimited dry toast and noodles. With snacks and second helpings prohibited, the oarsmen consumed "three big meals a day with dry toast the largest part of each" during training.[95]

The oarsmen soon became acquainted with the village of Grünau. Its lovely, tree-shaded streets—like the rest of Berlin—were clean and orderly, and even weeks before the regatta opened, the Olympic spirit was everywhere in evidence. "Every house had its flags, and there was something homely in the comparatively narrow streets of Grünau and nearby Köpenick," noted the *Times* of London. Loudspeakers were strung up in the trees along the main thoroughfare, where open cafés catered to tourists and locals. The town was idyllic, as illustrated by the scenes in a home movie filmed that month by Hungarian businessman

Laszlo Antos. Antos's film captures the delivery of beer kegs by a Schultheiss truck and then cuts to a sweeping shot across the Langer See showing the enormous empty grandstand with crews practicing on the water below. Spectators gather on the promenade, watching oarsmen practice in small boats from Germany, Japan, Italy, and elsewhere. The film makes clear the beauty of the forested regatta venue, where the riverbank was shaded by ancient elms, oaks, and birches. Antos's film lacks audio, but remembrances of the town by the oarsmen included the sounds of "German marching music—*boom, boom, boom*—all day long," emitting from numerous loudspeakers.[96] Despite the loudspeakers, flags, and festival atmosphere, the area around Grünau symbolized a calm oasis in contrast with the jammed scene in Berlin. The Washington oarsmen walked around the town but also spent a lot of time waiting on the lawn near the boathouse for their practices to begin. During these down periods, "there was not much to do except watch the leaves and grass grow," remembered Joe Rantz. Grünau, he continued, "didn't have [that] Berlin feel." Even so, what distractions Grünau and Köpenick offered were minimized for the crew. "We were pretty well focused on what we were doing. We weren't there as tourists," Jim McMillin recalled.[97]

In their quite limited interaction with the people of Grünau, the rowers found the local Germans to be "simple, friendly people." They especially appreciated playing with children, and they tried their best to converse in their limited German. "The oarsmen got the impression that these people were not all that enthused with Hitler," Lee Miller, a University of Washington student, wrote after interviewing several of them in 1982. "But nobody spoke against him. The people of Grünau told the Husky oarsmen that if Hitler told them to fight, they would—but they hoped the Americans would be on their side this time."[98]

Soon the contours of the racecourse became familiar as they started practicing on the river. As they paddled downriver toward the start line from the finish line grandstand, they could see the river widen after a small promontory. This promontory contained a noticeable hillock located about fifteen hundred meters from the start line. Passing it, the crews would have about five hundred meters to go to the finish line. In that last five hundred meters, the full panorama of the regatta stadium, and boathouses would open to the left, with the finish line floating grandstand on the right. The grandstand had been constructed by the army, and it was attached to the nearby riverbank by two pedestrian bridges floating on aluminum pontoons. At the far end of the grandstand was the finish line. A giant placard, with the word ZIEL emblazoned upon it, indicated the racecourse's end. Just above ZIEL was a second placard, with the words REIHENFOLGE BEI 1000 MTN painted on it. That sign ("Order at 1,000 Meters")

Aerial view of the Grünau racecourse, showing the floating grandstand at lower left and the promontory on the right. (From the U.S. National Archives.)

would alert the spectators in the grandstand across the river of the respective positions of the crews as they crossed the midway point of each race.[99]

Grünau's racecourse had a long history. Developed by the Berlin Regatta Society in 1880, Grünau became established as the center of German rowing before the start of the twentieth century. Regattas drew thousands to the small suburb, and soon boathouses and a wooden grandstand for spectators were erected.[100] The Olympics required substantial investment and upgrades, including the construction of an entirely new, enormous "center" boathouse, with a specially constructed terrace supporting the Führer's balcony. The old grandstand was significantly refurbished, and the new floating grandstand was installed directly across the river to double spectator capacity.[101]

German broadcast engineers were familiar with the Grünau racecourse. From the early 1930s on, the broadcast of rowing regattas both locally and nationally allowed them to test relay technologies and improve the infrastructure.[102]

Engineers installing broadcast equipment on the roof of the grandstand in Grünau. (From the German Broadcasting Archive, Rundfunkmitarbeiter auf dem Dach der Zieltribüne in Grünau [DRA/ ID-1425399].)

By 1936, German radio engineers, like their British and U.S. colleagues, had a long history of broadcasting rowing. The first network sports broadcast in German history occurred on 21 July 1925, when on "an unbearably hot day" a group of musicians abandoned their studio to play in a small garden alongside the Dortmund–Ems Canal in Münster. Pulling his microphone outside—still tethered to the telephone line—an unnamed announcer was delighted to discover a rowing regatta being contested on the canal, which he then described to the audience.[103] The Olympics, however, required accommodating significantly more broadcasting personnel than had ever covered a regatta. Telefunken and RRG engineers, working with the army and the Berlin organizing committee, constructed broadcast platforms above the grandstand with additional platforms on the porch above the shell bays of one boathouse. The platform at the boathouse looked a bit like a fenced porch, and it offered a nicely panoramic view of the finish line. The elevated location above the grandstand gave a sweeping perspective down the course and across to the finish line, allowing the broadcasters "an optimal view of the finish of the boats in tight decisions."[104] The location also had the secondary—but important—effect of making the expected Nazi leadership more clearly visible to the broadcasters.

The broadcasters, in turn, could be watched by the spectators below. To the right of the main boathouse, at about the eighteen-hundred-meter mark on the course and directly across from the floating grandstand, were two older boathouses. Racks for more than two hundred seventy shells, boats, and launches could be found in the bays of the three boathouses. In front of the boathouses, past the small grassy lawn, was a long promenade that stretched more than two hundred meters along the final length of the racecourse. The promenade provided standing room for more than ten thousand fans, pushing the total capacity to more than forty thousand spectators in the finish line area.[105]

The grandstand, boathouses, and promenade on one side and the massive floating grandstand across the course on the opposite bank gave the finish line area the aura of a large, open stadium. Rowing into the final five hundred meters of the race, crews would enter a tunnel of noise as tens of thousands of people cheered at close range. The only space and protection from the crowd would come from the distance separating water level from the grandstands. In some ways, this funneling effect and rising finish-line noise could be reminiscent of Poughkeepsie, but in others it would be entirely different. The single biggest difference was the widths of the respective rivers; the Hudson, at Poughkeepsie, was more than one quarter of a mile wide, and towering palisades accentuated the valley in which the rowers raced. The Grünau course on the Langer See was much tighter and more compressed. It soon became clear after the first couple of practice rows that the stadia, boathouses, and crowded promenade would seem to pop up from nowhere after passing the promontory as the finish line neared. Although the course seemed constricted, German army engineers had actually widened and shaped the river to ensure six boats could race simultaneously for the gold for the first time in Olympic history.[106]

Media preparations at Grünau were equally expansive. Leni Riefenstahl hired veteran cameramen, among them Helmuth von Stwolinski, Walter Frenz, and Heinz von Jaworsky, to facilitate the rowing production for her film. But the regatta course presented difficulties for capturing racing drama. Perhaps the most serious obstacle Riefenstahl faced was the inability to capture facial close-ups and other shots from inside the shells during competition. Several ideas were proposed, including shooting closely from motorboats and zooming in from towers lining the racecourse. There would be cameramen on both grandstands as well. Finally, an observation balloon was planned to track the race as it moved up the river. The filmmakers also rigged an eight-oared shell with cameras to capture the oarsmen and coxswains in action. Preparatory shots, taken in advance of the regatta, could be intercut with the actual racing in the final production. But ultimately the eight-oared shell proved unworkable because the size and weight of the cameras made balance almost impossible.[107]

On 26 June Riefenstahl and her team attended to the Berlin regatta to test "slow motion shots, panning shots, and tracking-shots," as well as starts and finishes. The film crew returned for additional experimentation and rehearsal at the German national rowing championships on 15 July 1936. Those tests confirmed Riefenstahl's suspicion that some manner of filming inside the crew shell would be necessary to heighten the drama. The rowing shots, she concluded, would require a more human dimension and scale. Riefenstahl and her team decided to request permission from each team to place a cameraman in the stroke's seat, then the coxswain's seat, for brief practice rows. The teams— wearing their racing uniforms—would paddle on the course as cameraman Heinz von Jaworsky recorded the action. "I remember I sat on that [seat] with the camera and did the rowing movement which shows what the man, the first rower would see—the coxswain, who was wearing a little megaphone, shouting at them" he recalled. "Since I had done lots of rowing myself . . . it was not unfamiliar to me." As von Jaworsky carefully slid back and forth on his slide in time with the rowers, he did his best to steady the spring-wound Bell and Howell handheld Eyemo camera in front of his face.[108] The resulting shots—including close-ups of Don Hume's and Bob Moch's faces—ultimately made up some of the most dramatic footage in Riefenstahl's *Olympia*.

Riefenstahl's cameramen were required to share space atop the course's towers with stadium announcers, a setup that bothered the mercurial film director. Grünau's venue management needed to accommodate all media requests within very tightly constricted spaces (on the water, above the racecourse in towers, atop the grandstand, and in the designated press seats) without impinging upon the athletic contests. Tension between the athletic organizations, the venue management, and the media was bound to occur. To ease the relationships and facilitate communication, shortly before the Olympic canoe races began, the full media contingent took a tour of the venue. Chugging upriver in a large tour boat, the sixty reporters, filmmakers, and broadcasters were familiarized with the media planning. The deck above the boathouse, where Hitler and the other dignitaries would be seated, was indicated, as were the small platforms at the boathouse and above the reconditioned grandstand where radio microphones would be placed. Newspaper reporters saw their reserved press section in the grandstand, and guides pointed out the local Olympic Fire Cauldron set up high on the Müggelberg (a set of nearby hills viewable from the river). The flame, it was explained, would be ignited by a torch relayed from the Olympic stadium cauldron to inaugurate the canoe competition on 7 August. It would be extinguished upon the conclusion of the rowing regatta on 14 August.[109]

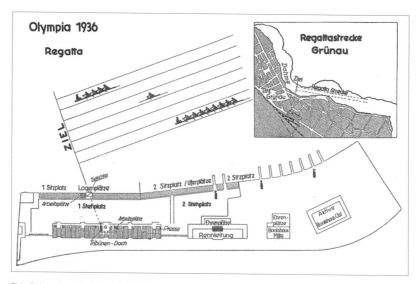

This Reichs-Rundfunk-Gesellschaft graphic illustrates microphone placement and platforms above the grandstand and boathouse in Grünau. (From the German Broadcasting Archive, Reichs-Rundfunk-Gesellschaft, *Broadcasting Leader*, p. 71.)

During the regatta, it was explained, the crowds and broadcasters would be kept abreast of the progress of the racing through a system of stadium announcements. Spotters along the course, equipped with shortwave transmitters, would call the races as the boats passed. Spotters' broadcasts would be transmitted directly to speakers along the promenade and the grandstand. For the broadcasters, the elevated platform and use of binoculars would likely suffice for the second half of the race, but just in case they had problems seeing the first part of the races, local relay broadcasts would continually blare updates. The use of the new microphones would filter out almost all the ambient noises, and so the broadcasters would not have to worry about interference with their calls (the crowd noise transmissions would be mixed under the Olympic stadium). The total number of live transmissions via dedicated cables out of Grünau on race day would be capped at seven, but because more than seven broadcasters might request live broadcast capability, on the day of the finals the RRG scheduled its "flying broadcasting squad" to be available. This squad consisted of as many as twenty "transmitting cars" with shortwave relay apparatus "drawn together from all over the Reich" that would guarantee the capability of live broadcasting for any organization demanding it.[110]

The RRG employed several new techniques and apparatuses for covering river-based events. Along the course the network placed several floating platforms, created by the joining of two pontoon boats with a wooden deck, and a raised microphone covered with a windscreen next to a relay transmitter. Being mobile, these pontoon barges could be loaded with equipment and broadcast personnel, motored to strategic intervals on the racecourse, and then anchored to provide relay coverage. After the race, the pontoons could then be returned to be safely docked in case of inclement weather.[111]

Scheduling calm practice times on the river became difficult as canoeists and crew teams began regularly practicing, the venue management completed construction, and the media contingent started working on the course. Making it even more problematic was that the Langer See remained "part of a public water-way and thus open to water traffic" during these preparatory days. Coaches and team managers complained to the venue administration about boat traffic to no avail.[112] Tension on the water increased.

When the U.S. Olympians first arrived, however, the river was generally quiet. Only the Australian and Canadian crews beat the Huskies to Grünau. The Aussies were a big, beefy squad made up of policemen from the Sydney Rowing Club. They had ventured first to England for the Royal Henley Regatta on their way to Germany. Upon arrival in Henley, however, they were barred from racing. Officials classified the Australians as "professionals," that is—they worked with their hands, doing manual or similar labor that would give them an advantage over the "young men of sedentary occupation," that constituted the rowing class in England.[113] The Australians, angered by the slight, would not forgive the British.

The Sydney policemen were a fun-loving group, and what they lacked in rowing style they made up for in enthusiasm and good humor. Their size and spirit fooled some of the journalists who saw them row earlier in England and Europe. Robert Perrier, a reporter for *L'Auto*, considered the foremost sports journal in France, warned his U.S. colleagues that "if the Olympic finals are won by eight policemen from Sydney, Australia, don't say you weren't warned." Other observers also noted the Australian crew's impressive physical gifts and conditioning. "We got kind of chummy with the Australian bunch," Jim McMillin later recalled.[114] That friendliness can be credited in no small part to the dismissive attitude the Washington oarsmen held toward their down under rivals. McMillin later recalled a particularly memorable encounter with the Australians soon after arrival:

> We were rowing up the course, oh, maybe 26 or 27 strokes a minute, something like that, and about halfway through the course we stopped rowing. I thought, "what the hell we stopping for?" Turned around, there's this Australian police

crew, taking a time trial. And we were rowing them down. And so we stopped so we wouldn't interfere with them. And anyway, when we got in, they came on over and introduced themselves. They knew they weren't going to win the race. They thought we probably would. Their main message was: just beat the Goddamn limeys.[115]

Soon after the U.S. crew joined the Canadians and Australians in Köpenick, the Swiss, South African, and Dutch rowers arrived.

The teams generally interacted well, and after dinner each night the squads would remain in the dining hall to socialize, sing songs, and attempt communication. One night the Yugoslav team was singing, but with each chorus of the song—which the U.S. oarsmen could not translate—the Yugoslavs would glare at the Yanks. Thinking they were being insulted, the Washington rowers stood up and approached the Yugoslavs with clenched fists. Things calmed down—but not before the Australian policemen almost joined in the fray. "There were signs of a possible free-for-all fight," George Pocock remembered, "but nothing came of it."[116]

As his team settled in, Ulbrickson faced several challenges. Most worrisome was the health of Hume, Adam, and White. The trip across the Atlantic had severely aggravated the chest cold that began as sniffles shortly after the Poughkeepsie Regatta. Hume had a history of respiratory illness affecting his rowing, but after his freshman year—during which he missed almost two weeks of training with a very severe infection—he had proven able to work through the occasional outbreaks. But this case seemed different. He was listless, lacked appetite, looked pale, and just wanted to sleep. Although Ulbrickson did not weigh him immediately upon arrival in Germany, it was clear that Hume had lost more weight than either Adam or White (who were on the mend). Aside from the health of his athletes, there was the shell repair, shellac varnish coating, and other rigging work that George Pocock needed to get done on the *Husky Clipper*. Then there were the logistics. AOC informed the rowing committee that all financial obligation to the athletes ended once competition ceased. As soon as the rowers finished their final race, in other words, they would be on their own in Europe. Ulbrickson was infuriated to find this out so late, and, making the situation even more dire, when he, "Monk" Terry, and others inquired about passage back to the United States, they discovered every boat leaving Germany was fully booked for ten days after competition ended. "Some of my boys haven't enough money to buy food over three days," Ulbrickson told the Associated Press. "We seem to be the stepchildren of the Olympic outfit," he grumbled.[117]

The initial rowing practices were rough. "It had been quite a while," McMillin recalled, "probably a week in the states where we didn't row, and then seven or eight days at sea, so it was a good two weeks or more that we hadn't really rowed any.... [I]t felt good to get on the water and in our own shell, except those two weeks showed, because we were pretty rusty for quite a while," he explained. "It was quite a penalty, to be away from rowing that long." During those first practices, first with ill Don Hume stroking the eight, and then when substitute Don Coy replaced Hume for a few practices, things "weren't going well," Moch recalled.[118]

On the morning before the opening ceremony, on the last day of July, Hume returned to practice. To reacclimate to Hume's rhythm, the stroke rating remained low and the workout lasted only thirty minutes. Observers watching their workout that morning considered it "satisfactory." Ulbrickson had earlier planned a time trial for 31 July, but Hume's condition forced postponement. Hume's return coincided with a noticeable uptick in energy and activity around Grünau. That day, the French, Czechoslovaks, and Austrians arrived, bringing the number of competing nations up to thirteen. The fourteenth team, the British, would arrive the following morning.[119]

The U.S. oarsmen and coach started sizing up each crew upon arrival. One of the first crews the U.S. crew encountered, after the Australians, was the Italian one. They were impressed. "Since their first look at the Italians," the *New York Times* reported, "the Huskies have just about decided that there is where the opposition lies."[120] The Italian squad was filled with tall, experienced, and exceptionally strong oarsmen. They were the oldest and biggest crew in the regatta. Four years earlier in Los Angeles, four of the nine—coxswain Cesare Milani, stroke Enrico Garzelli, Dino Barsotti, and Guglielmo del Bimbo—were outrowed by the University of California's crew in the closest finish in Olympic eights history. Between 1932 and 1936 Italy's Fascist government prioritized athletic success, with developmental funds flowing freely to club, party, and university organizations promising victory in Berlin. The crew had won the right to represent Italy by beating numerous excellent domestic squads. "Almost every Italian lake and river is fairly smothered with oarsmen," Grantland Rice wrote, "and it will take something better than normal to offset all this stamina, speed, and rowing skill" in Berlin.[121] The *New Yorker*'s rowing columnist concurred, remembering a conversation with "a rowing enthusiast who toured Europe" in 1935:

> He said, speaking of Olympic prospects, "Watch out for the Italians." I would have been watching out for the Italians anyway, because they lost the 1932 race in something pretty close to a dead heat, but it seems interest in L'Arte del Remo is even keener than it was then, and they developed a half-dozen promising crews, all rowing that short, high stroke which is so well adapted to their size

and weight. Most of the oarsmen are university men, but the rowing clubs are independent. They are able to secure a pretty good quality of coaching, both amateur and professional, and they think nothing of going out on the water twice a day all summer.[122]

The Italians looked strong and rhythmic on the water throughout the training period leading up to the racing. The Germans also looked impressive, but the same *New Yorker* columnist considered them overrated. Although "the Rhine is covered with boatloads of earnest Aryan oarsmen," he wrote, they row "an undistinguished, methodical, completely Teutonic stroke" that would hamper the crew in Olympic competition with U.S., British, and Italian oarsmen.[123]

While the Washington crew settled in, the broadcasts from Berlin had started airing regularly on CBS and NBC. The networks had irregularly covered the torch relay and other events connected to the Olympics, but the regular series of broadcasts began once the U.S. athletes arrived at their quarters in the Olympic Village.[124] On 29 July, NBC and the RRG collaborated on a cultural broadcast from Berlin's Pergamon Museum.[125] Bill Slater, speaking quietly into his microphone, described the scene at the gigantic party to celebrate the Olympic arts festival, and he gave the U.S. audience a sense of his first week in Germany. The event at the museum, Slater explained, opened with a solemn moment of silence to commemorate the memory of all who died in the Great War. "It was a very moving ceremony," Slater reported. Finally, Slater offered U.S. listeners a word-picture of Berlin on the eve of the games. "Tens of thousands surrounded the street Unter den Linden. Tens of thousands stood in the great open square between the State Opera House—which was floodlit—and the Memorial of the Unknown Soldier, and tens of thousands lined the road that led to the Pergamon Museum," he said. "They cheered the well-known leaders of the Party and the Government; they cheered also, and watched with interest, the many foreign guests of note. . . . Everywhere anyone goes in Berlin there is a great sense of joyful freedom. Everybody seems to think that this is a wonderful holiday for all those who are in Berlin. . . . The only thing we lack is the true Olympic weather. It has been raining on and off, there have been storms for the last few days."[126]

The following night Slater broadcast live from the welcoming ceremony sponsored by the Reich Ministry for Public Enlightenment and Propaganda. Reich Minister Goebbels officially welcomed the foreign press and broadcast community to Berlin. "Hello, America, NBC calling again from Berlin," Slater began. "We have a lot of news tonight, a lot of festivities," he continued. He described the scene from his perch on a balcony, "overlooking a very brilliant scene at the press reception here." Then he turned over the microphone to "Mr.

Roderich Dietze," whom he called "the official announcer of the Olympic Games for this year and a member of NBC's staff for the reporting of these Games." Dietze greeted his "NBC listeners in the States" and summarized the "marvelous speeches" given at the event, primarily the talks by Walter Funk, the secretary of state, and Goebbels. The party that listeners could hear, Dietze explained, was "for the representatives of the movie people, the film people, and naturally, the broadcasters. I think there are about 100 of them," he continued, "from all the different countries of the Games." Dietze then returned the microphone to Slater, who offered "a few official items of news" to conclude the broadcast. Slater concluded by previewing the opening ceremonies to take place two days later, explaining that the U.S. men's and women's teams practiced marching for a while earlier in the day in an attempt "to make a more military showing, and a better showing, in comparison with the delegations of other nations in the opening parade . . . than was shown by the Americans at Los Angeles back in nineteen-hundred and thirty-two." Slater then discussed Jesse Owens, Archie Williams, and other track-and-field athletes, but just as he began to mention the participants in the fifteen-hundred-meter race he was cut off. An announcer in New York City closed the program with the identification required by regulations: "a special shortwave rebroadcast, this program was a Red Network presentation of the National Broadcast Company and was heard in America via RCA Communications Incorporated."[127]

Though U.S. broadcasters did not carry Goebbels's remarks live, the German RRG did, and one can listen to a one-minute-twenty-second recorded excerpt of his twelve-minute talk on the Worldwide Web.[128] Rather than ignore accusations of propaganda excess and strict censorship being reported in the foreign press, Goebbels addressed the issue directly. "In the past few months, Germany has been accused of the intention to operate the Olympic Games as propaganda for the state," he explained. "I can assure you, gentlemen, that this is not the case, because if it were the case, I would probably know." Some slight tittering in the audience could be heard (recorded by the RRG as "subdued laughter") followed by applause. After concluding his official remarks, Goebbels answered questions. His surprisingly honest and candid responses to the often critical inquiries posed by foreign journalists revealed his calculated brilliance. Responding to criticism of press censorship, the Nazi media chief claimed censorship produced beneficial results in the German polity. In the years since the Nazis assumed power, he explained, new media rules enabled the government to mold a unified, open, and unreserved public opinion out of the "spiritual anarchy" that preceded Nazi rule in Germany.[129] Goebbels denied "any propaganda motives were connected with the Games" and decried "the critical stories about the 'new' Germany spread outside" the nation by "emigrants." The Associated Press called his talk "remarkably frank." He asked sportswriters to observe Germany "as it actually is" and to "tell the world about it." His disarming demeanor, and welcoming words, effectively framed the Nazi worldview for foreign consumption before the games.[130]

Finally, on 1 August 1936, the Berlin Olympic Games officially opened. As early as six in the morning the streets began crowding with excited Berliners, anticipating the arrival and procession of the Olympic torch, the parade of dignitaries west toward the giant stadium, and the masses of tourists crowding the avenues, buses, and electric trains. French coxswain Noël Vandernotte left Köpenick early to catch the torch run through the streets of Berlin. "There were enormous crowds, down the alleys and streets, but no one spoke in the street. Not a word," he recalled. "The atmosphere was strange." He remembered a feeling he would later describe as "heavy" or "oppressive"—a feeling created by the Sturmabteilung men in uniform, the uncountable Hitler Youth everywhere, and the swastika armbands in evidence.[131] The quiet public that morning surprised and spooked the young Frenchman, and years later it would be one of his most enduring memories from Berlin.

The Olympic torch is run through the streets of Berlin, 1 August 1936. (From the U.S. National Archives.)

The public looked on, eager to get to the stadium and start the celebration. Standing among the lakes and forest of West Berlin, the Olympic stadium was a marvel. Because it sat in a slight depression, it appeared "nestled in the earth" to French ambassador André François-Poncet, who thought "it lacked the imposing eminence of the Colosseum in Rome." But after venturing up the wide ramp to his seat near the Tribune of Honor, the sight of the perfectly manicured field and immaculate seating areas struck him as "strikingly noble." It was, he thought, the most modern and well-designed sporting venue in the world.[132]

At noon the stadium gates opened, and by 2 p.m. the huge crowd was already in evidence.[133] The world's athletes were being bused out to the Maifeld, the expansive grass field bordering the promenade leading into the stadium, to assemble for the opening ceremonies. To make sure the parade of athletes would be error-free, organizers had workers lining up each contingent carefully in their assigned spaces on the field in the order of entrance. The athletes arrived hours ahead of time. The U.S. team was instructed to stand at attention for the arrival of dignitaries, but the rigid stance soon wore on them. "We finally gave up and sat down," remembered McMillin. "Our crew. Probably some of the other Americans, too, because we just couldn't stand that long so we figured the hell with it, and when the brass came through we were sitting there and we just waved at them."[134]

The crowds soon swarmed the Maifeld and Reichssportfeld area. Ticket-holders, curious onlookers, journalists, and members of the Olympic family all buzzed in around the giant stadium. Soon the bowl began to fill, and the press box and broadcast cabins hummed with activity. Officials scurried about the tribune of honor, preparing for Hitler's arrival. The air was electric with anticipation.

The U.S. oarsmen only sat on the ground for a short time because a current of excitement soon passed through the assembled teams. Hitler's open Mercedes was drawing near the stadium, and it would shortly pass the athletes lined up against the rope barrier. The oarsmen rose and moved closer to the restraining rope. All the Olympic athletes had been instructed to maintain proper decorum and remain at attention, but the excitement of the moment overtook the U.S. team. Bob Moch later recalled that moment:

> All these athletes and officials from the different countries stood straight as a rod as these officials came down in the middle, and we were supposed to stand there at attention, but then the United States squad broke ranks and ran up along the rope to get a better look. Everybody else held ranks, but we didn't. We ran so we could get a better look at all of them, and when they passed we went back and took our original positions.[135]

George Pocock watched Hitler's limousine draw up closer to the athletes. He saw the Führer dismount and stride toward the stadium. Hitler was "so close I could have touched him," an amazed Pocock remembered. With guards closely in tow, the dictator entered the arena. It erupted. Pocock described the noise of Hitler's arrival as "blood-curdling, spine-tingling, frantic screaming," from 120,000 people.[136]

Paul Wolff, an inventor working for Leica cameras, was perched high atop the roof of the press gallery on the lip of the great bowl. He scanned the spectators, the towers of the Marathon Gate to the west, and the Olympic cauldron. He heard the "blast of trumpets, and the flags of fifty-three competing nations rose at their masts" and checked his watch. It was precisely 3:56 p.m. The Greek team marched into the stadium, under the gray cloudy skies, and the enormous gathering began cheering. As teams continued streaming in, each one paused momentarily before the Tribune of Honor, where Hitler and Olympic dignitaries were assembled, and then moved past, around the track, and on to designated locations surrounding the field.[137] Applause was continuous and steady, raining down on the athletes.

Waiting outside between two long ropes approximating the width of the stadium's marathon gate, the oarsmen heard a curious roar. Unexpectedly, the French team had apparently given the fascist salute as it passed by Hitler's reviewing stand. The gesture surprised and delighted the German spectators. The newspaper reporters and radio broadcasters also were surprised by such a friendly gesture coming from Germany's most longstanding nemesis. The whole thing, Noël Vandernotte later contended, resulted from misunderstanding and miscommunication. The French athletes had been instructed to raise the "Olympic" salute, with their hand extended horizontally from the shoulder. The salute, a French historian later noted, "resembled nothing so much as the Nazi gesture." The collective misinterpretation by the public raised a frenzy "as unexpected as [it was] disproportionate." "We received an incredible ovation, a once-in-a-lifetime ovation. Even Hitler was surprised," recalled Vandernotte. The French athletes, disconcerted, were furious. "Nobody told us" that the salute could be misinterpreted, Vandernotte remembered, calling the whole scene "awkward and unwelcome . . . nobody said anything [to us]. It's further proof that no one in France or in the Delegation, no one really knew what was happening in Germany." The French ambassador, who witnessed the salute, later claimed it was clearly not the Nazi salute, and the German cheers represented a "wholly mistaken enthusiasm."[138]

The U.S. team made no such mistake. They had been instructed aboard the S.S. *Manhattan* not to dip the flag upon passing the tribune of honor, and their

The opening ceremonies of the 1936 Berlin Olympics, 1 August 1936. (From the U.S. National Archives.)

salute would be the simple removal of their hats. On the *Manhattan* the parade order had been given, and here, jammed together between the ropes set to the width of the stadium's marathon gate, the athletes were herded into order. The men's track-and-field squad would enter first, then the swimmers (both men and women), followed by the boxers, wrestlers, oarsmen, equestrian athletes, women's track-and-field team, gymnasts, and the rest of the competitors.[139] Lined up and ready to go, the U.S. rowing team waited. They would be the second-to-last team to enter, and so the athletes and officials watched as the long line of officials and foreign teams snaked their way around the stanchion holding the restraining rope and up the central pathway toward the stadium's marathon entrance. Finally, the time came for the U.S. contingent to march. For the oarsmen from Seattle, the march into the stadium and around the track was thrilling. Roger Morris peered up at Hitler just as the team passed the dictator's tribune. "He was pretty fat," a surprised Morris later recalled thinking, describing the German dictator as "chunky." He had not been missing many meals, Morris thought. As the team paraded in front of Hitler, the flag of the United States remained high and the men removed their hats and placed them over their hearts. The biggest impression left was of disorder; while other teams

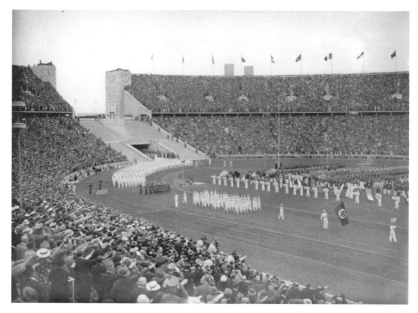

German athletes parade into the Olympic stadium in the opening ceremonies of the 1936 Berlin Olympics. (From the U.S. National Archives.)

marched in lockstep, or at military cadence, the U.S. contingent relished avoiding strict regimentation. They "strolled past, deliberately out of step," George Pocock remembered.[140]

The U.S. radio networks missed the entrance of the U.S. team. CBS and NBC scheduled only one-hour broadcasts. To ensure they would not miss Hitler's official opening, the taking of the Olympic oath by the athletes, the conclusion of the torch relay, and the music of Richard Strauss, they elected to omit the parade of nations. CBS cut in at 11:56 a.m. Eastern, 4:56 p.m. Berlin time, about an hour after the athletes began the parade, and NBC joined soon after. César Saerchinger opened the CBS broadcast by marveling at the German team, which was just finishing the parade. The Germans, he said, were "beautifully dressed in white with black ties, white trousers, white caps, and they're marching in very smartly. The whole audience is standing with their hands raised up. It's the most astonishing sight I've ever seen."[141] After offering some observations about the stadium and the weather, Saerchinger introduced the U.S. audience to Hitler. "In just a minute or two, Herr Hitler, the Chancellor of Germany, will open the Games officially," the CBS correspondent said. "He's down below me here on

Hitler opens the Berlin
Olympic Games, 1 August
1936. (From the U.S. National
Archives.)

a platform, I can see him quite clearly, he's dressed in a brown uniform and
he's got a red armband on," Saerchinger continued. "One of the most dramatic
things this afternoon was Hitler's arrival. You would hear them cheering miles
away before he arrived, the cheers would then get louder, louder, and louder.
And there was—the whole place went mad when he arrived, absolutely balmy,
the whole lot of them," Saerchinger recalled for the audience.[142]

A few moments later a distinct voice could be heard under Saerchinger's
narrative. "Mein Führer!" it calls, before launching into a speech in German.
Saerchinger introduced the new speaker as Hitler, but then quickly corrected
himself. "It wasn't Hitler, it was Theodor Lewald [organizer of the games]
who is speaking in the arena in front of Hitler." Lewald continued speaking.
As his speech droned on, Saerchinger kept jumping in to announce Hitler's
imminent opening of the games. "Well, now, that I think is the end of Dr.
Lewald's speech," he said, sounding annoyed. "No, no, it isn't, he's going on

still. I understood when I started that that speech was going to take about one minute. It's now taken considerably longer than that." As Lewald continued, Saerchinger began to fret about the broadcast window. "This speech is still going on, and it looks like it's never going to stop," he told the U.S. audience a few minutes later. When it finally ended, he described the athletes chatting with each other, "all bored stiff by that speech, just as bored as I was." Just then a hoarse voice could be heard through the stadium loudspeakers, slightly cut off by Saerchinger's last comment. "That was Herr Hitler! Announcing it opened! Now they are cheering him! They are cheering Herr Hitler, and that last bit that you just heard was Herr Hitler himself!" he yelled. His excitement became palpable as thousands of birds were released, followed by the entry of the last runner with the Olympic torch aloft. "He's got his torch, he's a fair young man, he's in white shorts, running in. . . . He's holding it high, taking long steps," narrated Saerchinger. "He did it, he lights it, the whole thing is in flames. . . . Oh a wonderful sight, wonderful," he continued. The Olympic hymn, composed and conducted by Strauss, clearly could be discerned in the background as Saerchinger returned the broadcast to New York. There, in a CBS studio, Robert Trout interviewed a group of former Olympians, including Gertrude Ederle and Abel Kiviat.[143]

The broadcast then returned to Berlin, where Saerchinger introduced Ted Husing and Bill Henry. In his crisp and rapid style, Husing offered a preview of all the biggest events. "Now comes our time to sign off," Bill Henry said, starting to wrap up the broadcast. "I'm going to say goodbye to you now, after I hand the microphone to Ted Husing to bid you all au revoir until tomorrow because we're coming back to you at 12:30 tomorrow." Just then Husing jumped in. "It begins tomorrow. Hang on to your seats, it's going to be hot stuff for another week! Here we go!" "That was Ted Husing," Saerchinger interjected. "Now say goodbye Bill Henry." "Goodbye America, and I'm sorry you couldn't be here to see this wonderful show. I'm glad to have been able to tell you something about it," Henry said. "And now we return you to America," said Saerchinger in closing.[144]

For the Germans, the broadcast of the opening ceremonies had been in preparation for years. It represented the pinnacle of Nazi broadcasting, combining everything from the technical innovation and expansion of the Zeesen shortwave plant to the increase in nationalistic programming broadcast to every German home. The opening ceremonies broadcast, more than any other program, introduced Nazi broadcasting to Germany and the world. The broadcast, and ensuing Olympic programs, offered many rural and impoverished Germans their first immersive experience in Nazi radio programming. Germans

German radio broadcasters working in a press box studio in the Olympic stadium. (From *Die Olympischen Spiele 1936 in Berlin und Garmisch-Partenkirchen.*)

everywhere—in communal groups, in private homes, or even out in cafés—listened. The nation's "ears were attuned to the microphones which carried the proceedings to the most remote corner of the country," noted a reporter for the *New York Herald Tribune*.[145] The program was announced live by the team of Paul Laven and Rolf Wernicke. The partnering of Laven and Wernicke represented typical Nazi shrewdness. Laven had worked for the RRG before the Nazi takeover, and he had developed a following during the years of broadcasting in the Weimar Republic. Wernicke was a young, "genuine Nazi reporter," whose voice was enthusiastic and delivery excitable.[146] Their partnership on one of the biggest broadcasts in German history was intended to transfer some of Laven's authentic popularity to his younger Nazi partner.

The opening ceremonies broadcast proved to be one of the finest shortwave relay productions in the first decade of U.S. network radio. "Trade listeners were highly impressed with the way the networks handled the pageantry . . . of the Olympics, with the pickup of the amplifiers in the stadium coming through with exceptional clarity," noted *Variety*.[147] The signal proved surprisingly strong and the voices from Berlin sounded clear and crisp. The reception was described in the *New York Times* as "almost perfect."[148]

For the oarsmen on the field, the most important moment in the ceremony occurred when the flag bearers of each team stood in a wide semicircle with their teams behind them awaiting the administration of the Olympic oath. The flags were dipped as the athletes recited the oath:

> We swear, at these Olympic Games, to compete honorably and fairly, and to obey the rules of the Games. We will take part with valiant spirit, for the honor of our countries and the glory of sport.[149]

With the oath administered, each team's flag-bearer raised the team standard and the large procession reassembled on the track. The teams proceeded back out to the great grassy field from which they entered earlier in the afternoon. The oarsmen piled in to their bus back to Köpenick, where training resumed the following morning.[150]

With the closing of the opening ceremonies, the games were ready for the world's attention. The city of Berlin buzzed with activity. Olympic athletes began performing or settled into training regimens awaiting their competition. The filmmakers, broadcasters, newsreel cameramen, and newspaper reporters started their feverish schedule of recording history as it occurred. The most complex broadcasting production ever envisioned fully took to the airwaves, ready to transport hundreds of millions of listeners to the German capital. A remarkable moment at the nexus of twentieth-century sport and media history had arrived.

CHAPTER 4

Live from Hitler's Reich

Transmitting the Games and the Listener's Experience

The opening ceremony broadcasts primed global audiences for two weeks of Olympic experience. Newspaper journalists composed copy in the press box as athletes, officials, and spectators streamed from the enormous concrete bowl. The time lag between Europe and North America helped U.S. newspaper reporters, as telegraphic reports could be sped across the ocean in time for same-day coverage in evening editions.[1] For U.S. network radio broadcasters, the opening of the games inaugurated a grueling work schedule. For two weeks, radio commentators covered live events daily while summarizing results nightly in résumé programs. These programs created indelible memories in the minds of millions of U.S. listeners and listeners around the world.

Generally, both CBS and NBC transmitted daily résumés live from Berlin at 11 p.m. so they would air at 6:00 p.m. on the U.S. East Coast. Bill Slater, Eduard Roderich Dietze, and occasionally Max Jordan would give results and interview athletes for NBC, and the CBS broadcast team of César Saerchinger, Bill Henry, and Ted Husing offered a similar program. Except in unusual circumstances (such as when events ran long, prohibiting broadcasters from returning to the stadium), daily summaries were transmitted from small, glass-partitioned studios built into the press box of the Olympic stadium's giant bowl. The Olympic summaries served two functions: They provided results, and they promoted upcoming broadcasts.

By turning the Olympics into a daily serial program featuring celebrity athletes and suspenseful narratives, CBS and NBC hoped to reverse the trend of disappearing audiences occurring during the 1935–36 broadcast season. That year, for the first time since the inception of U.S. network radio, ratings revealed a significant drop in the number of Americans tuning into CBS and NBC. As Jim Ramsburg notes, the decline in listeners may not actually have occurred; new, more precise methods of surveying broadcast audiences were employed for the first time, and the analytics might simply have corrected previous overestimations.[2] Regardless of the reality, the lower ratings for CBS and NBC, and the establishment of the Mutual Broadcasting System as a truly national network in 1936, created an industrywide perception that CBS and NBC were losing listeners.[3] Radio manufacturers, retailers, CBS and NBC executives, and others in the industry hoped additional sports and global news programming in 1936 might enlarge the cumulative U.S. broadcast audience. NBC advertisements called the Olympic Games "the biggest of all summer radio shows," and network executives were encouraged when preliminary Olympic broadcasts—including torch relay reports and Olympic trials in various sports—garnered substantial audience interest.[4] NBC ultimately increased sports programming airtime by 34 percent in 1936 over 1935, with the Olympics and Olympic-themed programming the largest contribution to the increase.[5]

Daily Olympic radio résumés proved their promotional value during the winter games in Garmisch-Partenkirchen. Both CBS and NBC aired the programs, though NBC's relationship with the Reichs-Rundfunk-Gesellschaft (RRG) permitted more broadcasts than their junior rival could air. In general, however, winter games coverage did not require the scope and complexity required in Berlin. NBC transmitted only one live athletic contest across the Atlantic—the silver-medal ice-hockey match between Canada and the United States on 16 February 1936—and nightly summaries lasted only ten minutes. CBS broadcast only the opening and closing ceremonies and small portions of hockey games live, and several attempted transmissions were frustrated by adverse atmospheric conditions.[6] Facilities in Garmisch-Partenkirchen were limited, since it had fewer venues located in closer proximity, and neither CBS nor NBC committed the promotional resources, personnel, or airtime to making the winter games a notable broadcast event. NBC, for example, did not send Bill Slater or Max Jordan: All reporting, including the live call of the hockey game, was handled by the RRG's Dietze.[7]

NBC's hockey program, however, featured a problem that plagued the Berlin broadcasts from their inception. The timing of the game did not precisely match the preordered transmission schedule, and as the reserved airtime neared its

Reichs-Rundfunk-Gesellschaft
commentator Eduard Roderich
Dietze broadcast for NBC during
both the 1936 winter and summer
Olympic Games. (From the German
Broadcasting Archive/Max Kluge.)

end, Dietze—during the live broadcast—inquired on-air if his transmission could continue. "I'm not quite sure if you Americans are interested enough, or if the network can manage it, to stay on with my commentary until the third period is over," he said while nervously looking at the clock and calling the action. Lacking a feedback circuit, Dietze continued his broadcast unaware of whether his program continued airing in the United States. (NBC officials did, in fact, elect to stay with the game until the final whistle, when Canada's victory secured its silver medal.)[8]

Aligning broadcast schedules to Olympic events had proven enormously difficult throughout the two weeks of the Berlin Games. Both the BBC's Thomas Woodrooffe and CBS's César Saerchinger were forced to fumble through the opening ceremony when Dr. Lewald droned on unexpectedly, and for the following two weeks commentators in Berlin found themselves forced to speak around unexpected occurrences numerous times. Promoted live events were occasionally missed because of administrative delays, alterations to competition schedules, and other factors. Today, billions paid in rights fees ensure broadcasters' ability to influence scheduling, but in Berlin the organizing committee prioritized the live, in-venue experiences of athletes, officials, and spectators over the global radio audience.[9] This created significant frustrations for much of the world's broadcasting community. Although some organizations—such as Japan's NHK—used recordings extensively to ensure Olympic programming's efficient insertion into daily schedules, others, including the BBC and the U.S. networks, either severely limited or prohibited the use of recorded materials.[10]

When one compares the surviving Olympic broadcast recordings to the radio schedules printed in newspapers and NBC's official programming records, the slippages between planned coverage and the actual broadcasts are revealed.[11] One particularly exasperating case occurred on 4 August, when CBS promoted live coverage of Jesse Owens in the broad-jump competition. The broadcast opened from a New York City studio with the following announcement:

> We regret that atmospheric conditions have prevented our bringing you the program from the Olympics so far, however we anticipate these difficulties will be able to be overcome and that shortly we will be able to present our special feature.[12]

Jesse Owens wins the gold medal in the men's long jump, 4 August 1936. Technical and scheduling issues caused both CBS and NBC to cut away from Berlin before Owens set the Olympic record on his final attempt. (From *Die Olympischen Spiele 1936 in Berlin und Garmisch-Partenkirchen*.)

The time required to repair the signal severely cut into the airtime available for the program. A stand-by orchestra played two musical selections before the relay from Berlin could be secured. The CBS commentating team then gave detailed summaries of the day's events, followed by an abbreviated interview with gold-medalist Helen Stephens. A terrific roar could be heard from the stadium crowd just as the Stephens interview ended. "The crowd is getting a great thrill now from the announcement regarding the broad jumping across the field," Bill Henry explained, "but I see our time is almost up." He then tossed it back to César Saerchinger. "Friends, I'm sorry we couldn't give you . . . this broad jump," Saerchinger apologized, adding that "if you'll tune in at 12:30 New York time, you will probably get the results."[13]

Schedule mismatches and technical disruptions regularly occasioned on-air apologies from announcers in New York City studios and sportscasters in Berlin. These logistical challenges were not confined to the U.S. networks. The BBC scheduled coverage in very tight windows, thereby creating administrative problems in delivering the games to Great Britain and (through the Daventry shortwave plant) to the Empire. "Well, here we are, they've just finished the 400 meters hurdles, and I'm very sorry but according to some hitch on the lines on the continent we couldn't get through in time, as soon as we wanted to," the BBC's Woodrooffe opened one collaborative CBS–BBC broadcast.[14] The only broadcast organization largely immune to such issues was the RRG, which manipulated its schedule to prioritize Olympic reports.

The German network inundated its domestic airwaves with sports broadcasting. Special "Olympic Flash" broadcasts often interrupted other programming to report German victories, and the "Olympic Echo" show offered summaries, interviews, commentary, and recordings three times daily, from 12:45 p.m. to 1 p.m., 8 p.m. to 8:20 p.m., and 10:15 to 10:45 p.m. Most German Olympic commentaries were handled by the reporting team of Paul Laven and Rolf Wernicke. Both were well-known voices on Germany's national airwaves, and their broadcast collaboration was, according to the German Broadcasting Archive, "probably anything but random." The Nazi radio administration hoped Laven's established reputation and authentic popularity would transfer to the younger, more ideologically faithful Wernicke over the two weeks of broadcasts.[15]

For the foreign broadcasters, booking transmissions through the RRG was a streamlined process facilitated by the work of Kurt Rathke (in charge of "counseling and accommodation of foreign reporters"), Horst Cleinow (in charge of shortwave transmission), and Harald Diettrich (in charge of international program exchange and international service).[16] All worked under the direction of Kurt von Boeckmann. Von Boeckmann was not a typical Nazi. With his doctorate in law, and his experience leading the Research Institute for Cultural Morphology in Munich (before he moved into broadcasting), von Boeckmann's intelligence and cosmopolitan perspective proved rare among the RRG Nazi leadership. His "pleasant manners," command of multiple languages, and "rare adaptability" made him an "ideal choice" to manage visiting broadcasters. His selection as vice president of the International Broadcasting Union (IBU) attested to his popularity in the global broadcasting community.[17]

To arrange transmissions, commentators notified their German liaison and would then soon find that the required cables, circuits, microphones, and transmitters were reserved. Even transportation between venues and around Berlin would be arranged at no charge. Telegrams confirming bookings would be sent to the domestic headquarters of collaborating broadcast organizations. Foreign radio commentators were assigned assistants from the Olympic information office for translation and administrative support. One German radio magazine asked "Miss S.," the liaison assigned to work with Bill Slater, to recount her responsibilities:

> We are clock, notebook, and calendar for our foreign broadcasters. . . . Messenger, secretary, and guide—in short—girl for everything ["girl Friday"]. We pick up 'our' broadcaster from the hotel, we receive his mail, look through the programs, determine when and where they have to make their reports and make sure they arrive there punctually. We run the required errands for him, do the writing, translate and guide him and his wife through Berlin. At every broadcast we are there and observe with him, especially translating the results for him immediately. I had to bring eight or nine winners of gold medals from the arena to the microphone [for Slater]—which was not easy.[18]

The interview concluded by noting that throughout the games "helpers pressed exact broadcasting plans into [Slater's] hands. . . . [W]herever he went, everything was prepared."[19] Even before meeting their liaisons, foreign broadcasters were provided with special Olympic passports ensuring free entrance to any venue and guaranteed seating in the press box, a Broadcasting Guide, with full logistical details, and "Die deutsche Rundfunkaussprache," a German pronunciation guide to the names of more than 6,000 participants in the games.[20]

The German government and the Berlin Olympic Organizing Committee widely promoted broadcasting innovations in the foreign press. "The hearer will be able to learn more about the Olympic activities at one time than the actual spectator," explained one Canadian newspaper, noting that the fan in the stands "cannot possibly be in more places than one, whereas the radio audience will be able to listen to descriptions as they come from all arenas while the various contests are under way."[21] This idea—that listeners at home, on the other side of the planet, might be privy to a more holistic and immersive experience than actual ticketholders seated in the stadium—represented the promise of all future sports programming. To accomplish such a feat in 1936 required extensive planning, meticulous execution, and detailed coordination among a large group of broadcasters and their representative organizations.

Such support produced excellent results. Despite occasional technical or scheduling glitches, overall audio production and transmission proved remarkably effective for such a complex, multilateral event. The preliminary run during the Garmisch-Partenkirchen Winter Olympics, and extensive testing between the RRG and its global partners, ensured success. This commitment to achieving the most innovative and efficient transoceanic relay guaranteed that the Berlin Games would be both the most extensive and the most sophisticated intercontinental broadcast occurring before the Second World War.

Evidence of the technological success abounds in newspaper accounts and audience correspondence. Listeners around the world expressed surprise and delight at the clarity of the Berlin broadcasts. When the RRG tested shortwave transmission to Japan's Komura receiving station on 3 July, the surprised Japanese engineers heard the German signal "as clearly as they hear the radio broadcasts of JOAK radio station of Tokyo." "Germany sounds about as far away as Germantown," marveled the *Philadelphia Inquirer*'s radio columnist. A friend of Bill Henry's from Catalina Island wrote to the CBS sportscaster shortly after hearing a program. "Have just heard your broadcast from Berlin," Ernest Windle wrote. "It came in over KHJ just as clearly as if coming from a Los Angeles station. Congratulations." "The direct broadcasts for both NBC and CBS came in like a local station," one amazed resident of Perth, Australia, told the *New York Times*. *Variety* marveled at the clarity of the first week of broadcasts, noting "the almost uniformly good reception." Bill Slater's "voice, always clear and penetrating," wrote the *Brooklyn Daily Eagle*'s Thomas Rice, "was as distinct as if he had been in Radio City."[22]

The fidelity of the transmissions made the Berlin broadcasts a landmark. But the actual content—the live broadcasting of world historical events, the interviews, and the touristic reportage from Nazi Germany—proved even more engaging. Sports broadcasting, up to 1936, was shaped by distinctive developmental trajectories within each national radio system.[23] The Berlin Olympics proved foundational for modern sports broadcasting as it transitioned—in the United States, Great Britain, Germany, Japan, and elsewhere—from occasional appearances on national airwaves to an established and consistent programming genre. In the United States, CBS, NBC, and the newly established Mutual

Broadcasting System began truly competing in national network sports broadcasting only in the 1934–35 season.[24] For the BBC, live sports broadcasting started late because of strident opposition from the newspaper industry. Fearing declines in attendance, some national sport governing bodies hindered British broadcasting, to the extent that by the early 1930s "BBC live coverage of sport was almost at a standstill" according to one history.[25] The installation of Seymour Joly de Lotbinière as director of Outside Broadcasts in 1935 reversed this trend, leading directly to an increase in live sports reporting on Great Britain's airwaves. One year later, the BBC hired Angus Mackay, sports editor of the *Scotsman*, to be the network's first "sports sub-editor."[26] De Lotbinière insisted upon a more professional, prepared, and engaged style among his charges. "No single person had more influence on the style of radio commentary on the BBC," noted one history of British sports broadcasting. Between 1935 and 1938, the BBC more than doubled the number of live outside reports, with sports making up the vast majority of programs.[27]

The Berlin Olympics offered broadcast organizations an opportunity to increase sport and international news programming at minimal cost. They also allowed broadcasters to collaborate in new ways, with the result that audiences around the world were exposed to different broadcast styles. NBC's collaboration with the RRG, and the extensive use of Dietze, for example, introduced U.S. audiences to modes of German broadcast delivery. One review noted Dietze displayed "a pleasing voice, and a friendly personality" despite his "decidedly English" accent. *Variety* humorously chided Dietze for using British-isms such as "nil" rather than "nothing," "contra" instead of "against," and "trousers" rather than "pants."[28] Dietze further distinguished his broadcasts from those by U.S. commentators by habitually crediting on the air the RRG at the start of a transmission. The BBC–CBS programs, however, drew more press attention than the RRG–NBC collaboration.[29] The BBC announcers' more laconic and understated style, many noted, contrasted sharply with the speed and crisp diction of CBS's U.S. commentators.

The most famous collaborative program from Berlin took place on 3 August 1936, when Jesse Owens won the hundred-meter gold medal. That broadcast began with the BBC's Thomas Woodrooffe welcoming the audience. "I've got here Mr. Ted Husing, he's an American commentator, and he's going to follow the 100 meters race for you," Woodrooffe explained, introducing the CBS sportscaster to his BBC listeners. Husing thanked Woodrooffe and then reported the world record Owens achieved the previous day, in the preliminaries, was disallowed because of a favoring wind. He introduced each competitor in the finals, with occasional comments indicating his consciousness of addressing a transnational audience. "Osendarp, as those people in Britain know, won the British AAA championship two Saturdays ago," he explained. Husing's delivery throughout the broadcast remained uncharacteristically deliberate, with an emphatic enunciation, no doubt caused by a nervousness about appearing on the BBC. Bill Henry, seated near Husing and Woodrooffe in the small stadium box, later recalled Husing "stopped dead in his tracks" when he realized his rapid delivery and snappy patter were out of place on the British airwaves.[30] But even Husing's slower speed still outpaced his British partner's typical delivery.

Husing framed the race as the "battle of the three Americans and the three Europeans." Jesse Owens, Ralph Metcalfe (Husing called him "the midnight locomotive from Marquette"), and Frank Wycoff made up the U.S. team, and the Europeans consisted of the Dutch Tinus Osendarp, Lennart Strandberg, a Swede, and the German Erich Borchmeyer. Before returning the microphone to Woodrooffe, Husing prophesized the U.S. runners would sweep the medals, with Owens taking the gold. Woodrooffe then offered observations about the "general atmosphere" being "very sporting indeed." The sprinters then entered the arena. "I see them now, just coming out to the track, just loosening their muscles—the two Negroes," Woodrooffe added excitedly. "They run most beautifully, these Negroes, they've got the most lovely style of stride, one of the most graceful things I've ever seen, and the two Negroes—and Wycoff—the crowd is cheering them, and everyone is hoping we'll see another world record broken," he said. As the runners were "mucking about with their footholds . . . still in their sweat suits" Woodrooffe complained that the race was already fifteen minutes delayed. "When this race does come off, I think it's going to be a very exciting one, and I couldn't have thought of anyone better than Mr. Husing to tell you about it," he continued, stalling for time. He then offered a series of observations about the city of Berlin. "As I said, these two Negroes are the most graceful creatures on the track . . . I have ever seen in my life. They have the most graceful stride, [grace] hardly describes it—they seem not so much to be running as floating over the track," he repeated, waiting for the official's whistle calling the racers to the line. Finally, he handed the microphone back to Husing as the race was about to start. "And here they go, down on their marks," Husing whispered as silence enveloped the broadcast:

> This is the big hush that sets over the stadium. We've got to watch them very carefully now. They haven't come up yet. As soon as they do, we'll pick them up and spring them right up the track. They're still down on their mark. The wind is blowing here, it's a little bit chilly. They're set! The gun sounds and they're away! Jesse Owens gets out there with Metcalfe . . .

Just at that moment a tremendous roar from the crowd drowned out Husing. By the time Husing's voice returned, the race was closing on the finish line with Owens's win assured. "It's Owens, Metcalfe, and Osendarp!" Husing called out. Very quickly Husing handed the microphone back to Woodrooffe, who, conscious of the time, announced immediately "that's all we have time for today." He signed off by telling listeners to tune in the news to find out "whether they did break the world record or not."[31]

The RRG's domestic broadcast of the same race was, in many ways, quite similar to the BBC–CBS race call. Sportscaster Rolf Wernicke, a dedicated National Socialist who owed his career to his public support for Nazi ideals, highlighted the racial characteristics of the athletes. Wernicke compared the sprinters to animals ("splendid purebred racehorses") and then, like Husing, he framed the contest as a battle between the United States and Europe. Just as Husing quieted while awaiting the starter's pistol, Wernicke's voice also softened as the crowd hushed. Unlike the BBC–CBS call, however, the RRG's transmission was properly modulated and the crowd never eclipsed Wernicke's voice. Wernicke's race call transmits his excitement with crystal clarity while the roar of the spectators remains audible but not overwhelming. After the race, Wernicke demonstrated a spontaneous enthusiasm for Owens's achievement.

Jesse Owens (upper right) captures the 100 meters. (From Cigaretten-Bilderdienst, Hamburg-Bahrenfeld GmbH.)

As German scholar Hans Pöttker noted, Wernicke's ideological commitment to National Socialism was apparently overwhelmed by the experience of witnessing one of the twentieth century's most remarkable athletic achievements. He closed the RRG program with "restrained admiration," and even noticeable respect, for Owens.[32]

The most surprising aspect of the BBC's broadcast of the hundred-meter final was not the appearance of CBS's Husing but, rather, the absence of Harold Abrahams, England's top track-and-field commentator. Abrahams's biographer considered Husing's substitution for Abrahams attributable only to discrimination. Mark Ryan found Woodrooffe's later justification—that Husing's rapid delivery more effectively fit the speed of the race—unconvincing.[33] Immediately before the Olympic Games, Abrahams did an excellent broadcast of the British AAA championships at White City Stadium—an event widely seen as a Berlin preview.[34] His absence from the Owens broadcast ultimately possessed little historical significance, however, because Abrahams soon provided the BBC and British and U.S. audiences with perhaps the most memorable and historic broadcast from Berlin. That program, the live report of the fifteen-hundred-meter final, would later be widely recognized as a historic moment in the history of global sports broadcasting.

Journalists previewing the fifteen-hundred-meter race considered it one of the most exciting and competitive events on the Olympic schedule. Six of the top seven finishers from the 1932 Los Angeles final in the same event made the 1936 final, including gold-medalist Luigi Beccali of Italy and Glenn Cunningham of the United States, holder of the world's record in the mile. New Zealand's Jack Lovelock and Canada's Phil Edwards looked strong, and the U.S. competitors Gene Venzke and Archie San Romani, as well as Germany's Fritz Schaumburg, were all considered medal contenders. In fact, all twelve finalists possessed realistic medal aspirations—a rare occurrence in Olympic history. Everyone expected a historic race. The night before the contest, Abrahams expressed excitement and concern that his close friendship with Lovelock might bias his call. "I have every hope that [Lovelock] will win," he wrote his fiancée Sybil Evers. "If he does, I think I'll burst the microphone."[35]

The broadcast opened with Woodrooffe setting the stage, calling the event one of the greatest races scheduled in Berlin. A loud but indistinct chant briefly interrupted Woodrooffe's introduction. "That chanting you just heard is cheering for the arrival of Herr Hitler," he explained. A hush occurred, then the gun, and the race began. Abrahams tried to call the first lap, but with the runners bunched closely and the great distance from the box to the track he admitted his inability to provide good information. "An American [is] leading, I can't see who it is, but an American is leading," Abrahams explained as they made the far turn. "Coming down the stretch, I'll tell you who's leading in a moment. . . . They're all bunched together. . . . I think Cunningham's come up into the lead," he said. The atmosphere of the roaring crowd, the very fast race, and the tightly bunched competitors becomes electrifying even when listening to a recording decades later. Abrahams's voice started climbing. "God, this is going to be a race by the time they get to the last lap!" he yells. In retrospect, Abrahams did a poor job of providing the audience with key information. He bumbled through the leaders, failed to report lap times, and repeatedly apologized. "The time for 800 meters I've missed, I'm sorry," he explained as the runners—still tightly bunched—moved into the second half of the race. But what he lacked in cool delivery he more than made up for with an unaccustomed emotionalism. When Jack Lovelock finally emerged in the lead, Abrahams lost control and evolved from reporter to fan. "Lovelock just running perfectly now! C'mon Jack!" he screams. "Lovelock leads! 300 meters to go!" he yells. His emotional call of the race's last few seconds became one of the most famous moments in BBC history:

> Come on, Jack! . . . Lovelock leads! Lovelock! Lovelock! C'mon Jack, my God he's done it! Five yards, six yards, he's done it! Hurray! . . . Jack Lovelock ran in the most beautiful style! It was the most marvelous sight I've ever seen!

When Abrahams transitioned from detached reporter to electrified participant, he provided the template for all future iconic sports broadcasting moments. His "unbridled enthusiasm," Mark Ryan wrote, "made broadcasting history."[36] Every milestone sport broadcast call—from "The Giants win the pennant! The Giants win the pennant!" to "Do you believe in miracles?!"—captures the sportscaster's spontaneous astonishment in real time. Like Abrahams, those announcers effectively transmitted electric feelings directly to the audience. Live sports broadcasting, at its best, transforms audiences into participants, telescoping distance while injecting adrenaline via personal—even intimate—connections. This is radio as live experience, and this "liveness" remains radio's distinguishing characteristic. By combining authenticity, individuality, and enthusiasm, Abrahams's call can be recognized today as one of the earliest examples of genuinely thrilling sports broadcasting. Future sports reporting would remain indebted to this ex-athlete for his emotional outburst in Berlin. The race call, also broadcast to the United States over the airwaves of CBS, became an influential, memorable, and remarkable historical moment.

Such unabashed spontaneity was rare on both the British and the U.S. airwaves in 1936. Man-on-the-street interviews and *Vox Pop* programs were often

"Come on, Jack!" Jack Lovelock of New Zealand (in black, wearing number 467) prepares to take the lead. Harold Abrahams's emotional broadcast of the 1,500-meter final on the BBC (and over CBS in the United States) was a milestone in the history of sportscasting. (From *Die Olympischen Spiele 1936 in Berlin und Garmisch-Partenkirchen.*)

scripted, and even unrehearsed and apparently spontaneous discussion programs were carefully structured by networks and commercial sponsors.[37] Woodrooffe sensed immediately that Abrahams's unrestrained emotionalism violated an unwritten rule. He decided to address the issue immediately. "Now, [the race] sent the crowd mad, and as you may have heard it sent Harold Abrahams completely mad, and it sent me mad as well," Woodrooffe explained while wrapping up the program. By mentioning the engulfing hysteria in the stadium, and his own feelings, Woodrooffe subtly excused Abrahams's unprofessionalism.

Abrahams's performance, combined with de Lotbinière's call for a more uninhibited and engaged BBC commentating style, soon sparked public discussion of appropriate modes of live address over Britain's airwaves.[38] Emotional spontaneity and verbal informality threatened to promote individuality in a system that, up until 1936, prized formalized institutionalism and depersonalized professionalism. In its earliest years, BBC executives pondered—then rejected—instructing commentators to imitate the rapid-fire and self-consciously stylistic U.S. live sports commentary style. By design, by the mid-1930s, "there was rarely exaggeration, over-dramatisation or over-excitement," in BBC sportscasts.

But the Berlin broadcasts reignited debate. "Our English announcers have not yet learned to be natural," wrote one critic, noting that "the best of American announcers, strange though their English often appears, are much more successful in being themselves." But such "self-consciousness," *The Spectator*'s Basil Maine warned, could also provoke exaggerated verbosity. U.S. radio commentators, "so eager . . . to make no pause," will continue speaking "lest we should think that they had dried up . . . mentally." U.S. announcers, Maine concluded, were susceptible to "extemporization run amok." Yet between U.S. "whole-hearted spontaneity" and British "cold-blooded neutrality," he concluded, existed a medium that would benefit the BBC and its audience.[39]

To argue the significance of Abrahams's call is not to claim it was completely novel. Compelling memorable and emotional live sports broadcasting predated the 1936 Berlin Olympic Games. But Abrahams's call was heard live across the national BBC and CBS airwaves (and later overseas via recordings transmitted through the Daventry shortwave plant), making the cumulative worldwide radio audience for this specific program one of the largest ever assembled. The recording of Abrahams's call—and the citation of it in commemorative programs and books about sports broadcast history—attests to its foundational status and influential legacy.[40] Before Berlin, the apex of sports broadcasting style, as embodied by Ted Husing's delivery, was rapid but dispassionate with steady reportorial verbosity. "Husing was the first great technician as a sports broadcaster," remembered Brooklyn Dodger announcer Walter "Red" Barber.[41] "The Ted Husing style was noted for its control and accuracy," Walter Cronkite later recalled. "Described as being able to bring you to the edge of your chair without screaming, his flow of language was such that Husing rarely needed to use the same descriptive adjective twice."[42] Husing's live commentary, *Sports Illustrated*'s William Taaffe wrote, was "seamless, the words flowing off his tongue in perfect balance and harmony."[43] Precision mattered more than idiosyncrasy, volume, or partisanship. Husing perfected this style, and NBC hired Bill Slater and assigned him to Berlin precisely because Slater—more than any other NBC commentator—could replicate Husing's delivery.[44]

After Berlin, emotional spontaneity and explicit fandom became more popular on the world's airwaves. Correlation is not causation, and additional factors clearly pushed network managements to continue evolving sports broadcasting toward more personal and naturalistic styles of address. But Abrahams's call on 6 August 1936 remains historic because it so perfectly encapsulates, in one specific and memorable moment, the transition of sports broadcasting from its original incarnation into the future model.

Just as the BBC management promoted emotionalism on the airwaves, other national broadcasters—such as Japan's NHK and the RRG—also used the Berlin games to increase unfiltered emotional reporting. NHK sent four employees to Berlin, and although Japanese athletes performed well in several events, two live broadcasts proved particularly historic.[45] The swimming finals provided exciting racing that the NHK broadcast live, and later by recording, back to Japan. A German newspaper reporter, unable to understand the Japanese language, noted how animated and excited the NHK broadcasters appeared while calling the action from the swimming stadium. One specific swimming race remains a staple of Japanese broadcasting lore. Hideko Maehata captured the two-hundred-meter breaststroke, becoming the first Japanese female to win a gold medal in the Olympics. As the race neared its conclusion, Maehata and Germany's Martha Genenger matched each other stroke for stroke, bringing the swimming stadium's roaring crowd to its feet. NHK announcer Sansei Kasai "abandoned his regular detachment as a journalist to cheer on" the Japanese swimmer. Clearly audible above the crowd, Kasai started repeatedly yelling "Maehata ganbare! Maehata ganbare!" ["Go, Maehata!"]. The electrifying live broadcast was recorded and later rebroadcast and would eventually be released as a recording that sold enough copies to qualify as a bestseller. "It was a seminal

Hideko Maehata, the first Japanese woman to win a gold medal in the Olympic Games, receives her medal. Millions of Japanese radio listeners stayed up late to hear the live NHK broadcast of Hideko Maehata's victory in the 200-meter breaststroke on 11 August 1936. (From *Asahi Shinbun.*)

commentary performance, delivered at the birth of live sportscasting and talked about by generations of sportscasters since," states Hisateru Furuta's history of Japanese broadcasting.[46]

A second historic NHK broadcast occurred on 9 August 1936, when the marathon concluded Berlin's track-and-field events. The race was covered live, with twelve separate microphone pickups stationed along the racecourse, available for use by German, U.S., British, Japanese, Argentine, and other broadcasters. Korean Kitei Son,[47] running for Japan, was the surprise winner. As he entered the Olympic stadium and neared the finish line, a group of Japanese spectators seated in front of the broadcasters went wild, yelling "Bonsai! Bonsai! Bonsai!" The NHK announcers leaned out of their enclosure to mix the cheers with their excited call of the momentous victory.[48]

The marathon would be Ted Husing's final live sportscast from Berlin. Husing's "vacation" had already extended longer than originally planned, and he wanted to return to New York City in time to call an important heavyweight boxing match on CBS. The drama of the marathon—in which 1932 gold-medalist Juan Carlos Zabala of Argentina collapsed while attempting to become the first two-time Olympic champion—combined with Son's unexpected triumph made for an excellent program. Husing called it "one of the most remarkable races we've ever seen" before explaining that he had dispatched Woodrooffe to the finish line to see whether Son could be enticed up to the box for an interview. The exhausted Korean ignored the request, dodged Woodrooffe and the press, and, after gathering his clothes, stumbled to the dressing room beneath the stadium. In a final summary of the race, Husing noted that bronze medalist Shoryu Nan was "another Jap" medalist.[49]

Throughout the games, Husing—alone among the U.S. and British announcers—consistently referred to Japanese athletes as "Japs." "The Japs," Husing told the U.S. audience while calling the high-jump competition on 2 August, "use a hurdle-scissor [jump], which is amazing." The use of this pejorative epithet provided another reminder of the racial coding occurring regularly on the airwaves during the Olympics. The insult occurred elsewhere in a variety of programs, such as when U.S. diver Marshall Wayne previewed the platform diving championship. "The Americans' only competition will be from the Jap—or the boy from Japan, I might say," a stumbling Wayne told Bill Henry.[50] U.S. broadcasters often linked Japanese achievements to supposed inherent racial advantages—such as the ability of Japanese athletes to endure unmatched amounts of training.[51] Nor was explicitly attributing Japanese athletic success to racial characteristics limited to U.S. sportscasters. The RRG's Paul Laven, Horst Slesina, and Rolf Wernicke, when describing Japanese athletes (such as Kohei Murakoso, who unexpectedly led much of the ten-thousand-meter race), linked Japanese achievement to specific racial attributes.[52] Bill Henry called Murakoso, who eventually finished fourth behind three Finns, "a little sawed-off Japanese" in his CBS summary of the same race.[53]

The race mentioned most regularly, in numerous contexts throughout the games, was the "white" race. Husing, mimicking the Nazis, called bronze-medal sprinter Tinus Osendarp "the fastest white man in the world today" in one broadcast.[54] While previewing one swimming final, Bill Henry called swimmer Jack Medica "our outstanding white hope" against the Japanese.[55] By categorizing competitors and results by race, the U.S., British, and Nazi broadcasters conjured ethereal hierarchies of athletic achievement completely divorced from the reality of Olympic scorekeeping. In reestablishing racial identities erased by radio's lack of visual signification, radio commentators descriptively positioned themselves between listeners and events. In this sense, the Berlin sports broadcasts closely paralleled all U.S. broadcasting in the 1930s, in which racial and ethnic coding was explicit, required, and ubiquitous.[56]

Despite such clear verbal division, sportscasters and interviewees on CBS and NBC occasionally attempted to use the vehicle of athletic triumph to promote racial harmony. "I think it's only fair to say the colored people of the United States—and the white people—have good reason to be proud of [Cornelius] Johnson, [Jesse] Owens, [Ralph] Metcalfe, [John] Woodruff and [Dave] Allbritton—all colored boys, and deporting themselves in a manly and fine way," Jay O'Brien, a U.S. Olympic official, told one CBS audience.[57] Ultimately, the Berlin broadcasts served as a racial paradox. At the same time that explicit racial coding imposed racial stratification on the airwaves, the voices of black athletes like Archie Williams and Jesse Owens were treated with respect—and even reverence—by CBS and NBC interviewers. At a time when newspapers in the U.S. south still refused to report Olympic titles won by African Americans, the networks celebrated their achievements on the national airwaves.[58] By explicitly linking U.S. nationalism to African American athletic achievement, CBS and NBC sportscasters subtly transgressed established modes of racial representation on the U.S. airwaves.

Similarly, U.S. network programs from Berlin created new discursive spaces to discuss women's athletic achievements within the context of national superiority. The transmission of female voices on Olympic broadcasts paradoxically contained elements of transgression while remaining confined within accepted gender norms. Just as the Olympic programs implicitly challenged U.S. society's codified racism while remaining within acceptable channels of racial representation, the programs featuring female athletes implicitly addressed misogyny and equality while ensconced within established gender constructs. While always evidencing a consciousness of appropriate models of female address and decorum on the airwaves, the voices of U.S. female coaches and athletes created space for notably rare celebrations of women's athletic equality.

In an NBC preview broadcast, airing one week before the opening ceremonies, Bill Slater invited women's track coach Delores "Dee" Boeckmann to address "the mothers and fathers in America and all the sports fans interested in our girls." Slater queried Boeckmann about the experiences of the U.S. women in Berlin. "The girls loved the big greeting that they got from all the people here in Berlin," Boeckmann explained, before detailing the accommodations for the women in the gender-segregated women's Olympic village. Unlike most of the interviews with male athletes and coaches—which focused primarily on athletic contests and foreign competition—Slater's interview with Boeckmann explored such issues as the difference in European bedding and pillows, their effect on sleep, and the meals prepared in the women's village. "We got fried food, which we weren't used to, and the girls didn't like that," Boeckmann said, noting that the women also were denied the desserts served to the male athletes. Both the food and the bedding issues, she explained, were remedied quickly. When Boeckmann mentioned that "the girls" enjoyed walking around the Reich Sports Field, Henry cut in: "I didn't know they were allowed to leave the quarters"—just in case U.S. listeners might believe their female athletes could travel unchaperoned in Berlin. "They're not allowed to leave the outside big fence," Boeckmann quickly clarified. "We have a big fence all around the *Reichssportfeld*, and they have to have their passport to get out, and they must have the permission of the coach and the chaperone to go downtown shopping but they may walk around the stadium."[59] Her reminder that U.S. women would never be unchaperoned in Germany was typical of the protective and patronizing tenor of the entire interview. Its difference from a typical sportscast can be glimpsed from the following exchange:

> **BILL SLATER**: Well, what happens when they go downtown shopping? They speak a language that's a little bit different here. What happens when they want to go downtown shopping or visiting or seeing some of the very interesting sights here in Berlin?
> **DEE BOECKMANN**: Well, we have what are called runners over here. The German government has furnished runners over here and they are girls who have taken a very vigorous examination in many, many languages and they are dressed in a white linen suit with the Olympic circles on the pocket, and people know throughout the town of Berlin [that] they are very fine girls

and they take the girls downtown, they are their translators, and they take them to the very, very interesting parts of town, ask them what they want to buy, the souvenirs for their mothers and fathers and sisters and brothers and their sweethearts and uncles and aunts. So they take them to the shop and they help them find the little things that they want to take home.[60]

Boeckmann ended the interview by relaying the humorous adventure of Marion Lloyd, a U.S. fencer who entered the men's village without permission to do some banking. "All of a sudden there was a lot of noise in the bank and they asked her what she was doing there and how she got in," Boeckmann said.[61] Lloyd, Boeckmann explained, was the first woman to set foot in the men's athletes' village since the arrival of the competitors. In highlighting this single violation of the sanctity of gender segregation among the athletes, and detailing the response, NBC and Boeckmann provided reassurance that U.S. female athletes in Berlin would remain segregated, protected, and above reproach.

Throughout the games, the U.S. female athletes were simultaneously celebrated for their remarkable achievements and patronized by references to their appearance and by reinforcing restrictive gender norms. The Olympic programs provided one of the few spaces on the U.S. national airwaves where female and male athletic achievement could be comparatively discussed. Swimming, diving, track-and-field, and running results required explicit categorization by gender so as not to risk listener confusion. In placing women's and men's athletic achievements within the same context, the Berlin broadcasts were somewhat futuristic in their implicit promotion of gender equality. Such broadcast content could be controversial; even as late as 1936, discussion of appropriate modes of female athletic performance remained contentious. As Brad Austin notes, some "physical education organizations in the United States actively campaigned against women participating in international competitions and especially the Olympics" because of fears "that women would start to play sports for the wrong reasons, that the athletes would be exploited in almost countless ways, and that a societal focus on training and celebrating elite athletes would reduce the opportunities for all women to participate in athletics."[62] Many educators preferred the ideal of feminized physical education emphasizing cooperative values rather than the masculine version inculcating competitive values. Others, pointing to such Olympic stars as Mildred "Babe" Didrikson, celebrated women's athletic achievements as progressive.[63] But no such debate emerged on the national airwaves from Berlin. By ignoring the controversy, and normalizing and celebrating women's athletic achievement, CBS and NBC helped further the cause of gender equality.

Such support was implicit rather than explicit. Operating within a culture and society that circumscribed the representation of female athletes, the networks carefully contextualized and segregated female voices on the air. Stereotypically feminine concerns, such as the appropriate gifts to purchase for family members in Berlin's shops, predominated. Just as the reification of race was required by radio's lack of any visual element, gender, too, needed to be consistently emphasized for the listeners back home. By working within social constructs, network sportscasters replicated the gender constraints structuring U.S. network broadcasting in the 1930s. Whether on daytime serials, home economics programs, or even comedy and variety shows, CBS and NBC consistently propagated appropriate models of female decorum and behavior in attempts to reinforce cultural stereotypes and protect the national airwaves from radicalism. As radio scholars have pointed out, sometimes these efforts backfired.[64] But the imposition of tightly policed gender norms was an essential and integral aspect of U.S. broadcast procedure in the 1930s, and the Olympic programs were no exception.

CBS and NBC sportscasters repeatedly demonstrated consciousness of this responsibility. Questions directed toward female and male participants differed considerably in both delivery style and substance. Discussions of women's

The world's fastest humans. Helen Stephens and Jesse Owens, victors in the 100 meters. (From *Die Olympischen Spiele 1936 in Berlin und Garmisch-Partenkirchen*.)

athletics more often devolved into humor, as sports reporters and interviewees would shift tone after any discussion of men's athletics. A typical example occurred on 3 August, when Ted Husing asked U.S. Olympic Committee official Jay O'Brien about notable performances in the first days of the games:

TED HUSING: Say, the feminine side of our athletic picture is one that's often been neglected. How about you look at the women—after all, you're very handsome you know—[laughs].

JAY O'BRIEN: It would be like [you] Ted to get right to the ladies again [laughs]. Well, as a matter of fact, we had one great surprise—speaking of ladies—it was an attractive and charming surprise today. In the opening heat of the one hundred meters a *fraulein*, tall, sinewy, athletic-looking, ran a phenomenal time . . . and we all felt that this was [going to be] the winner. But in the following heat Miss Stephens, a so-called "farm girl"—age twenty-one, about five feet eleven, weighing about one-hundred and fifty-five pounds—no hips, fine shoulders—I'm just trying to give you a [*indistinct*] description of this young lady—stepped out and broke the world's record. In the repeating heat, she broke it again.[65]

Despite O'Brien's tone, much of the reporting on Stephens tended to be admiring and respectful.

"I clocked the young lady in what seemed to be impossible time," Bill Henry told the CBS audience when discussing her world record in the preliminaries. "I can tell you there are a lot of fellas running for colleges in the United States today who can't run 100 meters in eleven and four-tenths seconds," Henry explained, calling her feat "the most remarkable performance of all time" for a female sprinter.[66] But the respectful treatment accorded Stephens was largely anomalous. More typical was the tone taken by Bill Henry when interviewing Marjorie Gestring on 13 August, shortly after her surprise victory in the springboard diving competition made her the youngest Olympic gold medalist in history:

BILL HENRY: I have the young lady right here who was victorious and it is a great pleasure to me to live up to a promise which I made to her a good many months ago that if she won this championship she'd get a chance to talk to the United States—and so here is Marjorie Gestring. Marjorie, you can at least say hello.

MARJORIE GESTRING: Hello, everybody. I'm awfully happy that I won and I owe all my success and my championship to hard work and the hard cooperation of my coach—and I hope my Daddy is listening in!

HENRY: Well, I'm sure that he is, Marjorie, and I think the people will be interested in knowing that you are not an old broken-down woman here who has had forty or fifty years of competition, you had better tell the people first of all, how old you are, secondly, how long you've been diving, and thirdly where you live.

GESTRING: I live in Los Angeles, California, and I'm thirteen years old. I started diving when I was ten years old.

HENRY: Well, Marjorie, I think people will be interested in knowing where you go to school, and just what grade you are in school.

GESTRING: I go to Horace Mann Junior High and I'm in the eight [*indistinct*] nine.[67]

Critics in the press lauded the Gestring interview for both its delightful spontaneity and Gestring's endearing innocence.[68] What Henry's interview omitted, however, was any detailed discussion of the outstanding final dive that propelled her into first place.

When incorporating discourse of gender or race in their Berlin broadcasts, U.S. sportscasters attempted to minimize conflict as much as possible. Geopolitical tensions, such as the outbreak of the Spanish Civil War, were ignored or downplayed, as were questions of misogyny and racism. Offense was given only to foreigners, and, even then, it was sparingly applied. Labeling Kitei Son a "Jap" on the U.S. airwaves, for example, was clearly offensive. But perhaps more offensive to the Korean marathon victor was the omission of any discussion of the Japanese occupation of his homeland. The only time Son's Korean heritage arose in the CBS broadcast was when Bill Henry introduced him as a "Japanese boy, who, incidentally, was born in Korea."[69] Son's victory was otherwise hailed as a Japanese triumph by a Japanese subject. Similarly, the RRG's Paul Laven called Son "a Korean student" only one time, near the end of the marathon broadcast, after other German announcers continually referred to him as Japanese throughout the race.[70] By avoiding discussion of Korea's occupation, and by minimizing Son's heritage, sportscasters from the United States and Germany excluded international political controversy from their broadcasts. Racial discussion could be seamlessly interwoven into programs, but global conflict caused by colonial occupation and annexation appeared unspeakable, lest such discussion detract from Olympic themes of peace and international cooperation.

When listening to the surviving recordings of the CBS and NBC broadcasts, one is struck by the almost complete absence of reportage on the most widely publicized and well-known controversies connected to the games. This is one of the most remarkable facets of the Olympic broadcasts; they are, in some ways, more notable for what they omit than for what they contain. The largest controversies—and, in some cases, the most important news—that U.S. audiences read about in their newspapers went largely unnoted on the airwaves. Studies of newspaper reporting from Berlin note the multitude of ways the U.S. press framed questions surrounding the boycott movement, racial issues catalyzed by Jesse Owens's triumphs, and other controversies before, during, and after the games.[71] No such analysis of the network radio journalism transmitted from Berlin exists.

Perhaps this failure can be attributed to the fact that so little independent, critical, and investigative reporting made it onto the national airwaves. The number of broadcasters in Berlin was tiny in comparison with the number of newspaper reporters, and the requirement to be tethered to microphones for several daily broadcasts limited reporting opportunities. One newspaper columnist noted that Bill Slater expected to rely upon his wife "to scribble down some notes for her husband's benefit" during live broadcasts.[72] The CBS crew similarly relied on the uncredited labor of Claire Trask, who had served as an early CBS stringer in Berlin, for assistance throughout the games.[73] This lack of personnel unquestionably contributed to the inability to produce significant reportage during the games.

Yet such an explanation assumes that with the proper resources and personnel, the radio announcers would have sought to compete journalistically with the press. The record shows that, even when presented with ample opportunity, NBC and CBS sportscasters actively avoided independent and investigative reportage. Three of the most sensational stories from Berlin—all widely reported in the press—were either completely omitted or severely minimized in radio broadcasts. Eleanor Holm Jarrett's expulsion from the Olympic team was never discussed (or even reported) on the airwaves. In coverage of women's swimming events, where Jarrett had been scheduled to compete, her name was mentioned only in connection with her world's record (in the backstroke) and 1932 gold medal.[74] Bill Slater later told the press that he agreed with Jarrett's punishment, yet he refused to discuss it on the air and revealed his thoughts only upon returning to the United States.[75] Nor did the CBS or NBC sportscasters report on the controversy surrounding the substitution of Sam Stoller and Marty Glickman on the U.S. 4 × 100 relay team. Stoller and Glickman, the only two Jewish sprinters to earn spots on the U.S. squad, were replaced by Jesse Owens and Ralph Metcalfe shortly before the relay competition commenced. The change, widely reported in the press, was barely alluded to on the airwaves. Without ever explicitly mentioning Glickman or Stoller, Bill Henry simply stated that the "American team . . . had a rather surprising personality which had not been expected" when Jesse Owens, Ralph Metcalfe, Foy Draper, and Frank Wycoff ran in the preliminary heat. Ted Husing never once mentioned Glickman or Stoller when calling the final live. When Bill Henry interviewed Draper a few hours later, once again the replacement of the Jewish athletes went unrecognized.[76]

The third controversy ignored in broadcast coverage concerned the two U.S. boxers dismissed from the U.S. team, ostensibly for "homesickness." (The two had been apprehended shoplifting and were returned to the United States to avoid facing arrest in Germany.)[77] Even when CBS reported extensively from the boxing finals—where the U.S. team performed poorly—the absence of two top fighters remained unremarkable to the sportscasters.

Other controversies were implicitly addressed in subtle ways. The failed boycott movement, and its leadership, were entirely absent from the broadcasts, but effusive praise lavished on the German hosts can be interpreted as an indictment of those who sought to deprive U.S. athletes—and their fans listening at home—of such a marvelous experience. Before the games opened, Bill Slater called Berlin "a magnificent place, a place bedecked by flags, gala bunting and a holiday atmosphere."[78] His admiration for the German people and Olympic organizing committee was so pervasive that at one point an NBC executive in New York asked Slater to use the word "splendid" less often.[79] U.S. listeners could easily imagine the German capital as a carefree fantasyland. "Everywhere anyone goes in Berlin there is a great sense of joyful freedom," Roderich Dietze informed NBC's U.S. audience on 30 July.[80] "It is as though Berlin has become the playground of the whole world," Max Jordan explained in one broadcast.[81]

Commentary about Berlin, the operation of the games, and the German people tended to the complimentary. "Last night on Unter den Linden I visited one of the little newsreel theaters," Ted Husing told his CBS audience. Sitting through a thirty-minute newsreel encapsulating the first week of the games, Husing was surprised to witness the moviegoers seeming to interact with the stadium crowd projected on the screen. "It was one of those peculiar things where you hear the hubbub of the uproar from the picture, and then there would follow in the theater a hand-clapping and some amount of applause," he explained. The generous cheers offered the U.S. competitors surprised him as well. "Each picture of Jesse Owens received a salvo of applause," he added.[82] While praising Berliners on the airwaves, Husing published a different perspective in a front-page article in *Variety*. The bars and cabarets of Berlin were lively and fun, with music that sounded, at its best, "New Yorky [*sic*]," he explained. But "entertainment in these places is usually floperoo," he judged. Husing expressed surprise that so few Hollywood or Broadway celebrities traveled to Berlin when he considered its global prominence in the world's media in August 1936. The "American influx" of tourists, he complained, was limited to "gawky hinterlanders." He wrote that the city itself was jammed and "hotternell" as huge crowds marveled at "the flag festooned avenues and buildings, the huge platzes flying myriad banners and night-lighted broad avenues" that created "a wonderland for the natives who gape with wonder." "Imagine the dough thrown out in printing and bunting—not to mention the site costs as well as coverage costs for 40 radio countries and all the press! Staggering!" he exclaimed. Berlin, the recently divorced Husing concluded, was a "great place for a torchy guy . . . what with the barmaids in evening dress who sit and talk to you as you stupefy yourself."[83] Husing undoubtedly realized that such candid descriptions and such a revealing account of his personal experiences would be unwelcome on the airwaves of CBS. The contrast between Husing's honesty in *Variety* and his circumspect verbalizations on CBS offers an illustrative example of the relative amount of open discursive space in the two media.

Throughout the broadcasts from Berlin, U.S. athletes, officials, and sports-casters often unfavorably compared U.S. facilities and sport audiences with their German counterparts. Bill Henry interviewed sprinter Foy Draper about the stadium atmosphere following the final day of track-and-field events:

> **BILL HENRY:** You had a chance to see very much of the meet. Have you felt that this was a good crowd, or what do you think of it?
>
> **FOY DRAPER:** Well, Bill it sort of makes me ashamed to be an American when we call ourselves a sports-loving public. We come out here day after day and what is supposedly a dull day and instead of finding 15 or 20 thousand people, why I'm surprised to find over 100 thousand people at every meet.[84]

Others joined Draper in praising the Germans. "For the complete brilliance of an athletic contest, nothing I think can surpass what they have done here in the way of an athletic plant, in the way of taking care of the spectators, for the loudspeaker system is beyond all comprehension and beyond compare," Hus-ing told the CBS audience only minutes before calling the 4 × 100 meter relay in which Jesse Owens captured his fourth gold medal.[85] Before arriving in Berlin, Bill Slater told *Funk-Wacht Nordfunk*, "he had actually thought he could compare German and American broadcasting. But already on the first day he realized that this would be impossible because [the German broadcast production] could not be compared to any existing broadcasting achievement."[86] Such admiration was not limited to the pages of a German periodical. On NBC's final Olympic broadcast, Max Jordan acknowledged how "the Reichs-Rundfunk-Gesellschaft, the German broadcasting system, had made elaborate arrangements to secure the best possible teamwork with NBC." "Their work," Jordan told the U.S. audi-ence, "was really unparalleled in the history of radio."[87]

The U.S. radio networks demonstrated a remarkable deference to both Ger-man and U.S. authorities on the airwaves. This was another way their perfor-mance contrasted with that of the press. Newspapers, for example, reported on shockingly draconian German legal judgments, Nazi religious repression, and the surveillance and censorship practices of German propaganda authorities.[88]

None of these stories made it onto the U.S. national airwaves. Nor did CBS or NBC report the anti-Nazi protests briefly disrupting Olympic torch-relay ceremonies in Vienna and Prague—news the press deemed worthy of publication—even when they produced live broadcasts from those cities.[89] When U.S. newspapers reported on the illnesses suffered by U.S. athletes in cold and rainy Berlin, the radio networks countered with correctives. "Contrary of some reports that have been sent out," Bill Slater told an NBC audience a few days before the opening ceremony, "the American team is in excellent condition and I talked that over with Jackie Weber, the trainer, today."[90]

Part of this hesitancy to report critical, controversial, or negative news must be attributed to the relative underdevelopment of U.S. broadcast journalism in 1936. Conflict between the U.S. newspaper and radio industries erupted in the early 1930s in what later became known as the "Press–Radio War." The tension between the old and the new media intensified significantly when the Depression decimated advertising revenue. Executives from both industries met in New York City in December 1933 to settle their differences about the future of news distribution. The resulting agreement, called the Biltmore Agreement after the hotel in which it was signed, severely hampered the growth of independent broadcast journalism. The networks agreed to restrictions on both newsgathering and programming in order to benefit from increased publicity offered by the newspaper industry. Although the radio networks would soon violate the Biltmore Agreement's provisions, the contract served to restrict the growth and independence of broadcast journalism throughout the mid-1930s. Radio news was often produced, owned, and even censored by commercial sponsors who preferred goodwill to controversy.[91]

Attempts to bat down negative Olympic news started before the games opened and continued throughout the festival. The CBS and NBC microphones were regularly turned over to authorities seeking to redress criticism in the press. When Jesse Owens's frustration with the U.S. Olympic Committee was revealed in the newspapers, for example, neither CBS nor NBC aired his complaints. NBC, however, turned over a fifteen-minute program to Avery Brundage to publicly rebut Owens's charges.[92] When a jury of appeal revoked the Peruvian soccer team's 4–2 victory over Austria under specious circumstances, and the entire Peruvian Olympic team left Berlin in protest, Bill Henry read the Olympic committee's official ruling without once detailing the Peruvians' specific objections. "It's too bad that the Peruvians have withdrawn from the games, but I don't think that in the long run it will make too much difference," he concluded.[93]

The official line on any issue—as stated by the Berlin organizing committee, the International Olympic Committee, or the American Olympic

Committee—was consistently propagated on the network airwaves. Occasional controversies occurring directly within a competition, however, could neither be ignored nor downplayed. In a broadcast from Deutschland Halle wrapping up the boxing competition, Saerchinger and Henry reported allegations of injustice in medal-round judging. But the entire discussion carefully sidestepped specific accusations, and neither broadcaster, unlike the newspaper reporters, actually leveled charges. Rather, they turned over the microphone to the clearly frustrated U.S. coach Johnny Behr. "Hello radio friends in America," Behr began. "This is a sad story for me to tell." He then reported that the U.S. boxers had underperformed, winning but one silver and one bronze. "I do not wish to offer an alibi, but the decisions were off-color. In fact, the worst that I have seen in my twenty-five years as a boxing official—both here and abroad [*sic*]," he continued. In particular, the decision to award Italian Ulderico Sergo the gold medal over Jackie Wilson of the United States, Behr claimed, stunned everyone present. Even Sergo's Italian coaches congratulated Wilson on his "victory" immediately after the match, he noted bitterly. Behr announced that fifteen nations would be withdrawing from the International Boxing Federation to create a new organization designed to remedy the injustice occurring in Berlin. "The strange thing is that these games are to create goodwill. They have done anything but that," Behr continued. "Three of our boys had their men on the canvas at least twice—for long counts—and they still lost the decisions! I will sure be glad to get [back] to the land of fair play, my home, the USA. Goodnight, friends." Bill Henry immediately jumped in. "This is not a criticism of a country, but [the federation's] idea of judging," he interjected. "I'm not blaming any one country," Behr clarified, "I'm blaming more than anything else the inefficiency of the judges who were handling the bouts." Henry concluded by telling the audience that Behr "had no ambition to come to the microphone this evening and deliver an awful yelp about the boxing situation," but CBS needed him to "make some kind of a statement in order that you might have the angle of the American boxers with regard to the boxing here at the Olympic Games."[94]

It should be noted that CBS and NBC aired discussion, and criticism, of Nazi Germany during the Berlin Olympic Games. But such programs originated within the United States, or outside Germany, and contrasted sharply with the laudatory programs from Berlin. These other programs raised significant issues about the games, and Nazi Germany, in schedule locations often near or adjacent to Olympic reports. For example, on 2 August 1936—the day after the opening ceremonies—NBC's University of Chicago Round Table aired discussion of international sportsmanship in a time slot immediately abutting Olympic coverage, though one radio critic found the discussants uninformed and the program uninteresting.[95] NBC scheduled a talk by Rabbi Stephen Wise, direct from Geneva, Switzerland, on 8 August, in another time period directly bordering Olympic coverage. Rabbi Wise's address and the Olympic coverage were never cross-referenced by NBC's announcers, but the juxtaposition of two programs centered thematically on Nazi Germany was unmistakable. Wise made the linkage even more explicit by warning that Hitlerism was the attempt to "eradicate and destroy the Jews of the world." Wise further explained that the establishment of the World Jewish Congress, for which he had traveled to Geneva, was primarily an attempt to arouse "the conscience of mankind" to Hitler's destructive and vindictive threat to global humanity.[96]

Unfortunately, the lack of program ratings or other audience metrics prevents us from precisely measuring the communicative impact of Rabbi Wise's talk. Whether an average NBC listener could detect the subtle and unstated thematic linkage between the Olympic Games and the violence of the Nazi regime as described by Rabbi Wise is simply unknowable. But what can be reconstructed, to some extent, by reference to memoirs, contemporaneous journalism, letters, and other historical materials, is the experience of listening to the Berlin Games on the radio.

The thrill of listening to CBS's Olympic broadcasts, wrote one United Press reporter, was the excitement of participating in "sports history as it is written."[97] Listeners were clearly conscious of their role as both witnesses to, and participants in, historic occurrences. The technological innovations ensuring that broadcasts would be heard with remarkable fidelity tightly linked sportscasters and listeners. Through such aural cues as the stadium's roar, or the remarks made by friends and family gathered around the radio, listeners could easily imagine themselves within a global community of simultaneous participation. The programs from Berlin were "excellent," wrote one British radio critic, who then attempted to describe this participatory excitement:

> Apart from the commentary the listener gets plenty of extraneous interest. He will be listening avidly for the start of a race when a roar of cheering rises, and he gathers that some notability has just arrived or some athlete is being crowned. He wonders what those who are just getting on their marks think of it; he is full of excitement himself; he must feel glad to hear Olympic records being broken day by day while he sits in the armchair collecting thrills.[98]

So many of the broadcasts from Berlin proved powerfully stirring that listeners recalled feelings associated with them for decades. In particular, broadcasts featuring Jesse Owens—in England, Germany, and the United States—would be referenced by listeners for years to come. Radio's intimacy made audiences of millions develop seemingly personal links to Owens and others who appeared personable and approachable on the airwaves. Athletes relished their new-found celebrity, and print journalists enjoyed chronicling their experiences with the new medium. The radio connections seemed at once global and personal, instantaneous and historic.

Sportswriter John Tunis would later capture this listening experience in his young-adult bestseller, *The Duke Decides*. Set in Berlin during the games, one chapter tells the fictional story of James "Duke" Wellington's gold-medal performance in the fifteen-hundred-meter race by matching Wellington's thoughts in the stadium during the race with his family's experience listening to it through the radio announcer's call. The announcer's "voice, clear and sharp, went across Germany, across the wide sea, across the British Isles, across an ocean, across two thousand miles of land and into the living room of that home in Waterloo, Iowa." Listening to the games, Wellington's parents are transported to "another world" only to be interrupted because "Aunt Kate" keeps telephoning, reminding them to tune in. "She hasn't turned her radio off day and night all week," Wellington's father complained.[99] The fictional scene, and the whole chapter, effectively captures the reality of broadcast excitement. It relays the imaginative and dramatic power attracting so many listeners to Olympic broadcasts.

Critics and listeners alike noticed and remarked upon the feeling of personal intrusion they experienced in listening to the direct communication between athletes and their families through the medium of radio. Millions of listeners seemingly eavesdropped on the deeply emotional and personal links created by the microphone acting as a telephone. Most of the interviews demonstrated the athletes' recognition of addressing millions of strangers as well as their most cherished relatives. "Hello America, and particularly Fulton Missouri and all my friends," Helen Stephens began a typical interview on CBS.[100] "I want to say hello to Grandma!" were the first words spoken over the airwaves by Archie Williams after his victory in the four-hundred-meter race. *The Oakland Tribune*'s Jack Jernegan happened to be with Williams's seventy-five-year-old grandmother at that precise moment. She had "her ear glued to the radio," he wrote, and "all of his family were so excited they could hardly sit still."[101] Although most interviews appeared formulaic—and, in fact, a few seemed scripted, as athletes and coaches stumbled over words—occasional appearances of authentic emotional depth made a few interviews particularly memorable. After hearing Jesse Owens address the NBC audience on 8 August, a columnist for the *New York Amsterdam News* thought he "seemed quite homesick."[102] A few days later, Rudy Vallee and NBC surprised Owens by inviting his wife (and baby daughter) to his top-rated variety program when he connected with the Olympic champion in London for an interview. Taken aback by his wife's voice, which he heard through a feedback circuit, a subdued Owens sounded more human and less rehearsed than in his more typical appearances.[103]

The radio programs transmitting the achievements of African-American athletes thrilled and inspired millions. Senator Edward Brooke of Massachusetts later recalled his feelings. Ralph Metcalfe, Brooke recalled, "thrilled those of us who heard of his exploits on the radio . . . and made young blacks like myself proud of our race and proud of our nation."[104] "Jesse Owens blasted open the door to a world of possibilities of what I could become," remembered an African-American coal miner. "He made me believe anything was possible."[105] Many African-Americans, especially the ones in the rural South, when reminiscing about radio in the 1920s and 1930s recalled that the "radio broadcasts of Jesse Owens's 1936 Olympic performance in Berlin resulted in many celebrations. . . . Rural blacks organized picnics, musicals, and parties to celebrate the positive image of blackness presented by African American athletes."[106] Another African-American radio listener later wrote "it would be hard to overestimate the exultation in the black community" when hearing the performance of Jesse Owens in Berlin.[107]

Other contemporaneous reports and memoirs relate similar inspirational feelings generated by listening to the Berlin Games on the radio. When the "Olympic games began in August, I sat at home on pins and needles" listening to the triumphs of Jesse Owens, one young German woman later remembered. One week later, after leaving for vacation at Krumme Lanke, she "could no longer sit quietly" in her "cabin just listening to the games on the radio. I had enough money for a bus ticket. So I went straight to the stadium."[108] Another woman recalled, when a seven-year-old in the Saxony town of Dahlen, tuning into the BBC's broadcast, rather than the RRG's, to both improve her English and fully capture the thrill of Owens's victory.[109]

In the United States, the press chronicled the thrill of listeners enjoying the live events and interviews. Jessie Owens's mother, Emma Mae Owens, tuned into Berlin on a shortwave receiver to catch the broad jump. She was joined on the porch of her frame duplex cottage by Owens's sisters, brothers, nieces, and neighbors and two newspaper reporters. "Mrs. Owens sat close to the radio with her ears straining to catch every word and her nervous hands twisting a small handkerchief into a thousand wrinkles," one witness reported. Her anxiety only intensified when the broadcast cut off before Owens's final jump won the gold. Mrs. Owens had to be informed of her son's victory by telephone from a New York City newspaper minutes later.[110]

Many of the descriptions of listening to the Berlin Games emphasize the communal nature of the activity. Families, friends, and neighbors gathered around to catch the broadcasts, whether in the United States, England, Japan, or elsewhere. Like millions of Japanese, the family of Hideko Maehata stayed up all night to catch the live broadcast of Maehata's gold-medal-winning swim. "We were all nervous and our palms sweaty," remembered Maehata's cousin Tomizo Hase. Listening intensely to the famous call by Sansei Kasai, the family's emotions erupted with the announcement of Maehata's victory. "What a heavenly feeling that was; some of us even started crying in joy, saying, 'she's done great!'" recalled Hase.[111]

Berlin itself was entirely enveloped in the broadcasts. Speakers placed atop columns along the Unter den Linden, in plazas and railroad and underground stations, made the RRG broadcasts almost inescapable. People might catch the sportscast unintentionally while waiting for a bus, walking home from work, or even just sitting in cafés. In its ubiquity and popularity, the RRG's Berlin Olympic broadcasts fulfilled the communal promise and nationalistic purpose of broadcasting as envisioned by Eugen Hadamovsky and the Nazi radio administration.[112]

Radio listening was communal not only in urban areas, but also in a transnational sense. The Nazi administration defined broadcasting as a phenomenon distinguished by its nationalist characteristics, but the transnational and global scope of the radio transmissions was always an important consideration in Olympic broadcast planning. German shortwave broadcasts in English were intended to entertain and impress Americans, Australians, and the Anglophone world. The BBC was always mindful of the global reach of its shortwave Olympic transmissions as well. The experience of comparing German, British, and U.S. sportscasts delighted those few U.S. listeners with shortwave receivers capable of listening to multiple versions of the same events. Bill Ray of the *Oakland Tribune* particularly appreciated the ambient noises heard on "these direct [German shortwave] broadcasts from the Olympic Stadium." "The huge crowd makes a noise with volume that would set any Big Game crowd to shame as it is terrific," he noted. He also enjoyed contrasting Bill Slater's "American style" reports with the "very different German and British descriptions" available on shortwave.[113] "The evening short-wave transmissions from Berlin are replete with interesting sidelights 'auf Deutscher weise'," noted the *New York Times*.[114] Direct German shortwave transmissions included interesting sounds unavailable elsewhere; for example, Ray noted that at 11 p.m. every night Californians with shortwave receivers could catch the 7 a.m. "reveille bugle call that awakens the Olympiad participants in the Olympic Village." Owners of shortwave receivers could also enjoy the BBC's rebroadcast of recorded events every day.[115] U.S. radio retailers used shortwave programs to entice curious listeners into their stores. One Berkeley, California, radio store invited people to catch "live Olympic games reports . . . direct from Berlin" during a weeklong "open house" demonstration of new Philco receivers featuring automatic shortwave tuning. Roskin Distributors in Boston did the same, with the owner explaining to the *Boston Globe* that "the power of the Berlin short-wave stations has been tremendously increased . . . with the result that the program from Germany comes into American homes with room-filling volume."[116]

Ownership of shortwave receivers in the United States (and elsewhere) remained a rarity in 1936.[117] To promote distribution of RRG Olympic broadcasts more widely, German radio authorities encouraged radio stations and networks around the world to convert the RRG's shortwave signal for rebroadcast on standard AM bands. In the United States, the Federal Communications Commission still categorized shortwave rebroadcast relay as an "experimental" technology.[118] This classification prohibited commercialization of any overseas relay, but the networks were able to evade this problematic designation. For example, CBS's regular time announcements were sponsored by a watch company. "It is now five p.m., Bulova watch time," a CBS announcer would typically intone, adding "the Public Events and Special Features Department of the Columbia network brings you a transoceanic broadcast from the Olympic Games in Berlin at this time."[119] When the management of WBNX, New York, asked to rebroadcast English-language RRG Olympic programming, the Nazi government "extended permission to . . . sell any broadcasts of the games." Perhaps mindful of the FCC stricture, WBNX resold the RRG programs to local advertisers at cost. "The only added charge that WBNX is asking of advertisers is the cost of the line from . . . [RCA's control room in] Radio City to WBNX's studios, a matter of a few miles," reported *Variety*.[120]

The RRG rebroadcast on WBNX meant that listeners in New York City could tune in Berlin events, minimally, on WBNX, CBS, NBC, or the BBC. Such redundancy was not uncommon in the global context. Radio listeners in Canada, for instance, possessed multiple options for listening to the games. The Canadian Broadcasting Corporation, in summer 1936, was still in a developmental stage. Canadian listeners experienced the games primarily through the U.S. networks or rebroadcasts of international shortwave transmissions on local stations. Listeners in Toronto, for instance, could hear the BBC–CBS programs through radio station CFRB's affiliation with CBS, or they could tune in NBC affiliates in Canada or near the border, or catch the BBC or RRG shortwave rebroadcasts.[121]

U.S. broadcasts occasionally irritated Canadian listeners. Mike Rodden, the assistant sports editor of Toronto's *Globe and Mail,* listened to the CBS broadcast of the four-hundred-meter hurdles race on 4 August 1936. "The estimable Mr. Husing, now broadcasting from Berlin, Germany, is 'sold' on the idea that most of the United States athletes are in a class by themselves," Rodden wrote, and at CBS "there is nobody arising to issue any denials." Husing, he suggested, "might also pay tribute to the gallant contenders who are almost but not quite as good as their conquerors" in some events. Despite his nationalism, Rodden thought Husing "did a neat job" on the program, as "his running accounts of the races were thrilling." But Rodden remained bothered by Husing's unfamiliarity with Canadian Johnny Loaring. Loaring, a student at the University of Western Ontario, clearly caught the CBS announcer by surprise when he surged forward in the middle of the race, and Husing's ignorance about Loaring became clear in his concluding summary when he could offer nothing about the silver medalist.[122]

Much criticism in the U.S. press echoed Rodden's critique that the commentators could have prepared more effectively. "The spot news announcing by Bill Slater for NBC markedly improved as regards substance but not much in form," the *Brooklyn Daily Eagle*'s radio critic noted toward the end of the games. "He told the American listeners more of what they wanted to know and what was right before him, but not as much as he could have told." In particular, Slater, despite his "excellent voice" and knowledge of athletics, lacked "a smooth delivery and sufficient vocabulary." At times, Thomas Rice wrote, he became "wearisome tautological." Rice was surprised to catch Ted Husing on CBS "only once and that for such a short period I could not get a line on him." But he reserved his most severe criticism for the BBC's Abrahams. Abrahams, when describing the three-thousand-meter steeplechase, "did not know the runners, said so and proved it" on the air. "Many of the English announcers are admirable," Rice concluded, "but Abrahams was pretty sad."[123] Two weeks later, Rice reported that numerous readers expressed disagreement with his critique of Slater. "They boosted him to the skies" in their letters, reported the radio critic.[124]

Like Rice's correspondents, most radio critics polled by *Variety* who followed the initial broadcasts were impressed. Despite CBS's employment of Ted Husing, and its seemingly advantageous tie-in to the BBC, most early reviews favored NBC, with *Variety*'s critic describing NBC's product as "far superior."[125] Bill Slater, in particular, was often lauded. "The sports announcer you've been hearing and liking is Bill Slater," the *Oakland Tribune*'s radio columnist wrote in a short biography of the commentator published immediately after the opening ceremony.[126] Despite such initial attention on Slater, *Variety* concluded that most radio critics agreed that both Henry and Slater were "rated as giving nifty accounts of themselves in the various pickups." The one exception to this generally positive press was César Saerchinger, who, *Variety* noted, "overtalks his comments and impresses little from the expert angle."[127]

An issue facing the CBS team of Saerchinger, Husing, and Henry was the consciousness of cross-border or transnational address in several broadcasts. Knowing that many of their programs would be relayed in Great Britain and across the British Empire clearly affected the tone, content, and delivery of their sportscasts. Such transnational production was a hallmark of the Berlin Olympic Games, and it was not limited to the BBC–CBS partnership, or links between U.S. sportscasters and the Canadian audience. Max Jordan, in a summary program after the closing ceremonies, reported that Argentina's Radio Prieto scheduled the most shortwave relays of any broadcasting organization (NBC was second).[128] Based in Buenos Aires, Radio Prieto was a successful commercial station that by 1934 radiated a diverse programming schedule through South America's most powerful signal. It pioneered transoceanic sports relays, starting with the 1928 Amsterdam Olympics, and upon Hitler's assumption of power began offering a weekly "German Hour" to foster closer ties with the RRG. The "German Hour" brought Nazi notables, including Rudolf Hess, to the microphone to address German residents in Argentina. One of those German descendants, Alfredo Schroeder, was a partner in Radio Prieto. Schroeder traveled to Berlin where he "personally oversaw the Radio Prieto broadcasts of the 1936 Berlin Olympics." He hired popular sports reporter Alfredo Aróstegui to cover the games, but from the start Schroeder, Aróstegui, and their RRG partners planned on broadcasts extending beyond Argentina's borders. Occasionally the Peruvian and Paraguayan national broadcast systems linked directly into Radio Prieto's feeds to deliver live programs back to their listeners.[129]

For all the global, intercontinental, and transnational reach of the Berlin broadcasts, the one nation explicitly excluded from the games as both participant and broadcaster was the Soviet Union. The outbreak of the Spanish Civil War, mere days before the games opened, heightened the already considerable enmity between the Fascist and Bolshevik regimes.[130] In speeches and publications, Eugen Hadamovsky had regularly contrasted what he termed the "Salon Bolsheviks" of the Weimer Republic's radio administration with National Socialism's more authentically democratic ("völkisch") approach to broadcasting.[131] Soviet radio, he argued, represented a dangerous contagion in Nazi Germany. Though listening to the BBC had not been outlawed in Germany, tuning in Moscow's shortwave relay could place a listener in legal jeopardy. During the Olympics, the Nazi press reported that one unlucky resident of Hamm who was caught spreading rumors gathered from Moscow radio was convicted and sentenced to a year in jail.[132]

The first week of competition had presented the U.S. listening audience with indelible memories. Track-and-field victories by Owens, Stephens, and decathlete Glenn Morris radiated a celebratory atmosphere on the national airwaves. Interviews were notably joyful and occasionally humorous. But during the second week athletes from the United States began meeting new challenges—in the swimming pool, boxing ring, and elsewhere—causing consternation and frustration. In that week the Berlin programs devolved from celebratory to apologetic as Germany surpassed the United States atop the medal count. "I think that every credit and every honor should be given to Germany for developing a marvelous all-around team," Bill Henry told the CBS audience the night before the closing ceremony. "They have won their medals in a wide variety of sports and shown themselves to be a fine sporting nation." But he concluded his broadcast by reminding listeners that the "laws and rules of the Olympic Games . . . officially prohibit national standings . . . of any kind."[133] The U.S. announcers began to sound more strained and hoarse over the air in the second week, as the cold and rainy weather and exhausting work schedule clearly wore them down. The soldiers and uniformed civilians everywhere, the constant surveillance, and the foreboding sense of war's inevitability also began to sour the experience for U.S. reporters.[134]

Bill Slater had had enough. He ran into problems with NBC management back in New York City despite the good press his performances garnered. The precise source of this tension was never clarified. It was rumored, later, that Slater's difficulties stemmed from an argument over his expense accounting in Berlin. But NBC management also criticized his broadcasts by cable, and Slater did himself no favors by unfavorably comparing U.S. to German broadcasting in the pages of a popular German radio magazine. He also got scooped by Bill Henry, who enjoyed a close relationship to the American Olympic Committee, on several stories surrounding Jesse Owens's future and tour of Europe after the games concluded.[135] Slater's troubles may also have simply been the result of an ongoing personality conflict with John Royal, his NBC boss. "Both were headstrong men, but Royal was the boss," Red Barber remembered.[136]

Whatever the cause, on the morning of Friday, 14 August, Slater met Max Jordan for breakfast before departing for England.[137] He wanted to broadcast the White City track-and-field meet, featuring Jesse Owens, scheduled for the following afternoon. Going over the last few production details with Jordan,

Slater felt relieved to depart the Nazi capital. He left the rowing finals later that evening—an important broadcast that had been widely promoted—in the hands of Jordan and Dietze.

Slater's decision to skip the Grünau regatta had profound ramifications for both his career and NBC's production of the Berlin Games. The rowing finals at Grünau, and their live broadcast to the United States, would become one of the most memorable events to occur in Berlin, and over the U.S. airwaves, in 1936.

CHAPTER 5

Six Minutes in Grünau

The Olympic Regatta as the High Spot
of the Berlin Games

On Friday, 14 August, Max Jordan met Bill Slater at a café in Berlin's Lehrter Bahnhof to send him off to London. Jordan later remembered Slater "had seen enough of the 'hidden' Germany to discount all the Nazi flag-waving and Hitler-cheering he had gone through at the Olympic Games." "Why don't they revolt? We wouldn't stand for all this browbeating and bullying in America. I know that. Why do they stand for it here?" Slater asked. At that moment, three armed Nazi guards sat down at the next table. The whole café quieted. "It was as though a chill had come over those present," Jordan remembered. "In a nutshell, there was the answer to Bill's question."[1]

Back in New York City, NBC management had expected Slater to stay in Germany to broadcast the highly anticipated Grünau regatta. Press releases publicizing Slater's live coverage had been distributed, and his name appeared in newspapers around the United States promoting the broadcast. But Slater had had enough of Germany and preferred to call the next day's track meet in London, leaving the rowing to Jordan and Roderich Dietze. His last-minute decision scrambled the final days of NBC's Berlin coverage, offering an advantage to CBS. The junior network had begun promoting live coverage from Grünau even before the Olympics opened by prominently featuring rowing in press releases about the games.[2]

Widespread newspaper coverage created additional publicity for the regatta and further primed the audience for the broadcast. The popularity of

"Washington Crew Carries Hopes of America": The *Seattle Daily Times* notes millions of Americans will be listening to the live radio broadcast of the Olympic rowing final on 14 August 1936.

intercollegiate racing made rowing one of the few Olympic events with guaranteed audience interest once Jesse Owens left Berlin. CBS and NBC executives could presume listener familiarity with Al Ulbrickson and the Husky crew. The oarsmen's health, their practice rows, and the coach's thoughts about the regatta were featured regularly on the nation's sports pages. On the day the regatta opened with scull and small-boat racing on 11 August, *Chicago Tribune* readers were greeted by a large advertisement featuring Ulbrickson in the sports section. General Foods had recently inaugurated a sports-themed marketing campaign to introduce "Huskies," a new whole-wheat-flake breakfast cereal. Advertisements featured star athletes (such as Lou Gehrig of the New York Yankees) holding a spoon while offering praise for the healthy and tasty breakfast treat. "My vote goes to Huskies!" the text above a grinning Al Ulbrickson read. Next to Ulbrickson an illustration of the "University of Washington HUSKIES crew, this year's OLYMPIC crew" was depicted with the rowers finishing a stroke. (The exaggerated layback pictured, however, was more typical of the Glendon style than the Conibear stroke the crew actually used.)

The rowing finals at Grünau also were anticipated and promoted widely in Argentina, Germany, Italy, England, and elsewhere.[3] Broadcast preparations were extensive. The Germans had originally installed just seven speaker

On 11 August 1936—the first day of the Olympic regatta—this advertisement for Huskies Cereal featuring Coach Al Ulbrickson and the University of Washington crew appeared in the *Chicago Tribune*.

platforms for foreign broadcasters, but they quickly found that insufficient. Additional platforms were erected on top of the grandstand, but even then the demand for transmission facilities exceeded supply. During the regatta, the RRG sent its "flying broadcasting squad" out to the racecourse to accommodate the commentators. The supplemental vans composing the squad were "drawn together from all over the Reich" and carried shortwave relay transmitters. They guaranteed live broadcast capability for all the organizations seeking to transmit. Additional mobile recording facilities also were made available.[4]

The competing teams continued their training patterns as broadcast preparations were finalized. At the police barracks in Köpenick, Washington's oarsmen settled into their regimen soon after the opening ceremonies. Despite Ulbrickson's attempts to establish routines in eating, sleeping, and training, the oarsmen found occasional time to enjoy themselves. "One Sunday when we were not rowing we went in and saw some really great track and field events," Gordon Adam recalled. "We saw the 1,500 meters and one of the relay races at the stadium." To further break the monotony, the oarsmen played tricks on each other, and occasionally on their German hosts. A group of German police trainees lived one floor above the U.S. crew, and they often awoke the Washington oarsmen with their antics late at night. Fed up with the noise, one night Moch called together his crew and hatched a plan. They found two five-gallon buckets and filled them with water. The crew crowded around the window directly above the school's main entrance. When the police trainees returned ("rowdy again"), Moch hissed "Now!" His teammates poured the water down and dashed madly back to their rooms. They closed their doors and "hopped back into bed" only to hear a racket in the hallway a few minutes later. When Moch stepped out into the hallway, he saw the German officers "soaking wet, running up and down the corridor." They were furious, yelling in German, but soon left their U.S. neighbors and returned to their quarters.[5]

Interaction with their fellow U.S. oarsmen—the scullers and small-boat rowers—was limited. Though the entire squad bunked at the Police Training School, the Washington crew had its own army bus equipped with a sergeant as driver and a supervising lieutenant. "They were at our beck and call when we wanted to go row, which we did usually twice a day. They took us to Grünau and then brought us back," Gordon Adam recalled.[6] The one squad that did occasionally train with Washington was the four-with-coxswain from Riverside Boat Club in Boston. Made up of current and former Harvard rowers, the Riverside four had defeated four oarsmen from the University of Washington's junior varsity for the right to represent the United States. The Riverside oarsmen often shared with the Huskies the bus to the course, and George Pocock, Al Ulbrickson, and

"Monk" Terry, Riverside's coach, had become friends on the trip across the Atlantic. They shared observations about each other's crews during practices, and Ulbrickson eventually invited Terry to have the crews practice together. "They thought we were a very fine four," remembered Riverside's Edward Bennett. Ulbrickson used the Riverside boat as a "stalking horse for Washington's eight" during practice. The four would wait at the thousand-meter mark on the racecourse, and Terry would signal them to start racing a few seconds before the Washington crew drew astern. The Riverside and Washington shells would then battle over the last thousand meters of the racecourse. The exercise was designed to accustom the Huskies to rowing from behind in a short sprint race. The practices helped the Huskies gain closing speed and the confidence to barrel through an opponent as the finish line drew near. The problem, for both squads, was that the Riverside crew often outperformed the Huskies, even though they never actually won. By simply staying close to the world's fastest crew for three minutes, Riverside's rowers grew complacent. The practices "ruined us," Bennett remembered. "Overconfidence. We were walking on air and could only go downhill" when faced with adversity in a race. A fourth-place finish in their second heat eliminated Riverside from medal contention.[7]

The Huskies also began interacting with their competition in the days leading up to the regatta. Both in the shell bays, and back at the police barracks, mingling became unavoidable. "The German crew was fine," Moch recalled:

> I remember going down to the shell house to take the boat apart, to take the riggers off, and the German coxswain was there. He couldn't speak any English, and I couldn't speak any German, but we were kind of looking at each other's boat, and pointing at it, and so forth, and then he stopped when we got to our boat, down near where the coxswain sits, and he pointed. He saw that piece of iron bark alongside of me, alongside of the coxswain, that I used to hammer on with the dowels, and he looked at that, and he pointed to the bark and he pointed to the dowel and he said, "Good," "Sur Good." He could hear those knockers clear across the racecourse. We got along fine with the men. No problem at all.[8]

One memorable moment of tension arose during those practice weeks. Coming in from a row, Moch discovered the German shell stowed on the Huskies' rack in the shell bay. Angered, he had his oarsmen pick up the German boat and rest it on slings outside the boathouse. "Not a word was ever said about it," but the slight made the Huskies irate. "The Americans' impression was that German oarsmen were good on the water but arrogant off it," wrote rowing historian Christopher Dodd.[9]

The Huskies were not alone in finding the German crews arrogant. German arrogance annoyed the French oarsmen as well. Coxswain Noël Vandernotte recalled that for himself and his teammates, Germany's new emphasis on athletic success incited tension rather than collegiality around the boathouse. In particular, the French oarsmen resented the obvious professionalism of the Germans. "What could we do, we rowers, mere amateurs, facing that German armada?" he later remembered thinking. "Those Reich rowers were state athletes.... How do you compete with German rowers practicing every day from morning to evening?" Vandernotte had heard a rumor that the German Reich "increased the budget dedicated to the sport [of rowing] from five million marks to one hundred million marks" since the Nazis came to power.[10] Watching the behavior of the Germans and Italians on and off the water, Ulbrickson and Pocock shared Vandernotte's thoughts. "It didn't take us long to realize we were competing against governments," Pocock recalled.[11]

As racing neared, each crew sized up their opponents. "Everyone was friendly," recalled one British oarsman, who watched as the Italian and U.S. crews occasionally played to the media. Newsreel cameras, photographers, and reporters descended on the rowing venue, and the Italian crew began wearing "scarfs [sic] on their heads like pirates." One afternoon the Washington rowers donned Indian-feather headdresses, and an image of Moch, George Hunt, John White, and Joe Rantz was published widely.[12]

The Japanese eight, from Tokyo Imperial University, were impressed by the size and strength of the German, Italian, U.S., and Australian oarsmen. Upon his return to Tokyo, oarsman Yoshitoru Suzuki told the press his squad was "pitted against insurmountable odds" because of the "physical advantages of the other oarsmen." He estimated that the competition was, on average, "50 pounds heavier and five inches taller than" his crew.[13] Suzuki's squad was the most distinctive at Grünau. Although they were smaller, their equipment and rigging were scaled to match their size. In particular, their oars were significantly shorter—even shorter than would be appropriate for a Western crew of the same height. The reason for the short oars soon became apparent on the water. *New York Times* columnist Arthur Daley was standing near Al Ulbrickson one day as the Japanese cruised up the river. "Wait until you get a look at the Jap boat," Ulbrickson told Daley, smiling. "They try to hit 40 or 50 all the time, rowing furiously and getting nowhere." They reminded him of a duck, Ulbrickson continued, flapping its wings furiously on a lake's surface, unable to get aloft.[14] The Japanese squad unveiled its unorthodox high-rating strategy in the Marlowe-on-Thames and Royal Henley regattas earlier that summer. The goal, their coach explained, was to get opponents "to match the Japanese

From left: Joe Rantz, Jim McMillin, Robert Moch, John White, and George Hunt in Indian headdresses. (From the *XIth Olympic Games Berlin, 1936: Official Report*.)

shell's fast pitch with the view to wearing them out."[15] It failed in England, where the Swiss crew from Zurich decisively defeated Tokyo Imperial University in a Grand Challenge Cup race.[16]

That same Swiss crew surprised the British by winning at Henley. The oarsmen from the Zurich Rowing Club were fine technicians, having honed their stroke by sculling. Journalists watching them practice were impressed by their strength and style. "The Swiss are managing to make their presence felt here with considerable emphasis," noted the *New York Times*.[17] But the Swiss entered several oarsmen in both the eights competition and small-boat races, making them susceptible to exhaustion from competing in multiple events. Like the Swiss, the Hungarian crew looked smooth and syncopated while rowing in practice. Employing a variant of the British style, the Hungarians had surprised the rowing world by setting the Grünau course record while capturing the European championship earlier that summer. The Australian and Japanese eights, euphemistically labeled "erratic" in one regatta preview, appeared to perform at a level below the rest of the competition.[18]

The crews most concerning to Ulbrickson were the Germans, Italians, Swiss, and British.[19] "When we saw these experienced, nationally subsidized crews from Italy and Germany, we knew it was going to be pretty tough," Gordon

Adam told an interviewer in 1988. The British Leander boat, consisting of six Cambridge and two Oxford University rowers, had compiled a mixed record that summer. They easily dispatched a strong Union Boat Club squad from Boston at Henley but then fell to the Zurich club in a surprise upset. The Swiss eight "rowed beautifully together, and were amazingly powerful. . . . The prospects of a British victory in the forthcoming Olympic eights were not improved" by such a poor showing, *The Observer* dolefully noted.[20]

Heading into the Olympic regatta, the British press questioned the Leander crew's resilience. Reversing Henley's results was "doubtful," the *Manchester Guardian* noted, because "the Swiss are exceptionally fast, even judged by Olympic standards."[21] Although the British eight contained several excellent oarsmen, including stroke Ran Laurie, between Henley and Grünau there was talk of substituting rowers and changing the lineup to increase the boat's speed.[22] Such a suggestion, barely a month before the Olympic regatta (when all other crews were settled and practicing) seemed a troubling omen for the British. Watching the Leander boat practice in Germany, however, impressed Ulbrickson. When the draw for the preliminary heats was announced, he and Pocock identified the British as their chief competition.[23] The other eights in the heat—France, Japan, and Czechoslovakia—concerned them far less.

The *Husky Clipper* regained its speed as the oarsmen began their second week of training. The colds suffered by White and Adam aboard the *Manhattan* had all but disappeared, and even Don Hume's health problems—widely reported in the newspapers—eased a bit. Hume's recovery contrasted with press reports, some of which reported a hospital admission on 29 July.[24] Bill Henry tried to dispel these rumors in a CBS broadcast on 3 August. "I'm sure that everyone will be interested to know that Don Hume . . . has completely recovered, is in good health, he is not being dragged out to the hospital as has been reported, but today he was able to row over at Grünau and will undoubtedly be able to pull a mighty strong oar for the United States," Henry reported in that night's summary program.[25] Despite Henry's assurances, Hume's lingering illness threatened the boat's speed. Ulbrickson decided to replace Hume for a few practices with Don Coy, one of the spares, but the boat did not respond well.[26] "That didn't work," Jim McMillin remembered, "the boat just didn't feel right."[27] Hume recovered a bit and soon resumed stroking the boat under the watchful eyes of Pocock and Ulbrickson.

The oarsmen soon started to look—and feel—like champions for the first time since arriving in Germany. The day after Henry's broadcast, the Huskies turned in a 6:36 time trial while battling a slight chop and quartering headwind. They neither elevated the stroke rating nor sprinted, and Ulbrickson told the press he thought his crew had finally recaptured the form they showed in the Olympic trials.[28] He once described the racecourse on the Dahme as "smooth" and the water "light," and he knew the times would be fast when racing started. Despite the fact that the Olympic canoe and kayak competitions, occurring at the venue, complicated scheduling, practices throughout that week intensified. Traffic on the river soon became an issue, as the river's hundreds of boats barely avoided collisions. George Pocock placed a big protective rubber ball on the bow of the *Husky Clipper*. The boat continued improving, and on Friday, 7 August, they rowed a time trial in 6:09—matching the Hungarian's course record—without putting "their full steam on."[29] They looked sharp.

The practices accustomed the coaches, coxswains, and oarsmen to the idiosyncrasies of the course. It soon became clear that the inside lanes (numbers 1 and 2) possessed a distinct advantage. Protected by the promontory and hillock, boats racing up the course in those two lanes enjoyed calmer water and less wind than those relegated to the outside lanes. Olympic officials and coaches from Canada, Great Britain, the United States, and Australia met with the German organizers to discuss the problem as the regatta drew near. On 5 August the Anglophone teams officially protested the plan to race six boats across when such an obvious discrepancy existed, but the protest was immediately dismissed. Bob Hunter, the Canadian coach, "was particularly bitter" about his lane assignment in the preliminary heat. Not only would his oarsmen battle Italians, Hungarians, Australians, and Brazilians, but they would be forced to do so while rowing through more difficult conditions. "We are drawn in lane five, the outside lane," Hunter complained to the *Toronto Globe and Mail*. "On this course the difference between lane one and lane five is several boats' lengths because of the prevailing sidewind," he explained. "Crews of the three inside lanes have an immense advantage," he continued, "because they will be protected from the wind over three-quarters of the course." The British, U.S., Canadian, and Australian officials all "held out for a draw that would bring together only four boats in each heat, but got nowhere in the committee room."[30]

Concerns about the course and lane assignments were eased for the Huskies by the relative weakness of their preliminary heat. Only England represented a significant challenge, and in the boathouse before the race, Ulbrickson told Moch to monitor the British closely. The balancing act—just as it was back in Princeton, and Poughkeepsie before that—would be to keep the stroke rating steady and low in the first half of the race without letting the British take too large a lead. Ulbrickson told Moch not to worry about the other crews, even if they jumped out to early leads. It was the British who required close watching.

The Berlin regatta, with its large number of participants and racecourse allowing six boats to race simultaneously, was the most challenging Olympic rowing championship up to that time. Never had the eight-oared rowing field been so strong. Only the three winners in the preliminary heats passed through to the finals, earning a day to rest. Losers were relegated to new heats contested on Thursday, 13 August. The three winners of these *repêchage,* or second-chance, heats would then join the three earlier victors to contest the medal race. The six-lane racecourse, combined with the challenging racing schedule, the uneven racing conditions, and the large number of competing teams, made the Grünau regatta a daunting test. Grantland Rice offered the consensus of the U.S. sportswriters when he wrote that Washington faced "the hardest fight any American crew has ever faced."[31]

Just before racing began, Bob Moch circulated among the crews in an attempt to bring an old U.S. rowing custom to the Olympics. Dating back to the nineteenth century, U.S. oarsmen traditionally bet their shirts on the outcome of races. In championship regattas, victors would receive shirts from each loser (the victorious stroke would receive a shirt from each losing stroke, the winning coxswain would receive a shirt from each losing coxswain, etc.).[32] Rowing shirts, in U.S. intercollegiate crew, continue to represent victory to the present time. This traditional wager is so old that it predates the establishment, in 1906, of the Intercollegiate Athletic Association of the United States, the forerunner of the National Collegiate Athletic Association (NCAA). The NCAA's prohibition of athletes betting on their own contests (NCAA bylaw 10.3) contains an exception for "long-standing demonstrated tradition in a particular sport" inserted specifically to recognize the "exchanging of shirts in the sport of rowing."[33]

The tradition, however, was limited to the United States, and most of the athletes Moch approached in Germany were dismissive. "The Germans were the only crew that complied with the American custom," the *New Yorker's* Eugene Kinkead wrote. "The English said they didn't want to, and after trying to get the idea of rowing for shirts across to the coxswains of the Hungarian, Brazilian, Japanese, and other foreign crews, Bob Moch . . . decided to let the whole thing drop."[34] Aside from difficulties in translation, Moch's attempts likely failed because Washington's oarsmen preferred racing in dingy and stained workout shirts rather than Olympic uniforms. Dating back to their season-opening victory in Seattle, each oarsman wore his same preferred grimy shirt—or no shirt, as during the Olympic trials—on race day. Even the majesty of the Olympics could not override their superstition. The Husky oarsmen went to the starting line wearing dirty, mismatched shirts in both their Olympic races.[35]

"Out in Grünau, on the Havel Lakes, they are getting the boats ready for rowing tomorrow," César Saerchinger told the CBS audience the night before the regatta opened. Crew racing could not start soon enough. Henry and Saerchinger had spent several days chronicling German victories, while the U.S. team fell behind the Germans in the medal standings. Athletes from the United States were underperforming in several sports, making reporting the results a dispiriting exercise. "There are some forty nations that are broadcasting reports of the Games," Bill Henry told the audience, "and tonight, I imagine that most of them have more encouraging reports to give than I have for the United States, because our American teams have not had the best of luck today."[36] Rowing's popularity, and the strength of the Washington crew, promised U.S. listeners some relief from the roll of bad news.

The first day of the regatta did not go well for the Americans. The initial results, in sculling and small-boat racing, were dismal.[37] "We have work here for a man who is accustomed to burials at sea," joked Henry. "It looks as though the American hopes in the aquatic events are not as high as they might be. We had competition today in two or three events at Grünau, which was the start of the rowing competition, and the Americans have not done very well."[38] The biggest surprise for the U.S. oarsmen were the Germans. Despite a traditionally middling Olympic history, the German navy surprised everyone when the regatta began. "Our previous opinion of German oarsmen was that the majority were mediocre," wrote Henry Penn Burke, chairman of the American Rowing Committee, "and inclined to be overweight."[39]

Going into the preliminary heat on 12 August, Al Ulbrickson was asked about his strategy. The winner of each preliminary heat would earn a day of rest, with each of the other crews racing in *repêchage* heats the following day. Only the winner of those second-chance heats would meet the three victors in the preliminary races in the finals. "We'll take no chances," he told the press. "We intend to shoot the works and win the heat, thus gain an extra day's rest before Friday's final. The boys have satisfied me they have regained their condition and are rowing as well as when they won the final tryout."[40] The race appearing most competitive on the first day included the Italian, Hungarian, Brazilian, and Canadian crews. Only the Brazilians were given little chance. In the third heat, the Germans and Swiss were expected to battle while leaving the Yugoslavs and Danes behind.[41]

The German crowds were ready for racing. Arriving early in Grünau, they filled the grandstand, milled around the promenade, munched on pretzels and quaffed beers, and prepared to cheer on their oarsmen. The atmosphere was festive, and soon the crowd began the organized chanting and cheering that resounded across venues during the last week of the games. Originally, members of the organizing committee had been bothered by the lack of any distinguishable cheers from the stadium's enormous crowds. The loudest and most distinct chant, much to their dismay, celebrated a U.S. competitor. "You could hear the chant, through the stands, of thousands of people, raising their voices and repeating in unison: 'Owv-ens!, Owv-ens!' meaning 'Owens.' The W sounded like a V, of course, in German," remembered Marty Glickman. "There was this kind of massed, unrehearsed cheering for Jesse Owens. I think Hitler was enormously embarrassed by it," Glickman recalled.[42] To remedy this lack of a "spontaneous yell for German athletes," the journal *SportBlatt* solicited reader suggestions. The most popular submissions included *"Deutschland! Deutschland! Heil! Heil! Heil!"* and *"Deutsch-Eagle, fliegen zum Sieg!"* ("German eagle, fly to victory!") or *"Alle für in Deutschland Ehre!"* ("All for Germany's Honor!").[43] The most popular chant, which soon erupted at the aquatic stadium in rhythm with swimmers' strokes, was a shortened version of the top suggestion. It was adaptable to the rhythm of the rowing stroke as well, and beginning on the first day of racing, as German boats closed on the finish line, great roars of *Deutsch*-Land! *Deutsch*-Land! rained down upon the racecourse and echoed across the water.

After three long weeks of practice, the Huskies were ready. In the final days, Ulbrickson eased off the length of their workouts and tapered his demands. The boat mostly worked on starting and sprinting short intervals. On 12 August, when Moch called out "Hands on!" the oarsmen stopped their small talk, grabbed the *Husky Clipper*, and swung it over their heads. They gently placed the shell in the water, fastened their oars in the oarlocks, carefully took their seats, and tied their feet to the stretchers. Pushing off the dock, they paddled down the river. Ulbrickson walked back up the dock and on to the bank, making his way up to the boathouse porch from where he could scan down the racecourse. The grandstand was not full, but the twenty-five thousand people in attendance made a terrific noise with each earlier race.[44]

The atmosphere in Grünau, wrote the *New York Times*'s Frederick Birchall, was oddly British. "There is an English Derby touch to the [Olympic] rowing," he wrote, noting that "the crowd mills around in front of the stands much in the fashion of the horse-racing addicts who gather around the stands and rails at Epsom." This patina of British sports culture extended even to fashion. "English boating caps are also prominent at Grünau," Birchall wrote, "but instead of John Bull features beneath them they cover heads exceedingly Germanic."[45] The grandstands and promenade contained several loudspeaker towers rigged to relay the shortwave call of the race as it proceeded up the course. A newly designed crystal microphone, waterproofed by encasement with its preampli-fier in sponge rubber, guaranteed quality race calls from the motor launches following the action up the river.[46]

The first day of racing in Grünau set patterns repeated each ensuing day. The most vexing issue, aside from being assigned to unprotected lanes, con-cerned the starting commands. Using a hand-held megaphone, the official starter, standing on a platform above a large covered pontoon, would yell out the French commands. But in sweeping his megaphone across the six lanes, the oarsmen and coxswains in the outside lanes found it difficult to hear. On the first day of the regatta, the Riverside Boat Club four was left behind as the French, Yugoslav, and Polish shells rocketed off the line. "The referee's 'are you ready?-go!' sounded so much like one word the U.S. oarsmen were left holding their oars while their rivals jumped off," the *Boston Globe* reported. The Riverside crew never recovered from the horrible start.[47]

Shortly after 5:15 p.m. local time, on Wednesday, 12 August 1936, the Huskies started competing in the 1936 Berlin Olympic Games. Despite being warned about the problematic starting commands, the crew was caught fumbling at the start. They were last off the line as the other shells burst forth on the command "*Départe!*"[48] Two oars washed out by pushing whitewater on the first stroke, slowing the boat. This maladroit start was magnified by the electrifying blasts of the Japanese crew, which flew off the line at an unbelievable fifty strokes per minute. Although the other boats settled to a racing pace of approximately 36 strokes per minute about two hundred meters in, the Japanese kept splash-ing away. They were still ahead at the five-hundred-meter-mark, pounding furiously at 46 strokes per minute. At eight hundred meters, the Japanese led but were clearly tiring. The Leander crew then made its first move.[49] Moch, mindful of the shifting dynamic, called forth a move to remain in contact with the British as both boats passed the collapsing Japanese shell. The *Husky Clip-per* was running smoothly, and the British—despite rapidly moving out from the Japanese—added little to their lead as the crews all swarmed toward the midway point. Moch had earlier decided to drop the stroke rate, first from 38 to 36 strokes per minute, and then, when the British shell failed to open more space, down to 34 strokes per minute. Closing in on the fifteen-hundred-meter mark, the Czech, French, and Japanese boats had all faded. "Great Britain took the lead, we were probably half a length behind most of the way, but we would row a little harder, take a couple of big tens, maybe a big twenty [strokes], and force them to row harder," remembered Moch.[50]

Moving into the last quarter of the race, this pressuring strategy seemed to be working. Washington understroked the British eight but continually applied pressure with small bursts of power. Finally, the Huskies raised their stroke rating and gained a few seats. Much to their surprise, however, the British countered effectively. "All of our races . . . we just made up our minds to sprint the last 500 meters," Jim McMillin recalled, "and we didn't have any trouble going by the opposition. This time, Great Britain didn't come back. And they didn't come back. And they didn't come back." The Leander crew parried every challenge. With little time left in the race, both boats raised their stroke ratings and started flying. The gap between the two leaders and the three trailing boats widened with each stroke. Finally, with "maybe 300 meters to go, we raised the stroke and passed them," Moch recalled, but the British eight "just busted their fannies to win that boat race." The British eight clawed back at the U.S. eight, but it was too late. Now rowing 42 strokes per minute, the *Husky Clipper*'s bow jumped with each rip of the oar and the shell moved like an "express train, crushing England." The finish line, with its big ZIEL sign, loomed over both boats as they raced past. In the last several strokes the *Husky Clipper* stretched a tiny lead into about half a boat length. Remarkably, both boats plowed across the line maintaining their synchronicity and discipline. "It was probably the most perfect race we ever rowed," Moch recalled. Watching from the shore, Ulbrickson silently counted out twenty-one strokes in the final thirty seconds. That 42 stroke rate was "the highest beat they ever had rowed."[51]

The climactic duel punished both crews. Crossing the line, the oarsmen in both shells doubled over, recoiling in pain. Don Hume started to heave and then closed his eyes and collapsed over his oar. Bob Moch, just a few feet from Hume's face, could not tell whether Hume had completely lost consciousness. Hume "slumped and looked to be just about 'out'," reported the Associated Press, "but braced after [Moch] . . . doused him with water." Hume responded by opening his eyes but otherwise showed no emotion or movement. The oarsmen gingerly took up their oars, and the remaining crowd of about ten thousand spectators "cheered Washington as the crew paddled from the finish to its boat house."[52]

The race had gone precisely according to plan, according to Ulbrickson, though there was one surprise: "the time was much faster than we thought would be necessary." "I couldn't ask for a better rowed race," he concluded before turning and heading back toward the dock with George Pocock. But when a United Press reporter caught up with him, Ulbrickson admitted the race had been "too close for comfort." "When they are that close, I'm glad when they're over," he said.[53] The assembled coaches and officials in the rowing community knew they had witnessed a fantastic finish to an excellent race. But the significance of the contest emerged only when the times were announced. Washington won in 6:00.8, with the British clocking in at 6:02.1.[54]

Six minutes and eight-tenths of one second: the Huskies had rowed the fastest (non-wind-aided) time in history. They had achieved the universal goal of a six-minute sprint race—something akin, in 1936, to the four-minute running mile. Rowing two thousand meters in six minutes required perfect synchronization and maximum physical force. Everything had to click perfectly. It necessitated the best equipment, oarsmen applying flawless technique, and tight, strict rhythm. Washington won in the fastest time ever rowed at the Olympic Games, beating California's 6:03.2 in Los Angeles. It was easily the fastest race rowed on the Grünau course, eclipsing the record of 6:09.0 set by the Hungarians. Six minutes for two thousand meters was "unheard of," wrote Royal Brougham. It "shattered nearly every 2,000-meter record."[55]

After Ulbrickson greeted the rowers, checked on Hume, and ensured the *Husky Clipper* was safely stowed, he addressed the reporters waiting alongside the boathouse. Hume "said he felt fine before the race," Ulbrickson reported, but he "was a mighty sick boy for a while." "We're keeping him wrapped up," he said, "and also keeping our fingers crossed." In the British camp the defeat, though dispiriting, was not completely disheartening. The Leander crew had been assembled late and rowed together less than their rivals. They had the second-fastest time on the day, easily smashing both the course and Olympic records. "Unless they feel the strain," noted *The Times* of London, "the added experience of rowing together in a serious race may have improved rather than lessened their chances."[56] Many in Grünau (including the Huskies) came away certain the Leander boat was the second-fastest in the world.

In the other heats, the Hungarians and Italians separated from the pack early and dueled down the course. Holding off a furious charge by the Italians in the last hundred meters, the Hungarians secured a spot in the finals and a day of rest. In the final preliminary, the Swiss crew and German eight, much like the Hungarians and Italians, demonstrated clear superiority over the competition by the midway mark and then traded moves through the final thousand meters. In another close finish, the Zurich club just barely beat the German Viking crew and passed through to the finals.[57]

Neither CBS nor NBC broadcast the preliminary races. But that night Bill Henry offered the CBS audience the good news from Grünau. "I'm sure that everyone will be interested to know that our oarsmen, after a rather dismal start yesterday . . . came back in pretty good shape," he said. "Our eight-oared crew from the University of Washington rowed a marvelous race today and made the finest time that has ever been made over a 2,000-meter course by an eight-oared crew, and they had to, in order to beat the English team," he reported.

> The English team, the Leander club, rowed 2,000 meters in six minutes two and one-tenth seconds, and in order to defeat them, the American team, from the University of Washington, had to row six minutes, and eight-tenths of a second, which is some fifteen or twenty seconds faster than any eight-oared crew has ever rowed that distance in the Olympic Games before. All of the rowing is excellent. Hungary won their heat in six minutes and seven seconds, and Switzerland won theirs in six minutes and eight seconds.[58]

Henry never mentioned Hume's collapse at the end of the race.

Despite his confidence, Ulbrickson knew Hume was in terrible shape. Wrapped in a blanket, shivering on the floor of the boathouse, Hume waited for the bus back to Köpenick. He was barely conscious. Later that night, his flu-like symptoms kept him dizzy, nauseated, and unable to sleep.[59] When dawn arrived on 13 August, he looked even more haggard and pale. His weight had dropped seven pounds, and his cough became pronounced as the respiratory illness settled in his chest. He went to breakfast with the crew the following morning but could not stomach any food. Ulbrickson saw his stroke and sent him back to bed. A reporter spied Hume and asked whether he would be able to row in the finals. Hume "insisted he would be all right."[60]

Ulbrickson and Pocock ruled out rowing on the day off.

At some point on 13 August, Ulbrickson was approached by Bob Hunter, the Canadian coach. "How can we beat those Limeys?" asked Hunter. "Get out front and stay there," Ulbrickson advised. It may have been gamesmanship, designed to exhaust both crews, but Hunter apparently followed Ulbrickson's suggestion. In the third and final *repêchage,* the Hamiltonians from Ontario blasted off the line and led more than half the race. The British eventually reeled them back in and moved into the lead, but not before expending far too much valuable energy. "The British had a hell of a time beating the Canadians on the second day," McMillin recalled. "They had really . . . two tough races."[61] The British won and moved on, eliminating the Canadian eight.

The race between the Canadians and British was by far the fastest *repêchage.* The Canadian squad's time would have won either of the day's two earlier contests. In the first *repêchage,* the Germans easily eliminated the Australians, Czechs, and Danes, winning by more than ten seconds. In the second race, the Italians handled the Japanese, Yugoslavs, and Brazilians without difficulty, securing their berth in the finals.[62] When the racing ended at close to 7 p.m. on

Thursday, 13 August 1936, the championship final was set. Wednesday's victors: the United States, Switzerland, and Hungary would be joined by Great Britain, Germany, and Italy in a little less than twenty-three hours.

Going into the finals, the U.S. coach and his oarsmen were primarily concerned with the British. They were aware of the other crews but felt confident that none possessed the potential speed of the Leander crew. But the U.S. crew was also mindful that the Fédération Internationale des Sociétés d'Aviron (FISA), the international rowing organization charged with supervising the racing, had elected to employ a seeding structure for each race after the preliminaries.[63] Previously, all lane assignments occurred by blind draws. In the 1936 finals, however, shells earning the fastest times in the preliminary races, the United States (lane 6) and Great Britain (lane 5), were assigned to the outside of the course, and the boat with the slowest qualifying win (Germany) would enjoy the protection of lane 1. Next to the Germans, in lane 2, were the Italians, with the Swiss and Hungarians occupying the two middle lanes. Such obvious favoritism aroused suspicion and frustration, but, like Hume's illness and the rainy, windy conditions, the U.S. team considered the unjust assignment merely another obstacle to overcome.[64]

Throughout most of the morning on Friday, 14 August 1936, torrents of rain poured down on Berlin. The storm, however, "had little or no effect upon the attendance." Thousands of spectators stood under trees and umbrellas or pulled jackets over their heads as they lined the route out to Grünau. They hoped to see the Führer and other Nazi dignitaries passing by on the way to the regatta venue. Hitler and his entourage arrived after the first race had finished, but they quickly settled into their box to witness the regatta.[65]

The racing delighted the German leaders. One after another, German scullers and small-boat oarsmen propelled their craft to victory. As each race climaxed near the finish line, the euphoric crowd resumed chants of *Deutsch-Land! Deutsch-Land!* Particularly enjoyable for the German leader was Germany's victory in the four without coxswain, because the victory snapped Great Britain's string of four successive gold medals in the event. Hitler enjoyed the races while animatedly chatting with Josef Goebbels, General Werner von Blomberg, Reich Minister of the Interior Wilhelm Frick, Reich Minister of Food and Agriculture Walther Darré, and Ambassador and former Chancellor Franz von Papen. The engrossed attention of these Nazi leaders was overshadowed, however, by the antics of rotund General Hermann Göring. "When the German crew won the two oars race," César Saerchinger told the CBS audience with a laugh, "Göring was leaning forward and holding on to the banister in front of him, pulling it back and forth as though he was rowing, so that everyone was afraid he was

In these images from a German newsreel, Adolf Hitler, Hermann Göring, and others cheer a German rowing victory, Grünau, 14 August 1936. Note radio microphone at right. (From the Steven Spielberg Film and Video Archive, United States Holocaust Memorial Museum.)

In this image from a German newsreel Adolf Hitler watches the eight-oared crew Olympic final at Grünau, 14 August 1936. (From the Steven Spielberg Film and Video Archive, United States Holocaust Memorial Museum.)

going to pull the banister off. They say it was the most jolly sight they have seen from General Göring in some time," he reported.[66]

Before the racing of the eights, the only discordant note for the German authorities occurred in the double sculls race. Germans Willi Kaidel and Joachim Pirsch held off the veteran British pair of Jack Beresford and Leslie Southwood for most of the race. But the wily British veterans remained within striking distance, and, with less than five hundred meters to go, the British scullers caught the Germans. The boats dueled until the British pulled away just before the finish line.[67] Although the U.S. networks did not broadcast the race, the tight finish made it one of the most memorable BBC and RRG broadcasts from Grünau. "They are coming closer now—they have only got 300 meters to go," the BBC commentator called out as the crowd roared. "They are just passing the 1700 meter-mark and Great Britain and Germany are even. . . . The other pairs have dropped back, . . . As they approach us now here, these two crews pass . . . dead level. . . . This is a wonderful race! Great Britain has forged ahead only a few feet! . . . Great Britain has gone on to win by about a length and a half!" The

RRG's call echoed this exciting finish. "They are even! Great Britain attacks but Germany is equal. . . . Great Britain goes ahead but now [hear] the roar of the tens of thousands here in the grandstand! They still have 500 meters to row. Who will be victorious? . . . Germany is tiring! Great Britain passes and already leads by a half-a-length. . . . They are out-rowing the Germans with long strokes. . . . Great Britain wins—one-and-one-half lengths over the Germans, three lengths back—the Poles!"[68] The victory of Southwood and Beresford occurred shortly before the CBS team came on the air, and it cheered the U.S. broadcasters who were tired of German celebrations. "We had had to stand up for the German anthem and the 'Horst Wessel' song [the Nazi Party anthem] after every event, until we were nauseated," recalled Saerchinger.[69]

The Washington oarsmen awoke earlier that morning, ate breakfast, and rested in their rooms. George Pocock caught sight of Hume that morning and conferred privately with Ulbrickson. "He won't make it, Al," Pocock quietly said. "And we can't win with seven men against eight." Waiting all morning and past noon to race was excruciating. "Time dragged on," Ulbrickson recalled. When asked how he felt, Hume gave everyone the same reply: "not so hot." Ulbrickson was on the verge of replacing his stroke when Bob Moch called the oarsmen to a meeting in Hume's room. There were very few words spoken. "We've come a long way for this one, Don," Moch said. "We don't want you to miss it. Set the pace for us, and we'll pull you through." In that moment, in that room, the oarsmen made a commitment to each other. Emotions ran high. There was a brief pause of silence. "Okay," Hume whispered. The rowers then met with Ulbrickson. The discussion did not last long. It was the normally quiet John White who spoke. "Tie him in," White said. "We'll get him across the finish line." "We told Ulbrickson . . . strap him in, we'll get him there," McMillin remembered.[70]

The Washington contingent was surprised to see a supportive face from Seattle when they finally went downstairs to board their bus. Vernon McKenzie, dean of the University of Washington's School of Journalism, had flown over that morning from London to watch their race. "I rode to the races in the bus with the crew," McKenzie later told an interviewer. Their faces betrayed anxiety and concern. The enormous crowds congesting the streets made the drive difficult, and "the boys were worked up to a pretty high pitch. They were delayed a bit by the German police in trying to get to their shell house, and this made them even more nervous," McKenzie recalled. The only oarsman seemingly immune to the pressure was Hume, who sat impassively with his eyes closed.[71] After last-minute instructions from Ulbrickson, the oarsmen scooped up the *Husky Clipper*, put it in the water, retrieved their oars and placed them in the oarlocks, and shoved off to warm up for their final race together.

At precisely six o'clock in Berlin, one o'clock in New York City, and nine in the morning in Seattle on 14 August 1936, the CBS staff announcer in New York City opened the Grünau program. "The Public Events and Special Features Department of the Columbia network brings another transoceanic broadcast from Berlin, the scene of the Olympic Games," he began in customary style. After a short pause, César Saerchinger's voice came in clearly in midsentence: "—are taking place this afternoon. It is six o'clock in the afternoon, it has been raining nearly all day, and just now it's beginning to clear up," Saerchinger intoned. "We've had a good many races so far, and most of them have been won by Germany." Saerchinger set the scene by describing the perspective from his perch atop the grandstand: "Opposite us is another grandstand with all the flags of the nations, a very gay scene and there are, in spite of the rain, out here just simply untold thousands of people, all the dignitaries of the government are here, and the excitement has been simply terrific."[72]

The rain and gray skies, Don Hume's illness, and being relegated to the least-protected lane all combined to sap some of the customary confidence in the *Husky Clipper* as they paddled to the start line. "I don't think we were

The German crew prepares to race in the Olympic final, 14 August 1936. The Italian crew can be seen in the background. (From the U.S. National Archives.)

that confident on the final day," Gordon Adam remembered. "We were running scared from start to finish, believe me."[73]

The shell pulled up to the starting pier. Each eight maneuvered into position. The shells briefly adjusted their bows to point properly down their lanes, with coxswains raising their hands to indicate that they were not fully prepared. In the *Husky Clipper* some of the oarsmen removed their warmup sweatshirts and others fiddled with their clothing. The Belgian starting official harshly warned the U.S. crew to quickly prepare to race.[74] With the boats properly pointed, each of the coxswains dropped their hands to signal readiness to the referee. Up on the grandstand, Bill Henry peered down toward the start line. "The crews are still fooling around up at the start, they have not yet started this eight-oared crew race which to the Americans is always the climax of the Olympic regatta," he told the national audience.[75]

Once again, the Washington crew flailed at the start. The official starter began his commands by looking toward the Huskies in lane six. "*Monsieurs, attention!*" he called. "We thought he was going to say something [again] to us," McMillin recalled, "so we were just sitting there." The official then swept his megaphone toward the other lanes while barking out the starting commands.

The race begins. The University of Washington crew is on the far right. The promontory and hillock protecting lanes 1 and 2 can be seen on the left. (From the U.S. National Archives.)

"*Êtes-vous prêts?*" he called out. "*Départe!*" "They are just announcing it—They're off!" Bill Henry called into his microphone.[76]

The Huskies did not move, and the British also were surprised. The other shells, however, all jumped into action. "Somebody heard the British take off next to us, and said, 'Jesus, let's get out of here, the race has started!' We were probably about a stroke and a half late getting started . . . it was a scramble," McMillin remembered. Ulbrickson later estimated the sloppy start cost the Huskies half a boat length. The rowers tried to regain equilibrium and recapture their magic, but the boat did not feel right. Within the first minute of the race Moch sensed something was off.[77]

As all the crews settled into race pace, the German boat was popping ahead in the protected lane. "They have just started now and Germany is leading at 100 meters," Henry announced. He described "the excitement of the crowd" as they followed the race through the announcements on the loudspeakers. Down the course, Switzerland seized the lead with an early move, and the British eight matched them. Germany fell to third, and Washington clearly fell into last place. "We all know the Washington crew which is representing the United States is probably the slowest starting crew in the world. It gives everybody heart-failure," he explained with a small laugh. "They always stagger along far in the rear until the race is pretty far along and they are doing that now."[78]

Inside the shell, however, the customary confidence was missing. "After we'd gone about 300 meters we were behind by half a length, or three-quarters of a length, and it was pretty obvious to me at that time . . . we were in trouble," Moch recalled. The *Husky Clipper* remained behind the pack, with only the tired British eight trailing ("at this early stage," one witness recalled of the Leander crew, "exhaustion could be seen on their faces"). Although Washington was rowing a solid 34 strokes per minute, it lacked its usual speed. "I can remember, somewhere about the middle of the race, I knew we were not doing well and we were behind," McMillin remembered. "I thought: *God, we've come all this way from Seattle, and to end up our season like this it can't happen.*"[79]

Moch shared that foreboding feeling. He decided to act:

> I asked Don to take the stroke up. And no response. His eyes were closed, his jaw was open, his jaw was slack, and his wide mouth was open. He was rowing but he didn't know what he was doing. He was out of it. I kept yelling at him, and by that time, you know, when he comes forward to make the catch, he's maybe 18 inches from the megaphone, and I yelled right in his face. No expression at all.[80]

The struggle continued as the race passed the five-hundred-meter mark. "They have now gone nearly eight hundred meters and again the lead has switched,"

Henry told the CBS audience. "Italy is now leading with Germany second and Switzerland third and the United States dragging along, not out of the race by any means, but not in the first three." As the race closed toward the midpoint, however, Henry could detect an overall tightening of the contest. "I should say that there's not over one length space dividing the six crews," he said with some clear excitement in his voice.[81]

At the thousand-meter mark, Italy and Germany began dueling with moves. The Italians crossed first, in 3:06.3, followed by Germany in 3:07.8. Still protected from the headwind, they started sliding away from the pack. The Swiss crossed next, more than two second back, with the U.S. boat—barely ahead of the British—in fifth place. From his vantage point above the grandstand, Henry detected movement in the U.S. boat. Washington "is trailing just a trifle," he explained, "but is pretty close up." "There cannot possibly be more than a length or a length and a half between the first crew, the Italian crew . . . and the American crew which is on the outside and which to this point appears to be fairly well in the rear," he called out.[82] As the boats crossed the thousand-meter mark, the German announcer's voice over the loudspeaker became more animated. The

The Italian crew (left) leads the German crew (right) as the boats enter the last 500 meters on 14 August 1936. (From the U.S. National Archives.)

racecourse commentator was "having a fine hysteric over" calling out the duel between the German and Italian shells, wrote Paul Gallico, while the U.S. shell remained an afterthought.[83]

Staying near the British, Italian, and German shells continued costing the Washington squad. The stroke rating, Moch noticed, was stuck at about 34½ strokes per minute. Moch knew he needed it raised, but Hume remained unresponsive. "A big minute for the folks back home!" he yelled, banging his small dowels on the side of the boat. The rate rose to 35 but barely stuck.[84] The *Husky Clipper* continued skimming along, not losing ground but not gaining on the leaders either. The pressure was mounting—on Moch and on the oarsmen, who all felt something was wrong.

"With 800 meters to go I had a choice to make," Moch recalled. "I thought to myself: I've got to do something. I guess I've got to have the seven-man stroke the boat, take the stroke up, and hope Don can feel it and move, and would follow. . . . I made up my mind to do it." Just as Moch was going to transfer the pacing of the boat over to Joe Rantz—something he'd never done before—"Don came forward, to the catch, his eyes popped open and his jaw clamped shut," Moch remembered. "The stroke went up and we flew."[85]

From above the grandstand, Bill Henry noticed the change. As he called out the move being made by the Huskies, his voice registered unmistakable excitement. "The United States is beginning to pick up quite rapidly now! That good old Washington rush at the finish that they've been bringing up is coming up very rapidly now—I can see that they have passed Great Britain, I should say that they had passed Hungary without any question they are coming up very close now to the Italian crew which is still in the lead!"[86]

The *Husky Clipper* finally came together. The boat moved with power and purpose as Hume smoothly elevated the stroke rating. The other seven oarsmen sensed the surge and responded in kind. Moch yelled at the top of his lungs, his face contorted and his hands, grasping the small wooden knockers, banging on the side of the shell. The oarsmen started hearing the crowd. They knew they were running out of time.

As they crossed into the last five hundred meters and neared the grandstand and promenade, the chant could be heard echoing across the water: *Deutsch*-Land! *Deutsch*-Land! in time with the German boat's strokes. The Germans and Italians continued their duel, but having passed the promontory both shells lost protection from the quartering headwind and slowed. Washington applied the pressure to the Germans and Italians just as the two boats in the inside lanes were slowed by the equal conditions. Bill Henry couldn't believe his eyes. "It looks as though the United States is beginning to pour it on now, the Washington crew is driving hard on the outside of the course, they are coming very close now to getting into the lead! They have about 500 meters to go, perhaps a little less than 500 meters and there is no question in the world [but] that Washington has made up a tremendous amount of distance!"[87]

"The crowd is beginning to yell—they are now very close to the end of the grandstand!" Henry bellowed into his microphone. "The American crew is coming up very, very fast, they are coming very close to being in the lead now—I think that they have passed Germany—Germany and Italy are pushing hard very close on this side, and I believe the United States is going into the lead!" Over the RRG airwaves a commentator called out: "Still Italy! Then Germany! Now England! Ah, the Americans—their powerful spurts are irresistible! Their oars rip massively through the water!"[88]

The overwhelming roar enveloped the crews. Inside the *Husky Clipper* panic began to creep in. "Higher! Higher!" Bob Moch yelled, pushing his crew to raise the stroke rating. In the five-seat, Jim McMillin "used the F-word." "*Let's get out of here!*" he cried. But nobody heard him. Sitting just two seats up the boat, Gordon Adam "couldn't hear a sound except the large crowd chanting 'Deutschland!' at the top of their lungs," he recalled. "It was just a din." Moch knew the race had perhaps forty strokes left, but peering across the lanes he wasn't confident his shell had passed the Germans and Italians. Instinctively, without processing it, Moch called for an early final sprint. For the first time in his career as a coxswain—in his final race—he lied to his crew. "Twenty strokes left!" he screamed, banging on the side of the shell. He started counting down knowing that reaching the finish line would require additional strokes. "I'd countdown to maybe fifteen, and then start over at eighteen, then I'd countdown to maybe thirteen and start over at fifteen," Moch remembered. "And the stroke just kept going up and up and up, thank goodness. By the time we got to the finish line I don't think those guys could have taken two more strokes."[89]

The sprinting shells pulled abreast—and then passed—the grandstand. Henry could not tell "one length difference between the first five crews." "The American crew is in front, they are not leading by more than a deck-length, it is very, very close!" he called. The oarsmen ignored the stinging pain convulsing their muscles and remained disciplined and tightly rhythmic. Moch continually called the rating up while counting down the strokes, and he watched in amazement as the rating reached 45 strokes per minute for the first time in the crew's history. Perhaps even more remarkably, the boat skimmed fast enough over the water to clear its puddles at that rating. "Forty meters to go," Henry yelled, "twenty meters to go, ten meters to go, and the United States wins with

75,000 people cheered on the crews as they closed on the finish line, 14 August 1936. (From the U.S. National Archives.)

Italy second, Germany third, Great Britain fourth and Hungary fifth, and not one boat length between the first five crews!"[90] Crossing the finish line, amid the crowd's enormous roar, the oarsmen stopped rowing. Their blades skimmed the water. George Hunt briefly raised his arm "in a token of triumph" before slumping over. Hume pitched forward, and Gordon Adam collapsed, seemingly passed out. All the oarsmen writhed in tremendous pain.[91] The six boats plowed to a stop in the water, and the crowd, which only moments before had been roaring, quieted. "We sat there and as soon as we could get our breath somebody in our crew said, 'who won?'" Gordon Adam remembered. "Well, we did I think," Roger Morris quietly replied.[92] Moch recalled the tension further down the boat:

> For four or five seconds nobody said a word. Totally out, totally exhausted, and I remember Joe [Rantz] or Shorty [Hunt] or Don [Hume], one of the three in the stern said: "Did we win?" and I said, "I think so, but I'm not sure."[93]

Adam described the wait as interminable. The announcer's voice boomed from the loudspeaker: *Achtung! Achtung! Erst: U-S-A.*[94]

Henry's emphatic call transmitted his amazement at the event he had just described. His mind grasped for superlatives to describe the race. "Don Hume . . . stroked that great crew from the northwest to the outstanding victory of the Olympic games," he said, calling the event "one of the most thrilling races I have seen in my life." Inside the shell, the rowers were delirious. "God, we were out of gas at the end of that twenty, the first twenty, you know," McMillin said. "How I struggled through that last twenty I don't know, but the tanks were running on vapor." Bill Henry was certain he witnessed victory by the Washington crew, but down at water level, where the oarsmen were doubled over or contorting from the pain, the final result was not immediately clear to McMillin:

> We didn't know who won. I heard Bob say, when we stopped rowing, in a very faint voice, "I think we won." But he didn't know whether we did or not. The only thing I saw was on the shoreline was one of the fellows from the university, he was an oarsman, but he wasn't a participant, he was right on the finish line and he was jumping ten feet in the air. So we saw him and figured maybe we did win.[95]

Henry described the scene for the U.S. audience. "The German stroke is still collapsed," he said, "a couple of fellas in the Hungarian crew are laying flat in the boat, a couple of the Swiss boys are out." The oarsman McMillin spied offered one clue that Washington triumphed. Soon, the rower on the shore was joined by more celebrating U.S. spectators. "Some Americans down here are having a fit," Henry reported with a laugh. "Everybody is looking at them! They are yelling at the top of their voices."[96]

Al Ulbrickson watched the climax of the race perched atop a chair on the porch above a shell bay. When he first caught sight of his crew on the outside of the course, "he thought it was great, his crew coming down the course all by itself." The hill had blocked his view, though, and "suddenly the Germans and Italians popped out from behind the promontory." He "was shocked" by the differential between the three leading crews.[97] He began jumping up and down on the chair, urging his boat forward, a cigarette tightly clenched between his teeth. He worked his jaws back and forth "as furiously as locomotive pistons" until he bit the cigarette in two.[98] As the *Husky Clipper* entered the final stretch, beneath the massive floating grandstand, Ulbrickson yelled: "*Now! Now! Now!*"[99] He pumped his fist and continued jumping with excitement as the shell passed his perch and crossed the finish line.

Paul Gallico, watching from the press box in the grandstand, was awed by the Huskies' final sprint. "The big rangy kids in the outside shell," he wrote, were "slugging that water and plowing it back . . . faster and faster. . . . They would

This photo, published in a German cigarette company's review of the Olympics, appears to show the German eight ahead of the U.S. crew at the finish line in Grünau, 14 August 1936. (From *Die Olympischen Spiele 1936 in Berlin und Garmisch-Partenkirchen.*)

hook that river and then heave the shell ahead." "A couple of those kids couldn't breathe but they could still row," he wrote with amazement. In the final seconds of the race, the *Times* of London reported, the U.S. team "went from good to better in every way." A consensus quickly emerged that something historic had just occurred. Bill Henry called it "the outstanding victory of the Olympic games," and Grantland Rice later remembered it as "the high spot" of the Olympics. The *Official Report of the Olympic Games* later called it "the finest and the most interesting race of the Olympic Regatta."[100]

The Washington oarsmen kept the shell motionless, waiting for a small motor launch to pull up. Officials handed sweatshirts to the crew, and Don Hume quickly donned two. As buglers began a triumphant blast, they paddled over to the pontoon dock, past the waiting German and Italian shells, for the brief victory ceremony. After shaking hands with the many officials on the dock, a massive wreath was given to Moch, who quickly pushed it on to Hume. Bill Henry, watching Hume struggle with the wreath, began laughing. "Now they've hung an enormous wreath [laughing] around stroke Hume [laughing] who's

Minutes after the race, the victorious University of Washington crew prepares to greet Olympic officials on 14 August 1936. (From the U.S. National Archives.)

hardly strong enough to sit up in the boat. This is liable to knock him overboard! He's sitting up there with a great big wreath about the size of a tire on a truck wrapped around his neck," reported Henry. Then an emotional moment:

> There's the "Star Spangled Banner," and I'll stand at attention if you don't mind, now they play it and I hope that you can hear it. There are 25,000 Germans here standing, giving the Nazi salute towards the American crew, the Italian crew is standing out there with their hands raised in the *Fascisti* salute. The officials gathered around are likewise raising their hands and behind me you hear a celestial choir who have been waiting all afternoon for this opportunity to sing the "Star Spangled Banner."[101]

The band reached the end of the anthem—and continued playing the last part a second time. The extended anthem caused some confusion, but the spectators and rival oarsmen maintained their salutes. "I think the German crew is going to break their arms, they've had their arms extended out there during this entire time and so have the 25,000 people here on the shore," Henry reported with a chuckle. "It's a very beautiful and a very colorful sight, and one that we're all mighty glad to see over here."[102]

In this image from a German newsreel, the crowd celebrates the Olympic victors with the Nazi salute in Grünau, 14 August 1936. (From the Steven Spielberg Film and Video Archive, United States Holocaust Memorial Museum.)

As the Huskies pulled their boat from the dock, the band struck up "Stars and Stripes Forever," much to the delight of Henry, as the sound clearly wafted into his microphone and played under his commentary. The *Husky Clipper* did a victory lap in front of the grandstand, and when it ended the German crew gave the Huskies a cheer. There were no medals given out at Grünau; that official ceremony would occur the following day, in the Olympic stadium. As the Washington oarsmen headed back to the dock, they drew close to the Italian boat. The Italians once again saluted, and then, after carefully maneuvering their shells together, the rowers stretched out their arms and shook hands.[103]

Al Ulbrickson had run down to greet his oarsmen. He was speechless. His face registered a mix of relief, pride, and exhaustion. He briefly lowered his head to compose himself. He strode over to Roger Morris in the bow. Morris had the gigantic laurel wreath draped around his neck and body. "Where did you pick up the hay?" Ulbrickson asked. Morris's face beamed as he gestured back to the course. "I picked it up downstream," he answered.[104]

Hitler and the Nazi leadership remained in their box while the U.S. crew paddled in front of the grandstand and over to the dock. The German armada had completed the greatest performance in the history of Olympic rowing, despite the outcome of the final race. Grantland Rice later claimed to have caught a glimpse of Hitler as the crews sprinted toward the finish line. The German dictator, he wrote, was "standing, urging on the German crew with body English," as the boats tore down toward the finish.[105] The United Press's correspondent turned to look for Hitler's reaction just after the race concluded but noticed nothing out of the ordinary. In general, when Hitler watched Germans lose, his "expression hardened and he scowled."[106] But any anger Hitler may have felt was clearly tempered by the euphoria generated by five gold medals and the repetitive playing of the two German anthems. Josef Goebbels noted the "exciting" racing in his diary. "Everyone is pleased, especially the *Führer* who is beside himself," he wrote. "This is a Jubilee! The crowd," he concluded, was "wonderful."[107] Hitler and the Nazi leadership remained on their reviewing platform after the race, departing only "after witnessing the presentation of . . . laurel wreaths to members of the winning Washington team."[108]

Sharply contrasting any Nazi disappointment was the emotional response of Gaston Moch, Bob Moch's father, who listened to the race on CBS back in Montesano, Washington. Tuning in early, he found it on CBS and felt lucky to catch it. "The broadcast direct from Germany came in fine, at exactly 9 a.m. here the race started, [though] it had been advertised for 9:15 a.m.," he wrote the following day. His letter to his son captures the excitement of his listening experience:

> I thought the race on Wednesday with England was a thriller but the one yesterday was about all we could stand. . . . The broadcast direct from Germany came in fine, at exactly 9 a.m. here the race started, it had been advertised for 9:15 a.m. I stayed home and Mrs. Melville opened the store, we were going to sit down and have breakfast when the returns started coming and the announcement that the race would start at nine so, Mom, Sis and I gathered around the radio and what thrills we did get but you certainly came in in fine style and we jumped, hugged, cried and laughed all at the same time. It was the most exciting moment that I have ever experienced, you and those Huskies certainly put on the most marvelous fight I ever heard of, we are so darn proud that we just don't know how to act.[109]

Later that night, CBS brought Moch and Hume from Grünau to the stadium for an interview. Calling the race "one of the wildest eight-oared crew races certainly that I've ever seen, and that I believe anyone has ever seen," Bill Henry introduced the two. Henry asked Hume "how he feels about having won this victory." "Well, I'm happy and I know all the rest of them are happy," a tired Hume replied. "This, this race is one of those tough ones that you only want to row about once a year." Henry asked Hume about the health of the crew, and then turned to Moch. "Were you absolutely sure you could catch those fellas, and how far were you behind at the half-way point?" he asked. "At the half-way point about half-a-length, but later than that, about 500 meters to go, we were about a length behind," Moch explained. "Looked kind of blue there but the fellas sure came through in great style. They're a bunch of competitors from the word go. It was certainly the toughest race I've ever been in and the fellas came through in great style." Henry then asked whether the Washington strategy was "to hold back just to be dramatic." "Now tell the truth," he said, "is this the way you fellows like to row those races?" "No," responded Moch emphatically. "We'd rather be out ahead a lot sooner than that. However, if we have to do it, then we have to do it." Henry then closed the program by tossing it back to New York.[110]

On the other side of the planet, Gaston Moch heard the interview while attending a Montesano Chamber of Commerce meeting. Just before the broadcast, he wrote, the room hushed. "At 1 o'clock the Olympic Review came direct from Germany. Hume spoke and then another thrill when you got on, it was so quite [*sic*] in the room you could have heard a pin drop and your voice sounded great, it came in fine, and everyone enjoyed it."[111]

The victory of the Washington crew denied the Germans the opportunity to cap the most dominating performance in Olympic rowing history. Many left Grünau stunned and impressed by the German achievements. "Germany's brilliant rowing on the Langer See; her supremacy among the twos and fours, with and without coxes; her trial-heat defeat of the English double-scullers, her licking Switzerland, which had beaten the British at Henley, and her nearly licking Washington, astounded everybody," wrote Janet Flanner in the *New Yorker*.[112] Many competitors, though not surprised, also were impressed by German dominance. "The Germans won five of the seven titles up for grabs," remembered French medalist Vandernotte. "It's almost a miracle that we captured two bronze medals."[113]

Author Thomas Wolfe enjoyed the regatta but he considered the rousing celebration among the U.S. spectators after Washington's victory to be excessive. Wolfe jotted his thoughts in the small notebook he carried at all times. "Since the end of the Games I have read and heard certain American sneers to the effect that in the future Olympics 'freak' events and 'phoney' competitions should be banned," he scrawled. "All this is pretty feeble," he concluded, noting that "thrilling and beautiful [horse] riding contests" in which the Germans dominated were fully the equal of "the shot, throwing the hammer, hurling the javelin, throwing the discus, etc." The U.S. response to the Grünau regatta particularly bothered him:

> It would . . . be interesting to us "non-experts" to know why the exacting, skillful, and individualized contests in scull rowing, two men with and without coxswain—four with and without, etc.—are to be regarded as "freakish" and of no importance in the games, while the mechanized perfection of the Eights is all that matters. If—as we sometimes say—sport is a matter of individual competition, individual excellence—it would seem that in the division of rowing, the Germans have beaten us at our own game.[114]

Wolfe's claim that U.S. sports fans downplayed rowing outside the eights was supported by newspaper reportage summarizing the regatta. News of Germany's "unprecedented sweep of five first places" was often buried deep within lengthy narratives of Washington's thrilling victory.[115] The Huskies' achievement provided a small modicum of redemption, as in the final two days of the games—in the rowing and equestrian events—Germans captured nine gold medals in contrast with the one won in Grünau. Avery Brundage's summary of the regatta, broadcast on NBC, also minimized German dominance. "Our eight-oared crew demonstrated its superiority over those of other nations," he told the network audience. "Of course," he apologetically continued, "we must understand that rowing, in the United States, generally is not as well-developed as it is in these European countries, especially in Germany."[116]

The Olympic regatta proved memorable and historic not only for the participants and journalists, but also for those listening around the world. In the United States, the broadcast was heard by millions over CBS. Unlike many events occurring in Berlin, however, the live call of the eight-oared final turned out to be a CBS exclusive. In the confusion surrounding Bill Slater's departure, Roderich Dietze traveled out to Grünau to broadcast for NBC. NBC's programming records show that Dietze transmitted from Germany for thirty minutes from 12:45 p.m. to 1:15 p.m. (New York time). But almost all of NBC's stations had scheduled the relay circuit to open at 1:15 p.m.—about seven minutes after the race concluded. CBS's broadcast also had originally been scheduled for 1:15 p.m., but quick thinking on the part of Saerchinger had saved the program. Just minutes before the race was to begin, he dashed to a telephone, called CBS headquarters in New York City, and opened the circuit early.[117]

The schedule confusion was the likely outcome of multiple factors. The *repêchage* races for the eight-oared crews started the evening before at 6:15 p.m. Throughout the games, multiple contests ran long, delaying events scheduled later in programs. Gaston Moch likely saw the large banner headline in the *Seattle Times* on 13 August 1936 reading "Millions to Hear Broadcast of Olympic Crew Race." "Tomorrow morning, between 9:15 and 9:45, the Olympic crew race will be broadcast from Berlin through the stations of the National Broadcasting Company," the article began.[118] The elder Moch's surprise to catch the race right at 9 a.m. indicates the confusion that many listeners in the Pacific Northwest must have felt.

We cannot establish with certainty how many people heard the broadcast, and how many missed it, but it nevertheless is clear that a scheduling error caused NBC to hand CBS one of the most dramatic and memorable exclusive Olympic programs in U.S. broadcasting history. "What a chance!" wrote CBS's Saerchinger. "We were the only American radio commentators to catch that race, with millions of Americans listening to us."[119]

Conclusion

The Berlin Olympic Games and
Global Sports Broadcasting

On 15 August 1936, the Washington oarsmen were bused into Berlin to receive their gold medals in front of more than 100,000 spectators in the Olympic Stadium. Even the overcast sky and thirty-minute delay—occasioned by the overtime period in the final soccer match between Italy and Austria—could not damper their excitement. When the soccer concluded, the rowing victors were called to a platform to receive their gold medals and the oak sapling awarded to all Berlin victors. Bob Moch ascended the podium with his teammates lined up, in order, behind him. The Huskies were flanked by the Italian and German squads.[1]

The national anthem and flag raising provoked a tremendous upsurge of emotion. "We had one big thrill" in Berlin, Bob Moch recalled. "It was a thrill to stand on that podium . . . that brought tears to your eyes, and a lot of emotion. To see your flag go up and the 'Star Spangled Banner' played—that was an emotional time."[2] "It's quite a thrill," Gordon Adam remembered, "to see the stars and stripes hoisted to the highest flag and to listen to 'The Star-Spangled Banner.' That stays with you."[3] "They played the national anthem, and the U.S. flag going up, and this big billboard listing our crew and stuff," McMillin recalled in an interview in 2004. His voice choking with emotion, he paused to collect himself. "It had a tremendous effect on me, and the rest of us," he said quietly.[4]

"The splendid victory of our Eight-Oared crew," wrote Henry Penn Burke, chairman of the Rowing Committee, "was the one bright spot in the program and saved the U.S.A. from the humiliation of being white-washed."[5] The performance of the German oarsmen surprised and humiliated the U.S. rowing community. It also provided the German media and nation with one of the most successful days in the Olympic festival. Beating the British and Americans pleased the Germans, and, to some extent, helped salvage the games from the performance of Jesse Owens. "The thousands at Grünau were spared the humiliation of the torrent of American victories witnessed in the track and field events," Christopher Dodd wrote, explaining how the regatta's results provided Germany as much relief as delight.[6] The U.S. press celebrated the Huskies' triumph while minimizing German results, and the German press did exactly the opposite. Profiles of German oarsmen appeared widely as their triumphs filled the pages of newspapers, magazines, and special-edition programs and publications. It "rained gold" in Grünau, reported the *Berliner Illustrierte Zeitung*.[7] Nothing existed like the German performance in "Olympic rowing history since its inception," noted a German cigarette company's Olympic publication. "A single day brought more gold medals to German rowing than [the last] 36 years combined. And the impossible happened: USA, whose [rowing] position seemed as similarly unassailable as in athletics and swimming, was overthrown by German royalty."[8]

After the close of the games, most members of the crew toured Europe and then returned to the United States. Joe Rantz joined most of the Olympic team aboard the S.S. *President Roosevelt*, but the other oarsmen decided to take advantage of subsidized tours and the "travel marks" they had been allotted to explore Germany and Europe. Bob Moch, Roger Morris, and Charley Day bicycled through southern Germany, parts of Switzerland, and France before crossing back, while Jim McMillin, Gordon Adam, and John White rode a train down to Nuremberg to tour the Rhine. The three eventually split up, with Adam heading to Scotland to visit his father's family and McMillin and White visiting the Netherlands and northern France. Four of the oarsmen reunited in a French port to catch a liner back to New York. "I ended up in LeHavre, France, with a boat ticket, and train ticket—from New York to Seattle—and seven bucks," recalled Jim McMillin.[9]

Over the year, the story of the squad's Grünau triumph was regularly featured in U.S. newspapers and magazines and on local and national radio programs. The final race, and radio program, provided such a dramatic and heroic narrative that for a short period the oarsmen became nationally known for the remarkable feat. "Washington won, in dirty shirts and filthy rain, with a sprint up to the line that nearly killed all Americans present, including the crew," wrote Janet Flanner of *The New Yorker* in a typical recounting. "They were *heiled* by the Olympics' greatest assemblage of what Berlin calls its royal family—Herren Hitler, Goering, Goebbels, von Blomberg, Frick, Darré, and von Papen."[10] The following summer, as the Poughkeepsie Regatta neared, media attention intensified. The eight gold medalists defended their intercollegiate championship having lost only their coxswain, and articles in *Life*, *Time*, *The New Yorker*, *Collier's*, and elsewhere celebrated the crew.[11] Both CBS and NBC exploited the crew's fame by airing preview broadcasts on the eve of the regatta for the first time. NBC's program, transmitted live from Washington's boathouse on the Hudson, included Bill Stern interviewing Al Ulbrickson about the Olympics and rowing in Europe versus America.[12] The following evening Washington easily swept the river. What the varsity race broadcast lacked in drama it made up for in new broadcasting technique, as Royal Brougham called the event for NBC from a rented TWA cloud-duster.[13] By 1938 CBS signed an exclusive deal with the Intercollegiate Rowing Association and was promoting its race coverage widely. Next to a drawing of an eight-oared crew, an advertisement in *Broadcasting* proclaimed

CBS AUDIENCE FIRST TO LEARN ANSWER

Greatest meeting of collegiate crews in the country is the annual regatta at Poughkeepsie on the Hudson. Rowing enthusiasts wonder if this year, with its bumper crop of good crews, will produce a successful challenger to Washington's supremacy. Columbia's audience, early in the evening of June 27, will be the first to learn the answer. For Columbia alone will be seated in the officials' launches, on the train, and at reserved vantage points along the course . . . broadcasting the race *as it happens!*[14]

Rowing's apex on the U.S. airwaves occurred in 1938. That year, the last of Washington's 1936 Olympic heroes raced on the Hudson. "If [Don] Hume does pace Washington to victory this year," noted the *New Yorker* in its preview, "he will become one of only two men who have been able to stroke a winning varsity crew three times at Poughkeepsie."[15] Unfortunately for Hume, however, the Huskies were beaten by both the U.S. Naval Academy and California.

National interest in intercollegiate rowing was diminished by the cancellation of the 1940 Olympics, and it was further decreased by the wartime suspension of the Poughkeepsie Regatta in 1942. Though the regatta resumed in 1947, the sport never again enjoyed nationwide media coverage or enormous national popularity. Rowing, which always emphasized anonymous, cooperative teamwork over individual celebrity, failed to effectively transition to the postwar era of electronic media. As advertisers and networks pursued bankable athletic stars appearing weekly on radio, and later television, crew racing disappeared from the national airwaves. The third-rated ABC network, spun off NBC during the war, carried the regatta in 1947 and 1948. In 1949, after ABC proved unable to locate a national sponsor, the regatta disappeared from the national airwaves.[16]

The networks lost interest in rowing for the same reason that they lost interest in other sustaining sports and entertainment programs airing regularly throughout the 1920s and 1930s. The advertising climate in U.S. radio changed significantly after 1935 and intensified even further immediately after the war. The commercial imperative in postwar network radio eliminated numerous broadcasts of historical significance.[17] The growing demand by sponsors for more time dedicated to specific sports such as college football and boxing left other athletic contests with less national media opportunities.[18] Parallel historical trajectories to rowing broadcasts can be discerned elsewhere. The Davis Cup tennis matches, for example, aired over the national airwaves regularly in the 1930s.[19] Like the Poughkeepsie Regatta, the Davis Cup championships were often employed to test innovative mass communication technologies, such as global shortwave relay. But when advertisers began purchasing sports with larger, more predictable, and more loyal audiences, the Davis Cup championships disappeared from national network radio shortly after the war.[20] Their historical significance in the development of U.S. broadcasting proved unable to keep the Davis Cup and Poughkeepsie Regatta broadcasts on the network schedules.

This postwar evolution of network sports broadcasting gave rise to a new generation of sports broadcasters. Bill Slater discovered that NBC would not continue his tenure upon his return from Europe, and his career as a network sportscaster never fully recovered from Berlin. It is not entirely clear why NBC's programming director, John Royal, terminated Slater's employment shortly after his return to the United States. Years later, Bill Stern (who replaced Slater at NBC), published the rumor that Royal accused Slater of padding his Berlin expenses. Walter "Red" Barber, who became director of CBS Sports in 1946, attributed the Slater–Royal clash to a personality conflict between two headstrong men. The NBC archival materials at the Library of Congress and the Wisconsin Historical Society shed little light on the subject, as they contain no materials on Slater between 1936 and his return to the network as a game show host and part-time replacement sportscaster in the late 1940s.

Royal was clearly dissatisfied with Slater's work in Berlin. Slater, it should be noted, made many questionable decisions while in Germany. More than any other U.S. broadcaster, Slater publicly praised Germany and the German radio administration during the games. He gave an interview to *Funk-Wacht Nordfunk*, a popular German radio guide, praising the Nazis. Slater's decision to skip the Grünau regatta and create the situation resulting in CBS landing an exclusive broadcast of one of the most widely anticipated events from Berlin undoubtedly also hurt his relationship with management.

Ted Husing, like Slater, left Berlin early. He rushed back to New York City after the Olympic marathon in order to broadcast one of the year's most anticipated sporting events: the Joe Louis–Jack Sharkey heavyweight bout in Yankee Stadium. Husing arrived in Manhattan on 18 August 1936, and later that night he was ringside in the Bronx calling the fight for CBS.[21]

Husing's reign as the most popular U.S. sports commentator continued through the Second World War. In the postwar transition, however, his professionalism and work ethic began to slip. His colleagues noticed increasingly erratic behavior, as the growing popularity of Stern's NBC broadcasts intensified an already considerable professional paranoia. His drinking also continued to be problematic. In 1946, exhausted by the constant travel, his rivalry with Stern and NBC, and growing tension with CBS management, Husing left the network. He accepted an offer from New York station WHN to return to his broadcasting

CBS Sportscaster Ted Husing at Yankee Stadium in August 1936. Husing left Berlin early to return to the United States in time to call the Jack Sharkey–Joe Louis fight. (CBS publicity photograph.)

roots in music. He spun discs while intermixing patter and commercial chat and overnight became the most famous U.S. disc jockey. His salary skyrocketed from $27,500 to $250,000 (more than $2.6 million in 2015 dollars).[22]

Husing's good fortune, however, did not last long. Soon he returned to his intemperate and occasionally truculent behavior, and conflicts with station management erupted. His behavior, work habits, and even his health continued declining. A brain tumor was soon diagnosed. Although not cancerous, the primitive excision surgeries cost Husing his eyesight and created speech issues. By the end of the 1950s he had become an invalid, living in Southern California with his mother after the failure of yet another marriage. CBS's Bill Paley quietly paid the mounting medical expenses Husing could no longer afford. Before completely losing his eyesight and becoming fully disabled, Husing appeared on the NBC television program "This is Your Life," on 7 June 1958.[23] Host Ralph Edwards ushered Jesse Owens onstage to greet Husing and reminisce about Berlin. But one story from the 1936 trip to Germany would not be disclosed. Husing's most important legacy—his altruism—remained secret. Though Ted Husing preferred not to reveal his efforts, his father never forgot. "Uncle Henry [Husing], Ted's father, took great delight in telling us for years afterwards: 'so, the *goy* saved your life!'—he just loved to say that," Stanley Wertheim later recalled with a chuckle. But Ted Husing never publicly acknowledged his role in saving the Wertheim family from Nazi extermination. It remained a tightly guarded family secret he carried to the grave on 10 August 1962.[24]

Husing's CBS colleague, César Saerchinger, was granted a sabbatical in early 1937. He spent much of that year traveling and compiling a book of his adventures as the first U.S. overseas network radio correspondent. CBS sent its young director of talks, Edward R. Murrow, to Europe to substitute for Saerchinger. Murrow's outstanding managerial skills quickly became apparent. He hired William L. Shirer and successfully challenged NBC's exclusive arrangements with many European broadcasters. Saerchinger eventually moved to NBC, where he broadcast as a roving correspondent and news commentator during the Second World War.[25]

Bill Henry, the third man in the CBS booth, returned to California and continued working for the *Los Angeles Times* and broadcasting for CBS. He celebrated the success of the Berlin Games in public appearances while continuing to attack the defunct boycott movement. That campaign, Henry told an audience in Oxnard, California, that fall, was little more than an opportunity for "some cheap politicians in this country . . . to throw stones at Hitler's head."[26] He maintained close ties to the International Olympic Committee (IOC), regularly traveling to Europe to meet with and advise IOC members. In summer 1939, while in Europe to broadcast Olympic preview programs for CBS, Henry's visit was overtaken by events. The Second World War erupted during his stay in England, and he seamlessly transitioned from sports reporter to war correspondent. His radio connection proved essential in securing access to the British Expeditionary Force as it left for France. "If hadn't had been for the Columbia Broadcasting System I'd never have made it," he wrote a friend, "as the British Army didn't want to take a mob of newspapermen" over to France. "It is a good thing to have this CBS connection," he continued, "as it is a tough racket for a lone wolf newspaperman to do anything here."[27]

Like Henry, numerous radio announcers and sports commentators around the world transitioned to war reporting with the eruption of global conflict. The Reichs-Rundfunk-Gesellschaft's (RRG's) most popular soccer commentator, Balduin Naumann, joined the official war news medium, Propaganda Kompagnie, in 1940 to produce combat reports for German listeners. Arno Hellmis, the sportscaster made famous in Germany for his shortwave relays of Max Schmeling's boxing matches, was killed while reporting the German invasion of France.[28] After returning to the United States, Bill Henry spent most of the war broadcasting from CBS's Washington, DC, bureau. Beginning in 1943, he offered a popular five-minute prime-time summary of war news titled "Bill Henry and the News." Perhaps Henry's most famous war broadcast occurred on 12 April 1945, when he broke the news of President Franklin D. Roosevelt's death.[29] Later that year, Henry resumed his duties at the *Los Angeles Times* and played an integral but little-known role in cleansing the Nazi stain from the Olympic movement. He published an "approved history" of the games in 1948, timed to the resumption of the quadrennial festival in London. The book downplayed Nazi innovations and the organizing success of the Berlin Olympiad while celebrating the achievements of Jesse Owens and the other black U.S. athletes.[30]

Leveraging Jesse Owens's celebrity to redeem the Olympic movement remained effective throughout the postwar era. The electric memory of Owens as the first person to "defeat" Hitler retained magical resonance. The Cleveland sprinter became a transcendent figure, having achieved a level of global celebrity unmatched by any athlete in the interwar era. Radio created the medium whereby hundreds of millions of listeners simultaneously experienced and shared his triumphs. In his radio interviews, Owens always maintained a personable vocal presence exuding warmth and goodwill. His resonant voice delivered disarming words with a charming modesty, regardless of whether the listening audience resided in Germany, the United States, or elsewhere. Even listeners with a limited command of English could enjoy listening to the world's greatest athlete.[31]

The economic value of Owens's global celebrity, however, would always be circumscribed by U.S. racism. Owens's life after 1936 became an ongoing series of struggles to achieve financial remuneration commensurate with his public stature.[32] Despite his embodiment of national pride—and his stature as the living refutation of Hitlerian ideals—Owens was never offered the lucrative opportunities extended to such other 1936 Olympic stars as Glenn Morris, who signed contracts with NBC, a Hollywood studio, and the National Football League, or Eleanor Holm Jarrett, who also went to Hollywood.[33] Holm (who divorced bandleader Art Jarrett shortly after the Berlin Games) lived long enough to see her image transformed from unrepentant party girl to feminist icon. Her Berlin rebellion eventually eclipsed her fame as a world-class swimmer. Featured prominently in a 1999 HBO documentary about women's athletics, Holm attended a screening at the White House. The octogenarian spent the evening flirting "outrageously with President Clinton, at one time cooing to him, 'you are one good-looking dude,'" recalled sportswriter Frank Deford. Holm died at her home in Miami at the age of 91 in 2004.[34]

Over the decades, Jesse Owens became an all-purpose "goodwill ambassador" for the Olympic movement. As such, he transitioned into a redemptive figure, useful to the likes of Leni Riefenstahl, Avery Brundage, filmmaker Bud Greenspan, and others attempting to purify the Olympic ideal by obscuring the Nazi legacy. As the Berlin Games receded further from living memory, Owens evolved into an increasingly distant figure from another world. His persona proved useful as political cover to uphold increasingly anachronistic ideals in the face of Cold War criticism, Black Power protests, and attempts to revisit the failure of the 1936 boycott movement. "When Americans look back to the 1936 Olympics," sportswriter Red Smith wrote during the Olympic boycott debate of 1980, "they take pleasure only in the memory of Jesse Owens' four gold medals." Outside of that, Smith wrote, "we are ashamed at having been guests at Adolf Hitler's big party."[35] To erase this memory of collaboration with Nazi authorities, Owens became synonymous with the 1936 Olympic Games in public memory. This powerful legacy derived principally from the newest global medium of the 1930s: radio. During the month of August 1936, Jesse Owens may have been the most famous person in the world. His athletic triumphs were experienced live by the largest cohort of humanity ever assembled. Yet in the final year of his life he was making commercials for American Express that opened with a simple question: "Do you know me?"[36] He died from complications of lung cancer on 31 March 1980.

The legacy of Jesse Owens furthered the aims of the Olympic movement and remains resonant today.[37] It has also facilitated the research of scholars seeking to unapologetically analyze the Berlin Olympics. Owens's humanistic superiority is regularly counterpoised to the racist ideology of National Socialism to create a safe context for inquiry. This dichotomous framework continues to structure both popular discourse and historical analysis. Yet such constriction by moral judgment risks hindering research and limiting the complexity of the historical record. Contextualizing, and accurately crediting, Nazi achievement remains a fraught and sensitive issue. It is probable that the innovations in mass communication and global broadcasting created by the Nazi regime have remained largely unexplored in the historical record for this reason. Yet the Berlin Games were, by far, the most complex and large-scale multilateral global broadcast event occurring before the Second World War. They were arguably the most important series of broadcasts in the interwar years. The fact that engineers at the BBC, RCA, and the Japanese network NHK all recorded numerous Berlin events—not a common practice in 1936—attests to a contemporaneous consciousness of their historic importance.[38] Their elision, or outright omission, from histories of U.S. and British broadcasting represents an inexplicable void in mass media scholarship.

In their employment of innovative broadcast technology and production practices, the Nazi media organizations developed the model for global sports broadcast production that remains in place today. The ambivalence about crediting Nazi broadcast achievements is nowhere more clearly in evidence than in the exhibition curated by the Olympic Museum in 2015 to commemorate the history of the live broadcasting of the Olympic Games.[39] Berlin is represented solely by the inclusion of the introduction of the new Siemens condenser microphone. The installation of sophisticated directional antennae and greater power at the Zeesen shortwave plant that allowed for clear global transmission are not mentioned. Yet these shortwave transmission improvements successfully facilitated outreach to the global audience, just as satellite technology would serve the same purpose when introduced in the television age. The network circuitry relayed into the 40-Nations Switchboard, combined with the administrative innovations implemented by the management of the Olympia Weltsender Berlin headquarters, became the model for all future Olympic International Broadcast Centers.[40] The assignment of local administrative liaisons for all overseas broadcasting partners, begun in Berlin, continues to the present as part of the responsibility of all Olympic host broadcasting organizations working under the supervision of the Olympic Broadcasting Services.[41] All global sports broadcasting—whether the Olympic Games, the World Cup, or other multilateral live programming—remains deeply indebted to the model pioneered in Berlin. Yet just as the invention of the Olympic torch relay as a

Nazi innovation remains rarely acknowledged in public discourse, the origins of the contemporary system for multilateral live broadcast production remains largely unknown to the average sports fan enjoying live sports programming in his or her home.

Scholarly examination of the relationship between the U.S. media industries and the Nazi government remains contentious. Recent investigations into the relationship between Hollywood and Hitler sparked a particularly virulent debate.[42] The issue of collaboration in broadcasting, however, is paradoxically both simpler and more complex. Did CBS, NBC, the BBC, NHK, Radio Prieto, and almost forty other broadcasting organizations closely collaborate with the Nazi Reich Ministry for Public Enlightenment and Propaganda to promote the "new Germany" around the globe? Yes—they unequivocally did. They had few alternatives, for transoceanic broadcast relay in the 1930s required far more cooperation than any other contemporaneous media industry. Because of the technological, physical, and material infrastructure required for broadcast production, cooperation was a necessity. No foreign broadcast organization could possibly have installed their own panoply of required network circuitry and transmission apparatus inside Nazi Germany. The only choice was collaborate or omit live broadcasts from the games. On the sixty-second and final NBC Olympic transmission, airing after the conclusion of the closing ceremonies, Max Jordan explained the NBC-RRG partnership to the U.S. audience: "The Reichs Rundfunk Gesellschaft . . . made elaborate arrangements to secure the best possible teamwork with NBC," he explained.

> Their work was really unparalleled in the history of radio. Never before had the Olympic Games been broadcast. And here were 67 foreign broadcasting reporters, who had gathered from the four corners of the globe, all clamoring for facilities, microphones, cable lines, and shortwave transmitters. NBC, together with Radio Prieto, Buenos Aires, Argentina, was on top of the list with the largest number of broadcasts done by any single organization except of course, the German company, which was employing all of its fifteen national stations practically during the whole day, and an additional seventeen speakers to broadcast overseas to Australia and South Africa, to China and the Philippines, to Iceland and South America. The German engineers estimate that a total of 5,000 individual broadcasts, in thirty different languages, were arranged during the Games. *Five thousand broadcasts.* That meant that every single phase of the Games could be witnessed by listeners in every corner of the globe. And again: NBC gave the most complete coverage. Not only were the events of the day summarized daily by Bill Slater and Roderick Dietze over coast-to-coast networks, but whenever important events were concluded the winners immediately were brought up to NBC microphones.[43]

It should be noted that Jordan's unrestrained praise omitted the technical glitches, missed events, and other issues that inevitably arise in live broadcast production. The Berlin Games were truly "unparalleled in the history of radio" but they were also imperfect. Their very liveness—the suspense created by connection in real time—made the broadcasts both more spontaneous and less flawless than the more typically scripted and rehearsed programs of the era.

Max Jordan's inclusion of Dietze on the NBC team signifies just how closely the two broadcasting organizations were aligned. That Dietze worked for the RRG and was "the official announcer of the Olympic Games," was not hidden from the NBC audience. Dietze, unlike almost all RRG employees in 1936, was not a party member, and his political views were later characterized as "comparatively moderate." But his even temperament, his educational background in engineering, and his multilingual skills all combined to uniquely place him within the Propaganda Ministry. After the Olympics, his career trajectory within German radio rose rapidly and by May 1940, he would have authority over all English-language German radio propaganda. He worked throughout the war supervising such British and U.S. "radio traitors" as William Joyce, Robert Best, and Mildred Gillars. During the war his personal loyalty to the German regime intensified. As Germany collapsed in late April 1945, Dietze escaped to Hamburg, where he personally used the microphone to transmit a final English-language broadcast. He offered a tribute "to the great leader of the German people, Adolf Hitler, whose memory, I believe, will be immortal in the minds of every German. . . . The name of Adolf Hitler will be eternal," he continued, and "it will never be eradicated from the hearts and the minds of Germany's youth. And whenever we think of Germany's greatness, of Germany's unity, of the nation of all Germans, of the Reich which is eternal, we will think of Adolf Hitler, the man who united the Germans for the first time in history." Dietze was arrested by the British military on 12 May 1945 and spent six months in a prison. After denazification, he returned to broadcasting, working with West German broadcast organizations until his death on 25 May 1960.[44]

That NBC extensively used an RRG employee loyal to the National Socialist regime for 1936 Olympic broadcasts is unquestionably an embarrassment. But focusing on collaboration between the U.S. networks and the German propagandists leaves the mistaken impression that the networks never aired criticism of the German government in 1936. This is not true. Rabbi Stephen Wise addressed the national audience with criticism of the German regime, and in a variety of other venues critical and independent perspectives on Nazi Germany received airtime in summer 1936. Both CBS and NBC, for example, broadcast the acceptance speech by Earl Browder, general secretary of the Communist Party of the United States of America, upon his nomination as the party's presidential candidate on 28 June 1936. That speech explicitly criticized the German Nazi administration.[45] As Douglas Craig, David Goodman, and other radio scholars note, political discourse on the U.S. airwaves in the Depression was far more diverse, critical, and fertile than would become the norm in less than a decade.[46]

The Olympic broadcasts themselves, though produced in collaboration with the Nazi regime, could also implicitly critique German propaganda. By celebrating the victories of Owens, David Albritton, Archie Williams, John Woodruff, and other African Americans, CBS and NBC implicitly challenged Nazi racial theory. This is the paradox of the Berlin broadcasts: They simultaneously promoted, and undermined, the Nazi mass communication message. The simple dichotomous conclusion that the U.S. networks *either* collaborated with *or* opposed the Nazi administration elides too much historical evidence that CBS and NBC did both. To blame the network broadcasters for not openly and explicitly criticizing their hosts on the airwaves while using their microphones, transmitters, circuitry, and studios evidences little sensitivity to the historical or technical complexity of the issue. Even Ambassador William E. Dodd, who disdained the Nazis, carefully circumscribed his criticism in an interview on NBC after the closing ceremonies. "The Olympic Games, now coming to a conclusion here, have been about the most interesting ever held," he said, pointedly refusing to compliment the Nazis. "Our Committee management has been good," he added. Perhaps realizing that he said nothing at all about the games, or Germany, Dodd closed by noting "the stadium is a marvelous structure."[47]

The sensitive issue of Olympic broadcasting's collaboration with repressive and authoritarian regimes continues to this day. The enormous rights fees now paid to the IOC, and the close cooperation with the host nation's organizers, have drawn the world's broadcasters together even more tightly than in 1936. The issue of cooperation with antidemocratic or dictatorial regimes when broadcasting the games arises often, as when NBC broadcast the Sochi winter games from Vladimir Putin's Russia, or the 2008 summer games from Communist Beijing.[48] In both cases, NBC was criticized for not doing more to broadcast independent and critical reporting from the host nations. Just as in 1936, the Olympic broadcaster preferred to deflect this criticism with patriotic narratives of heroic athletic performance.[49] The Olympic movement, since its inception, has demonstrated few qualms about such nationalistic exploitation of the games. The founder of the modern Olympics, Baron Pierre de Coubertin, made this attitude clear in response to a question about propaganda after the Berlin festival. "What's the difference between propaganda for tourism—like in the Los Angeles Olympics of 1932—or for a political regime?" he responded.[50]

Although the IOC can be criticized for such equivalence, this candid admission demonstrates that the leaders of the Olympic movement have always valued participation and interchange above moral judgment. The Olympics, from 1936 on, have brought together the world's broadcasters to exchange ideas, discover new technologies, and learn new production routines. Best practices in broadcasting are rapidly disseminated around the globe by this ephemeral industrial community of technicians, engineers, and sportscasters summoned into existence for two weeks every four years. These multilateral mass communication congresses have real effects. "The Berlin Olympics dominated the summer of 1936 on the radio" in Japan, and numerous cultural programs about Germany were relayed as well as the sports broadcasts, noted media scholar Jane Robbins. The NHK's visitors to Germany were particularly impressed with the condenser microphones, which they "brought back to Japan after the Olympics in order to assist NHK's research into radio equipment." This experience in Berlin proved influential and directly inspired the NHK's greater attention toward overseas broadcasting.[51]

Olympic programs have proven consistently useful in the context of domestic broadcast competition as well. For CBS and Radio Prieto, relaying live Olympic events created brand value and audience loyalty in the competitive commercial environments of U.S. and Argentine radio broadcasting. In the case of CBS, this branding worked. In 1936 the chain aired 108 hours of sports, and in 1937 this increased to 140½ hours. Audiences increased, advertisers noticed, and in promotional materials the junior chain assured "its listeners that they may continue to depend upon CBS as 'the network for sports.'"[52] CBS's increase in both global and sports programming did not go unnoticed. "Columbia doubled its world coverage in 1936 over 1935," wrote the radio critic of the *Pittsburgh Press*, concluding that "the CBS network has done more to bring the world to Pittsburgh homes than any other group of stations."[53] The memorable and exclusive broadcast from Grünau undoubtedly played a role in CBS's developing reputation for international news and sports programming in the late 1930s.

Today, the Olympic brand is so powerful it has become synonymous with NBC's brand identity. The U.S. network signed a deal in 2014 with the IOC assuring the continued partnership through 2032. The price was $7.75 billion, making it the most expensive global broadcast property in the network's history.[54] The deal may ultimately prove profitable, as the Olympics remain one of the last remnants of the mass audience universe.[55] In a world of fracturing audiences and numerous alternative new media distribution channels, from the global perspective the Olympic Games retain a remarkable power to attract every demographic in huge numbers. NBC will continue to leverage this appeal by manufacturing heroic narratives and creating new instant athletic celebrities in Rio de Janeiro, Tokyo, and beyond.

Olympic celebrity, the Husky oarsmen eventually discovered, could be fleeting. Attention from the national media eventually disappeared. They remained an important part of the regional sports history of the Pacific Northwest, but even there their fame diminished considerably over the decades. When Charles M. Gates published *The First Century at the University of Washington* in 1961, he included no mention of the victory in Grünau despite describing the importance of rowing in the school's history.[56] But in rowing history, their place is assured. The crew was inducted in the National Rowing Foundation's Hall of Fame in 1971, with seven of the nine members traveling to New York City to accept the honor.[57]

The rowers occasionally appeared in Seattle's newspapers or were interviewed on radio or television programs, especially in connection with anniversaries of the victory. On the fortieth anniversary they recreated a shirtless pose from 1936, and ten years later they celebrated the fiftieth anniversary with a commemorative row.[58] By then the first of the rowers—Charley Day—had died. Day had gone to medical school and become a doctor, but his smoking habit led to incurable lung cancer. Al Ulbrickson lived long enough to be inducted in the inaugural class of the University of Washington's Athletic Hall of Fame in 1979, passing away at the age of seventy-seven in 1980.[59]

In 1999, Dan Raley, the sports editor of the *Seattle Post-Intelligencer*, named the Grünau gold-medal race "Seattle's defining sports moment of the century."[60] By then, only Don Hume, Joe Rantz, Jim McMillin, Roger Morris, and Bob Moch survived to be interviewed. One by one they passed away, until Roger Morris—the first to cross the finish line—was the last surviving member of the crew. He died on 22 July 2009.[61]

Lives can be measured in time and space. Several of the oarsmen lived into their late eighties and early nineties, but their lives would largely be defined by six minutes and twenty-six seconds occurring on 14 August 1936. On that day they rowed two kilometers faster than any crew in the world. They were more than five thousand miles from home. But they were linked to their families—and millions of U.S. listeners—via the new technologies of shortwave relay and radio broadcasting. Their very personal achievement became magnified, and millions experienced their triumph and shared pride in their success. Eighty years later, thanks to broadcasting, the essence of the Olympic Games remains this live, instantaneous translation of personal athletic achievement into shared national, and even global, experience.

Notes

Prologue

1. César Saerchinger, *Hello America! Radio Adventures in Europe* (Boston, MA: Houghton Mifflin, 1938), 189–90. Saerchinger's memoir contains numerous errors, however, and the present narrative is based on multiple sources. Saerchinger claims the broadcast was retarded one hour and he sought to delay rather than advance the program's open. But the recorded broadcast indicates the race occurred between 6:02 p.m. and 6:08 p.m. Berlin time. CBS and NBC promoted the broadcast for 6:15 p.m. Berlin time. At least one listener tuned in early and was surprised to find the live race call before the scheduled time printed in the newspaper.

2. Cooper C. Graham, *Leni Riefenstahl and Olympia* (Metuchen, NJ: Scarecrow Press, 1986), 123.

3. Gordon B. Adam, *An Olympian's Oral History: Gordon B. Adam, 1936 Olympic Games, Rowing* (Los Angeles: Amateur Athletic Foundation of Los Angeles, 1988), 16, http://www.la84foundation.org/6oic/OralHistory/OHAdam.pdf.

4. Jim McMillin interview, 19 October 2004, 12.

Introduction

1. Grantland Rice, "U.S. Victory in Rowing at Olympics Rated High Spot," *Baltimore Sun*, 21 January 1937, 14; Olympics Roundup," 14 August 1936, Call Number: RWC 6247 A1–2, in NBC Radio Collection, Recorded Sound Reference Center, Library of Congress [hereafter: NBCR-LC].

2. Richard Gaither Walser, *Thomas Wolfe Interviewed 1929–1938* (Baton Rouge: Louisiana State University Press, 1985), 109.

3. "This was Seattle's defining sports moment of the century," wrote *Seattle Post-Intelligencer* sports editor Dan Raley in 1999. Dan Raley, "Events of the Century," *Seattle Post-Intelligencer*, 21 December 1999, http://www.seattlepi.com/sports/article/Events -of-the-century-3835569.php. The story of the 1936 Olympic eight would gain more national attention with the 2013 publication of Daniel James Brown, *The Boys in the Boat: Nine Americans and Their Epic Quest for Gold at the 1936 Berlin Olympics* (New York, NY: Viking, 2013).

4. "German Government Aids Television," *Electronics*, January 1935, 10.

5. Jerome S. Berg, *On the Short Waves, 1923–1945: Broadcast Listening in the Pioneer Days of Radio* (Jefferson, NC: McFarland, 1999), 73–74; H. J. P. Bergmeier and Rainer E. Lotz, *Hitler's Airwaves: The Inside Story of Nazi Radio Broadcasting and Propaganda Swing* (New Haven, CT: Yale University Press, 1997), 35–38; H. Mogel, "The World Broadcasting System, Berlin," *Electronics*, May 1934, 163.

6. On television, see Douglas Lee Battema, "Going for the Gold: A History of the Olympic Games and United States Television, 1956–1988," PhD diss., University of Wisconsin, 2002; Michael E. Geisler, "Nazis into Democrats? The *Internationale Früh-schoppen* and the Case of Werner Höfer," in *Medien—Politik—Geschichte,* ed. Moshe Zuckermann (Göttingen, Germany: Wallstein Verlag, 2003), 232–33; Stephen R. Wenn, "A History of the International Olympic Committee and Television, 1936–1980," PhD diss., Pennsylvania State University, 1993. On newspaper coverage, see Robert Drake, "Jesse Who? Race, the Southern Press, and the 1936 Olympic Games," *American Journalism* 28, no. 4 (2011): 81–110; Pamela C. Laucella, "An Analysis of Mainstream, Black, and Communist Press Coverage of Jesse Owens in the 1936 Berlin Olympic Games," PhD diss., University of North Carolina at Chapel Hill, 2004; Deborah E. Lipstadt, *Beyond Belief: The American Press and the Coming of the Holocaust, 1933–1945* (New York, NY: Simon and Schuster, 1993), 63–86; John D. Stevens, "The Black Press and the 1936 Olympics," *American Journalism* 14, no. 1 (1997): 97–102. On film, see Taylor Downing, *Olympia* (London, U.K.: British Film Institute, 1992); Cooper C. Graham, *Leni Riefenstahl and Olympia* (Metuchen, NJ: Scarecrow Press, 1986); David B. Hinton, *The Films of Leni Riefenstahl* (Metuchen, NJ: Scarecrow Press, 2000).

7. "Televising the Olympics," *Broadcasting,* 15 September 1936, 22.

8. "Radio and Public Address at the Berlin Olympics," *Radio-Craft*, November 1936, 268; Elihu Katz and Daniel Dayan, *Media Events: The Live Broadcasting of History* (Cambridge, MA: Harvard University Press, 1992).

9. Susan J. Douglas, *Listening In* (New York, NY: Times Books, 1999), 22–39; Marshall McLuhan, *Understanding Media* (Cambridge, MA: MIT Press, 1994), 297–307; Edward D. Miller, *Emergency Broadcasting and 1930s American Radio* (Philadelphia, PA: Temple University Press, 2003).

10. On "liveness," see Andrew Crisell, *Liveness and Recording in the Media* (New York, NY: Palgrave Macmillan, 2012); Alexander Russo, *Points on the Dial: Golden Age Radio*

beyond the Networks (Durham, NC: Duke University Press, 2010); Paddy Scannell, *Radio, Television and Modern Life* (Cambridge, MA: Blackwell, 1996); Scannell, "The *Brains* Trust: A Historical Study of the Management of Liveness on Radio," in *Media Organization and Production* ed. Simon Cottle (London: Sage, 2003), 99–112; Jeffrey Sconce, *Haunted Media: Electronic Presence from Telegraphy to Television* (Durham, NC: Duke University Press, 2000).

11. The Scott Full-Range Hi-Fidelity All-Wave Receiver advertisement on page 2 of the January 1936 edition of *All-Wave Radio* promotes the Berlin Olympics as a unique listening opportunity; "Listen to the Olympics" [advertisement] *Toronto Globe and Mail*, 11 August 1936, 8; "Here's the Real Reason Why People Buy Radios—NBC Programs!" [advertisement], *Radio Today*, May 1936, 2; "NBC Programs Are Working for You. . . . Are You Using Them?" [advertisement] *Radio Today*, June 1936, 2.

12. "Al Michaels Recalls Earthquake at 1989 World Series in Bay Area after 25 Years," ThePostGame.com, 14 October 2014, http://www.thepostgame.com/blog/throwback/201410/al-michaels-1989-world-series-earthquake-candlestick-san-francisco-oakland-mlb; "ABC 1989 World Series Game 3 Earthquake," Youtube.com, https://www.youtube.com/watch?v=Z8ExMRocoaM.

13. Jonathan Finn, "Anatomy of a Dead Heat: Visual Evidence at the 2012 US Olympic Trials," *International Journal of the History of Sport* 31 no. 9 (2014): 976–93; Ray Gamache, *A History of Sports Highlights: Replayed Plays from Edison to ESPN* (Jefferson, NC: McFarland, 2010).

14. Michael J. Socolow, "'Always in Friendly Competition': NBC and CBS in the First Decade of National Broadcasting," in *NBC: America's Network*, ed. Michele Hilmes (Berkeley: University of California Press, 2007), 25–43.

15. Saerchinger, *Hello America!* 190.

16. NBC estimate in Thomas C. McCray to Max Jordan, 26 December 1946, Folder 23, Box 284, William F. Brooks Papers, NBC Collection, Wisconsin Historical Society, Madison, WI [hereafter: NBC-WHS]. CBS estimate from Columbia Broadcasting System, *We Now Take You to. . . .* (New York, NY: Columbia Broadcasting System, 1937), 124–27.

17. Columbia Broadcasting System, *We Now Take You To*, 3.

18. Max Jordan to John W. Elwood, 24 February 1933, Folder 2, Box 18, NBC-WHS.

19. William L. Shirer, *20th Century Journey: A Memoir of a Life and the Times*, vol. 2, *The Nightmare Years, 1930–1940* (Boston, MA: Little, Brown, 1984), 277. On the exclusivity contract between NBC and RRG, see Robert J. Landry, "Edward R. Murrow," *Scribner's*, December 1938, 10.

20. "Networks Plan Complete Olympic Games Coverage," *Broadcasting*, 1 August 1936, 45. While the RRG cooperated extensively with CBS, RCA Communications (a subsidiary of NBC's parent company, the Radio Corporation of America) refused CBS access to its shortwave facilities. CBS was forced to employ an inferior German Postal and Telegraph relay to AT&T facilities instead.

21. Roger Moorhouse, *Berlin at War* (New York, NY: Basic Books, 2011), 206; "Vorbereitungen—Olympia-Koffer," *Die Olympischen Spiele 1936 im NS-Rundfunk*, http://1936.dra.de/index.php?id=124#zitat273; Jane M. J. Robbins, *Tokyo Calling: Japanese Overseas Radio Broadcasting, 1937–1945* (Fucecchio, Italy: European Press Academic, 2001), 36–38; Hisateru Furuta, *Broadcasting in Japan: The Twentieth Century Journey from Radio to Multimedia* (Tokyo, Japan: NHK Broadcasting Culture Research Institute, 2002), 45–47; Robert Howard Claxton, *From Parsifal to Perón: Early Radio in Argentina, 1920–1944* (Gainesville: University Press of Florida, 2007), 46–47; Arnd Krüger, "The Ministry of Popular Enlightenment and Propaganda and the Nazi Olympics of 1936," in *Fourth International Symposium of Olympic Research* (1998), 40, http://library.la84.org/SportsLibrary/ISOR/ISOR1998g.pdf.

22. Christopher Hilton, *Hitler's Olympics: The 1936 Berlin Olympic Games* (Stroud, U.K.: Sutton, 2006); Arnd Krüger and William Murray, eds., *The Nazi Olympics: Sport, Politics, and Appeasement in the 1930s* (Urbana: University of Illinois Press, 2003); David Clay Large, *Nazi Games: The Olympics of 1936* (New York, NY: W. W. Norton, 2007); Guy Walters, *Berlin Games: How the Nazis Stole the Olympic Dream* (New York, NY: William Morrow, 2006). Biographies and autobiographies of participants include William J. Baker, *Jesse Owens: An American Life* (New York, NY: Free Press, 1986); Marty Glickman, *The Fastest Kid on the Block* (Syracuse, NY: Syracuse University Press, 2007); Sharon Kinney-Hanson, *The Life of Helen Stephens: The Fulton Flash* (Carbondale: Southern Illinois University Press, 2004); Jeremy Schaap, *Triumph: The Untold Story of Jesse Owens and Hitler's Olympics* (Boston, MA: Houghton Mifflin, 2007).

23. British Pathé, "Poughkeepsie Regatta (1934)," Youtube.com, http://www.youtube.com/watch?v=YrayUl2ZNhc; British Pathé, "The American Varsity Boat Race (1927)," Youtube.com, http://www.youtube.com/watch?v=q6594J4FhIU.

24. Michael J. Socolow, "Live from 'America's Rhineland': The Poughkeepsie Regatta and Early American Network Sports Broadcasting, 1925–1940," *Journal of Sport History* 43, no. 2 (2016): 149–67.

25. Edward B. Husing, *Ten Years before the Mike* (New York, NY: Farrar and Rinehart, 1935); A. A. Schechter, *I Live on Air* (New York, NY: Frederick A. Stokes, 1941); Helen Sioussat, *Mikes Don't Bite* (New York, NY: L. B. Fischer, 1943).

26. On the 2-million-mark figure, see Heinz Pohle, *Der Rundfunk als Instrument der Politik: Zur Geschichte des deutschen Rundfunks von 1923–38* (Hamburg, Germany: Verlag Hans Bredow-Institut, 1955), 415–18; Z. A. B. Zeman, *Nazi Propaganda* (London, U.K.: Oxford University Press, 1964), 110. Currency conversion from marks to dollars via "Historical Dollar-to-Marks Conversion Page," http://www.history.ucsb.edu/faculty/marcuse/projects/currency.htm. Translation to present dollars via Bureau of Labor Statistic CPI Inflation Calculator: http://data.bls.gov/cgi-bin/cpicalc.pl?cost1=806000&year1=1936&year2=2015. One example of an RRG announcer used by BBC, NBC, and other national broadcasters during the Olympic Games was Eduard Roderich Dietze. See "Dietze, Eduard Roderich," in *Die Olympischen Spiele 1936 im NS-Rundfunk*, http://1936.dra.de/?id=66.

27. Fritz Stern, *Five Germanys I Have Known* (New York, NY: Macmillan, 2007), 119; André François-Poncet, *The Fateful Years* (New York, NY: Howard Fertig, 1972), 203. See also Frederic C. Tubach and Sally Patterson, *German Voices: Memories of Life during Hitler's Third Reich* (Berkeley: University of California Press, 2011), 34.

28. Adolf Hitler and H. R. Trevor-Roper, *Hitler's Secret Conversations, 1941–1944* (New York, NY: Signet, 1953), 404.

29. "Adolf Hitler," Folder 319: Obituaries, National Broadcasting Company History Files, Motion Picture, Broadcasting and Recorded Sound Division, Library of Congress [hereafter: NBCHF-LC].

30. David Margolick, *Beyond Glory: Joe Louis vs. Max Schmeling and a World on the Brink* (New York: Knopf, 2005).

31. "Wide Radio Hook-Up to Carry the Fight," *New York Times*, 21 June 1932, 26.

32. "50,000,000 Will Hear Big Fight as 82 Stations Send It on the Air," *New York Times*, 22 September 1927, 21; "England to Hear Golf Reports on Short Waves over Radio," *New York Times*, 14 June 1927, 36.

33. "Fight Broadcast to Argentina; Great Feat, Say Radio Experts," *New York Times*, 12 September 1924, 18. See also Jerome S. Berg, *The Early Shortwave Stations: A Broadcasting History through 1945* (Jefferson, NC: McFarland, 2013), 35–42; Steven P. Phippsa, "The Commercial Development of Short Wave Radio in the United States, 1920–1926," *Historical Journal of Film, Radio and Television* 11, no. 3 (1991): 215–28; Elena Razlogova, *The Listener's Voice: Early Radio and the American Public* (Philadelphia: University of Pennsylvania Press, 2011), 11–32. Others argue the first intercontinental sports relay occurred in 1926, including E. P. J. Shurick, *The First Quarter-Century of American Broadcasting* (Kansas City, MO: Midland, 1946), 123. It should be noted that the 1923 Luis Firpo–Jack Dempsey heavyweight championship match was relayed wirelessly to Argentina in Morse code and an "instant translation" provided "round-by-round" descriptions to a large audience via Radio Sudamérica—but this was a recreated, not live, broadcast. See Matthew B. Karush, *Culture of Class: Radio and Cinema in the Making of a Divided Argentina, 1920–1946* (Durham, NC: Duke University Press, 2012), 61; Andrea Matallana, *Locos por la Radio: Una Historia Social de la Radiofonía en la Argentina, 1923–1947* (Buenos Aires, Argentina: Editorial Prometeo, 2006), 39.

34. The Reminiscences of Irvin Reed Weir (February 1951), 18, Radio Pioneers Project, Columbia University Oral History Collection, New York City [hereafter: RPP-CU].

35. The Reminiscences of Donald G. Little (1951), 34, RPP-CU.

36. Walter C. Evans, "Now You'll Know How Rebroadcasting Is Handled," *Radio Age*, January 1926, 17. On shortwave relay experimentation, see also *Radio Corporation of America Annual Report, 1924* (1925), 8, in Folder 500, NBCHF-LC.

37. The Reminiscences of Raymond F. Guy (1951), 72–73, RPP-CU.

38. Robert W. McChesney, *Telecommunications, Mass Media, and Democracy: The Battle for Control of U.S. Broadcasting, 1928–35* (New York, NY: Oxford University Press, 1993); Philip T. Rosen, *The Modern Stentors: Radio Broadcasters and the Federal Government, 1920–1934* (Westport, CT: Greenwood Press, 1980).

39. "Engineering Department History," March 1948, 5, 15, File Folder No. 79, NBCHF-LC.

40. Saerchinger, *Hello America!* 270.

41. "Broadcasting Sports," *Electronics*, November 1930, 365.

42. On the success of the Lake Placid broadcasts, see Burke Miller to Phillips Carlin, 15 January 1932, Folder 63, Box 12, NBC-WHS; "Radio Will Carry Olympic Reports," *New York Times*, 31 January 1932, 1.

43. Saerchinger, *Hello America!* 184; "Oxford–Cambridge Boat Race to Be Re-Broadcast," *New York Sun*, 3 March 1934, 24. On BBC investment in international sports broadcasting between 1933 and 1935, see Simon J. Potter, *Broadcasting Empire: The BBC and the British World, 1922–1970* (New York, NY: Oxford University Press, 2012), 62–63.

44. For a description of how this policy affected U.S. radio journalists in Europe, see William L. Shirer, *20th Century Journey*, vol. 3, *A Native's Return, 1945–1988* (Boston, MA: Little, Brown, 1990), 85.

45. Joy Elizabeth Hayes, *Radio Nation: Communication, Popular Culture, and Nationalism in Mexico, 1920–1950* (Tucson: University of Arizona Press, 2000); Michele Hilmes, *Network Nations: A Transnational History of British and American Broadcasting* (New York, NY: Routledge, 2012); Kate Lacey, "Radio in the Great Depression: Promotional Culture, Public Service, and Propaganda," in *Radio Reader: Essays in the Cultural History of Radio*, ed. Michele Hilmes and Jason Loviglio (New York, NY: Routledge, 2002), 21–40; Joelle Neulander, *Programming National Identity: The Culture of Radio in 1930s France* (Baton Rouge: Louisiana State University Press, 2009).

46. Christopher S. Thompson, *Tour de France: A Cultural History* (Berkeley: University of California Press, 2008), 42–44; Mark Pegg, *Broadcasting and Society, 1918–1939* (London, U.K.: Croom Helm, 1983), 128; Furuta, *Broadcasting in Japan*, 39–41; Anne F. MacLennan, "Learning to Listen: Developing the Canadian Radio Audience in the 1930s," *Journal of Radio & Audio Media*, 20, no. 2 (2013): 318–20; Douglas, *Listening In*, 199–218.

47. "Berichterstattung der ausländischen Rundfunkstationen und des 'Deutschen Kurzwellensenders,'" *Die Olympischen Spiele 1936 im NS-Rundfunk*, http://1936.dra.de/index.php?id=8#c528.

48. Reichs-Rundfunk-Gesellschaft, *Olympia-Weltsender: Olympia World Station* (Berlin, Germany: Deutscher Verlag für Politik und Wirtschaft, 1937). On U.S. local stations rebroadcasting the RRG's English Olympics signal, see "McGlashan's Olympics," *Broadcasting*, 15 August 1936, 60; "Conquest Alliance V-P Scores FCC for 'Inconsistent' Policy in S.A." *Variety*, 29 July 1936, 34.

49. "Broadcasting's Biggest Job," *The Listener*, 29 July 1936, 199.

50. See, for example, "Die Olympischen Spiele 1936 im NS-Rundfunk: Eine rundfunkhistorische Dokumentation," *Die Olympischen Spiele 1936 im NS-Rundfunk*, http://1936.dra.de/. Broadcast materials produced by the Nazis, such as *Olympia-Weltsender: Olympia World Station*, lack such ambivalence.

51. Frederic C. Tubach and Sally Patterson, *German Voices: Memories of Life during Hitler's Third Reich* (Berkeley: University of California Press, 2011), 34.

Chapter 1. Rowing, Radio, and American Sports Broadcasting, 1925–36

1. Practices, lineups, weather, and other notes are derived from University of Washington Crew Log, 1936, Folder 7, Box 19, Thomas C. Mendenhall Collection, Mystic Seaport Museum and Library, Mystic, CT.

2. Jim McMillin interview, 19 October 2004, 5; Robert Moch interview, 12 October 2004, 5.

3. Jim Murray, "Yes, It All Began with a Boat Race," *Los Angeles Times*, 20 December 1985, http://articles.latimes.com/1985-12-20/sports/sp-5125_1_boat-race.

4. Robert F. Kelley, *American Rowing* (New York, NY: G. P. Putnam's Sons, 1932), 73; Ronald A. Smith, *Sports and Freedom: The Rise of Big-Time College Athletics* (New York, NY: Oxford University Press, 1990), 42–44.

5. Kelley, *American Rowing*, 73. On the 1875 Saratoga Regatta, see James Wellman and Walter B. Peet, *The Story of the Harvard–Yale Race 1852–1912* (New York, NY: Harper, 1912), 8–9; William Henry Nugent, "The Sports Section," *American Mercury*, March 1929, 329–38.

6. William J. Chipman, "Six Vanished Races," *IRA Regatta Program* (1948), 10, 37. On the Rowing Association of American Colleges, see Charles Van Patten Young, *The Cornell Navy: A Review* (Ithaca, NY: Taylor and Carpenter, 1907), 13, 20. It should be noted that many writers both at the time and later confused the Rowing Association of American Colleges with the later Intercollegiate Rowing Association. For example, see Wellman and Peet, *Harvard–Yale Race,* 9.

7. Chipman, "Six Vanished Races," 37. Others also attribute the withdrawal of Harvard and Yale to the inability of either to win. See Young, *Cornell Navy*, 20. One history of the Harvard–Yale race claims the withdrawal was due to the "rough water" and "uncertainty" around scheduling on the Saratoga, New York, racecourse, which was "the only one available for a race with so many participants": Wellman and Peet, *Harvard–Yale Race,* 9. "Ready for the Varsity Race," *New York Times*, 24 June 1894, 20.

8. See "Rowing," *The Spirit of the Times* (New York), 2 June 1883, 504. "The Oars," *Philadelphia Inquirer,* 28 December 1883, 4. On the organizational meeting of the new Inter-Collegiate Rowing Association, see "Intercollegiate Rowing Association," *Cornell Daily Sun*, 12 January 1883, 1. "About the College," *Columbia Spectator,* 11 January 1883, 10.

9. Chipman, "Six Vanished Races," 37. Thomas C. Mendenhall, *A Short History of American Rowing* (Boston, MA: Charles River, 1980); 25–26. Samuel Crowther, *Rowing and Track Athletics* (New York, NY: Macmillan, 1905), 110.

10. Kelley, *American Rowing*, 72.

11. Grace A. Trudie, *Around Cold Spring* (Charleston, SC: Arcadia, 2011), 8; Malcolm Roy, "Fifty Years of Poughkeepsie," *IRA Regatta Program* (1947), 12; Michael J. Socolow, "Live from 'America's Rhineland': The Poughkeepsie Regatta and Early American Network Sports Broadcasting, 1925–1940," *Journal of Sport History* 43, no. 2 (2016): 149–67.

12. Kelley, *American Rowing*, 137; Kelley, "Regatta, Rich in Tradition, Held Interest of the Entire Nation," *New York Times*, 13 January 1933, 20. It should be noted that Kelley

mistakenly dates the meeting as December 1895 when it actually occurred in December 1894. See Roy, "Fifty Years of Poughkeepsie," 12; John Mylod, *Biography of a River: The People and Legends of the Hudson Valley* (New York, NY: Hawthorn, 1969), 102; Joyce C. Ghee and Joan Spence, *Poughkeepsie, New York: Halfway up the Hudson* (Charleston, SC: Arcadia, 1997), 32; Robert B. Johnson and William Blaikie, *A History of Rowing in America* (New York, NY: Corbitt and Johnson, 1871), 49.

13. Roy, "Fifty Years of Poughkeepsie," 12; Allan Keller, *Life along the Hudson* (New York, NY: Fordham University Press, 1997), 196–98.

14. Mylod, *Biography of a River*, 100.

15. Roy, "Fifty Years of Poughkeepsie," 12.

16. Buhler, "History of Rowing"; Roy, "Fifty Years of Poughkeepsie," 12; Keller, *Life along the Hudson*, 196–98.

17. Harvey K. Flad and Clyde Griffen, *Main Street to Mainframes: Landscape and Social Change in Poughkeepsie* (Albany, NY: Excelsior Editions, 2009), 102; Mylod, *Biography of a River*, 102. See also Stanley Woodward, *Paper Tiger* (New York, NY: Atheneum, 1964), 171; R .F. K., "The Oarsmen," *New Yorker*, 16 June 1928, 69.

18. Samuel Crowther Jr., "The Ethics of American Rowing," *Outing Magazine*, July 1907, 500.

19. "Dean McClellan Advocates More Recreation Fields for University," *Pennsylvania Gazette*, 10 January 1919, 311.

20. Paul Gallico, *Farewell to Sport* (New York, NY: Alfred A. Knopf, 1938), 329.

21. Jimmy Cannon, *Nobody Asked Me* (New York, NY: Dial Press, 1951), 264.

22. Cannon, *Nobody Asked Me*, 266.

23. George A. Palmateer, "Regatta Thrills Are Lasting," *IRA Regatta Program* (1947), 8.

24. "Washington Crews Sweep Poughkeepsie Regatta for Second Successive Year," *Life*, 5 July 1937, 22.

25. Hugh Bradley, "Hugh Bradley Says," *New York Post*, 23 June 1936, 16; "Washington Crews Sweep Poughkeepsie."

26. Kelley, "Regatta," 20.

27. Mendenhall, *Short History*, 26.

28. "East against West at Poughkeepsie," *Literary Digest*, 26 June 1926, 48; Susan Saint Sing, *The Wonder Crew: The Untold Story of a Coach, Navy Rowing, and Olympic Immortality* (New York, NY: St. Martin's Press, 2008), 266–77.

29. Richard A. Glendon and Richard J. Glendon, *Rowing* (Philadelphia, PA: J. B. Lippincott, 1923); Saint Sing, *Wonder Crew*.

30. James C. Rice, "Making a Varsity Crew," *Outing*, June 1913, 314.

31. Duncan Norton-Taylor, "A Very Dangerous Girl," *Collier's Weekly*, 5 January 1935, 10–11. Representative fiction includes Corey Ford, "Crossed Oars," *Collier's*, 9 September 1933, 20–21; Edward Shenton, "The Hard Guy," *Collier's Weekly*, 30 June 1934, 7–9; Harry Sylvester, "Eight-Oared Crew," *Collier's Weekly*, 17 June 1939, 17–18. Nonfiction includes Alastair MacBain, "Riding Backward," *Collier's Weekly*, 15 June 1935, 12; Alastair MacBain, "Ready All!" *Collier's Weekly*, 27 June 1936, 14; Alastair MacBain, "Nobody Loves the Coxswain," *Collier's Weekly*, 12 June 1937, 17. The Harvard–Yale race

also figured in fiction and nonfiction pieces in this period. See Ralph D. Paine, "His Code of Honor," *Scribner's*, June 1916, 703–16.

32. On control of network programming by the advertising community, see Cynthia B. Meyers, *A Word from Our Sponsors: Admen, Advertising, and the Golden Age of Radio* (New York, NY: Fordham University Press, 2013).

33. The Reminiscences of Raymond F. Guy (1951), 72–73, Radio Pioneers Project, Columbia University Oral History Collection, New York City [hereafter: RPP]. See also Testimony of O. B. Hanson, Chief Engineer, NBC, Federal Communications Commission Docket No. 5060 (22 November 1938), 715–56; "Today's Radio Program," *New York Times*, 23 May 1925, 18; Kingsley Welles, "The Listeners' Point of View—Summer Radio Programs Are Attractive," *Radio Broadcast*, August 1925, 470; "When WJZ Was Portable," *Radio Broadcast*, August 1925, 486; Alfred N. Goldsmith and Austin C. Lescarboura, *This Thing Called Broadcasting* (New York, NY: Henry Holt, 1930), 211.

34. "Die Erste Sport-Übertragung," in *Rundfunk-Jahrbuch 1933* (Berlin, Germany: Reichs-Rundfunk-Gesellschaft, 1934), 130–31; *BBC Hand Book* (London, U.K.: British Broadcasting Company, 1928), 80.

35. "Plan to Use Radio Telephone for Bulletins at Regatta," *New York Times*, 10 June 1922, 15.

36. The Reminiscences of Raymond F. Guy (1951), 73, RPP.

37. "Telephone Aids Radio in Nationwide Broadcast of Big Rowing Classics," *Harlem Valley Times*, 13 August 1931, 10.

38. "Looking through the Studioscope," *What's on the Air*, June 1931, 10.

39. Ted Husing, *Ten Years before the Mic* (New York, NY: Farrar and Rinehart, 1935), 137–38.

40. Husing, *Ten Years*, 139–41; "Regatta Veiled in Mist and Words," *New York Times*, 30 June 1929, 14; Red Barber, *The Broadcasters* (New York, NY: Dial Press, 1970), 47. On Seattle's reaction to the broadcast, see Carroll M. Ebright to Broussais C. Beck, 4 March 1930, Folder 1, Box 1, Broussais C. Beck Papers, Special Collections, University of Washington Library, Seattle, WA [hereafter: BCB-WA].

41. Ky Ebright to Broussais C. Beck, 10 July 1934, Folder 1, Box 1, BCB-WA; Leonard Lyons, "The Lyons Den," *New York Post*, 21 June 1935, 11.

42. Thomas F. Moore, "Sports Announcer by Accident," *Sports Illustrated*, 12 October 1964, http://www.si.com/vault/1964/10/12/612615/sports-announcer-by-accident.

43. William Stewart to Sydney Strotz, 17 June 1934, and Graham McNamee to Burke Miller, 18 June 1934, Folder 40, Box 19, National Broadcasting Company Records, Wisconsin Historical Society, Madison, WI [hereafter: NBC-WHS]; Barber, *Broadcasters*, 43; David J. Halberstam, *Sports on New York Radio: A Play-by-Play History* (Lincolnwood, IL: Masters Press, 1999), 14–15.

44. In 1931 one trade magazine wrote of the "millions of chain listeners" who tuned in Ted Husing's CBS report of the regatta: "Looking through the Studioscope," 10.

45. Michael J. Socolow, "'Always in Friendly Competition': NBC and CBS in the First Decade of National Broadcasting," in *NBC: America's Network*, ed. Michele Hilmes (Berkeley: University of California Press, 2007), 25–43.

46. Robert W. McChesney, "Media Made Sport: A History of Sports Coverage in the U.S.," in *Media, Sports, and Society*, ed. Lawrence A. Wenner (Newbury Park, CA: Sage, 1989), 59–60.

47. John F. Royal to Richard C. Patterson, 1 October 1935, Folder 39, Box 35, NBC-WHS. Discussion of cooperation in not purchasing sporting events can be found in the minutes of the "Operating Committee Meeting—Chicago, September 17, 1934," 2, Folder 831, National Broadcasting Company History Files, Motion Picture, Broadcasting and Recorded Sound Division, Library of Congress, Washington, DC [hereafter: NBCHF-LC].

48. Abel Alan Schechter, *I Live on Air* (New York, NY: Frederick A. Stokes, 1941), 411–12.

49. Ibid., 411–12, 426.

50. "The Oarsmen," *New Yorker*, 27 June 1936, 70.

51. "Shell Chateau," 6 July 1935, NBC-Red. Recording in author's possession.

52. Al Ulbrickson, "Row, Damit, Row," *Esquire*, April 1934, 50; Matthew Klingle, *Emerald City: An Environmental History of Seattle* (New Haven, CT: Yale University Press, 2007), 169.

53. "Washington Crews Not Content to Rest upon Their Laurels," *Christian Science Monitor*, 28 April 1937, 10; Herbert Reed, "Rowing, the Real Team Sport," *The Outlook*, 21 April 1926, 604.

54. George Marvin, "Why Washington Wins," *The Outlook*, 1 July 1925, 333; "Washington Crews," 10.

55. Varsity Boat Club," Huskycrew.com, http://www.huskycrew.com/vbc.htm; Marvin, "Why Washington Wins," 332; "Washington Crews," 10; Gordon R. Newell, *Read All! George Yeoman Pocock and Crew Racing* (Seattle: University of Washington Press, 1987), 79–80.

56. "Washington Crews," 10.

57. George Pocock and Clarence Dirks, "One-Man Navy Yard," *Saturday Evening Post*, 25 June 1938, 16; Göran R. Buckhorn, "Dick's Red Coat," *Hear the Boat Sing*, 11 October 2009, http://hear-the-boat-sing.blogspot.com/2009/10/dicks-red-coat.html; Stewart Stokes, "It Was a Fearful Stroke, but They Made Their Old Boat Hum: A Social and Technical History of Rowing in England and the United States" (unpublished senior thesis, Colby College, Waterville, ME, 2010), 111–12, http://web.colby.edu/crew/files/2010/06/It-Was-A-Fearful-Stroke-Stews-Thesis.pdf; Newell, *Ready All!* 27; Pocock Singles Project, "Pocock History," http://www.pocockclassic.com/pocock/us.html.

58. Pocock and Dirks, "One-Man Navy Yard," 17, 43; Stokes, "Fearful Stroke," 112.

59. Al Ulbrickson and Clarence Dirks, "Rockne of Rowing," *Saturday Evening Post*, 19 June 1937, 14; "Rowing Begins at University of Washington on December 15, 1899," Historylink.org, http://www.historylink.org/_content/printer_friendly/pf_output.cfm?file_id=1647; Stokes, "Fearful Stroke," 109; Thomas C. Mendenhall, "Coaches and Coaching IV: Hiram Conibear," *The Oarsman*, September–October 1978, 22–29.

60. Ulbrickson and Dirks, "Rockne of Rowing," 14; Newell, *Ready All!* 76; Thomas C. Mendenhall, "The Old Man in the Felt Hat: Thomas D. Bolles," *The Oarsman*, September–October 1979, 12.

61. Ulbrickson and Dirks, "Rockne of Rowing," 94; Mendenhall, *Short History,* 32.

62. "Washington Crews," 10; Newell, *Ready All!* 78.

63. Newell, *Ready All!* 78; Ulbrickson, "Row, Damit, Row," 91; Ulbrickson and Dirks, "Rockne of Rowing," 95; Arch Campbell, "The Race That Changed World Rowing," 3–4 (unpublished manuscript, n.d.), Crew-Historical Features Folder, Box 2, University of Washington Intercollegiate Athletics Department Collection, Accession No. 97–096, University of Washington Special Collections, Seattle, WA.

64. Newell, *Ready All!* 76. On page 141, footnote 3, Newell notes that the stroke was called, at various times, the "Conibear stroke," the "Husky stroke," the "Washington stroke," and later the "American stroke" (overseas). There were several slight variations over the decades. For one such differentiation, see Donald F. Grant, "My Version of the Washington Stroke (Not the Conibear Stroke)," in Alvin E. Ulbrickson, "Rowing at the University of Washington, 1900–1960" (unpublished M.A. thesis, University of Washington, 1963), 208–10. "At the height of the discussion of [Conibear's] stroke," Robert Kelley writes, "there were those to hold that he had taken it from others." Specifically, some argued that it was a variant of an old Yale stroke taught by Bob Cook. See Kelley, *American Rowing*, 227–29. Others claim the Conibear stroke never existed, and the technique was a variant of George Pocock's "knowledge and style." See Stanley Richard Pocock, *"Way Enough!" Recollections of a Life in Rowing* (Seattle, WA: BLABLA, 2000), 55; Bill Pickard interview with author, Pocock Rowing Foundation, 7 March 2013.

65. Newell, *Ready All!* 82; Pocock, *"Way Enough!"* 3–4; "Callow Quits Washington for $15,000 Post at Pennsylvania," *Los Angeles Times*, 7 July 1927, B1; "Ulbrickson Picked to Coach Huskies," *New York Times*, 9 August 1927, 21.

66. Thomas C. Mendenhall, "The Dour Dane," *Rowing USA*, June–July 1982, 9–13; "The Record," in *Appreciation Night Program—Alvin M. Ulbrickson,1959*, Box 3, Varsity Boat Club Collection, Accession No. 3368, University of Washington Special Collections, Seattle, WA; "Yale Is in the Olympics, but Washington Is Good," *Literary Digest*, 12 July 1924, 60; Newell, *Ready All!* 100; "Husky Crew Drills Open," *Los Angeles Times*, 24 February 1936, 18.

67. Ulbrickson, "Row, Damit, Row," 50.

68. Ky Ebright to Broussais C. Beck, 2 June 1934, Folder 1, Box 1, BCB-WA. See also entry for 9 October 1933 in "Frosh Crew Log," Box 16, Varsity Boat Club Collection, Accession No. 3368–2, University of Washington Special Collections, Seattle, WA.

69. "Washington and California Set to Renew Rowing Rivalry Today," *New York Times*, 13 April 1935, 18.

70. "Husky Frosh Beat Field by Wide Margin," *Seattle Post-Intelligencer*, 17 June 1934, 1; Robert F. Kelley, "Poughkeepsie Revival; New London Survival," *Literary Digest*, 16 June 1934, 36; Stanley H. Woodward, "Mr. Callow Takes On the West," *Literary Digest*, 15 June

1935, 32; "Washington Rowing History—Men's 1930s," Washington Rowing Foundation, http://www.huskycrew.org/1930.htm; Lorin Peterson, "Without Benefit of Graft," *Columns*, May 1935, 57.

71. Robert Moch, first 1999 interview with Dan Raley; Moch 2004 interview, 3–4; McMillin interview, 4; John Romano, "California Crew Olympic Favorite," *Boston Globe*, 17 July 1935, 21.

72. McMillin interview, 4.

73. Moch 2004 interview, 4. On "Brougham's boys," see Moch, first 1999 interview; "New Names for Sports Scrap-Books," *Literary Digest*, 13 July 1935, 32.

74. "Varsity Crew Points for Berlin via Way Stations," *University of Washington Daily*, 6 January 1936, 3; Clarence Dirks, "Prospects Bright as Husky Varsity Crews Report Today," *Seattle Post-Intelligencer*, 13 January 1936, clips in Robert Moch Scrapbook, George Pocock Rowing Foundation, George Pocock Memorial Rowing Center, Seattle, WA [hereafter: RMS-GPRF].

75. Moch 2004 interview, 5.

76. Bud Withers, "Huskies' Last Surviving Member of 1936 Olympic-Gold Crew Team Dies," *Seattle Times*, 24 July 2009, http://seattletimes.nwsource.com/html/huskies/2009527676_crewobit24.html.

77. Royal Brougham, "The Morning After," *Seattle Post-Intelligencer*, 18 April 1936, 18; Moch, second 1999 interview with Dan Raley, 3.

78. "Dr. Charles Ward Day, 47, Prominent Physician, Dies," *Seattle Post-Intelligencer*, 27 May 1962, 33.

79. Brougham, "Morning After," 18 April 1936, 18. George Kirksey, "Ulbrickson Describes Husky Crewman," United Press clipping, 4 July 1936, in RMS-GPRF. Moch, first 1999 interview, 3.

80. Al Ulbrickson, as told to Clarence Dirks, "Cracked Oar Sweeps Hudson," *Ken*, 14 July 1938, 66; Lenny Anderson, "Shorty in Name—but Long on Memories," *Seattle Post-Intelligencer*, 7 March 1965, clip in Dan Raley file in author's possession.

81. Brougham, "Morning After," 18 April 1936, 18; Gordon B. Adam, *An Olympian's Oral History: Gordon B. Adam, 1936 Olympic Games, Rowing* (Los Angeles: Amateur Athletic Foundation of Los Angeles, 1988), 1–4, http://www.la84foundation.org/6oic/OralHistory/OHAdam.pdf.

82. "John G. White, Taken by Death," *Seattle Times*, 20 April 1949, 29; Moch, first 1999 interview, 3.

83. McMillin interview, 1–2; Brougham, "Morning After," 6 April 1936, 11; Brougham, "Morning After," 18 April 1936, 18.

84. Brougham, "Morning After," 18 April 1936, 18; Moch, first 1999 interview, 2.

85. Craig Smith, "Undefeated UW Rower Rantz Earned Gold," *Seattle Times*, 12 September 2007, http://seattletimes.nwsource.com/html/huskies/2003880103_obit12.html; Brougham, "Morning After," 18 April 1936, 18.

86. Brougham, "Morning After," 6 April 1936, 11; Newell, *Ready All!* 106; "The Oarsmen," *New Yorker*, 25 June 1938, 52; Moch 2004 interview, 4.

87. Marilyn Moch interview, 16 August 2012, 1–5; Eric Cohen, "Husky Legend Bob Moch: 1914–2005," *Husky Rowing News*, 16 February 2005, 3; Newell, *Ready All!* 137.

88. University of Washington Crew Log, entries for 27, 28, and 31 March 1936, Folder 7, Box 19, Thomas C. Mendall Collection, Mystic Seaport Museum and Library, Mystic, CT.

89. "Husky Crew Drills Open," *Los Angeles Times*, 24 February 1936, 18; "Ulbrickson Cautions Crew about Newspaper Publicity," *University of Washington Daily*, 17 January 1936, 3, RMS-GPRF; Newell, *Ready All!* 138–39.

90. Clarence Dirks, "California Varsity Will Include Six Major Stars," *Seattle Post-Intelligencer*, 5 April 1936, 21; Clarence Dirks, "Ebright Says Crew Faster," *Seattle Post-Intelligencer*, 14 April 1936, 13; Royal Brougham, "U.W. Crews Win All Three Races," *Seattle Post-Intelligencer*, 19 April 1936, 1, 17; Clarence Dirks, "Bear, Husky Boats Await Big Regatta," *Seattle Post-Intelligencer*, 17 April 1936, 10; Clarence Dirks, "50,000 to Witness Crew Races Today," *Seattle Post-Intelligencer*, 18 April 1936, 16.

91. Clarence Dirks, "U.W. Varsity Boat Wins by 3 Lengths," *Seattle Post-Intelligencer*, 19 April 1936, 16; John Kieran, "Sports of the Times," *New York Times*, 15 June 1936, 29; Brougham, "Morning After," 21 April 1936, 11; Brougham, "U.W. Crews Win," 1; "Huskies' Crew Favorite for Olympics," *Washington Post*, 20 April 1936, 16.

92. Brougham, "Morning After," 14 June 1936, 17; "Coaches Speak to Big Crowd," *Seattle Post-Intelligencer*, 11 June 1936, 25.

93. Clarence Dirks, "Husky Varsity and Jayvee to Race on Hudson," *Seattle Post-Intelligencer,* 21 April 1936, 11; "U.W. Students to Hold Tag Sale for Sweepsters Today," *Seattle Post-Intelligencer*, 22 April 1936, 15.

94. Brougham, "Morning After," 14 June 1936, 17; George M. Varnell, "Crews Head for Poughkeepsie Races," *Seattle Times*, 11 June 1936, 25, 26; Varnell, "U.W. Coaches Fatten Up Oarsmen on Trip," *Seattle Times*, 12 June 1936, 19; Brougham, "Huskies Eights Row at Chicago," *Seattle Post-Intelligencer*, 14 June 1936, 17; Varnell, "Miss Conibear Visits Huskies at Windy City," *Seattle Times*, 14 June 1936, 20; Varnell, "Husky Crews Work Out on Lake Michigan," *Seattle Times*, 13 June 1936, 14.

95. Robert F. Kelley, "Oarsmen of Washington and Navy Join Squads in Training at Poughkeepsie," *New York Times*, 15 June 1936, 29; George M. Varnell, "Varnell Says," *Seattle Times*, 16 June 1936, 18.

96. Bill Henry, "Bill Henry Says," *Los Angeles Times*, 15 June 1936, A9; Robert F. Kelley, "Well-Conditioned Penn Crew Arrives at Scene of College Regatta," *New York Times,* 5 June 1936, 27.

97. "Varnell Says," 18; Kelly, "Oarsmen of Washington and Navy," 29; Henry, "Bill Henry Says," A9; "Al Ulbrickson Says New Quarters Helped Huskies," *Poughkeepsie Eagle-Tribune*, 24 June 1936, 10; Brougham, "Morning After," 14 June 1936, 17; Clarence Dirks, "U.W. Gets New Training, Living Quarters on Hudson," *Seattle Post-Intelligencer*, 16 February 1936, 17.

98. Kieran, "Sports of the Times," 29; "Cracked Rib Forces Sweep Swinger Daggett Out of Bear Boat in Crew Trials," *Los Angeles Times*, 30 June 1936, A12.

99. Brougham, "Huskies Eights Row at Chicago," 18; "Rival Crews Eye Cornell," *Los Angeles Times*, 16 June 1936, A11; "Wind Works Havoc with Oar Workouts," *Los Angeles Times*, 18 June 1936, 15; Kelly, "Oarsmen of Washington and Navy," 29.

100. McMillin interview, 7–8.

101. James A. Burchard, "Varsity Coxswain Hero of Huskies Sweep of Hudson," *New York World-Telegram*, 23 June 1936, 20; "Coxswain," *New Yorker*, 18 July 1936, 8–9.

102. Bradley, "Hugh Bradley Says," 16; Franklin D. Roosevelt to Maxwell Stevenson, 16 June 1936, and Maxwell Stevenson to the Honorable Franklin D. Roosevelt, 10 June 1936, President's Personal File, No. 3615: Intercollegiate Rowing Association, Franklin D. Roosevelt Library, Hyde Park, NY; "Coach Ulbrickson Praises Oarsmen," *New York Times*, 23 June 1936, 29; "'Thought We'd Win,' Says Coach," *Los Angeles Times*, 23 June 1936, A11.

103. "Washington Wins First Race since Coach Graduated," *Hartford Current*, 23 June 1936, 14; "'Thought We'd Win,'" A11. Malcolm Roy, "Huskies Nearly Lost on Foul," *New York Sun*, 9 July 1936, 25.

104. Joe Williams, "West Steals Hudson Show," *New York World-Telegram*, 24 June 1936, 20.

105. Roy, "Huskies Nearly Lost," 25.

106. Moch 2004 interview, 6.

107. "Al Ulbrickson Says," 10; Herbert Allen, "Moch Brains Enable Huskie Beef to Score First 'Keepsie Sweep," *New York Post*, 23 June 1936, 16; James A. Burchard, "Varsity Coxswain Hero of Huskies Sweep of Hudson," *New York World-Telegram*, 23 June 1936, 20; Williams, "West Steals Hudson Show," 20.

108. Allen, "Moch Brains Enable Huskie Beef," 16; McMillin interview, 8; Burchard, "Varsity Coxswain," 20.

109. Moch 2004 interview, 6–7.

110. Bill Henry, "Washington Crews in Clean-Sweep Victory," *Los Angeles Times*, 23 June 1936, A11; George M. Varnell, "Memories of Crew: Al Recalls the Highlights of a Long, Honored Career," *Seattle Times*, 26 January 1959, 12; "Al Ulbrickson Says," 10.

111. Henry, "Washington Crews," A11.

112. Henry, "Washington Crews," A11; Brougham, "Morning After," 1 July 1936, 15; Williams, "West Steals Hudson Show," 20.

113. Henry, "Washington Crews," A11.

114. "Ulbrickson, Washington Coach, Calm after Crew Triumphs," *Poughkeepsie Eagle-News*, 23 June 1936, 10; Henry, "Washington Crews," A11; Mendenhall, "Dour Dane," 13.

115. Allen, "Moch Brains Enable Huskie Beef," 16; "Coach Ulbrickson Praises Oarsmen," 29.

116. Jim Lemmon, *The Log of Rowing at the University of California, Berkeley, 1870–1987* (Berkeley, CA: Western Heritage Press, 1989), 30–31.

117. "Coach Ulbrickson Praises Oarsmen," 29; Grantland Rice, "'Husky' Oarsmen Appear to Be Bound for Olympics," *Boston Globe*, 23 June 1936, 21.

118. "'Thought We'd Win,'" A11.

119. Aaron Stein, "Radio Offers Sports and Politics," *New York Post*, 23 June 1936, 14; Clarence Dirks, "Nation Hears Huskies on Program," *Seattle Post-Intelligencer*, 23 June 1936, 13.

Chapter 2. "Let's Go to Berlin"

1. "Coach Prefers Longer Route," *Los Angeles Times*, 30 June 1936, A12.

2. George M. Varnell, "Huskies Go to Work, Awaiting Olympic Trials," *Seattle Times*, 25 June 1936, 22.

3. Ibid.

4. "Penn Crew at Princeton," *New York Times*, 2 July 1936, 18.

5. "Cracked Rib Forces Sweep Swinger Daggett Out of Bear Boat in Crew Trials," *Los Angeles Times*, 30 June 1936, A12; Jim Lemmon, *The Log of Rowing at the University of California, Berkeley, 1870–1987* (Berkeley, CA: Western Heritage Press, 1989), 30–31; Intercollegiate Rowing Association, *Annual Regatta of the Intercollegiate Rowing Association, Poughkeepsie, June 22, 1936* (New York, NY: Intercollegiate Rowing Association, 1936), 15, http://library.marist.edu/archives/regatta/pdf_programs/1936_IRA_Program.pdf; Clarence Dirks, "California Varsity Will Include Six Major Stars," *Seattle Post-Intelligencer*, 5 April 1936, 21.

6. Robert F. Kelley, "Washington, the Favorite, Will Row against N.Y.A.C. and Tiger Eights in First Heat Today," *New York Times*, 4 July 1936, 7.

7. Intercollegiate Rowing Association, *Annual Regatta*, 8.

8. "One More River to Cross," *Poughkeepsie Eagle-News*, 15 June 1936, 7.

9. Kelley, "Washington, the Favorite," 7; Peter Mallory, "Joe Burk, Sculler," 8 January 2008, http://www.row2k.com/features/features.cfm?action=read&ID=357#.UAcbTZH5DDU.

10. Thomas C. Mendenhall, "The Dour Dane," *Rowing USA*, June–July 1982, 9–13; Thomas C. Mendenhall, "Rusty Callow" *The Oarsman*, September–October 1980, 5–6; Stanley H. Woodward, "Mr. Callow Takes On the West," *Literary Digest*, 15 June 1935, 32.

11. Frederick W. Rubien, ed., *Report of the American Olympic Committee, Games of the Xth Olympiad, Los Angeles, California, July 30–August 14, 1932, III Olympic Winter Games, Lake Placid, New York, February 4–13, 1932* (New York, NY: American Olympic Committee, 1933), 184.

12. Jim McMillin interview, 19 October 2004, 8; "Husky Coach Lauds Crew," *Los Angeles Times*, 2 July 1936, A9; Gordon B. Adam, *An Olympian's Oral History: Gordon B. Adam, 1936 Olympic Games, Rowing* (Los Angeles: Amateur Athletic Foundation of Los Angeles, 1988), 1–4, http://www.la84foundation.org/6oic/OralHistory/OHAdam.pdf.

13. Grantland Rice, "The Sportlight: Memories of Italy's 1932 Crew," *Boston Globe*, 25 June 1936, 22.

14. Royal Brougham, "Husky Varsity Wins Race," *Seattle Post-Intelligencer*, 5 July 1936, 15; "Eight-Oared Crews Meet in Olympic Test Today," *Los Angeles Times*, 4 July 1936, 11; McMillin interview, 5–6; Joe Rantz interview with Dan Raley (2nd 1999 interview), 3; "The Oarsmen," *New Yorker*, 6 June 1936, 63.

15. Robert F. Kelley, "Coast Crews Lead in Olympic Trials," *New York Times*, 5 July 1936, S1; "The Weather over the Nation and Abroad," *New York Times*, 5 July 1936, 11.

16. Brougham, "Husky Varsity Wins Race," 14; George M. Varnell, "Huskies, Bears Win Eight-Oared Heats," *Seattle Daily Times*, 5 July 1936, 13; Kelley, "Coast Crews Lead in Olympic Trials," S1.

17. Brougham, "Husky Varsity Wins Race," 1, 14.

18. McMillin interview, 8; Robert F. Kelley, "Splendid Race Establishes Washington Crew as U.S. Olympic Standard Bearer," *New York Times*, 6 July 1936, 19.

19. "Olympic Crew Trial Won by Huskies," *Washington Post*, 6 July 1936, 14; "Report of the Secretary, Frederick W. Rubien," in Frederick W. Rubien, ed., *Report of the American Olympic Committee: Games of the XIth Olympiad, Berlin, Germany, August 1–16, 1936; IVth Olympic Winter Games, Garmisch-Partenkirchen, Germany, February 6–16, 1936* (New York, NY: American Olympic Committee, 1936), 45 [hereafter: *Report of the American Olympic Committee, 1936*]; "Boat Races," Program Card, Entry for WJZ, 6 July 1936, 5:00–5:23 p.m., NBC Program Cards, NBC Collection, Library of Congress [hereafter: NBCPC-LC].

20. Royal Brougham, "Huskies Win Olympic Tryouts in Record Time," *Seattle Post-Intelligencer*, 6 July 1936, 13.

21. McMillin interview, 8; Bill Henry, "Washington Crew Wins Berlin Trip," *Los Angeles Times*, 6 July 1936, A9.

22. Grantland Rice, "Italian Eight Called Big Foe of Washington at Olympics," *Baltimore Sun*, 6 July 1936, 9.

23. "The Washington Team Wins the Finals of a Rowing Competition and Qualifies for the . . . HD Stock Footage," *Critical Past*, Youtube.com, https://www.youtube.com/watch?v=2QD09Be3gMA.

24. Brougham, "Huskies Win Olympic Tryouts," 1; "Olympic Crew Trial Won by Huskies"; George M. Varnell, "Washington Earns Games Berth," *Seattle Times*, 6 July 1936, 18.

25. Robert Moch interview, 12 October 2004, 17; "Boat Races," Program Card, entry for WJZ, 07/05/36, 5:00–5:23 p.m., NBCPC-LC.

26. Jack Cuddy, "Ulbrickson Says 'Mental Attitude' Won Olympic Crew Trials for Huskies," *Los Angeles Times*, 7 July 1936, A10.

27. "Callow Quits, Report Says," *Seattle Post-Intelligencer*, 7 July 1936, 15.

28. Henry, "Washington Crew Wins Berlin Trip"; George E. Timpson, "Washington Crew to Row for America at Olympics," *Christian Science Monitor*, 6 July 1936, 10.

29. In 1936 sprint racing distances were not yet standardized. U.S. sprint races measured 1¼ mile but international sprint racing measured 2,000 meters—about

thirty-eight feet less than the U.S. standard. Record is noted in "University of Washington Crews, 1899–1938," 9, Folder 9, Box 12, Thomas C. Mendenhall Collection, Mystic Seaport Museum and Library, Mystic, CT [hereafter: TCM-MSML].

30. "Huskies Give It Old Heave-Ho and Win Another Olympic Rowing Crown," *Los Angeles Times*, 15 August 1936, 9; Moch 2004 interview, 7.

31. Moch 2004 interview, 7–8. Eckmann made the trip east with the crew, and he was in both Poughkeepsie and Princeton. He had been named athletic director of the university in April 1936. See Royal Brougham, "The Morning After," *Seattle Post-Intelligencer*, 21 April 1936, 11.

32. Brougham, "Huskies Win Olympic Tryouts," 14.

33. "Olympic Crew Trial," 14.

34. Gordon R. Newell, *Ready All! George Yeoman Pocock and Crew Racing* (Seattle: University of Washington Press, 1987), 101.

35. Brougham, "Huskies Win Olympic Tryouts," 13.

36. George M. Varnell, "Varnell Says," *Seattle Times*, 10 July 1936, 14.

37. Adam, *An Olympian's Oral History*, 20–21; McMillin interview, 3.

38. Burke quoted in George M. Varnell, "Varnell Says," *Seattle Times*, 6 July 1936, 18.

39. "Washington Earns Games Berth," *Seattle Daily Times*, 6 July 1936, 18; "$6,000 in Rowing Fund," *New York Times*, 6 July 1936, 19.

40. "On to Berlin! Say Seattle Dollars! U of W Crew Needs $5,000," *Seattle Times*, 6 July 1936, 1.

41. Henry, "Washington Crew Wins Berlin Trip"; G. M. V., "Jim M'Millin New Skipper for U.W. Crew," *Seattle Times*, 6 July 1936, 18; McMillin interview, 9.

42. Brougham, "Huskies Win Olympic Tryouts," 13; Royal Brougham, "Husky Crew Eager to Hear of Drive," *Seattle Post-Intelligencer*, 7 July 1936, 15; "Olympic Fund Slump Eases," *Baltimore Sun*, 7 July 1936, 13.

43. "Huskies Go on Sightseeing Trip," *Seattle Times*, 8 July 1936, 16; "Nation's Greatest Oarsmen Climb High to Secure Birds-Eye View of Largest City," *Spokane Daily Chronicle*, 25 July 1936, 12; Malcolm Roy, "Huskies Nearly Lost on Foul," *New York Sun*, 9 July 1936, 25.

44. "On to Berlin!" *Seattle Times*, 6 July 1936, 1; "Husky Drive Going Over," *Seattle Post-Intelligencer*, 7 July 1936, 1.

45. Carolyn Marvin, "Avery Brundage and American Participation in the 1936 Olympic Games," *Journal of American Studies* 16, no. 1 (1982): 81–106. "Iron Chancellor" description on page 81.

46. Arnd Krüger, "United States of America: The Crucial Battle," in *The Nazi Olympics: Sport, Politics, and Appeasement in the 1930s,* ed. Arnd Krüger and William Murray (Urbana: University of Illinois Press, 2003), 60; "Report of the President, Avery Brundage," and "Report of the Treasurer, Gustavus T. Kirby," in *Report of the American Olympic Committee, 1936,* 37.

47. Maxine Davis, *The Lost Generation* (New York, NY: Macmillan, 1936), 41.

48. On Pegler's commentary, see Deborah E. Lipstadt, *Beyond Belief: The American Press and the Coming of the Holocaust, 1933–1945* (New York, NY: Simon and Schuster, 1993), 73–74.

49. "Storm over Berlin," *Literary Digest*, 31 August 1935, 34.

50. Hendrik Willem Van Loon, *Air-storming* (New York, NY: Harcourt, Brace, 1935), 166–68.

51. Cornelis van Minnen, *Van Loon: Popular Historian, Journalist, and FDR Confidant* (New York, NY: Palgrave Macmillan, 2005), 156.

52. John F. Royal to N. Van Doren, 15 November 1935, Folder 6, Box 40, NBC Collection, Wisconsin Historical Society, Madison, WI [hereafter: NBC-WHS].

53. Handwritten note, signed "DS" on R. C. Patterson to David Sarnoff, 7 November 1935, Folder 6, Box 40, NBC-WHS.

54. Royal had already discussed technical and logistical details with German representatives—including booking hotel rooms—on a trip to Berlin in summer 1935. See John F. Royal to R. C. Patterson, 7 November 1935, Folder 6, Box 40; and John F. Royal to Mr. R. C. Patterson, 15 November 1935, Folder 62, Box 12, NBC-WHS; William Lundell to John F. Royal, 9 November 1935, Folder 62, Box 12, NBC-WHS.

55. "Jews in America," *Fortune*, February 1936, 134. On Paley's sensitivity about his Judaism, see Sally Bedell Smith, *In All His Glory: The Life of William S. Paley, the Legendary Tycoon and His Brilliant Circle* (New York, NY: Simon and Schuster, 1990), 41–45, 145–47, 510.

56. "Mount Olympus," *Jewish Standard* [Jersey City, NJ], 18 October 1935, 1.

57. CBS Helsinki Broadcast, 4, Box 13, Bill Henry Collection, Occidental College, Los Angeles, CA [hereafter: BHC-OC].

58. CBS Helsinki Broadcast, 5, Box 13, BHC-OC; "Berlin," *Variety*, 28 August 1935, 52.

59. Bill Henry, "U.S. Writer at Loss Understand Attitude to Berlin Olympics," *Lethbridge Herald*, 14 August 1935, 13.

60. Bill Henry, "U.S. Olympic Games Entry Wins Support," *Salt Lake Tribune*, 13 August 1935, 11.

61. "Sherrill Decries Fight on Olympics," *New York Times*, 1 November 1935, 15.

62. "Advertising Club of New York Luncheon," NBC-WEAF Broadcast, 31 October 1936, Call Number: RWC 6819 A2, NBC Radio Collection, Recorded Sound Reference Center, Library of Congress [hereafter: NBCR-LC].

63. An acute sensitivity to the relationship between Jewish interests and the boycott movement existed—so much so that President Roosevelt refused to take sides. See Andrew Nagorski, *Hitlerland: American Eyewitnesses to the Nazi Rise to Power* (New York, NY: Simon and Schuster, 2012), 191.

64. "Hays Replies to Sherrill," *New York Times*, 1 November 1935, 15; "Nazi Aid Seen in Games," *New York Times*, 1 November 1935, 15.

65. Mark Ryan, *Running with Fire: The True Story of "Chariots of Fire" Hero Harold Abrahams* (London, U.K.: Robson Press, 2012), 194.

66. "Jesse Owens and the Nazi Olympics," episode 2, series 6, *Things We Forgot to Remember*, BBC Radio 4, 1 August 2011, http://www.bbc.co.uk/programmes/b00w1xwj. See also "Should We Send a Jew to Cover the Berlin Olympics?" *Sports Journalists' Association* [U.K.], 17 July 2012, http://www.sportsjournalists.co.uk/olympics/should-we-send-a-jew-to-cover-the-berlin-olympics/.

67. "Jesse Owens and the Nazi Olympics." See also Jemima Kiss, "Media: BBC Archives: The Past on File," *The Guardian* [U.K.], 20 April 2009, 7.

68. Krüger, "United States of America," 54–55.

69. Quoted in Marty Glickman, *The Fastest Kid on the Block* (Syracuse, NY: Syracuse University Press, 1996), 27. Brundage noted in the AOC's final report that a chief obstacle to financing the games consisted of "the active boycott by Jews and Communists." "Report of the Chairman of the Finance Committee, Avery Brundage," in *Report of the American Olympic Committee, 1936*, 73. See also Marvin, "Avery Brundage and American Participation," 81–109.

70. William J. Bingham, "The Olympic Games," *Harvard–Yale Regatta Program* (1936), 40. Box 3, Varsity Boat Club Records, Special Collections, University of Washington Library, Seattle, WA.

71. Norman Falahee, "Government or Game?" *Columns*, January 1936, 11.

72. Glickman, *Fastest Kid on the Block*, 13.

73. Transcript of John Woodruff interview at "African American Athletes," in the United States Holocaust Memorial Museum's online exhibition, "The Nazi Olympics: Berlin, 1936," http://www.ushmm.org/exhibition/olympics/.

74. Joe Rantz interview with Dan Raley (1999), 3; Adam, *An Olympian's Oral History*, 12.

75. Moch 2004 interview, 17.

76. Sharon Kinney Hanson, *The Life of Helen Stephens: The Fulton Flash* (Carbondale: University of Southern Illinois Press, 2004), 58–60.

77. Max Jordan to John F. Royal, 9 November 1935, and John F. Royal to R. C. Patterson, 12 November 1936, Folder 6, Box 40, NBC-WHS. On coverage plans, see Max Jordan to John F. Royal, 22 August 1935, and John F. Royal to R. C. Patterson, 7 November 1935, Folder 6, Box 40, NBC-WHS.

78. "Report of the President, Avery Brundage" and "Report of the Treasurer, Gustavus T. Kirby," in *Report of the American Olympic Committee, 1936*, 37, 59.

79. "Report of the President, Avery Brundage," in *Report of the American Olympic Committee, 1936*, 37.

80. "$5,000 Check Sent to Crew for Berlin Trip," *Seattle Daily Times*, 10 July 1936, 1.

81. "Olympics Past and Present," National Broadcasting Company, 10 July 1936, Folder 1, Box 491, NBC-WHS.

82. "Olympic Prospects with Bill Slater," NBC Program Card, Entry for WJZ, 15 April 1936–8 July 1936, 7:15 to 7:30 p.m., NBCPC-LC.

83. César Saerchinger, *Hello America! Radio Adventures in Europe* (Boston, MA: Houghton Mifflin, 1938), 190.

84. On German assistance to CBS and NBC, see Reichs-Rundfunk-Gesellschaft, *Olympia-Weltsender: Olympia World Station* (Berlin, Germany: Deutscher Verlag für Politik und Wirtschaft, 1937).

85. "Coxswain," *New Yorker*, 18 July 1936, 8.

86. Brougham, "Husky Crew Eager to Hear of Drive," 15 McMillin interview, 9; Moch 2004 interview, 8; Adam, *An Olympian's Oral History*, 9; Newell, *Ready All!* 101.

87. Newell, *Ready All!* 102; Adam, *An Olympian's Oral History*, 10.

88. "American Olympic Committee Handbook," reprinted in *Report of the American Olympic Committee, 1936*, 51.

89. "Report of Chairman of Administration Committee, A. C. Gilbert," in *Report of the American Olympic Committee, 1936*, 61–62.

90. Alexander M. Weyand, *The Olympic Pageant* (New York, NY: Macmillan, 1952), 253.

91. "Olympic Games, 1936," NBC Program Card, Entry for WEAF, 07/15/1936, 11:15–11:30 a.m., NBCPC-LC; C. E. Butterfield, "Radio Day by Day," *Rome* [NY] *Daily Sentinel*, 10 July 1936, 9.

92. Weyand, *Olympic Pageant*, 253.

93. Barbara J. Keys, "Spreading Peace, Democracy, and Coca Cola," *Diplomatic History* 28, no. 2 (2004): 191.

94. Guy Walters, *Berlin Games: How the Nazis Stole the Olympic Dream* (New York, NY: William Morrow, 2006), 153.

95. Walters, *Berlin Games*, 154; "Offer of $100,000 for Olympic Fund Spurned," *Los Angeles Times*, 17 July 1936, A9.

96. "Offer of $100,000," A9; Walters, *Berlin Games*, 154.

97. Alvin Ulbrickson and Richard L. Neuberger, "Now! Now! Now!" *Collier's*, 27 June 1937, 21.

98. "Offer of $100,000," A14; Walters, *Berlin Games*, 156.

99. "Report of Chairman of Uniform Committee, Frederick W. Rubien," *Report of the American Olympic Committee, 1936*, 77.

100. McMillin interview, 9–10; Adam, *An Olympian's Oral History*, 10–11.

101. Ulbrickson with Neuberger, "Now! Now! Now!" 56; J. P. Abramson, "Extra-Curricular Antics of Athletes Enlivened Olympians' Ocean Voyage, Called 'Best Ever,'" *New York Herald Tribune*, 2 August 1936, section 3, 3.

102. Adam, *An Olympian's Oral History*, 10; Moch 2004 interview, 8.

103. Craig Lambert, "Three Olympics," *Harvard Magazine*, September–October 1988, 61.

104. Walters, *Berlin Games*, 157.

105. Charles Fountain, *Sportswriter: The Life and Times of Grantland Rice* (New York, NY: Oxford University Press, 1993), 251.

106. David Clay Large, *Nazi Games: The Olympics of 1936* (New York, NY: W. W. Norton, 2007), 180–81.

107. See, for instance, "Arthur O. Mollner Interview" (May 1988), 11, http://www.la84foundation.org/6oic/OralHistory/OHMollner.pdf; Moch 2004 interview, 8.

108. "Report of Chairman of Transportation Committee, Daniel J. Ferris," in *Report of the American Olympic Committee, 1936*, 82; Moch 2004 interview, 9; "George Hunt Gives Views on Berlin, Nazis, Olympic Games," *Puyallup* [WA] *Press*, August 1936, 1.

109. Lawrence Terry to Tom Mendenhall, 25 August 1982, Folder 6, Box 17, TCM-MSML.

110. Arthur Daley, "Sports of the Times," *New York Times*, 7 March 1943, S2.

Chapter 3. Berlin 1936 as Global Broadcast Spectacle and Personal Experience

1. Al Ulbrickson, as told to Clarence Dirks, "Cracked Oar Sweeps Hudson," *Ken*, 14 July 1938, 66.

2. "Cracked Oar Sweeps Hudson," 66; "George Hunt Gives Views on Berlin, Nazis, Olympic Games," *Puyallup* [WA] *Press*, 21 August 1936, 1, 7; Gordon B. Adam, *An Olympian's Oral History: Gordon B. Adam, 1936 Olympic Games, Rowing* (Los Angeles, CA: Amateur Athletic Foundation of Los Angeles, 1988), 11, http://www.la84foundation .org/6oic/OralHistory/OHAdam.pdf; "Accord U.S. Team Fine Reception in Hamburg," *North Tonawanda* [NY] *Evening News*, 24 July 1936, 8.

3. Gordon R. Newell, *Ready All! George Yeoman Pocock and Crew Racing* (Seattle: University of Washington Press, 1987), 104; "George Hunt Gives Views."

4. "George Hunt Gives Views"; "Nazis Restrained during Olympics," *New York Sun*, 10 July 1936, 1; Genêt [Janet Flanner], "Berlin Letter," *New Yorker*, 1 August 1936, 40; Alexander M. Weyand, *The Olympic Pageant* (New York, NY: Macmillan, 1952), 251; William L. Shirer, *The Nightmare Years, 1930–1940* (Boston, MA: Little, Brown, 1984), 230. See also Arnd Krüger, "The Ministry of Popular Enlightenment and Propaganda and the Nazi Olympics of 1936," in *Fourth International Symposium of Olympic Research* (1998), 40, http://library.la84.org/SportsLibrary/ISOR/ISOR1998g.pdf.

5. Newell, *Ready All!* 104; Paul Gallico, "Two Mystery Ousters Thin Olympic Team," *Washington Post*, 30 July 1936, 15.

6. Arthur J. Daley, "Tens of Thousands Line Streets to Welcome U.S. Team to Berlin," *New York Times*, 25 July 1936, 7.

7. César Saerchinger, *Hello America! Radio Adventures in Europe* (Boston, MA: Houghton Mifflin, 1938), 190.

8. "George Hunt Gives Views"; Daley, "Tens of Thousands"; *Olympian's Oral History*, 11.

9. Albion Ross, "Berlin's Unter den Linden Jammed as Olympic Mania Grips the City," *New York Times*, 27 July 1936, 11; Daley, "Tens of Thousands"; Adam, *Olympian's Oral History*, 11; "George Hunt Gives Views."

10. Howard K. Smith, *Events Leading Up to My Death: The Life of a Twentieth-Century Reporter* (New York, NY: St. Martin's Press, 1996), 28. See also "Howard K. Smith on living in Germany in 1936—EMMYTVLEGENDS.ORG," Youtube.com, https://www .youtube.com/watch?v=QxbCFYmmlKs.

11. Marty Glickman, *Fastest Kid on the Block: The Marty Glickman Story* (Syracuse, NY: Syracuse University Press, 1999), 14.

12. Genêt, "Berlin Letter," 22 August 1936, 65. On "Travel Marks," see "Advertisement: American Express Travel Department," *Vogue*, 15 June 1936, 12.

13. "Half-Year Holidays for Nazis Olympic Victors," *New York Sun*, 17 August 1936, 28.

14. "Olympiad Bid Goes on the Air," *Los Angeles Times*, 23 May 1932, A1; "Pre-Olympic Hour with Will Rogers," *Brooklyn Daily Eagle*, 22 May 1932, E6. Barbara Keys argues these and other promotional appeals worked, as the 1932 games generated surplus gate receipts of $1.5 million. See Barbara J. Keys, "Spreading Peace, Democracy, and Coca Cola," *Diplomatic History* 28, no. 2 (2004): 170.

15. Michael J. Socolow, "'Always in Friendly Competition': NBC and CBS in the First Decade of National Broadcasting," in *NBC: America's Network*, ed. Michele Hilmes (Berkeley: University of California Press, 2007), 35.

16. Keys, "Spreading Peace, Democracy, and Coca Cola," 171. See also Barbara J. Keys, *Globalizing Sport: National Rivalry and International Community in the 1930s* (Cambridge, MA: Harvard University Press, 2006), 99–100.

17. "Olympic Radio Program," *New York Times*, 5 February 1932, 26.

18. Adolf Hitler and H. R. Trevor-Roper, *Hitler's Secret Conversations, 1941–1944* (New York, NY: Signet, 1953), 404.

19. "Storm over Berlin," *Literary Digest*, 31 August 1935, 34; John Kieran, "On Your Mark for the Olympic Games!" *New York Times*, 26 July 1936, S10; Alexander M. Weyand, *The Olympic Pageant* (New York, NY: Macmillan, 1952), 251.

20. *Olympian's Oral History*, 12–13; Amanda Smith, "Remembering the 1936 Berlin 'Nazi Olympics,'" *Bodysphere*, ABC Radio (Australia), 5 August 2015, http://www.abc.net.au/radionational/programs/bodysphere/remembering-the-1936-berlin-nazi-olympics/6674614; Henry McLemore, "Germany Turns Other Cheek to Unruly Olympic Guests," *Hammond* [IN] *Times*, 25 July 1936, 10.

21. Shirer, *Nightmare Years*, 232.

22. John W. Elwood to M. H. Aylesworth, 17 April 1933, Folder 4, Box 10, NBC-WHS; Max Jordan, *Beyond All Fronts* (Milwaukee, WI: Bruce, 1944), 94. On the career of Magnus, see "Kurt, Dr. Magnus" [webpage], http://www.stiftung-bg.de/kz-oranienburg/index.php?id=202.

23. "Broadcasts to Germany Every Other Friday," *Broadcasting*, 15 December 1931, 20; "Former Radio Chief a Suicide in Berlin," *New York Times*, 30 March 1933, 12; Horst J. P. Bergmeier and Rainer E. Lotz, *Hitler's Airwaves: The Inside Story of Nazi Radio Broadcasting and Propaganda Swing* (New Haven, CT: Yale University Press, 1997), 18; Jordan, *Beyond All Fronts*, 94; Kate Lacey, *Feminine Frequencies: Gender, German Radio, and the Public Sphere, 1923–1945* (Ann Arbor: University of Michigan Press, 1996), 100–101.

24. Carolyn Birdsall, *Nazi Soundscapes: Sound, Technology and Urban Space in Germany, 1933–1945* (Amsterdam, Netherlands: Amsterdam University Press, 2012), 53–54; Bergmeier and Lotz, *Hitler's Airwaves*, 18–19.

25. "Plan Ultra Short Net," *Broadcasting*, 15 July 1934, 28; Lacey, *Feminine Frequencies*, 101–4; Michael Zwerin, *Swing under the Nazis: Jazz as a Metaphor for Freedom* (New York,

NY: Rowman and Littlefield, 2000), 119–20; Horst Dressler-Andress, "German Broadcasting," *Annals of the American Academy of Political and Social Science*, 177 (1935): 63.

26. Jordan, *Beyond All Fronts*, 251.

27. Eugen Hadamovsky, *Propaganda and National Power* (New York, NY: Arno Press, 1972), 69, 56.

28. On Goebbels's belief in radio's supremacy as a mass communications medium, see Bergmeier and Lotz, *Hitler's Airwaves*, 6–8; David A. Welch, "Restructuring the Means of Communication in Nazi Germany," in *Readings in Propaganda and Persuasion: New and Classic Essays*, ed. Garth S. Jowett and Victoria O'Donnell (Thousand Oaks, CA: Sage, 2006), 128–30.

29. Bergmeier and Lotz, *Hitler's Airwaves*, 138–39; Michael Dregni, *Django: The Life and Music of a Gypsy Legend* (New York, NY: Oxford University Press, 2006), 157.

30. Dregni, *Django*, 64.

31. Eugen Hadamovsky, "Wireless and the Olympic Games," in *Olympia-Weltsender* (Berlin, Germany: Reichs-Rundfunk-Gesellschaft, 1937), 6.

32. Pierre Aycoberry, *The Social History of the Third Reich, 1933–1945* (New York, NY: New Press, 1999), 75.

33. See, for example, Ewald Grothe, "Die Olympischen Spiele von 1936—Höhepunkt der NS-Propaganda?" *Geschichte und Wissenschaft im Unterricht* 59 (2008): 291–307; Allen Guttmann, "Berlin, 1936: The Most Controversial Olympics," in *National Identity and Global Sports Events: Culture, Politics, and Spectacle in the Olympics and the Football World Cup*, ed. Alan Tomlinson and Christopher Young (Albany: State University of New York Press, 2006), 70–73.

34. Louis P. Lochner, *What about Germany?* (New York, NY: Dodd, Mead, 1942), 64.

35. Keys, "Spreading Peace, Democracy, and Coca Cola," 172.

36. Jeff Schutts, "'Die Erfrischende Pause': Marketing Coca-Cola in Hitler's Germany," in *Selling Modernity: Advertising in Twentieth-Century Germany*, ed. Pamela E. Swett, S. Jonathan Wiesen, and Jonathan R. Zatlin (Durham, NC: Duke University Press, 2007), 162. In the United States, former swimming gold medalist (and Hollywood celebrity) Johnny Weissmuller became the first Olympic athlete to endorse Coca-Cola in 1934 (Keys, "Spreading Peace, Democracy, and Coca Cola," 172).

37. Schutts, "Erfrischende Pause," 162.

38. Keys, "Spreading Peace, Democracy, and Coca Cola," 168.

39. Kate Lacey, "Radio in the Great Depression: Promotional Culture, Public Service, and Propaganda," in *Radio Reader: Essays in the Cultural History of Radio*, ed. Michele Hilmes and Jason Loviglio (New York, NY: Routledge, 2002), 21–40.

40. On the transition in U.S. radio, see Louis E. Carlat, "Sound Values: Radio Broadcasts of Classical Music and American Culture, 1922–1939," PhD diss., Johns Hopkins University, 1995. For the transition in German radio, see Bergmeier and Lotz, *Hitler's Airwaves*.

41. Lacey, *Feminine Frequencies*, 110; Susan J. Douglas, *Listening In* (New York, NY: Times Books, 1999); Donna L. Halper, *Invisible Stars: A Social History of Women in American*

Broadcasting (Armonk, NY: M. E. Sharpe, 2001); Michele Hilmes, *Radio Voices: American Broadcasting, 1922–1952* (Minneapolis: University of Minnesota Press, 1997); Allison McCracken, *Real Men Don't Sing: Crooning in American Culture* (Durham, NC: Duke University Press, 2015).

42. Suzanne Lommers, *Europe—On Air: Interwar Projects for Radio Broadcasting* (Amsterdam, Netherlands: Amsterdam University Press, 2012), 115–16.

43. "NBC Obtains Sole Right to Dirigible's Inaugural; Nets Cover 'Queen Mary'" *Broadcasting*, 1 April 1936, 30; "From the Zeppelin's Cabin," *Broadcasting*, 15 May 1936, 40; "Personal Notes," *Broadcasting*, 1 July 1936, 81; Herbert Lennartz, "Radio aboard the 'Hindenburg,'" *Radio News*, August 1936, 72.

44. On Baier's role in Berlin and assisting Jordan, see "Rundfunkmitarbeiter Sommerspiele 1936," *Die Olympischen Spiele 1936 im NS-Rundfunk*, http://1936.dra.de/?id=54; "One of the Party," *Broadcasting*, 4 August 1941, 38B.

45. David J. Halberstam, *Sports on New York Radio: A Play-by-Play History* (Lincolnwood, IL: Masters Press, 1999), 43–44; John Lewis, *Radio Master: The Life and Times of Sports Broadcasting Great Ted Husing* (Minneapolis, MN: Langdon Street Press, 2010), 174. Slater's style is described in "Olympic Cavalcade," *Motion Picture Daily*, 30 August 1948, 4.

46. On Slater's resemblance to Husing, see "Radio Dial Log," *Brooklyn Daily Eagle*, 6 July 1936, 8.

47. Robert West, *The Rape of Radio* (New York, NY: Rodin, 1941), 401; Lewis, *Radio Master*, 174; "Bill Slater Gets His Stories from the Stars," *Radio Mirror*, February 1948, 4; Ted Patterson, *The Golden Voices of Football* (Champaign, IL: Sports Publishing, 2004), 76; Marion Slater, "William E. Slater 1924," https://apps.westpointaog.org/Memorials/Article/7466/.

48. Ellipses in original. See Philco advertisement, *American Legion Monthly*, August 1936, 4.

49. Jordan, *Beyond All Fronts*, 162.

50. Shirer, *Nightmare Years*, 232.

51. Paul Gallico, "Gallico Tells How Hitler Dominates Olympic Games, Even Censoring His Stories," *Buffalo Courier Express*, 5 April 1936, 9.

52. Thomas Wolfe, *You Can't Go Home Again* (New York, NY: Harper and Row, 1940), 621.

53. Ibid., 625–27.

54. Ibid., 626.

55. Irene Awret, *They'll Have to Catch Me First: An Artist's Coming of Age in the Third Reich* (Madison: University of Wisconsin Press, 2004), 96.

56. Peter Gay, *My German Question: Growing Up in Nazi Berlin* (New Haven, CT: Yale University Press, 1999), 78–95; Frederic C. Tubach and Sally Patterson, *German Voices: Memories of Life during Hitler's Third Reich* (Berkeley: University of California Press, 2011), 40; Joachim Fest, *Not I: Memoirs of a German Childhood* (New York, NY: Other Press, 2014), 96.

57. John R. Tunis, "The Dictators Discover Sport," *Foreign Affairs*, July 1936, https://www.foreignaffairs.com/articles/russian-federation/1936-07-01/dictators -discover-sport.

58. "Speaking of Liberty," NBC, 14 August 1941, https://archive.org/details/ SpeakingOfLiberty.

59. Deborah E. Lipstadt, *Beyond Belief: The American Press and the Coming of the Holocaust, 1933–1945* (New York, NY: Simon and Schuster, 1993), 73–74.

60. Joe Williams, "Modern Germany an Enigma," *New York World-Telegram*, 14 August 1936, 16.

61. "World Will Listen: Elaborate Radio Plans for Olympiad," *Nottingham* [England] *Evening Post*, 16 July 1936, 3.

62. David H. Hosley, *As Good As Any: Foreign Correspondence on American Radio, 1930– 1940* (Westport, CT: Greenwood Press, 1984), 12–13.

63. Jordan, *Beyond All Fronts*, xi–xii, 166–68. Jordan notes "Karl Nord" was a pseudonym employed to protect his colleague.

64. "Ted Husing's Wife to Sue for Divorce," *New York Sun*, 10 July 1936, 1.

65. "Ted Husing Eases Up," *Variety*, 1 July 1936, 27; William L. Stuart, "The Radio Reporter," *Oakland Tribune*, 9 August 1936, 14; "Radio Dial Log," *Brooklyn Daily Eagle*, 6 July 1936, 8; "Eduard Roderich Dietze," *Die Olympischen Spiele 1936 im NS-Rundfunk*, http://1936.dra.de/?id=66. Dietze also regularly broadcast for the BBC. On CBS's use of the Berlin broadcasts to gain on NBC, see William B. Lewis, "CBS Program Division Reports for 1936, Plans for 1937," 22, in Box 3, William B. Lewis Papers, Boston University Archives, Boston, MA.

66. Ted Husing with Cy Rice, *My Eyes Are in My Heart* (New York, NY: Bernard Geis, 1959), 33.

67. "Girls to Play Ophelia," *Buffalo Courier-Express*, 12 July 1936, 2; "Americans in London," *Variety*, 5 August 1936, 12.

68. Stanley Wertheim interview, 13 May 2015; Lewis, *Radio Master*, 258–59. On Husing's feelings about his Judaism, see Husing and Rice, *My Eyes Are in My Heart*, 33–34.

69. Patricia Henry Yeomans, ed., *Behind the Headlines with Bill Henry, 1903–1970* (Los Angeles, CA: Ward Ritchie Press, 1972), 59.

70. *The XIth Olympic Games Berlin, 1936: Official Report*, 2 vols. (Berlin, Germany: Wilhelm Limpert, 1937), 1: 217–18 [hereafter: *Official Report*].

71. "Reich Radio to Link Nations for Games," *New York Times*, 19 July 1936, 17.

72. *Official Report*, 1: 336; H. Dewald, "Application of Lorenz Communication Technique at the Olympic Games, Germany, 1936," *Electrical Communication*, April 1937, 281–82; David Morton, *Off the Record: The Technology and Culture of Sound Recording in America* (New Brunswick, NJ: Rutgers University Press, 2000), 57–58; "World Will Listen."

73. Dewald, "Application of Lorenz," 282.

74. "Die Technischen Vorbereitungen des Rundfunks zur Olympiade," *Funk Wacht Nordland*, 19–25 July 1936, 9. [Translation is by Anette Ruppel Rodrigues.]

75. Examples of the variety in estimates: "The Engineer's Report," *Olympia-Weltsender*, 72; "Reich Radio to Link Nations for Games"; Z. A. B. Zeman, *Nazi Propaganda* (London, U.K.: Oxford University Press, 1964), 110.

76. "McGlashan's Olympics," *Broadcasting*, 15 August 1936, 60.

77. "Reich Radio to Link Nations for Games"; "Olympic Relays: American Stations Linked to 40-Nations Switchboard at Berlin Stadium," *New York Times*, 26 July 1936, S10.

78. "Berlin, 1936: A Condenser Microphone Used during the Games," in "Live! Broadcasting the Olympic Games," Olympic Museum, http://www.olympic.org/museum/interactive-documentary/broadcasting/#1940.

79. "Die Bedeutung der Rundfunktechnik für die Berichterstattung von den Olympischen Spielen 1936 in Garmisch-Partenkirchen und Berlin," *Die Olympischen Spiele 1936 im NS-Rundfunk*, http://1936.dra.de/index.php?id=144; Dewald, "Application of Lorenz," 282.

80. "Communication at the Olympiad," *Bell Laboratories Record*, September 1932, 14.

81. On NHK and 1932 Olympics, see Hisateru Furuta, *Broadcasting in Japan: The Twentieth Century Journey from Radio to Multimedia* (Tokyo, Japan: NHK Broadcasting Culture Research Institute, 2002), 45–46; Ryoto Ono, "Japan," in *The Museum of Broadcast Communications Encyclopedia of Radio*, 3 vols., ed. Christopher H. Sterling and Michael C. Keith (New York, NY: Taylor and Francis, 2004), 1: 833. Japan sent 130 athletes to Los Angeles, the largest foreign team (Keys, "Spreading Peace, Democracy, and Coca Cola" 177–78; Keys, *Globalizing Sport*, 111). The BBC originally contracted with CBS to carry the U.S. signal, but when CBS was refused live broadcast access, the deal fell through. See "Olympic Games: Running Commentary by Radio," *Citizen* [Gloucester, England], 30 March 1932, 6.

82. Keys, *Globalizing Sport*, 109–12. On the BBC–CBS negotiation, see "Olympic Games: Running Commentary." The BBC Year-Book covering 1 November 1931 to 31 October 1932 mentions neither Lake Placid nor Los Angeles under "Events of the Year," *B.B.C. Year-Book 1933* (London, U.K.: British Broadcasting Corporation, 1933), 215–24.

83. Jerome S. Berg, *On the Short Waves, 1923–1945: Broadcast Listening in the Pioneer Days of Radio* (Jefferson, NC: McFarland, 1999), 73–74; Bergmeier and Lotz, *Hitler's Airwaves*, 35–38; H. Mogel, "The World Broadcasting System, Berlin," *Electronics*, May 1934, 163; Dewald, "Application of Lorenz," 281–82.

84. "Olympic Relays."

85. "Germany Prepares for the Olympics" *Radio-Craft*, March 1936, 560.

86. César Saerchinger, "Propaganda Poisons Europe's Air," *Broadcasting*, 15 April 1938, 66.

87. "Reich Radio to Link Nations for Games."; Jordan, *Beyond All Fronts*, 164. *Official Report*, 1: 278–80, 335–50; Saerchinger, *Hello America!* 187; Shirer, *Nightmare Years*, 320; John McCoy, "Radio Sports Broadcasting in the United States, Britain, and Australia, 1920–1956 and Its Influence on the Olympic Games," *Journal of Olympic History* 5, no. 1 (1997): 23.

88. *The BBC Year-Book, 1937* (London, U.K.: British Broadcasting Corporation, 1934), 110.

89. Daley, "Tens of Thousands," 7.

90. "Unstarred Rowing Crew Champions," *Literary Digest*, 25 July 1936, 34.

91. *Official Report*, 1: 217–18.

92. Ibid., 1: 79, 218–20.

93. *Olympian's Oral History*, 12; "Oarsmen Find Foe Too Kind," *New York Post*, 30 July 1936, 22.

94. "Oarsmen Find Foe Too Kind," 22; *Official Report*, 1: 218.

95. Lawrence Terry to Tom Mendenhall, 25 August 1982, Folder 6, Box 17, Thomas C. Mendenhall Collection, Mystic Seaport Museum and Library, Mystic, CT; Lee Miller, "The Husky Crew at the Berlin Olympics, 1936," 13, University of Washington—Athletics—Crew: Pamphlet File, Allen Library Special Collections, University of Washington, Seattle, WA; "City's Olympic Athletes Speak to Kiwanians," *Puyallup* [WA] *Press*, 18 September 1936, 6.

96. "Olympic Event (Crew) at Lake Gruenau" (August 1936), Laszlo Antos Collection, Steven Spielberg Film and Video Archive, United States Holocaust Museum, Washington, DC, http://collections.ushmm.org/search/catalog/fv3674; "Perfect Course," *Olympic Games News Service*, 16 April 1935, 4; Miller, "Husky Crew," 3; "Olympic Games," *Times* [London, UK], 12 August 1936, 6.

97. Joe Rantz interview with Dan Raley (1999), 1; Jim McMillin interview, 19 October 2004, 15.

98. Miller, "Husky Crew," 4.

99. "Olympic Event (Crew) at Lake Gruenau."

100. "Grünauer Water Sports Museum," http://www.museumsportal-berlin.de/en/museums/grunauer-wassersportmuseum/.

101. *Official Report*, 1: 165; "Perfect Course," 4.

102. See, for example, the mobile shortwave transmitter placed in a motorboat to cover rowing races in 1933 in *Rundfunk-Jahrbuch 1933* (Berlin, Germany: Reichs-Rundfunk-Gesellschaft, 1934), 130–31.

103. "Die Erste Sport-Übertragung," in *Rundfunk-Jahrbuch 1933* (Berlin, Germany: Reichs-Rundfunk-Gesellschaft, 1934), 130–31.

104. "Zieltribüne in Grünau (DRA/ID-1425399)," *Olympische Sommerspiele 1936 in Berlin*, http://1936.dra.de/index.php?id=32.

105. *Official Report*, 1: 165; William J. Bingham, "The Olympic Games," *Harvard–Yale Regatta Program* (1936), 40; "Perfect Course," 4.

106. "Unstarred Rowing Crew Champions."

107. Cooper C. Graham, *Leni Riefenstahl and Olympia* (Metuchen, NJ: Scarecrow Press, 1986), 49–51, 120, 122; *Official Report*, 1: 330.

108. Graham, *Leni Riefenstahl and Olympia*, 50.

109. *Official Report*, 1: 121, 321.

110. *Official Report*, 1: 349.

111. A photo of the pontoon boat with shortwave relay can be found at "Sportreporter berichten aus einem Boot von der Regattastrecke in Grünau (DRA/ID-1425391)," *Rundfunktechnik bei den Olympischen Spielen 1936,* http://1936.dra.de/index.php?id=31. A photograph of one pontoon boat can be found at "Regattastrecke in Grünau (DRA/ Anton Pankofer/ID-1458828)" http://1936.dra.de/index.php?id=32.

112. *Official Report,* 1: 191.

113. "First Olympic Games Team in Berlin," *Times* [London, UK] 24 June 1936, 6; Newell, *Ready All!* 104.

114. "The Oarsmen," *New Yorker,* 4 July 1936, 41; on Perrier, *L'Auto,* and 1936 Olympics, see W. J. Murray, "France, Coubertin and the Nazi Olympics: The Response," *Olympika* 1 (1992): 46, 58; "Slow Trial Is Rowed by Washington Eight," *New York Times,* 1 August 1936, 6; McMillin interview, 15.

115. McMillin interview, 15.

116. Newell, *Ready All!* 105.

117. "Oarsmen Find Foe Too Kind," 22.

118. McMillin interview, 11; Moch, second 1999 interview with Dan Raley, 2.

119. "Hume Returns to Washington Crew for Drill," *Chicago Tribune,* 1 August 1936, 19; "Americans Recovering from Illnesses as Games Start," *Binghamton* [NY] *Press,* 1 August 1936, 1, 13; "Hume Back in Shell, Huskies Look Better," *New York Post,* 31 July 1936, 17.

120. "Slow Trial," 6.

121. Grantland Rice, "The Sportlight: Memories of Italy's 1932 Crew," *Boston Globe,* 25 June 1936, 22.

122. "The Oarsmen," *New Yorker,* 18 April 1936, 62.

123. Ibid.

124. "The Games of the XI Olympiad [1936 Berlin Olympics]: International Re-Broadcast," NBC Broadcast, 29 July 1936, Catalog ID: RB 13559, Paley Center for the Media Collection, New York, NY [hereafter: PCM-NY].

125. "Rede des Reichspropagandaministers Joseph Goebbels anlässlich der Eröffnung des 'Internationalen Kunstwettbewerbs,'" http://1936.dra.de/index.php?id=37.

126. "The Games of the XI Olympiad [1936 Berlin Olympics]: International Re-Broadcast," NBC Broadcast, 29 July 1936, Catalog ID: RB 1753, PCM-NY.

127. "The Games of the XI Olympiad [1936 Berlin Olympics]: International Re-Broadcast," NBC Broadcast, 30 July 1936, Catalog ID: RB 13558, PCM-NY.

128. "Ansprache des Reichspropagandaministers Joseph Goebbels vor Vertretern der ausländischen Presse," *Die Olympischen Spiele 1936 im NS-Rundfunk,* http://1936.dra .de/index.php?id=139#zitat456.

129. Ibid.

130. Ibid.; "Half Million to Hear Hitler," *New York Post,* 31 July 1936, 17.

131. Fabrice Abgrall and François Thomazeau, *1936: La France à l'Épreuve des Jeux Olympiques de Berlin* (Paris, France: Alvik, 2006), 173.

132. André François-Poncet, *The Fateful Years* (New York, NY: Howard Fertig, 1972), 204.

133. Abgrall and Thomazeau, *1936: La France à l'Épreuve*, 174.

134. McMillin interview, 11.

135. Robert Moch interview, 12 October 2004, 9.

136. Newell, *Ready All!* 105–6.

137. Paul Wolff, "What I Saw at the Olympics," in *Dr. Paul Wolff's Leica Sport Shots* (New York, NY: William Morrow, 1937), n.p.

138. Abgrall and Thomazeau, *1936: La France à l'Épreuve*, 175–76; Poncet, *Fateful Years*, 205.

139. Arthur J. Daley, "Training Violations Evoke Warning to Olympic Team," *New York Times*, 19 July 1936, S1.

140. Roger Morris interview with Dan Raley (1999), 1; Newell, *Ready All!* 106.

141. "Games of the XI Olympiad, The [1936 Berlin Olympics]: Opening Day and Opening Ceremony (Radio)," WABC—CBS, 1 August 1936, Catalog ID: RB 4941, PCM-NY.

142. Ibid.

143. Ibid.

144. Ibid.

145. Al Laney, "Nazis' Fervor Finds Climax in Olympic Rites," *New York Herald-Tribune*, 2 August 1936, 1.

146. "Hörzitate Sommerspiele," *Die Olympischen Spiele 1936 im NS-Rundfunk, DR*, http://1936.dra.de/index.php?id=38.

147. "Programs from Germany's Olympics Sound Pretty Good to U.S. Radio Trade," *Variety*, 5 August 1936, 34.

148. "100 Stations Carry Olympic Broadcast," *New York Times*, 2 August 1936, S3.

149. David Clay Large, *Nazi Games: The Olympics of 1936* (New York, NY: W. W. Norton, 2007), 199.

150. Ibid.

Chapter 4. Live from Hitler's Reich

1. David Welky, *Everything Was Better in America: Print Culture in the Great Depression* (Urbana: University of Illinois Press, 2008), 56.

2. Cooperative Analysis of Broadcasting, *Ten Years of Network Program Analysis* (New York, NY: Cooperative Analysis of Broadcasting, 1939), 36–39; Jim Ramsburg, *Network Radio Ratings, 1932–1953: A History of Prime Time Programs through the Ratings of Nielsen, Crossley, and Hooper* (Jefferson, NC: McFarland, 2012), 48.

3. Michael J. Socolow, "'Always in Friendly Competition': NBC and CBS in the First Decade of National Broadcasting," in *NBC: America's Network*, ed. Michele Hilmes (Berkeley: University of California Press, 2007), 25–43.

4. "Radio's New Rally," *Radio Today,* April 1936, 5; H. L. M. Capron, "Clear Out Old Models," *Radio Today,* May 1936, 22; "Here's the Real Reason Why People Buy Radios—NBC Programs!" [advertisement], *Radio Today,* May 1936, 2; "Ethered for Air," *Radio Today,* July 1936, 14.

5. National Broadcasting Company, *35 Hours a Day!* (New York, NY: National Broadcasting Company, 1937), 11, 38–39.

6. "Storm Interrupts Short-Wave Radio: Magnetic Disturbance Halts the Rebroadcast of the Olympic Games from Germany," *New York Times,* 15 February 1936, 18; Columbia Broadcasting System, *We Now Take You to . . .* (New York, NY: Columbia Broadcasting System, 1937), 124; César Saerchinger, *Hello America! Radio Adventures in Europe* (Boston, MA: Houghton Mifflin, 1938), 187–88.

7. CBS used sportswriter Paul Gallico, already covering the games for the *New York Daily News,* rather than send Bill Henry or Ted Husing. Columbia Broadcasting System, *We Now Take You to,* 124.

8. "Olympic Winter Games," 16 February 1936, NBC-Red, Recording RWC 6198 B2, NBC Radio Collection, Recorded Sound Reference Center, Library of Congress [hereafter: NBCR-LC].

9. For example, when Herman Göring arrived early to the swimming stadium, organizers swapped the France–Sweden match for the Germany–Austria match to accommodate the Nazi leader (Frederick T. Birchall, "Young Olympic Diving Champion Gives Grown-Up Radio Interview," *New York Times,* 13 August 1936, 13).

10. The BBC used recordings extensively in their shortwave global service but not as often on the domestic network. See Bill Ray, "Short Rayves," *Oakland Tribune,* 5 August 1936, 16; "Along Short-Wave Trails," *New York Times,* 26 July 1936, 10.

11. The NBC Collection at the Library of Congress holds the network's program files on microfiche.

12. "The Games of the XI Olympiad [1936 Berlin Olympics]: International Re-Broadcast," WABC-CBS Broadcast, 4 August 1936, Catalog ID: RB 1337, Paley Center for the Media, New York, NY [hereafter: PCM-NY].

13. Ibid.

14. Ibid. For the BBC's scheduling live coverage of the 400-meter race, see "National Programme Daventry," *Radio Times,* 4 August 1936, http://genome.ch.bbc.co.uk/dc8f20b38a9c4a458f23e314b67eacb8.

15. "Die Rundfunkberichterstattung von den XI. Olympischen Sommerspielen in Berlin vom 1–16. August 1936," http://1936.dra.de/index.php?id=8.

16. "Rundfunkmitarbeiter Sommerspiele 1936," *Die Olympischen Spiele 1936 im NS-Rundfunk,* http://1936.dra.de/?id=54; Max Jordan, *Beyond All Fronts* (Milwaukee, WI: Bruce, 1944), 136.

17. Suzanne Lommers, *Europe—On Air: Interwar Projects for Radio Broadcasting* (Amsterdam, Netherlands: Amsterdam University Press, 2012), 227–29.

18. "Die Olympischen Spiele im Rundfunk," *Funk-Wacht Nordfunk,* 23–29 August 1936, 9.

19. Ibid., 9.

20. Reichs-Rundfunk-Gesellschaft, *Olympia-Weltsender: Olympia World Station* (Berlin, Germany: Deutscher Verlag für Politik und Wirtschaft, 1937), 67.

21. "Radio Flashes: Olympic Broadcasts," *Winnipeg Free Press,* 4 July 1936, 18.

22. "Berlin Broadcast Test Successful," *Japan Times and Mail,* 4 July 1936, 4; George Lilley, "Tuning the 'Thrill' Bands," *Philadelphia Inquirer,* 9 August 1936, 20; Ernest Windle to Bill Henry, 25 July 1936, Box 13, Bill Henry Papers, Occidental College, Los Angeles, CA; S. C. Rosier, "Eavesdropping on Home," *New York Times,* 18 October 1936, 12; "Programs from Germany's Olympics Sound Pretty Good to U.S. Radio Trade," *Variety,* 5 August 1936, 34; Thomas S. Rice, "Airing the Olympics," *Brooklyn Daily Eagle,* 9 August 1936, C7.

23. Dick Booth, *Talking of Sport: The Story of Radio Commentary* (Cheltenham, U.K.: SportsBooks, 2008).

24. Robert W. McChesney, "Media Made Sport: A History of Sports Coverage in the U.S.," in *Media, Sports, and Society,* ed. Lawrence A. Wenner (Newbury Park, CA: Sage, 1989), 59–60.

25. Quote is from Booth, *Talking of Sport,* 126. See also Asa Briggs, *The History of Broadcasting in the United Kingdom,* vol. 2, *The Golden Age of Wireless* (New York, NY: Oxford University Press, 1965), 111–13; Mike Huggins, "BBC Radio and Sport, 1922–1939," *Contemporary British History* 21, no. 4 (2007): 497.

26. Huggins, "BBC Radio and Sport," 500.

27. Booth, *Talking of Sport,* 39, 50, 63; Briggs, *Broadcasting in the United Kingdom,* 2: 76.

28. "Follow-Up Comment," *Variety,* 12 August 1936, 40.

29. "Pants and Cricket," *Variety,* 12 August 1936, 36.

30. Bill Henry, "Olympic Coverage," *Broadcasting,* 2 August 1948, 40; William Mellors Henry and Patricia Henry, *Behind the Headlines with Bill Henry, 1903–1970* (Los Angeles, CA: Ward Ritchie Press, 1972), 175.

31. "The Games of the XI Olympiad [1936 Berlin Olympics]: International Re-Broadcast," BBC-CBS Broadcast, 3 August 1936, Catalog ID: RB 4942, PCM-NY.

32. "Hörzitate Sommerspiele," in *Die Olympischen Spiele 1936 im NS-Rundfunk,* http://1936.dra.de/index.php?id=38. The recording of the race can be found at http://1936.dra.de/uploads/mp3/B004755116.mp3.

33. Mark Ryan, *Running with Fire: The True Story of "Chariots of Fire" Hero Harold Abrahams* (London, U.K.: Robson Press, 2012), 223–25.

34. "Arts and Popular Culture," *Courier and Advertiser* [Dundee, Scotland], 11 July 1936, 6; "Broadcasting," *Times* [London, England], 11 July 1936, 19.

35. Ryan, *Running with Fire,* 225.

36. Ryan, *Running with Fire,* 227; Booth, *Talking of Sport,* 72–73.

37. David Cardiff, "The Serious and the Popular: Aspects of the Evolution of Style in the Radio Talk 1928–1939," in *Media, Culture, and Society: A Critical Reader,* ed. Richard Collins (London, U.K.: Sage, 1986), 228–46; Jason Loviglio, *Radio's Intimate Public: Network Broadcasting and Mass-Mediated Democracy* (Minneapolis: University of Minnesota

Press, 2005), 38–56; Theo van Leeuwen, *Introducing Social Semiotics* (London, U.K.: Routledge, 2004), 157.

38. Harold Abrahams, "Athletic Roundup 1924–1954," in *Sports Report: Number 2*, ed. Eamonn Andrews and Angus Mackey (London, U.K.: William Heinemann, 1954), 36–48.

39. Quote on lack of exaggeration is from Huggins, "BBC Radio and Sport," 509; Basil Maine, *The B.B.C. and Its Audience* (London, U.K.: Thomas Nelson and Sons, 1939), 88–91.

40. See, for instance, "Jesse Owens and the Nazi Olympics," episode 2, series 6, "Things We Forgot to Remember," 1 August 2011, BBC Radio 4, http://www.bbc.co.uk/programmes/b00w1xwj.

41. Red Barber, *The Broadcasters* (New York, NY: Dial Press, 1970), 43.

42. "CBS Radio at 50: An Autobiography in Sound," CBS Radio, 18 September 1977, Catalog ID: R77:0499, PCM-NY.

43. William Taaffe, "Giant of the Airwaves: Ted Husing Stood Out among Early Sportscasters," *Sports Illustrated*, 2 April 1990, http://www.si.com/vault/1990/04/02/121753/giant-of-the-airwaves-ted-husing-stood-out-among-early-sportscasters.

44. "Radio Dial Log," *Brooklyn Daily Eagle*, 6 July 1936, 8.

45. Kosai Mitsumi, Tanomogi Shinroku, Yamamoto Teru, and Sansei Kasai made up the NHK contingent in Berlin.

46. Cameron Clark, "Focus on Rekion: NHK Radio Women's 200 Meter Breaststroke," Japanese Collections, University of Libraries Blogs, Ohio State University, http://library.osu.edu/blogs/japanese/2015/02/02/focus-on-rekion-nhk-radio-womens-200-meter-breaststroke/; Hisateru Furuta, *Broadcasting in Japan: The Twentieth Century Journey from Radio to Multimedia* (Tokyo, Japan: NHK Broadcasting Culture Research Institute, 2002), 46–47 (quote is from p. 47); Robin Kietlinski, *Japanese Women and Sport: Beyond Baseball and Sumo* (New York, NY: Bloomsbury Academic, 2011), 72–73; Robin Orlansky, "Moving Forward: Sports and Gender in Modern Japan," *Graduate Journal of Asia-Pacific Studies* 5, no. 1 (2007): 78; "Die Olympischen Spiele im Rundfunk," *Funk-Wacht Nordfunk*, 23–29 August 1936, 9.

47. On 15 December 2011 the IOC announced that in its official website listing of Olympic medalists the entry for the late Son Kitei, a Japanese citizen and a 1936 Berlin Olympics marathon gold medalist, would be changed to Sohn Kee-Chung, the Korean version of his name. The record also will include a note explaining that he was a native of the Korean peninsula, a Japanese colony at the time (http://japanrunningnews.blogspot.com/2011/12/ioc-changes-name-listing-of-1936.html). Thus, IOC records now say Sohn Kee-Chung won the marathon. See also Kunihiko Oda, "IOC Approves Korean Spelling for 1936 Marathon Champ," *Asahi Shimbun*, 20 December 2011, http://ajw.asahi.com/article/behind_news/sports/AJ201112200009.

48. "Olympischen Spiele im Rundfunk"; "Besonderheiten bei der Rundfunkübertragung des Marathonlaufs," *Die Olympischen Spiele 1936 im NS-Rundfunk*, http://1936.dra.de/index.php?id=128#zitat321; "The Games of the XI Olympiad [1936 Berlin

Olympics]: International Re-Broadcast," BBC-CBS Broadcast, 9 August 1936, Catalog ID: RB 4947, PCM-NY.

49. "Olympics Roundup," CBS Broadcast, 9 August 1936, Call Number RWC 6246 A1, NBCR-LC.

50. "The Games of the XI Olympiad [1936 Berlin Olympics]: International Re-Broadcast," WABC-CBS Broadcast, 2 August 1936, Catalog ID: RB 4940, PCM-NY; "The Games of the XI Olympiad [1936 Berlin Olympics]: International Re-Broadcast," WABC-CBS Broadcast, 10 August 1936, Catalog ID: RB 4947, PCM-NY.

51. "The Games of the XI Olympiad [1936 Berlin Olympics]: International Re-Broadcast," WABC-CBS Broadcast, 13 August 1936, Catalog ID: RB 4947, PCM-NY.

52. "Reportage vom 10.000m-Lauf der Männer (Ausschnitte)," 2 August 1936, *Die Olympischen Spiele 1936 im NS-Rundfunk,* http://1936.dra.de/index.php?id=128#zitat284.

53. "Olympics Roundup," WABC-CBS Broadcast, 7 August 1936, Call Number: RWC 6245 B1, NBCR-LC.

54. "The Games of the XI Olympiad [1936 Berlin Olympics]: International Re-Broadcast," WABC-CBS Broadcast, 9 August 1936, Catalog ID: RB 4947, PCM-NY.

55. "The Games of the XI Olympiad [1936 Berlin Olympics]: International Re-Broadcast," WABC-CBS Broadcast, 13 August 1936, Catalog ID: RB 4947, PCM-NY.

56. Susan J. Douglas, *Listening In* (New York, NY: Times Books, 1999), 17–20; Michele Hilmes, *Radio Voices: American Broadcasting, 1922–1952* (Minneapolis: University of Minnesota Press, 1997), 1–33, 75–96.

57. "Olympics Roundup," BBC-CBS Broadcast, 3 August 1936, Call Number: RWC 6244 A2, NBCR-LC.

58. Robert Drake, "Jesse Who? Race, the Southern Press, and the 1936 Olympic Games," *American Journalism* 28, no. 4 (2011): 81–110.

59. "The Games of the XI Olympiad [1936 Berlin Olympics]: International Re-Broadcast," NBC Broadcast, 25 July 1936, Catalog ID: RB 13559, PCM-NY.

60. Ibid.

61. Ibid.

62. Brad Austin, *Democratic Sports: Men's and Women's College Athletics during the Great Depression* (Fayetteville: University of Arkansas Press, 2015), 109–10.

63. Ibid., 103–72.

64. Douglas, *Listening In,* 83–123; Hilmes, *Radio Voices,* 151–82.

65. "Olympics Roundup," WABC-CBS Broadcast, 3 August 1936, Call Number: RWC 6244 A2, NBCR-LC.

66. "Olympics Roundup," WABC-CBS Broadcast, 3 August 1936, Call Number: RWC 6244 A1, NBCR-LC.

67. "The Games of the XI Olympiad [1936 Berlin Olympics]: International Re-Broadcast," WABC-CBS Broadcast, 13 August 1936, Catalog ID: RB 4947, PCM-NY.

68. Birchall, "Young Olympic Diving Champion."

69. "The Games of the XI Olympiad [1936 Berlin Olympics]: International Re-Broadcast," WABC-CBS Broadcast, 9 August 1936, Catalog ID: RB 4947, PCM-NY.

70. "Besonderheiten bei der Rundfunkübertragung des Marathonlaufs."

71. Drake, "Jesse Who?" 81–110; Pamela C. Laucella, "An Analysis of Mainstream, Black, and Communist Press Coverage of Jesse Owens in the 1936 Berlin Olympic Games," PhD diss., University of North Carolina at Chapel Hill, 2004; Welky, *Everything Was Better*, 45–66.

72. Jo Ranson, "Radio Dial Log," *Brooklyn Daily Eagle*, 10 April 1936, 23.

73. Husing thanks "Claire" on "Olympics Roundup," WABC-CBS Broadcast, 8 August 1936, Call Number RWC 6245 A3, NBCR-LC. On Trask and CBS, see Steve Wick, *The Long Night: William L. Shirer and the Rise and Fall of the Third Reich* (New York, NY: Macmillan, 2011), 100.

74. See, for example, "The Games of the XI Olympiad [1936 Berlin Olympics]: International Re-Broadcast," CBS Broadcast, 13 August 1936, Catalog ID: RB 4947, PCM-NY.

75. "Slater of Adelphi Backs Olympic Ban on Eleanor Jarrett," *Brooklyn Daily Eagle*, 1 September 1936, 11.

76. The 4 × 100 meter race is reported and discussed on the following recordings: "Olympics Roundup," WABC-CBS Broadcast, 8 August 1936, Call Number: RWC 6220 B3, NBCR-LC; and "Olympics Roundup," WABC-CBS Broadcast, 8 August 1936, Call Number: RWC 6245 B4, NBCR-LC. The Foy Draper interview about the relay occurs in "The Games of the XI Olympiad [1936 Berlin Olympics]: International Re-Broadcast," CBS Broadcast, 9 August 1936, Catalog ID: RB 4947, PCM-NY.

77. David Clay Large, *Nazi Games: The Olympics of 1936* (New York, NY: W. W. Norton, 2007), 181; Judith A. Steeh and Judith Holmes, *Olympiad 1936: Blaze of Glory for Hitler's Reich* (New York, NY: Ballantine, 1971), 93.

78. "The Games of the XI Olympiad [1936 Berlin Olympics]: International Re-Broadcast," NBC Broadcast, 29 July 1936, Catalog ID: RB 1753, PCM-NY.

79. Cable reprinted in Reichs-Rundfunk-Gesellschaft, *Olympia-Weltsender*, 112.

80. "The Games of the XI Olympiad [1936 Berlin Olympics]: International Re-Broadcast," NBC Broadcast, 30 July 1936, Catalog ID: RB 1753, PCM-NY.

81. "Olympic Games," NBC Broadcast, 16 August 1936, Call Number: RWC 5901 A4-B1, NBCR-LC.

82. "Olympics Roundup," WABC-CBS Broadcast, 8 August 1936, Call Number: RWC 6220 B3, NBCR-LC.

83. Ted Husing, "Wandering Broadwayite Broadcasts His Lowdown on Olympiad Berlin," *Variety*, 12 August 1936, 1, 62.

84. "The Games of the XI Olympiad [1936 Berlin Olympics]: International Re-Broadcast," BBC-CBS Broadcast, 9 August 1936, Catalog ID: RB 4947, PCM-NY.

85. "Olympics Roundup," WABC-CBS Broadcast, 8 August 1936, Call Number: RWC 6220 B3, NBCR-LC.

86. "Olympischen Spiele im Rundfunk," 9.

87. "The Games of the XI Olympiad [1936 Berlin Olympics]: International Re-Broadcast," NBC Broadcast, 16 August 1936, Catalog ID: RB 13560, PCM-NY.

88. On German legal system, see Joe Williams, "Modern Germany an Enigma," *New York World-Telegram,* 14 August 1936, 16; "Nazi Crime," *Variety,* 29 July 1936, 47. On censorship and surveillance, see "Paper Says Reporters Shadowed at Olympics," *Toronto Globe and Mail,* 7 August 1936, 6; "Sportswriters Outsmart Nazis," *Variety,* 12 August 1936, 54; Ralph W. Barnes, "Nazis Purge Berlin of Sights Unpleasant to Olympic Visitors," *New York Herald-Tribune,* 2 August 1936, section 2, 1.

89. "Anti-Nazi Riots in Prague," *New York Herald-Tribune,* 31 July 1936, 4; "Torch Ceremony Excites Anti-Fascist Outbursts," *New York Herald-Tribune,* 31 July 1936, 21. The broadcast from Prague on the night of the ceremony, with no mention of riots, can be heard on the recording "The Games of the XI Olympiad [1936 Berlin Olympics]: International Re-Broadcast," NBC Broadcast, 30 July 1936, Catalog ID: RB 13559, PCM-NY.

90. "The Games of the XI Olympiad [1936 Berlin Olympics]: International Re-Broadcast," NBC Broadcast, 30 July 1936, Catalog ID: RB 13558, PCM-NY.

91. Gwenyth L. Jackaway, *Media at War: Radio's Challenge to the Newspapers, 1924–1939* (Westport, CT: Praeger, 1995); George E. Lott Jr., "The Press–Radio War of the 1930s," *Journal of Broadcasting* 14, no. 3 (1970): 275–86.

92. "Address by Avery Brundage," NBC Broadcast, 17 August 1936, Call Number: RWC 6384 A4, NBCR-LC. The dispute between Owens and Brundage concerned the events Owens (supposedly) committed to attend in a post-Olympic European tour to benefit the Amateur Athletic Union (AAU). See Herb Graffis, "Clowns on High Olympus," *Esquire,* November 1936, 64.

93. "Olympics Roundup," CBS Broadcast, 13 August 1936, Call Number: RWC 6246 B1, NBCR-LC.

94. "Olympics Roundup," CBS Broadcast, 15 August 1936, Call Number: RWC 5650 B3–4, NBCR-LC. On newspaper reports of the controversy, see Paul Gallico, "'We Wuz Robbed! Rings Out in Olympic Fights," *San Francisco Chronicle,* 12 August 1936, 19.

95. Thomas S. Rice, "The Olympic Broadcasts," *Brooklyn Daily Eagle,* 16 August 1936, C7; "Radio Features," *New York Herald-Tribune,* 2 August 1936, section 5, 7.

96. "World Jewish Conference Program," NBC Broadcast, 8 August 1936, Call Number: RWC 6245 B3, NBCR-LC.

97. "Olympic Broadcasts," *Delphi* [IN] *Citizen,* 30 July 1936, 2

98. "Review of Broadcasting," *Manchester* [UK] *Guardian,* 8 August 1936, 12.

99. John R. Tunis, *The Duke Decides* (New York, NY: Harcourt, Brace, 1939), 185.

100. "The Games of the XI Olympiad [1936 Berlin Olympics]: International Re-Broadcast," CBS Broadcast, 4 August 1936, Catalog ID: RB 1337, PCM-NY.

101. Jack Jernegan, "Archie Gives Family a Thrill," *Oakland Tribune,* 8 April 1936, 8.

102. Ida Mae Ryan, "Along Radio Row," *New York Amsterdam News,* 8 August 1936, 11.

103. "The Rudy Vallee Show," NBC Broadcast, 13 August 1936, Call Number: RWB 7283 A1–4, NBCR-LC.

104. United States, 95th Congress, 2nd Session, Memorial Services Held in the House of Representatives and Senate of the United States, together with remarks

presented in eulogy of Ralph H. Metcalfe, late Representative from Illinois (Washington, DC: U.S. Government Printing Office, 1978), 82.

105. Robert Armstead, S. L. Gardner, *Black Days, Black Dust: The Memories of an African American Coal Miner* (Knoxville: University of Tennessee Press, 2002), 60.

106. Valerie Grim, "African American Rural Culture, 1900–1950," in *African American Life in the Rural South, 1900–1950,* ed. R. Douglas Hurt (Columbia: University of Missouri Press, 2003), 125–26.

107. Philip G. Hubbard, *My Iowa Journey: The Life Story of the University of Iowa's First African American Professor* (Iowa City: University of Iowa Press, 1999), 22.

108. Irene Awret, *They'll Have to Catch Me First: An Artist's Coming of Age in the Third Reich* (Madison: University of Wisconsin Press, 2004), 96–97.

109. Lisa Farringer Parker, *Angels in the Darkness: A Family's Triumph over Hitler and World War II Berlin, 1935–1949* (Tucson, AZ: Wheatmark, 2011), 29–30.

110. Levi Jolley, "Ma Owens Hasn't Had Good Meal since Sunday," *Baltimore Afro-American,* 8 August 1936, 1.

111. "[Begin Japanology] Season 4, EP17: Hideko Maehata 2011–06–02," Youtube .com, https://youtu.be/Z5_yc4jRm7s.

112. Peter Fritzsche, *Life and Death in the Third Reich* (Cambridge, MA: Harvard University Press, 2009), 67–68.

113. Bill Ray, "Short Rayves," *Oakland Tribune,* 5 August 1936, 16.

114. "Along Short-Wave Trails," *New York Times,* 9 August 1936, 10.

115. Bill Ray, "Short Rayves," *Oakland Tribune,* 5 August 1936, 16; quote is from Bill Ray, "Short Rayves," *Oakland Tribune,* 10 August 1936, 21.

116. "Apple Radio Store to Hold Open House," *Berkeley Daily Gazette,* 3 August 1936, 16; "What We Hear," *Boston Globe,* 9 August 1936, D6.

117. Harwood L. Childs, "America's Short-Wave Audience," in *Propaganda by Short Wave,* ed. Harwood L. Childs and John B. Whitton (Princeton, NJ: Princeton University Press, 1943), 326.

118. Jerome S. Berg, *On the Short Waves, 1923–1945: Broadcast Listening in the Pioneer Days of Radio* (Jefferson, NC: McFarland, 1999), 95–97.

119. "The Games of the XI Olympiad [1936 Berlin Olympics]: International Re-Broadcast," WABC-CBS, 10 August 1936, Catalog ID 4947, PCM-NY. The FCC allowed commercialization of shortwave relay as of 1939 (Berg, *On the Short Waves,* 57–58).

120. "Conquest Alliance V-P Scores FCC for 'Inconsistent' Policy in S.A.," *Variety,* 29 July 1936, 34.

121. "Radio," *Toronto Globe and Mail,* 11 August 1936, 8. On the development of Canadian network radio development in this period, see Anne F. MacLennan, "Learning to Listen: Developing the Canadian Radio Audience in the 1930s," *Journal of Radio and Audio Media,* 20, no. 2 (2013): 311–26.

122. Mike Rodden, "On the Highway of Sport," *Toronto Globe and Mail,* 5 August 1936, 6.

123. Thomas S. Rice, "The Olympic Broadcasts," *Brooklyn Daily Eagle,* 16 August 1936, C7.

124. Thomas S. Rice, "The Olympic Broadcasts," *Brooklyn Daily Eagle,* 30 August 1936, C7.

125. "Nearly 19 Hours Given Olympics," *Variety,* 12 August 1936, 41.

126. William L. Stuart, "The Radio Reporter . . .," *Screen and Radio Weekly* (insert in *Oakland Tribune*), 2 August 1936, 14.

127. "Programs from Germany's Olympics."

128. "The Games of the XI Olympiad [1936 Berlin Olympics]: International Re-Broadcast," NBC Broadcast, 16 August 1936, Catalog ID: RB 13560, PCM-NY.

129. "Der Aufmarsch des Ausland-Rundfunks zu den Olympischen Spielen," *Funk-Wacht Nordfunk,* 19–25 July 1936, 9; Robert Howard Claxton, *From Parsifal to Perón: Early Radio in Argentina, 1920–1944* (Gainesville: University Press of Florida, 2007), 46–47.

130. Some radio correspondents scheduled to report from Berlin left for Spain upon the outbreak of hostilities. See David H. Holsey, *As Good As Any: Foreign Correspondence on American Radio, 1930–1940* (Westport, CT: Greenwood Press, 1984), 26.

131. "Reichsleiter Eugen Hadamovsky über den Volkssender 1936," *Funk-Wacht Nordfunk,* 14–20 June 1936, 10.

132. "Silence the Best Policy," *Syracuse Herald,* 12 August 1936, 16.

133. "Olympics Roundup," CBS Broadcast, 15 August 1936, Call Number: RWC 5650 B3–4, NBCR-LC.

134. "Slater of Adelphi Backs Olympic Ban on Eleanor Jarrett," 11; Jordan, *Beyond All Fronts,* 167.

135. For an example of a Bill Henry exclusive, see "Olympics Roundup," WABC-CBS Broadcast, 10 August 1936, Call Number: RWC 6245 B2, NBCR-LC.

136. Barber, *The Broadcasters,* 50; David J. Halberstam, *Sports on New York Radio: A Play-by-Play History* (Lincolnwood, IL: Masters Press, 1999), 43–44; Bill Stern, *The Taste of Ashes* (New York, NY: Henry Holt, 1958), 61.

137. Jordan, *Beyond All Fronts,* 167.

Chapter 5. Six Minutes in Grünau

1. Max Jordan, *Beyond All Fronts* (Milwaukee, WI: Bruce, 1944), 168.

2. "NBC–CBS' Olymp. Games Coverage," *Variety,* 15 July 1936, 62.

3. Reichs-Rundfunk-Gesellschaft, *Olympia-Weltsender: Olympia World Station* (Berlin, Germany: Deutscher Verlag für Politik und Wirtschaft, 1937), 103–4.

4. *The XIth Olympic Games Berlin, 1936: Official Report,* 2 vols. (Berlin, Germany: Wilhelm Limpert, 1937), 1: 347–49 [hereafter: *Official Report*]; "Wettkampfreportagen-Rudern, Segeln," *Die Olympischen Spiele 1936 im NS-Rundfunk,* http://1936.dra.de/index.php?id=130.

5. Gordon B. Adam, *An Olympian's Oral History: Gordon B. Adam, 1936 Olympic Games, Rowing* (Los Angeles, CA: Amateur Athletic Foundation of Los Angeles, 1988), 12, http://www.la84foundation.org/6oic/OralHistory/OHAdam.pdf; Bob Moch, first 1999 interview with Dan Raley, 4.

6. Adam, *An Olympian's Oral History,* 12.

7. Craig Lambert, "Three Olympics," *Harvard Magazine*, September–October 1988, 63; Robert Garver in collaboration with Kate Sullivan, "A Brief History of Riverside Boat Club" (2008), 33, https://riversideboatclub.com/files/RBC%20History.pdf.

8. Robert Moch interview, 12 October 2004, 14.

9. Arthur Daley, "Sports of the Times," *New York Times*, 7 March 1943, S2; Christopher Dodd, *The Story of World Rowing* (London, U.K.: Stanley Paul, 1992), 169.

10. Fabrice Abgrall and François Thomazeau, *1936: La France à l'Épreuve des Jeux Olympiques de Berlin* (Paris, France: Alvik, 2006), 80, 167.

11. Gordon R. Newell, *Ready All! George Yeoman Pocock and Crew Racing* (Seattle: University of Washington Press, 1987), 104.

12. Dodd, *World Rowing*, 181. The image can be seen at Michael J. Socolow, "Six Minutes in Berlin," *Slate.com*, 23 July 2012, http://www.slate.com/articles/sports/fivering_circus/2012/07/_1936_olympics_rowing_the_greatest_underdog_nazi_defeating_american_olympic_victory_you_ve_never_heard_of_.html.

13. "Teidai Oarsman Back from Olympic Games," *Japan Times and Mail*, 28 August 1936, 5.

14. Arthur Daley, "Sports of the Times," *New York Times*, 25 January 1944, 22.

15. "Japanese Crew Beaten by Swiss," *Japan Times and Mail*, 4 July 1936, 1, 5; "Japanese Crew Is Heavy Favorite in Henley Regatta," *Japan Times and Mail*, 1 July 1936, 5.

16. "Finals Day at Henley," *Observer*, 5 July 1936, 29.

17. Frederick T. Birchall, "Young Olympic Diving Champion Gives Grown-Up Radio Interview," *New York Times*, 13 August 1936, 13.

18. "American Crew Oozes Power in Trial Spin," *Los Angeles Times*, 5 August 1936, A13.

19. "U. of W. Eight Has First Trial," *Toronto Globe and Mail*, 1 August 1936, 7; Elmer Dulmage, "Olympic Rowing Plans Protested," *Toronto Globe and Mail*, 6 August 1936, 6.

20. Adam, *An Olympian's Oral History*, 16; "Finals Day at Henley," *Observer*, 5 July 1936, 29.

21. "Games and Players: Our Oarsmen for Berlin," *Manchester* [UK] *Guardian*, 14 July 1936, 3.

22. "British Crews at Berlin: Leander Selected," *Manchester* [UK] *Guardian*, 7 July 1936, 4.

23. Dodd, *World Rowing*, 183.

24. Paul Gallico, "Two Mystery Ousters Thin Olympic Team," *Washington Post*, 30 July 1936, 15.

25. "Olympics Roundup," WABC-CBS Broadcast, 3 August 1936, Call Number: 6244 A2, NBC Radio Collection, Recorded Sound Reference Center, Library of Congress [hereafter: NBCR-LC].

26. Lee Miller, "The Husky Crew at the Berlin Olympics, 1936," 13, University of Washington—Athletics—Crew: Pamphlet File, Allen Library Special Collections, University of Washington, Seattle.

27. Jim McMillin interview, 19 October 2004, 11.

28. "American Crew Oozes Power."

29. "Husky Oarsmen in Last Drill as Race Nears," *Seattle Times*, 12 August 1936, 14 (quote on speed); Bob Cahen, "Washington at the Olympic Games," *Columns*, November 1936, 8 (Ulbrickson quote); Miller, "Husky Crew," 13.

30. Dulmage, "Olympic Rowing Plans Protested," 6; see also *Official Report*, 2: 1003.

31. Grantland Rice, "'Husky' Oarsmen Appear to Be Bound for Olympics," *Boston Globe*, 23 June 1936, 21.

32. "How Columbia Won Seventy-Two Shirts," *Literary Digest*, 6 July 1929, 48.

33. Neil H. Huffey, "College Sports Wagering: A Case Study about Gambling on College Athletics and the Motivations and Consequences Surrounding Legislation Wanting to Ban Wagering on College Sports," masters paper, University of Nevada, Las Vegas, 2001, 37.

34. Eugene Kinkead, "The Oarsmen," *New Yorker*, 26 June 1937, 64; George M. Varnell, "Varnell Says," *Seattle Times*, 13 September 1936, 27.

35. Cahen, "Washington at the Olympic Games," 8.

36. "The Games of the XI Olympiad [1936 Berlin Olympics]: International Re-Broadcast," CBS Broadcast, 10 August 1936, Catalog ID: RB 4947, Paley Center for the Media Collection, New York City, NY [hereafter: PCM-NY].

37. "Germans Dominate Olympics Regatta: Cambridge Crew Misunderstands Starter and Is Left Behind," *Boston Globe*, 12 August 1936, 25; "Germans Lead in Pairs, Fours and Single Sculls," *San Francisco Chronicle*, 12 August 1936, 19.

38. "Olympics Roundup," CBS Broadcast, 11 August 1936, Call Number: RWC 6246 A4, NBCR-LC.

39. Henry Penn Burke, "Report of Chairman of Rowing Committee," in *Report of the American Olympic Committee: Games of the XIth Olympiad, Berlin, Germany, August 1–16, 1936: IVth Olympic Winter Games, Garmisch-Partenkirchen, Germany, February 6–16, 1936*, ed. Frederick W. Rubien (New York, NY: American Olympic Committee, 1936), 243.

40. "Yank Boats Lose Trial," *Los Angeles Times*, 12 August 1936, 9, 12.

41. "Germans Dominate Olympics Regatta," 25.

42. "Jesse Owens and the Nazi Olympics," *Things We Forgot to Remember*, BBC Radio 4, 1 August 2011, http://www.bbc.co.uk/programmes/b00w1xwj.

43. "Germans Fail to Organize Olympic Cheering Sections," *Toronto Globe and Mail*, 4 August 1936, 6.

44. Royal Brougham, "U. Crew Wins Olympic Trial," *Seattle Post-Intelligencer*, 13 August 1936, 1.

45. Birchall, "Young Olympic Diving Champion," 13.

46. "Broadcasting the Olympics," *Broadcasting*, 15 August 1936, 57; "Radio and Public Address at the Berlin Olympics," *Radio-Craft*, November 1936, 300.

47. "Germans Dominate Olympics Regatta," 25; Arthur Daley, "Sports of the Times," *New York Times*, 25 January 1944, 22. On the starter's platform, see Dodd, *World Rowing*, 181.

48. Burke, "Report of Chairman of Rowing Committee," 245.

49. Arthur J. Daley, "Grunau Rowing Course Mark Smashed by Washington in Beating British Crew," *New York Times*, 13 August 1936, 14.

50. Moch 2004 interview, 10.

51. McMillin interview, 12; Moch 2004 interview, 10; Royal Brougham, "U. Crew Wins Olympic Trial," *Seattle Post-Intelligencer*, 13 August 1936, 1, 15; "U.S. Eight Wins in Drive," *San Francisco Chronicle*, 13 August 1936, 25.

52. "Hume Big Worry, Husky Stroke Faces Test," *Seattle Post-Intelligencer*, 13 August 1936, 15; "Huskies Reach Rowing Final," *New York World-Telegram*, 12 August 1936, 31.

53. "Hume Big Worry"; "Huskies Reach Rowing Final."

54. *Official Report*, 2: 1018.

55. Brougham, "U. Crew Wins Olympic Trial," 1.

56. "Olympic Games," *Times* [London, UK], 13 August 1936, 6.

57. Ibid., 6; *Official Report*, 2: 1018.

58. "The Games of the XI Olympiad [1936 Berlin Olympics]: International Re-Broadcast," CBS Broadcast, 12 August 1936, Catalog ID: RB 4947, PCM-NY.

59. Miller, "Husky Crew," 12, 14.

60. "Hume's Illness Perils Husky Crew Chances in Olympics," *Seattle Times*, 14 August 1936, 1.

61. "Olympic Games: The Regatta at Grunau," *Times* [London, UK], 14 August 1936, 6; McMillin interview, 12.

62. *Official Report*, 2: 1018; "Japan Is Beaten," *Japan Times and Mail*, 16 August 1936, 5.

63. *Official Report*, 2: 1000.

64. Cahen, "Washington at the Olympic Games," 8.

65. *Official Report*, 2: 1001–2.

66. "Olympics Roundup," 14 August 1936, Call Number: RWC 6247 A1–2, NBCR-LC.

67. "Olympic Games," *Times* [London, UK], 15 August 1936, 6.

68. "Der Doppelzweier Geht durchs Ziel," in *Olympia-Weltsender: Olympia World Station*, 106; Neither *Olympia-Weltsender* nor the BBC listing for the event specifies the commentator. See "Olympic Games—Rowing," National Programme Daventry, 14 August 1936, http://genome.ch.bbc.co.uk/8ff088e5a610482092babd6f5bf0f99b.

69. César Saerchinger, *Hello America! Radio Adventures in Europe* (Boston, MA: Houghton Mifflin, 1938), 189.

70. Al Ulbrickson and Clarence Dirks, "Rockne of Rowing," *Saturday Evening Post*, 19 June 1937, 97; Blaine Newnham, "Nine UW Rowers Who Showed Up Hitler in 1936 and Won Gold," *Seattle Times*, 11 May 2004, http://community.seattletimes.nwsource.com/archive/?date=20040511&slug=blai11; McMillin interview, 11.

71. "European Scene," *Columns*, November 1936, 11.

72. "Olympics Roundup," 14 August 1936, Call Number: RWC 6247 A1–2, NBCR-LC.

73. Adam, *An Olympian's Oral History*, 16.

74. Cahen, "Washington at the Olympic Games," 9.

75. "Olympics Roundup," 14 August 1936, Call Number: RWC 6247 A1–2, NBCR-LC.

76. Ibid. Although the customary starting commands in 1936 were "Êtes-vous prêts?" followed by "Partez!" the starting official substituted "Départe!" for "Partez!" This caused confusion for all the American rowers. See Burke, "Report of Chairman of Rowing Committee," 242.

77. Ulbrickson and Dirks, "Rockne of Rowing," 97; McMillin interview, 13.

78. "Olympics Roundup," 14 August 1936, Call Number: RWC 6247 A1–2, NBCR-LC.

79. Moch 2004 interview, 11; Guy Walters, *Berlin Games: How the Nazis Stole the Olympic Dream* (New York, NY: William Morrow, 2006), 285; McMillin interview, 13.

80. Moch 2004 interview, 11.

81. "Olympics Roundup," 14 August 1936, Call Number: RWC 6247 A1–2, NBCR-LC.

82. Ibid.

83. Paul Gallico, "Row Husky Shell to Victory," *San Francisco Chronicle*, 15 August 1936, 23; *Die Olympischen Spiele 1936 in Berlin und Garmisch-Partenkirchen* (Hamburg-Bahrenfeld, Germany: Cigaretten-Bilderdienst, 1936), 86.

84. Miller, "Husky Crew," 15.

85. Moch 2004 interview, 12.

86. "Olympics Roundup," 14 August 1936, Call Number: RWC 6247 A1–2, NBCR-LC.

87. Ibid.

88. "Olympics Roundup," 14 August 1936, Call Number: RWC 6247 A1–2, NBCR-LC. The Deutsches Rundfunkarchiv does not have the recording of the race. These words were reprinted in *Die Olympischen Spiele 1936 in Berlin und Garmisch-Partenkirchen*, 87–88. The race call on the RRG appears to have been a relay of the running commentary produced for the loudspeakers in Grünau. See "Wettkampfreportagen-Rudern, Segeln," in *Die Olympischen Spiele 1936 im NS-Rundfunk*, http://1936.dra.de/index.php?id=130.

89. McMillin interview, 13; Adam, *An Olympian's Oral History*, 15; Moch 2004 interview, 12; Dodd, *World Rowing*, 183.

90. "Olympics Roundup," 14 August 1936, Call Number: RWC 6247 A1–2, NBCR-LC; Miller, "Husky Crew," 16.

91. "Washington Oarsmen Win to Retain Crown for U.S." *New York World-Telegram*, 14 August 1936, 18.

92. Adam, *An Olympian's Oral History*, 15.

93. Moch 2004 interview, 13.

94. Adam, *An Olympian's Oral History*, 15.

95. McMillin interview, 14.

96. "Olympics Roundup," 14 August 1936, Call Number: RWC 6247 A1–2, NBCR-LC.

97. Miller, "Husky Crew," 16.

98. Bill Henry, "Washington Crew Wins Olympic Crown," *Los Angeles Times*, 15 August 1936, 9.

99. Alvin Ulbrickson with Richard L. Neuberger, "Now! Now! Now!" *Collier's*, 26 June 1937, 21.

100. Gallico, "Row Husky Shell to Victory," 23; "Olympic Games," *Times* [London, UK], 15 August 1936, 6; *The XIth Olympic Games Berlin, 1936: Official Report*, 2 vols. (Berlin, Germany: Wilhelm Limpert, 1937), 2: 1003.

101. "Olympics Roundup," 14 August 1936, Call Number: RWC 6247 A1–2, NBCR-LC; Saerchinger, *Hello America!* 190.

102. "Olympics Roundup," 14 August 1936, Call Number: RWC 6247 A1–2, NBCR-LC.

103. "Washington Oarsmen Win,"18.

104. Dodd, *World Rowing*, 184; Arthur J. Daley, "Fifth Successive Olympic Eight-Oared Rowing Title Is Captured by U.S.," *New York Times*, 15 August 1936, 7; Walters, *Berlin Games*, 285.

105. Grantland Rice, "U.S. Victory in Rowing at Olympics Rated High Spot," *Baltimore Sun*, 21 January 1937, 14.

106. André François-Poncet, *The Fateful Years* (New York, NY: Howard Fertig, 1972), 205; Stephen H. Roberts, *The House That Hitler Built* (New York, NY: Harper and Brothers, 1938), 18–19.

107. Entry for 15 August 1936 in *Die Tagebücher von Joseph Goebbels,* vol. 1, *Aufzeichnungen 1923–1941* (Munich, Germany: K. G. Saur, 1998), 159.

108. "Washington Oarsmen Win," 18.

109. Gaston Moch to Bob Moch, 15 August 1936, in Robert Moch Scrapbook, George Pocock Rowing Foundation, George Pocock Memorial Rowing Center, Seattle, WA [hereafter: RMS-GPRF].

110. "The Games of the XI Olympiad [1936 Berlin Olympics]: International Re-Broadcast," WABC-CBS Broadcast, 14 August 1936, Catalog ID: RB 4948, PCM-NY.

111. Gaston Moch to Bob Moch, 15 August 1936, RMS-GPRF.

112. Genêt [Janet Flanner], "Berlin Letter," *New Yorker*, 22 August 1936, 64–65.

113. Abgrall and Thomazeau, *1936: France à l'Épreuve*, 180.

114. Thomas Wolfe, *The Notebooks of Thomas Wolfe*, 2 vols., ed. Richard S. Kennedy and Paschal Reeves (Chapel Hill: University of North Carolina Press, 1970), 2: 822.

115. "Washington Oarsmen Win," 1, 18.

116. "Olympic Games," NBC Broadcast, 16 August 1936, Call Number: RWC 5901 A4–B1, NBCR-LC.

117. Saerchinger, *Hello America!* 190.

118. "Millions to Hear Broadcast of Olympic Crew Race," *Seattle Times*, 13 August 1936, 8.

119. Saerchinger, *Hello America!* 190.

Conclusion

1. "Huskies' Coxswain Taken on Last Ride," *New York Times*, 16 August 1936, S2.

2. Robert Moch interview, 12 October 2004, 15.

3. Gordon B. Adam, *An Olympian's Oral History: Gordon B. Adam, 1936 Olympic Games, Rowing* (Los Angeles, CA: Amateur Athletic Foundation of Los Angeles, 1988), 15–16, http://www.la84foundation.org/6oic/OralHistory/OHAdam.pdf.

4. Jim McMillin interview, 19 October 2004, 13–14.

5. Henry Penn Burke, "Report of Chairman of Rowing Committee," in *Report of the American Olympic Committee: Games of the XIth Olympiad, Berlin, Germany, August 1–16, 1936: IVth Olympic Winter Games, Garmisch-Partenkirchen, Germany, February 6–16, 1936,* ed. Frederick W. Rubien (New York, NY: American Olympic Committee, 1936), 242.

6. Christopher Dodd, *The Story of World Rowing* (London, U.K.: Stanley Paul, 1992), 184.

7. "Goldregen in Grünau," *Berliner Illustrierte Zeitung—Die 16 Olympischen Tage,* August 1936, 75.

8. *Die Olympischen Spiele 1936 in Berlin und Garmisch-Partenkirchen* (Hamburg-Bahrenfeld, Germany: Cigaretten-Bilderdienst, 1936), 80.

9. McMillin interview, 15; "Huskies' Coxswain Taken on Last Ride," S2.

10. Genêt [Janet Flanner], "Berlin Letter," *New Yorker,* 22 August 1936, 65.

11. "Washington Crews Sweep Poughkeepsie Regatta for Second Successive Year," *Life,* 5 July 1937, 22; "The Oarsmen, *New Yorker,* 26 June 1937, 63–64; "Washington Wakes," *Time,* 5 July 1937, 26; Alvin Ulbrickson with Richard L. Neuberger, "Now! Now! Now!" *Collier's,* 27 June 1937, 21.

12. "Poughkeepsie Regatta," NBC Broadcast, 21 June 1937, Call Number: RWA 2416 A4, NBC Radio Collection, Recorded Sound Reference Center, Library of Congress [hereafter: NBCR-LC].

13. "Poughkeepsie Regatta," NBC Broadcast, 22 June 1937, Call Number: RWA 2416 A5, B1, NBCR-LC.

14. "The Only Network Broadcasting These Events As They Happen," [CBS advertisement] *Broadcasting,* 15 May 1938, 38–39. Italics in original.

15. "The Oarsmen," *New Yorker,* 25 June 1938, 52. The only rower to stroke three successive intercollegiate champions was John Patterson Gardiner of the University of Pennsylvania, who rowed with the champions of 1898, 1899, and 1900.

16. Michael J. Socolow, "Live from 'America's Rhineland': The Poughkeepsie Regatta and Early American Network Sports Broadcasting, 1925–1940," *Journal of Sport History* 43, no. 2 (2016): 149–67.

17. Erik Barnouw, *A History of Broadcasting in the United States,* vol. 2, *The Golden Web: 1933 to 1953* (New York, NY: Oxford University Press, 1968), 214; Michael J. Socolow, "Questioning Advertising's Influence over American Broadcasting: The Blue Book Controversy of 1945–1947," *Journal of Radio Studies* 9, no. 2 (2002): 282–302.

18. Bill Slater, "Forecasting Sportscasting," *The 1946 Radio Annual* (New York, NY: Radio Daily, 1946), 75.

19. Cesar Saerchinger, *Hello America! Radio Adventures in Europe* (Boston, MA: Houghton Mifflin, 1938), 184–86; John R. Tunis, "The Story of the Davis Cup," *Harper's,* September 1938, reprinted in John R. Tunis, *This Writing Game* (New York, NY: A. S. Barnes, 1941), 302. "A Résumé of CBS Broadcasting Activities during 1937," 18, Box 3, William B. Lewis Papers, Boston University Library.

20. In 1948, a "custom network" of eight stations was built for Davis Cup broadcasts and by 1950 the matches aired only on local stations by special arrangement.

See "Spaulding Sponsors Final Tennis Matches," *Broadcasting*, 30 August 1948, 23. "WQXR to Broadcast Davis Cup Matches," *Radio Daily*, 17 August 1950, 4. It should be noted that films of Davis Cup matches were a staple of early network television programming (unlike the Poughkeepsie Regatta). See Mary Gannon, "Esso Sponsorship of the NBC Newsreel," *Television*, September 1946, 15.

21. "Jack Sharkey vs. Joe Louis Fight," *Variety*, 26 August 1936, 77.

22. Red Barber, *The Broadcasters* (New York, NY: Dial Press, 1970), 36–37; William Taaffe, "Giant of the Airwaves: Ted Husing Stood Out among Early Sportscasters," *Sports Illustrated*, 2 April 1990, http://www.si.com/vault/1990/04/02/121753/giant-of-the-airwaves-ted-husing-stood-out-among-early-sportscasters.

23. "This Is Your Life"—Ted Husing (Part 1)" Youtube.com, https://www.youtube.com/watch?v=E1XQgxzWwNo.

24. John Lewis, *Radio Master: The Life and Times of Sports Broadcasting Great Ted Husing* (Minneapolis, MN: Langdon Street Press, 2010), 258–61; Stanley Wertheim interview, 13 May 2015.

25. David H. Holsey, *As Good As Any: Foreign Correspondence on American Radio, 1930–1940* (Westport, CT: Greenwood Press, 1984), 32; Ray Poindexter, *Golden Throats and Silver Tongues: The Radio Announcers* (Conway, AR: River Road Press, 1978), 148.

26. "Bill Henry Entertains Rotary Club Members," *Oxnard Daily Courier*, 20 October 1936, 1.

27. "Letter to Loyal Durand Hotchkiss from Bill Henry, World War II, September 25, 1939," *Bill Henry and the News*, http://billhenry.omeka.net/items/show/12.

28. Derrick Sington and Arthur Weidenfeld, *The Goebbels Experiment: A Study of the Nazi Propaganda Machine* (New Haven, CT: Yale University Press, 1943), 208.

29. "President Franklin D. Roosevelt: Death and Funeral, CBS Coverage (Radio)," CBS Broadcast, 12 April 1945, Catalog ID: R78:0007, Paley Center for the Media, New York [hereafter: PCM-NY]; "Radio," *Bill Henry and the News*, http://billhenry.omeka.net/exhibits/show/billhenryandthenews/broadcastjournalism/radio.

30. William Mellors Henry, *An Approved History of the Olympic Games* (New York, NY: G. P. Putnam's Sons, 1948).

31. "'Fliegenden Redaktion' im Olympischen Dorf: Interview mit Jesse Owens," *Die Olympischen Spiele 1936 im NS-Rundfunk*, http://1936.dra.de/index.php?id=122.

32. William J. Baker, *Jesse Owens: An American Life* (New York, NY: Free Press 1986); Donald MacRae, *In Black and White: The Untold Story of Joe Louis and Jesse Owens* (New York, NY: Scribner, 2002); Jeremy Schaap, *Triumph: The Untold Story of Jesse Owens and Hitler's Olympics* (Boston, MA: Houghton Mifflin, 2007).

33. Kristine Toohey and Anthony James Veal, *The Olympic Games: A Social Science Perspective* (Wallingford, Oxon, UK: CABI, 2000), 194–221; Barbara Fleming, *Fort Collins: The Miller Photographs* (Charleston, SC: Arcadia, 2009), 58.

34. "Dare to Compete: The Struggle of Women in Sports (TV)," HBO Broadcast, 8 March 1999, Catalog ID: T:61419, PCM-NY; Frank Deford, *Over Time: My Life as a Sportswriter* (New York, NY: Atlantic Monthly Press, 2012), 234; Richard Goldstein,

"Eleanor Holm Whalen, 30's Swimming Champion, Dies," *New York Times*, 2 February 2004, B7.

35. Red Smith, "Boycott the Moscow Olympics," in Red Smith, *The Red Smith Reader* (New York, NY: Random House, 1982), 50.

36. Craig Unger, "Media Notes from All Over: That Jesse Owens Commercial," *New York*, 14 April 1980, 9.

37. On 19 February 2016, as this book was being completed, Forecast Pictures released the movie "Race," starring Stephan James as Jesse Owens, in the United States and internationally. See "Race (2016)" IMDB, http://www.imdb.com/title/tt3499096/.

38. "Radio Collector's Items," *Variety*, 30 November 1938, 35.

39. *Live! Broadcasting the Olympic Games*, Olympic Museum, http://www.olympic.org/museum/interactive-documentary/broadcasting/.

40. "Übersee-Zentrale," in Reichs-Rundfunk-Gesellschaft, *Olympia-Weltsender: Olympia World Station* (Berlin, Germany: Deutscher Verlag für Politik und Wirtschaft, 1937), 110.

41. "Olympic Broadcasting Services," https://www.obs.tv/.

42. Alexander C. Kafka, "When Hollywood Held Hands with Hitler," *Chronicle Review*, 10 July 2013, http://chronicle.com/article/When-Hollywood-Held-Hands-With/140189/.

43. "The Games of the XI Olympiad [1936 Berlin Olympics]: International Re-Broadcast," NBC Broadcast, 16 August 1936, Catalog ID: RB 13560, PCM-NY.

44. H. J. P. Bergmeier and Rainer E. Lotz, *Hitler's Airwaves: The Inside Story of Nazi Radio Broadcasting and Propaganda Swing*, 88–90, 131–35; "Dietze, Eduard Roderich," *Die Olympischen Spiele 1936 im NS-Rundfunk*, http://1936.dra.de/?id=66.

45. Earl Browder, *What Is Communism?* (New York, NY: Workers Library Publishers, 1936), 75–77.

46. Douglas B. Craig, *Fireside Politics: Radio and Political Culture in the United States, 1920–1940* (Baltimore, MD: Johns Hopkins University Press, 2000), 131–33; David Goodman, *Radio's Civic Ambition: American Broadcasting and Democracy in the 1930s* (New York, NY: Oxford University Press, 2011); "Browder Heads Communist Slate," *New York Times*, 29 June 1936, 6.

47. "The Games of the XI Olympiad [1936 Berlin Olympics]: International Re-Broadcast," NBC Broadcast, 16 August 1936, Catalog ID: RB 13560, PCM-NY.

48. Elizabeth Hatfield, "Framing the Olympic Opening Ceremony: NBC's Use of Selectivity, Partiality and Structure in Presenting the Beijing Olympics," paper presented at the annual meeting of the NCA 95th Annual Convention, Chicago, IL, 11 November 2009; Mike Murphy, "Beijing's Olympian Deception: Echoes of Berlin, 1936," *National Post*, 31 March 2001, B3; Greg Vitiello, "How Host Nations Use the Olympics to Burnish Their Country's Public Image," *Television Quarterly* 38 (2008): 45–50.

49. Andrew Billings, Kenon Brown, and Natalie Brown-Devlin, "Sports Draped in the American Flag: Impact of the 2014 Winter Olympic Telecast on Nationalized Attitudes," *Mass Communication and Society* 18, no. 4 (2015): 377–98.

50. Guy Walters, *Berlin Games: How the Nazis Stole the Olympic Dream* (New York, NY: William Morrow, 2006), 303.

51. "Radio," *Japan Times and Mail*, 6 August 1936, 4; Jane M. J. Robbins, *Tokyo Calling: Japanese Overseas Radio Broadcasting, 1937–1945* (Fucecchio, Italy: European Press Academic, 2001), 36–38.

52. Columbia Broadcasting System, *A Résumé of CBS Broadcasting Activities during 1937* (New York, NY: Columbia Broadcasting System, 1938), 17–18.

53. Si Steinhauser, "Pitt and Duke Gridiron Classics Launch Big Broadcasts for 1937," *Pittsburgh Press*, 31 December 1936, 11.

54. Richard Sandomir, "NBC Extends Olympic Deal into Unknown," *New York Times*, 7 May 2014, http://www.nytimes.com/2014/05/08/sports/olympics/nbc-extends-olympic-tv-deal-through-2032.html?_r=0; "IOC Awards Olympic Games Broadcast Rights to NBCUniversal through to 2032," Olympic.org, 5 July 2014, http://www.olympic.org/news/ioc-awards-olympic-games-broadcast-rights-to-nbcuniversal-through-to-2032/230995.

55. Joanne Ostrow, "Why We Watch the Olympics: It's the Last Great Live TV Event," *Denver Post*, 22 July 2012, E1.

56. Charles M. Gates, *The First Century at the University of Washington* (Seattle: University of Washington Press, 1961), 98–100.

57. "Rowing Foundation Pays Tribute to the One-Time 'Young Giants Out of the Northwest'," *New York Times*, 23 January 1971, 23.

58. "Then (Olympic Champions) . . . Now (40 Years Later)," *Seattle Times*, 26 July 1976, 20; John Peoples, "Quite a Crew—1936 Huskies Gather to Row Back in Time," *Seattle Times*, 6 August 1986, H1.

59. "Alvin M. Ulbrickson, 77, Coached Olympic and Washington Crews," *New York Times*, 11 November 1980, D19.

60. Dan Raley, "Events of the Century," *Seattle Post-Intelligencer*, 21 December 1999, http://www.seattlepi.com/sports/article/Events-of-the-century-3835569.php.

61. Bud Withers, "Huskies' Last Surviving Member of 1936 Olympic-Gold Crew Team Dies," *Seattle Times*, 24 July 2009, http://www.seattletimes.com/sports/uw-huskies/huskies-last-surviving-member-of-1936-olympic-gold-crew-team-dies/.

Index

Page numbers in *italics* refer to illustrations.